JOHN WAYNE

JOHN WAYNE

The Man Behind the Myth

MICHAEL MUNN

THORNDIKE
WINDSOR

This Large Print edition is published by Thorndike Press®,
Waterville, Maine USA and by BBC Audiobooks, Ltd,
Bath, England.

Published in 2004 in the U.S. by arrangement with
NAL Signet, a member of Penguin Group (USA) Inc.

Published in 2004 in the U.K. by arrangement with Robson
Books (a trading division of Chrysalis Books Group plc).

U.S. Hardcover 0-7862-6583-3 (Biography)
U.K. Hardcover 0-7540-7993-7 (Windsor Large Print)

Copyright © Michael Munn, 2003

The text of this Large Print edition is unabridged.
Other aspects of the book may vary from the original edition.

Set in 16 pt. Plantin by Carleen Stearns.

Printed in the United States on permanent paper.

British Library Cataloguing-in-Publication Data available

**Library of Congress Control Number: 2004103183
ISBN 0-7862-6583-3 (lg. print : hc : alk. paper)**

For all the victims and heroes of 9/11

Contents

Foreword

I have a great affection for the man they called the Duke.

There are numerous actors I have a great admiration for, and there are a great many I think were better actors than Wayne. But I can think of only three I have real affection for, and John Wayne is one of them.

One reason simply has to do with his screen persona. I liked — and still like — watching Wayne on screen. Some of his work has touched my life. I can't think of another film that portrayed courage as inspiringly as *The Alamo*, which was the film that turned me on to Wayne in 1960 when I was just eight. I don't think the critics who savaged the film knew what they were talking about, and I say that with confidence, having been taught a valuable lesson from Laurence Olivier who said, "Critics, laddie, know fuck all!"

My affection grew when I met Wayne. I spent several days on the set of his only British film, *Brannigan*, which was filmed in London in the summer of 1974. The first day was spent largely in his trailer — just me and the Duke — talking about his life and work, and he also wanted to know all about me.

He took a liking to me, partly because I simply wanted to know everything I could learn about the filmmaking business he loved so much. My ambition in those days was to write and direct films. I think too he was impressed by my knowledge of his career and he patiently answered the countless questions I put to him. I knew that Wayne knew as much about moviemaking as anyone, but he said, "Kid, you're talking to the wrong fella. You wanna speak to [Howard] Hawks, or [Raoul] Walsh, or [Henry] Hathaway. It's a goddamn shame you didn't get the chance to speak to Pappy." I knew that when he spoke of "Pappy" — sometimes he called him "Coach" — he meant John Ford who had died the previous year.

He also listened while I made observations about his work, both positive and negative. Not once was he patronizing. He asked — or maybe he told — *Brannigan*'s director Douglas Hickox that I should be allowed to spend several days on the set of the film to observe the process of filmmaking. That way, I got to know Wayne better than I ever dreamed was possible.

Another reason for my affection was the fact that we shed a few tears together. That's not the kind of experience you can have and remain unaffected.

Being with John Wayne was a bit like being in a John Wayne film, because what you see on screen is pretty much what you get in real life. When I told him, "You somehow feel like you're an old friend to me," he said, "That's how I hope young people — *and* older people — think of me. When you come to see a picture of mine, I want you to know that I'm not going to do anything that will make you uncomfortable. I want you to know that you won't be disappointed in me. You may not like every film, and I've certainly made some stinkers, but it's important to me that my fans will always come back because they know I won't be mean, I won't be small, and like an old friend, I won't let them down."

During the days I spent on the set, I tried not to make a nuisance of myself by being in Wayne's face all the time. Every time he passed by me, he said, "Hi, kid, how ya doing?" and every day he made the effort to talk to me over a cup of coffee. He made me feel I *was* his friend. He'd ask me what I thought of the latest scene. I actually knew a bit about moviemaking because I'd worked with John Huston a bit, and I'd give my honest opinion. When a scene was being shot in Piccadilly Circus in which a red letter box (or "mailbox," if you're American) was used, I told Wayne that a letter box would not be located on a pedestrian island the way it was for the scene. He listened attentively with his arms crossed, and said, "You're right. But we've got to show the American audience London landmarks they recognize, or they won't believe it's London. And there was nowhere else to put the damn thing."

No matter what I said, he never put me down. Occasionally he said, "That's a damn good idea, kid. I'll talk to Hickox." I've no idea if any suggestions I made were actually used. But he somehow managed to make me feel important. How could I not feel affection for him?

Curiously, the idea to write this book partly came from Wayne back in 1974. I was already thinking of trying my hand at journalism, having been in film publicity since 1969 (which was the year Bob Hope told me that I was so nosy, I ought to be a reporter). I was always asking questions of everyone in the business, and I had learned a very valuable lesson early on from my boss at Cinerama, where I began working in the film industry in 1969 as a messenger boy. He told me to write down everything that was said to me by the many stars I was meeting so I would always have a precise record. I had a knack for remembering whole anecdotes and was able to write them accurately. In fact, when my tape recorder broke down while I was transcribing an interview I'd conducted with Tony Curtis in 1975, I had to write almost two hours of interview by memory: Curtis said he had never been so faithfully quoted.

When I turned up on the *Brannigan* location, I came armed with a small tape recorder given to me by film critic and author Alan Frank, who wanted me to collaborate with him on a book about film epics, and he urged me to tape any interviews I could get.

I had it in mind that I might someday write a book on Wayne, although I was more concerned about recording whatever Wayne said to me for my own personal posterity. Fortunately, he allowed me to record some of our conversations in his trailer, but from time to time, when the subject became too personal or confidential, he'd switch the machine off, and then when we were back to talking movies once more, he'd switch it on again. The words I didn't get on tape I wrote down at the earliest opportunity. Each day while I was on location, I jotted down virtually everything Duke said to me. Somewhat ironically, Wayne suggested that since I wanted to be a writer, I should make the most of my knowledge of cinema and try my hand at a book. I said, "Well, really, I'd like to do a book on you." He said, "Why not? Give it your best shot."

A few days later he turned up with a long list of names and phone numbers; people like Henry Hathaway, Howard Hawks, George Sherman, Maureen O'Hara, Claire Trevor, Paul Fix, and many others he said I ought to talk to. He said, "These people can tell you everything you want to know about making pictures, and about me." Consequently, I spent a lot of nights making transatlantic phone calls.

More than once he said, "Don't forget to call up those people I made a list of for you. They'll be expecting to hear from you."

"Don't worry, I won't forget."

There have been other biographies about John Wayne, most of them — with the exception of memoirs by his wife Pilar and daughter Aissa, as well as an account by Wayne's last secretary Pat Stacy — written by people who didn't actually know or meet Wayne. I think I got to know him quite well.

When I became a journalist toward the end of 1974, I began making concerted efforts to interview anyone who had ever worked with Wayne. When news came in 1979 that Wayne had been diagnosed with stomach cancer, I decided I needed to prepare a tribute, so I contacted all those I had originally called in 1974 who still survived. I also made contact with others, most of whom were willing to talk, some just prior to his death, some right after. I was working at *Photoplay* at the time and was asked by the editor to compile a tribute to John Wayne. But the one I wrote was never published.

I have continued to collect firsthand material on Wayne, and so almost thirty years after I met him, I've finally got around to writing my book on the Duke.

It took a long time for all sorts of reasons, but I became convinced the time was right just after the terrible disaster of 11

15

September 2001. As I watched the events of that day and the aftermath over the following weeks, as I heard stories of lives lost and of men and women who performed incredible acts of heroism, it became evident that old-fashioned American patriotism was flourishing. It made me think of John Wayne, what he spoke about and the message he put across in his films, especially in *The Alamo*.

Of course, John Wayne was just an actor. He didn't really die fighting at the Alamo, or win the battle for Iwo Jima. And yet, to the people of America, he was and remains a symbol of all that America should stand for. And not all of it was an illusion, despite what his critics say. He stood by his beliefs, and he fought for freedom not just on film, but in his life — and in the process he nearly lost his life.

I decided it was time to put the record straight about a number of aspects of his life in response to attempts to blight his reputation since his death, which he cannot answer himself. The main questions have been: why didn't he enlist during the Second World War, and what drove him to fight Communism so aggressively?

Those questions have answers, and they are not the ones his critics always aim for.

16

Along the way, I'll also straighten out some of the exaggerations about his early life and career. For some, it may seem to dilute the legend, but I think his life and career are remarkable enough without the embellishments, most of which came from early studio publicity notes — and also from the likes of John Ford. I don't happen to believe in John Ford's credo, "When the legend becomes fact, print the legend."

Wayne wasn't perfect. But as Maureen O'Hara said, "He was a beautiful human being." There were some great flaws in that beauty, and despite the admiration and, yes, the awe I held him in, he was, after all, just a human being (although when I met him, I made him laugh by saying "I've never met a living legend before"). But what came across — from my brief friendship with him and from hearing what most of the people I spoke to had to say — was that he was a man who *tried*, though not always succeeded, to do what was right. When, as Davy Crockett in *The Alamo*, he says, "There's right and there's wrong. You gotta do one or the other," he was speaking of his own philosophy. Good and bad were black-and-white. There were no gray areas. And maybe that philosophy was his biggest virtue and also his greatest flaw.

No one can deny Wayne had courage, something he displayed not merely on screen but in real life as he fought cancer twice. But he also faced death from forces just as deadly. Attempts were made on his life, which was a secret he kept — except from those who helped to protect him — for one reason: he did not want his family to know because he did not want any of them to worry about him or live in fear. In fact, against advice from the FBI, he refused to change his lifestyle and thereby give in to acts of terror. And that is an aspect of his life that is reflected in the courage and determination of the American people after 11 September.

Although the Wayne family home became something of a safe haven from the usual dangers celebrities feared — such as kidnappers and burglars — Wayne never took any extraordinary precautions to keep himself safe from any would-be assassins.

He continued to live his life *his* way. "America is the land of freedom," he said, "and that's the way I enjoy living."

Yes, John Wayne had real courage.

1

A Communist Conspiracy Revealed

As famed stuntman Yakima Canutt told me the story over a drink in the bar of a London hotel in 1976, it wasn't too difficult to imagine it as a scene straight out of a movie.

Two men were on their knees on the firm wet sand of the secluded beach. Their hands were cuffed behind them, their heads hung low, and their long shadows were thrown by headlights from a car, its engine still running, parked on a side road that ran down to the beach. Beside the car stood two FBI agents.

Big John Wayne stood a meter or two behind the kneeling men, a gun in his hand. Next to him stood his partner, a broad, short man with a crew cut, also with a gun in his hand. The weapons were aimed at the back of the heads of the two kneeling men who muttered pathetically in Russian. Wayne assumed that they were saying their last prayers to whichever god Soviet Communists revered.

But this was no movie scene. This was for real. The man with the crew cut standing next to Wayne was screenwriter James Edward Grant who could never have written a scene like this for Duke to play. Wayne had a policy of never shooting a man in the back in his films. Bad for the image.

"On the count of three," Wayne told Grant. "One — two — three," and then came the sound which the two Russians expected to be the last they would ever hear.

After both guns fired, it took several seconds for the two kneeling men, now shaking uncontrollably, to realize they were still alive.

Wayne turned to the federal agents. "You can have them now."

The G-men came forward, grabbed each Russian by an arm, and hauled them to their feet. The Russians looked quizzically at Wayne who held up his gun and said, "Blanks!"

"What do you want us to do with them?" asked one of the agents.

"Send them back to Russia."

Suddenly, in perfect English with a Midwestern American accent, one of the Russians cried out, "No! Please! Don't send us back to Stalin. We will both die."

"Don't worry," said the federal agent. "You won't be going back . . . yet. We've a few questions we want answered. And then — maybe — we'll let Stalin have you back."

"But you don't need to interrogate us. We can help you. We can work for you."

"Seems they're more afraid of their beloved Stalin than they are of you," Wayne said to the agents. To the Russians, he said, "Welcome to the land of the free."

The two federal agents led the Russians to the car and shoved them into the backseat.

"You won't forget our deal, will ya?" Wayne called out to the agents. "I don't care what you have to tell Hoover, but you'll keep my name out of this."

"If that's what you really want, Mr. Wayne. But these Commies came here to kill you. They failed this time, but those fucking Russkies may try again."

"Like I told you, I got a wife, an ex-wife, and four kids, and I don't want any of them knowing and having to worry for the rest of their lives. These Commies fucked it up this time. Maybe they'll think

21

twice before trying again."

"Maybe, Mr. Wayne."

"The name's Duke."

Wayne shook hands with the agents. Then they got in their car and backed up onto the highway.

Jimmy Grant handed his gun to Wayne. "I'm not used to handling these things. If they hadn't been loaded with blanks, I'm sure I'd have missed."

Wayne just grinned. Then they made their way up to the highway where Duke's car was parked.

As they drove off, Grant asked, "But suppose they do try again?"

"You better hope they don't," Wayne replied with a lopsided grin, "otherwise you might never work again."

As Yakima Canutt pointed out, "Duke was just a little too confident about that."

An old friend of mine, British actor Peter Cushing, had returned from Hong Kong where he had made a couple of lousy films in 1973. The quality of the films hardly mattered to him, but he was full of inspirational tales of courageous people who had escaped from the Republic of China to find a new life in Hong Kong. Among those people were some skilled technicians from the Chinese film industry which, during the 1960s, had been suffering from a period of decline under Communist control.

Peter, a gentle man in the truest sense, was moved as he told me, "I heard a great deal about the oppression of the Chinese people." And he asked, "Will the evil of Communism ever come to an end?" He spoke a great deal about the conditions the people of China lived under, and of the constraints that were put upon the artists of Chinese cinema. Out of this conversation came stories Peter had heard from a number of the Chinese immigrants of a plot hatched between Chairman Mao and Joseph Stalin to have a "big American film star" killed.

This was the first time I ever heard about it, and all Peter knew — "assuming the story is true," he added — was that the big American film star was renowned for two things: "He is known to hate Communists, and he's famous for being a screen cowboy. The first name that comes to mind is John Wayne. But surely that can't be true. Yet that's what these wonderful Chinese people told me. I wonder if it *was* John Wayne they meant."

There was only one way to find out. I

told John Wayne Peter's story. I didn't ask if it was true. I just told him what Peter Cushing had told me.

There we were, in John Wayne's trailer, with Wayne looking down at the floor and saying nothing for what seemed like an eternity. Then, in an almost hushed tone, he said to me, "Once the genie's out of the bottle, how ya gonna get it back in again?"

I didn't understand what he meant, and told him so.

He slapped his knee, looked me in the eye, and said, "Kid, I've been criticized for years because I've made my feelings known about those pinko bastards. I said it during the fifties and I've said it in the sixties, and I've stood up and said we were right to be in Vietnam. But those lefties, those so-called liberals, have tried to crucify me. Well, ya know something? They can't lay a glove on me with their mean-spirited words because I've faced worse than them.

"I'll be straight with you 'cos I like you, and you already know more than anyone should. This is between you and me. The Communists have been trying to kill me since 1949. But as you can see, they didn't do a very good job of it. I licked the Big C — and I licked those Commie bastards."

He then related an incident that occurred in 1966 when he was visiting troops in Vietnam and a sniper opened fire. It was not quite the same story that had been reported in the press.

He also told me that there had been attempts on his life on American soil, which, with the help of the FBI and "a few good friends like Jimmy Grant and Yakima Canutt," had been foiled. Grant was Wayne's favorite screenwriter, and Canutt, who died in 1986, remains the most famous stuntman in movie history. He was also one of Wayne's oldest and closest friends. "I owe my life to Yak," he said. "The agents told me I needed special protection. I said, 'Hell, I'm not gonna hide away for the rest of my life. This is the land of the free, and that's the way I'm gonna stay.' I'd say up to this point, I've succeeded right well."

I asked him if he thought he was now safe. He said, "As far as I'm concerned, I've always been safe. I'm not going through life looking over my shoulder."

Now it does seem that this could easily have been a great yarn Wayne had been spinning me. But, about two years after meeting Wayne, I interviewed Yakima Canutt. We sat and talked for a long time about Wayne, and how for years Wayne's ultraconservative politics had brought him his fair share of detractors, and a good proportion of supporters. The Communist witch hunt, which had raged in Hollywood during the McCarthy era — when actors, writers, and other artists had their names blackened because they were Communists, or had leftist views, or merely took the First Amendment — still stirred emotions in the movie world, and continues to do so.

John Wayne supported Senator McCarthy, and denounced Communism to the end of his days. When he made *The Alamo* it was a direct statement about American freedom — and therefore an indirect attack on Communism — and when he made *The Green Berets*, it was an unashamed assault on Communism. Those who didn't agree with Wayne's right-wing politics denounced him.

But, as I pointed out to Canutt, what Wayne's detractors probably never knew was that he had his own personal battle with the Communists who tried to have him killed.

Canutt was surprised to say the least, and asked, "How in hell did you know?"

"Because Duke told me. And he said he owed his life to you."

And so Canutt told me how he had been

instrumental in thwarting an attempt on Wayne's life.

I had thought that would be the last I'd hear about the Communist conspiracy, but to my surprise it came up again in 1983, and from someone who hardly knew John Wayne. He was Orson Welles.

It could never be said that Welles was a great fan of John Wayne, and he had no intention of enhancing the legend any further. We had been discussing the subject of the so-called Hollywood Ten and the Communist witch hunts, and the conversation had resulted in Welles suddenly saying, "Stalin was mad, of course. Should have been put in a straitjacket. Only a madman like Joseph Stalin would have tried to have John Wayne killed."

He eyed me as if to say, "That took you by surprise, didn't it?"

I decided it was prudent to let him think it did and I asked him what he meant. He went on to explain how he had heard about it from Soviet director Sergei Bondarchuk when making *Waterloo* in 1970. Through all this hearsay, Welles knew how, why, and when Stalin had made the decision to have Wayne killed. Had it not been for the fact that I already knew about the plot, I most certainly would have

27

taken Welles's storytelling with a generous pinch of salt.

But now I had what I consider to be as full an account of the Communist plot to kill John Wayne as I'm ever likely to get.

2

From Marion to Duke

"John Wayne was born Marion Michael Morrison," Claire Trevor told me.

The question of Wayne's real name was one I put to many who knew him, and Claire Trevor's mistake was a common one.

"Marion Michael Morrison was the name he was born with," said Henry Fonda.

"His parents must have had an odd sense of humor 'cos they named him Marion," said Yakima Canutt.

"But what was his middle name?" I asked Canutt.

"Michael."

"Marion Michael Morrison," said director George Sherman.

"Marion Mitchell Robinson," said actor John Carradine.

"They called him Marion, that's for

sure," said Ken Curtis, "and his middle name was Michael."

All of them got it wrong, and it isn't surprising. Much of Wayne's life and work is shrouded in myth and legend, even to those who knew him best.

The confusion is understandable. John Wayne told me, "My parents named me after my grandfather, Marion Mitchell Morrison. Only my middle name wasn't Mitchell. It was Robert. And that's the name on my birth certificate. My parents changed my middle name to Michael because they wanted my younger brother to be called Robert."

The legend is further complicated by the fact that in the 1925 Glendale High Yearbook, Wayne's picture, for reasons Wayne could never remember, bears the name Marion Mitchell Morrison, which has caused some film historians and biographers to mistakenly state his original name as being Marion Mitchell.

But Marion Robert it was when he was born on 26 May 1907 in Winterset, Iowa. And when his brother Robert was born on 8 December 1911, four-year-old Marion's middle name got unofficially changed to Michael, which is why Wayne's oldest son was called Michael.

"Well, I sure as hell wasn't going to name my firstborn Marion," Wayne told me with that famous crooked smile. "Any kid called Marion's gonna have a rough ride. And I should know."

Wayne's memories of his childhood are not particularly happy ones. He hated being called Marion, he couldn't understand why his middle name had to change just because he had a younger brother, and he resented his mother because for some reason Robert, not the firstborn son, became the apple of her eye.

Mother was Mary Brown — but always called Molly — born in Lincoln, Nebraska, in 1885. She was of Irish descent and known for being a dynamic, sometimes harping, and quick-tempered woman. Father was mild mannered, generous, and trusting Clyde Morrison from Monmouth, Illinois, of Scottish descent. His father was Marion Mitchell Morrison, apparently a hero of the American Civil War.

Just a few years after Clyde's birth in 1884, his family moved to Iowa where he grew up and served an apprenticeship as a pharmacist in Waterloo. It was there that he met Molly, who worked as a telephone operator. They were married on 29 September 1906, just eight months before

Marion was born. No one knows, or cares to reveal, whether Marion was born prematurely, or if Molly was already pregnant when she and Clyde married. But no one who knew them could ever claim they were a match made in heaven.

By the time Marion came into the world, Clyde was working as a pharmacist's clerk at a drugstore in Winterset. It seems there were marital problems almost from the beginning. While Clyde was easygoing and trusting of others, Molly was a dominant woman and definitely the head of the household. She constantly nagged Clyde, which upset Marion who began to feel insecure listening to his parents' constant arguments. It may well be that the incompatible couple had married in haste.

She wanted Clyde to progress in his work, and made sure that they saved enough money so he could buy his own store in nearby Earlham where the family made their new home. That's where Robert was born, named after Molly's father. Marion came to resent his mother's devotion to his younger brother, feeling unloved by her. Consequently, this made him grow closer to his father who taught him how to play football. In turn, Molly became increasingly impatient with

Marion who wanted little to do with Robert.

By most accounts, the store Clyde bought was a pharmacy. But according to Yakima Canutt, "Duke's father's store mainly sold paint and wallpaper, and it also sold patent medicine. I know that for a fact because Duke told me. But I also knew that Duke idolized his father and he felt that a pharmacist was a respectable profession and he preferred to remember his father as a pharmacist and not a seller of paint and wallpaper."

Years later, when Marion Michael Morrison became famous as John Wayne, stories emerged, often made up by studio publicists, which delved into his past and made a few changes to the true story. Young Marion, they said, discovered a great love of the countryside and would often go off on his own. "I hated the countryside when I was a kid," he told me, however. "The only reason I'd go off on my own was to run away from home because there was . . . well, a lot of unhappiness back then."

According to Canutt, "He ran away and was usually found and returned home. Other times he just came home on his own because he was hungry. And when he came home, it was back to a house where his parents were bickering. It was back to a town where the local bullies teased him about his name. What I believe is true — only this probably came about when he was a little older and not as a youngster of five or six as has been told — he enjoyed learning about the history of the old West. When we were working together on those early Westerns, he'd talk about the old West and of wagon trains and pioneers, of stagecoach robberies and heroic lawmen. And because his grandfather had fought in the Civil War, he immersed himself in the history of the war between the states.

"I reckon he must have been around ten or in his early teens when he discovered his love of American history. And it was good for him, because he learned what became so important to him and his image: the value of his country and the freedom it enjoyed. He was on his way to becoming an American patriot."

But before he was old enough to learn all that, he had learned how to keep silent about his deepest feelings. "He never complained to his mother about the lack of love he felt from her," said Canutt, "and he couldn't bring himself to let his father know how much he appreciated the patience and understanding he always showed him."

Wayne's inability to reveal his feelings was a trait he would instill in his own children, with the exception of one emotion. "The one feeling Duke encouraged in his children was showing love," said Canutt. "But he has never been able to abide people who bellyache and complain."

In 1914 the Morrisons moved to California. The reason for this move is in question. Most accounts say that Clyde was unwell — possibly with tuberculosis — and was told by his doctor to move to a much warmer and drier climate. But Wayne told me, "My father couldn't make a living as a pharmacist so I guess he decided he'd try his hand at homesteading. I guess he failed in business just because he was too generous to his customers and allowed them credit, much to my mother's displeasure, I may add. When much of the credit was not paid, he was forced to close the store."

And so the Morrisons left Iowa for California where Clyde took over the homestead that had belonged to his father. It was situated in Antelope Valley, an arid basin north of Los Angeles. The nearest town was Lancaster. Molly hated it there and complained about the primitive conditions she found herself having to endure.

Marion, who was just seven when they moved to the valley, also disliked it. Years later the story emerged that young Marion was in awe of the distant mountains that stretched for hundreds of miles, making him feel like a part of the old West. But I suspect that observation was one created by film publicists because it fitted the image of cowboy star John Wayne.

Henry Hathaway, who directed several of Wayne's films, including *True Grit*, told me during a transatlantic phone call, "That's the trouble with the studios in those days — when they found a star, they'd embellish biographical details, so you can never trust the 'official' versions." "I hated living in Antelope Valley," Wayne told me. "There were so many rattlesnakes, I had nightmares about them," he said. "We were living in little more than a rambling shack with no electricity. It was a hard life for all of us. I had to get up at five every morning to do my chores, while my father fought a losing battle growing crops in the poor soil, and what did grow was eaten by the jackrabbits."

Michael Wayne, Duke's oldest son, whom I met on the set of *Brannigan*, said of his father's family, "They were really quite poor and lived off tuna fish for about six months because evidently they got a good buy on several cases of tuna fish. After that, my father could never eat tuna."

So much of Wayne's childhood was clouded by stories that were tailored to fit the cowboy star that it becomes difficult separating fact from fiction. When he was barely more than seven, he was supposedly taught by his father to fire a rifle. Henry Hathaway said, "I think it's extremely questionable whether a pharmacist like Clyde would have even known how to use a rifle."

Marion apparently learned to swim using a local irrigation ditch, and he certainly had to learn to ride a horse. "I was riding as soon as I could walk," he said, which wasn't quite true, but it does fit snugly into the John Wayne legend.

"I had a horse called Jenny," he said, "and twice every week I rode over desert roads to pick up the mail and groceries from the general store in Lancaster. I also rode Jenny to school, which was in the same town." Wayne didn't say if he was particularly fond of Jenny, especially since she was little more than a scrawny nag. But despite making a career out of riding horses, he told me, "I've never really liked horses and I daresay not many of them liked me too much."

Poor Jenny's days ended when she became ill and thin, and had to be shot. Wayne said, "The nosy biddies of the town called the Humane Society and accused me, a seven-year-old, of not feeding my horse and watering him. This was proven to be a lie." (It didn't occur to me at the time, but Wayne referred to Jenny as "him" rather than "her.")

The Morrisons could not afford another horse, so Marion had to walk to school, and occasionally he would hitch a ride in a passing wagon. By now a loner who suffered from anxiety and shyness, he found making friends almost impossible. "I got into a lot of fights at school because my classmates laughed at my Midwestern accent and especially at my goddamn name. On many an occasion I came home from school covered in mud and blood, and got berated by my mother who gave me endless lectures on how I should behave like a gentleman. My father, however, praised me for my courage and taught me that a man must always stand up for himself. Unfortunately, I didn't usually win when I stood up for myself."

Clyde's advice may seem uncharacteristic coming from a man dominated by his wife, but Clyde learned to stand up to her. This led to constant arguments, and many nights Marion and Robert lay in bed, listening to their parents shouting at each other.

Conflict between them grew worse as Clyde's health improved (assuming it had been poor to start with). What is sure is that Clyde was no farmer and, in June 1916, he gave up tilling the soil and moved his family to Glendale, a suburb of Los Angeles, California, where he went to work as a clerk in the Glendale Pharmacy. Clyde's father had recently died and left a small inheritance, which gave the family a good start in Glendale.

Wayne said, "My father was well liked by the young people of the town and they called him Doc, because as well as dispensing medicine, he also gave what young people considered to be good advice. They'd go to him with their problems rather than to their own folks. He was a caring man, a selfless man. Thinking back after all these years, I don't think my mother, God rest her soul, deserved him. I only wish I'd learned then to let him know how much I loved him."

Marion was enrolled at Doran Elementary School and began attending the Presbyterian Church. "I liked Glendale," he said. "It was a town with a good community spirit. It kind of forced me out of my shell, and I joined the Boy Scouts, the YMCA, and the Masonic youth fraternity. When my father's inheritance ran out and we found we were short of money, I took odd jobs such as delivering newspapers and delivering prescriptions for the Glendale Pharmacy." He also acquired a dog, an Airedale: "We called him Duke. I loved that dog. He went with me everywhere, except to school and church. I used to go by the town's fire station where the firefighters began calling me Big Duke and the dog Little Duke. So everyone started calling me Duke, except my mother. I tell ya, I was real glad to be rid of that goddamn name.

"They were great guys, those firefighters. They used to give me milk. They'd say, 'Take it home for your cat,' even though they knew we had no cat. The milk was really for me. One day I got into a fight with a local bully and lost and got a black eye. One of the firefighters who was a former professional boxer gave me lessons in self-defense, and, ya know, before long I got to be pretty good with my fists."

40

★ ★ ★

In 1921 Duke Morrison began his freshman year at Glendale High. In his teens he had begun to grow rapidly upward, and before long he stood more than six feet tall. Although he was skinny, weighing just 140 pounds, he became star guard on the school football team. An intelligent young man, still a little shy but possessing a modest and unassuming manner, he started to win the admiration of his peers and began to achieve success in various aspects of his school life. He became class vice president in his sophomore and junior years, graduating to president as a senior, and he even wrote a sports column for the school paper.

It was in Glendale that Duke discovered movies. Not surprisingly, perhaps, his favorite pictures were Westerns. "I understand my fans because I had idols. They were Harry Carey and Tom Mix. Glendale was a popular location for picture makers, and I got to see a lot of scenes being filmed. I remember seeing Douglas Fairbanks filming a woodland scene for *Robin Hood.*

"I guess watching famous movie stars gave me some inspiration to try acting. I was a member of the school's dramatic society. I even got chosen as the school's representative in the Southern California Shakespeare Contest in 1925. I delivered Cardinal Wolsey's speech from *Henry VIII*." This is noted in the Glendale High School Yearbook of 1925. Among his plays at school were *The First Lady of the Land* in which he played a nobleman, and *Dulcey* as an old man.

It is unlikely that Duke Morrison possessed strong acting skills at this stage. School plays inevitably win praise more for the enthusiasm displayed by the cast than for any notable acting ability. The only evidence we have of his acting skills as a young man comes from his first speaking parts in films, namely *Salute* and *Words and Music* (both 1929), when he delivers his few lines with no conviction or credibility. However, I think Wayne made a point of emphasizing his high school plays and his attempt at Shakespeare in order to fend off the film critics, who often felt his greatest ability was to get on and off a horse with conviction.

But there seemed to be no desire to take up acting as a profession when he graduated in 1925. "When we moved to California, I discovered the ocean, and I loved it," he said. "My ambition was to become an officer in the United States Navy. I applied to the Naval Academy but was turned down."

Henry Hathaway cast doubt on this claim, saying, "I never heard Duke say his ambition was to join the Navy. I think that was an invention of either the studio or John Ford, who was in the Naval Reserve. Once a story like that gets the official stamp, it's hard for someone like John Wayne to turn around say it wasn't true. As far as I knew, his ambition was to become a lawyer. When he went to university, that's what he studied — law."

His high school grades were good enough for his acceptance to the University of Southern California (USC), but for a short while it looked like he would not be able to attend because the Morrison family simply couldn't afford it. He was saved when he received a football scholarship. During his first year at college, his parents finally separated and were divorced in 1929. Duke was relieved. Clyde eventually married a saleswoman at Webb's Department Store in Glendale, and Molly moved to Long Beach, taking Robert with her, where she lived for the rest of her days. Duke had little contact with either parent during his college years, when he was learning to become ever more independent. He was also becoming a high achiever at college.

When I spoke to one of Wayne's lifelong friends, actress Loretta Young, by telephone, she said, "Duke was no dummy, which a lot of people like to think. He did well academically during his freshman year, and he learned from his fraternity brothers how to drink and to play cards. I think that was the beginning of his preference for the company of men who could hold their liquor and play cards. Not that he didn't like girls. He found himself the center of attention from a number of college girls who warmed to his natural naïve charm and good looks. One of his girlfriends was my sister, Polly Ann Young. That's how I got to meet Duke, and we enjoyed a friendship that lasted many years. He always treated the girls he dated with good old-fashioned respect, never swearing in their presence and certainly never getting drunk. But in the company of men, it was a different story. He learned to hold his liquor, he swore when he felt like it, but he was never belligerent and was a nice guy, plain and simple."

Director Andrew V. McLaglen knew Wayne for many years and directed several of his later movies. When I had lunch with McLaglen at Pinewood Studios in 1978, where he was preparing to film *North Sea Hijack*, he said, "People think Duke was not an intellectual. Well, he was an intellectual. He read avidly and could hold a discussion about many subjects. He made himself aware of politics both nationally and internationally. Don't ever mistake John Wayne for being dumb, just because he was big and kind of slow. That was only a part of his screen persona."

George Sherman, who directed Wayne in a number of films, concurred when I spoke to him by telephone for a second time in 1979: "I knew Duke when he was still a young man and I can tell you that he was an extremely intelligent guy. He knew what the 1917 revolution in Russia was all about. He knew he didn't like Communists."

Another of Wayne's directors and friends, Raoul Walsh, told me in 1974, "I got to know Duke when he was still very young and the only thing he did that was stupid was to let himself get drunk too often. But when we were making *The Big Trail*, he proved he was very bright and articulate. When he spoke as a youngster, you knew he'd had a good education. He had to learn to drawl like a cowboy."

He developed his first political affiliations at USC. "When I was a sophomore at USC, I was a socialist, pretty much to the left," he said. "But not when I left the university. I quickly got wise. I'd read about what had happened to Russia in 1917 when the Communists took over. The average kid in college would like everybody to be able to have ice cream and cake with every meal as their God-given right. But as he gets older and gives more thought to his own and his fellow man's responsibility, he finds it just can't work the way he wanted it to because there are always some people who just won't carry their load. And the ones who whine about how hard they've got it are often the ones who won't carry their load. Communism just doesn't work."

Two of Duke's best friends at Glendale were Bob and Bill Bradbury, whose father, Robert N. Bradbury, was making short films featuring his sons. In 1926 Robert N. Bradbury made *Davy Crockett at the Fall of the Alamo*, with a featured part for his son Bob (who later took on the screen name of Bob Steele).

Wayne said, "I'd read up on the history of our country and I'd become fascinated with the story of the Alamo. To me it represented the fight for freedom, not just in America, but in all countries. Seeing Robert Bradbury's film was a real inspiration to me, and I guess it stuck with me until it became a passion of mine to make *The Alamo*. It's a story of freedom, and courage, and doing right in the face of adversity."

Legend has it that Duke Morrison was a star football player with the Trojans at USC and on his way to becoming an all-American football star. He certainly trained for a year under legendary football coach Howard Jones. It was through Jones that Duke met cowboy star Tom Mix who was under contract to the William Fox Studios in nearby Hollywood.

"When Tom Mix wanted the best seats to see the USC's Trojan football games, Jones arranged it," said Wayne. "In return, Mix promised Jones that he would find work for any of his players who needed summer jobs. So in the summer of 1926 me and my buddy Don Williams were sent to Fox."

There, legend has it, they drank and talked football with Mix, who decided to put Duke on the payroll as a personal trainer to help keep him in peak condition; their plan was that Duke would make Mix run two or three miles every day.

Henry Hathaway disputed that account, saying, "I'm not sure that Tom Mix actually took Duke on as a trainer. I think it's one of those stories that the studio put into his biographies because it made for a good story. And once it was in print, Wayne couldn't actually ever turn around and say that it wasn't true, so he went along with it."

It seems that, by 1974, Wayne was no longer sticking to the "official" version. He said, "I arrived at the studio and they put me straight to work carrying props. I got to meet Tom Mix at Fox. That was a real thrill for me. He used to like talking about football more than movies."

Duke Morrison was a tall, rather skinny young man, and it was probably doing all that work shifting props that helped him build up some of his muscles. His good looks inspired someone in the casting department to give him a job as an extra and even as a stuntman in a number of films.

"I do know that Tom Mix got him one of his first jobs as an extra in a Western at Fox called *The Great K & A Train Robbery* which starred Mix," said George Sherman.

There are unsubstantiated reports that Wayne was also an extra over at MGM in *Brown of Harvard* and *Bardelys the Magnificent*, and also at Warner Bros. in Michael Curtiz's biblical epic *Noah's Ark*. But since he was at work at Fox, these reports are unreliable. "I can't remember all the pictures I appeared in as an extra," he said. "That was a helluva long time ago."

When the summer was over, Duke went back to college and at a weekend party met Josephine Saenz, the daughter of Dr. Saenz, a wealthy Hispanic businessman and consul general in Los Angeles. Loretta Young recalled, "Although Josephine was a devout Catholic and a part of high society, she found Duke to be sincere and earnest, and a fresh change from the usual rich young men who tried to date her. Her family, however, did not approve of lowly Duke Morrison when he began dating their daughter. So they had to meet in secret, and despite her parents' objections, they became engaged."

According to virtually everything I've read about John Wayne, his dream of becoming an all-American ended with a shoulder injury. Some accounts say it happened while playing football; others that he hurt it surfing. Woody Strode, who appeared opposite Wayne in *The Man Who Shot Liberty Valance* (but is probably best remembered as the black gladiator Draba in *Spartacus*), played for the Los Angeles Rams before becoming an actor. He was of the opinion Duke Morrison had no chance of ever becoming an all-American. When I interviewed him in London in 1976 (where he was visiting briefly while en route to making a film in Italy), he told me, "Wayne was never a great football player, but somehow he got into the USC's hall of fame. I guess becoming the greatest movie star in the world will do that for you."

Coach Jones tried Duke first as a guard, which meant he had to be fast, but Duke never could run fast, so Jones moved him to tackle. When he failed at that too, he was dropped from the team at the end of the first year, and he lost his scholarship.

He may well have received a shoulder injury, but as Strode said, "It's unlikely, almost unthinkable, that a good coach would drop a promising all-American because of one injury. Duke just was not good enough to stay on the team."

George Sherman told me, "I don't know if Duke ever had a shoulder injury. All I can tell you is that when we first worked together, he never showed any sign of a weakened shoulder. But by 1939 he was already becoming less agile. For one thing, he suffered with back pain. My feeling is that if Duke said he hurt his shoulder, then it was true, but I don't believe that was the reason he was dropped from the college football team. He never could run particularly fast, and if you look at pictures of Wayne up to the time he made *The Big Trail* [in 1930], you can see that he was tall but not well built, which means he was never going to be a star football player. But it looked good to the fans in those early days to say he was, and it was something Duke was never going to dispute."

3

Call Him Wayne

With the football scholarship no longer available, Duke was unable to continue going to college. So he went back to Fox in the spring of 1927 to work in the property department, where he was well liked by the people he worked with for his casual and pleasant manner.

"When John Ford [then in his early thirties] needed an extra propman on *Mother Machree* [in 1928], I was given a very important job." Wayne laughed as he recalled, "My very important job was to release a gaggle of geese from their pens and herd them into camera shot. Now the coach was a pretty large man with a ferocious temper, and every time he called, 'Action!' the geese went everywhere. Well, that just made Pappy lose his temper with me, and I just stood there flustered and embarrassed as he told me that I was the most awkward fucking propman he'd ever known.

"So I got mad at him for yelling at me and cussing me, and I yelled and cussed right back. He said, 'You're a football player, aren't you?' I said, 'Yes,' and he said, 'Do you think you could block me?' and I said, 'Yes.' So he said, 'Get down on your three-point stance,' which is where you have one hand on the ground and the other in front of you. So I got down, and he kicked my hand away, and I went facedown in the dirt.

"Pappy and everyone just laughed, but I was steaming mad. I said, 'I'd like to try that again,' so I got down, but this time, I didn't wait for him to make a move. I just suddenly drove into him and sent him flying over tables and chairs — and there was horrified silence from everyone who obviously thought, 'That guy won't work here again.' But Pappy just laughed and said, 'You'll do all right, now get those fucking geese back in the pen and we'll try again.'

"Maybe 'cos I'd shown him he couldn't intimidate me, he took an instant liking to me and made sure I worked for him again on his next picture [*Four Sons*]. This time my very important job was to pick up piles of maple leaves and toss them into the air so they could be blown by a giant fan across the set to simulate autumn. After they shot the scene several times, I misunderstood a signal from Ford and thought the scene was over. So I began the very important job of sweeping up the leaves, and when I crossed in front of the camera, I realized they were still turning. Well, horror was written on every face around me and I figured I was in big trouble. But Pappy just laughed and did something to me he was famous for when he wanted to punish someone for their sins. He told me to bend over, which I did, and then he kicked me in the butt. He said, 'That's what we call assuming the position, so when I tell you to assume the position, you'll know what to do.' "

It's a great story, and one I'd like to assume is true. The problem is, Ford was a master storyteller, and as time went by, he invented tales about the stars he discovered, and those stars loyal to him, like Wayne, went along with everything Ford said.

For instance, when Ford made *Salute*, which was about a football rivalry between the army and the navy, Ford requested the use of twenty-five football players from the USC Trojans. His request was turned down, so, goes the story, he got Duke Morrison, who was to have his first talking part in the picture, to pull some strings. Duke supposedly went to the USC president and persuaded him to allow John Ford to borrow the players he needed.

On the morning the *Salute* cast and crew were ready to pull out of Los Angeles by train to head for the Naval Academy at Annapolis, an extra football player turned up by the name of Ward Bond.

Duke Morrison didn't like Bond and told him, "You're not getting on this train, Bond. You're too ugly to be in movies."

"Screw you, Duke," replied Bond, and shoved his way on to the train with the other football players.

At the Naval Academy, the players were taught how to drill and act like midshipmen. Finally, Ward Bond called out, "What is this bullshit, anyway?"

Ford asked Duke, "Who is that big ugly guy? The one with the liver lips and the big mouth."

"His name is Ward Bond," answered Duke. "He's just a big loudmouth who thinks he can play football."

"He sure is ugly," said Ford.

"He's a lousy football player too," said Duke.

"I'm going to use him," said Ford and, so the story goes, he invented a small part for Bond to play.

Henry Hathaway trashed this whole story for me: "Wayne had no pull with the university. He was probably totally forgotten by the university. There was no way he had the authority to cast the film. Only a studio executive could do that, and that's what really happened. No one was hand-picked by Duke; Ford chose his team from photographs the studio collected. And Ford never invented a part for Ward Bond. That part was already in the script. I tell you, that Jack Ford really knew how to blarney! And I can tell you, Wayne thought the world of Ward Bond."

It was just as well that John Ford knew how to blarney; he was carrying out secret activities for the navy. Wayne told me, "He was recruited by Rear Admiral Sims to work with Captain Ellis Zacharias [who was to become commander of the Eleventh Navy District in San Diego]. They were concerned over the rise of Japanese power in the Pacific. Zacharias ran a semiofficial intelligence unit using local Naval Reserve officers to collect information on Japanese and German influence in Mexico and the Far East. This information was passed to

J. Edgar Hoover and Vice Admiral T. S. Wilkinson.

"Ford happily conducted intelligence activities on his own initiative without pay or official recognition. I didn't know it then, but while we were filming *Salute*, he met with naval intelligence leaders and was given a mission to go to the Pacific. His official job was to research and film sequences for his next film, *Men Without Women*, but unofficially he was reporting on harbor access and defenses."

Morrison and Bond were both in *Men Without Women*, the story of a submarine damaged and trapped on the ocean floor with fourteen men on board. Another legend has built up around Wayne's involvement in this film. It's been claimed that when Ford was filming a scene in which the men of the submarine have to dive into choppy water, the stuntmen were too afraid to take the plunge. So Ford said, "Duke, get in the water," and Duke obliged by diving into the rough sea.

Wayne confirmed the story when I asked him about it, but Yakima Canutt said, "There's no doubt Duke was fearless and he did do a lot of his own stunts, but I'd be ashamed of any stuntman who couldn't do a simple thing like jump into the sea. That just doesn't sound right to me."

In the first few films Wayne appeared in at Fox, his roles were so small he received no billing. But when he played a student in a 1929 musical, *Words and Music*, he received credit, way down the cast list, as Duke Morrison. Although the studio found him occasional work as an extra, his main living was as a propman. But he was making friends on the Fox lot, and one of these was George O'Brien, one of the studio's leading romantic actors. O'Brien was able to get Duke a small role in the 1930 film *Rough Romance*, although he was still way down in the cast list, as he was in *Cheer Up and Smile*, also in 1930 and again playing a student.

"Through my friendships with John Ford and George O'Brien," Wayne told me, "I was made to feel like I belonged on the lot. I just loved going to work at Fox, and I began to feel this was my life."

Life for Duke Morrison was about to change forever — and so was his name.

Raoul Walsh told me, "When sound first came to movies in 1927, the studios thought that sound would be unsuitable for Westerns. They felt that sound meant you had to have plenty of talking, which is why they called the first sound films 'talkies,' and the studios asked, 'Who wanted to see a Western crammed with talking?' There was also the practical problem of filming with sound. The cameras were big and noisy and had to be enclosed in a box to prevent the noise being picked up by the microphones. The studios had converted all their stages to 'soundstages' where the heavy cameras could not be easily moved. Silent cameras were easy to move and pioneers of the cinema had developed techniques such as 'tracking shots' [whereby the camera moved along with the action].

"But I believed Westerns could be made with sound. I liked the idea of being able to hear hoofbeats and gunfire. But no one had tried filming outside of a studio soundstage. Then in 1929 I saw a Fox Movietone newsreel in which a longshoreman was interviewed in the open by means of recording equipment housed in a specially constructed wagon.

"I headed straight for the nearest phone and called a production executive at Fox and said, 'I want to make a Western with sound.'

"The executive said, 'Are you drunk?'

"I said, 'No. Get me a Fox Movietone News wagon.'

"So I got my wagon and I adapted a story called 'The Cisco Kid' into the first major sound Western [*In Old Arizona*]."

The film won an Oscar for its star, Warner Baxter, and Paramount quickly jumped on the Movietone bandwagon and made *The Virginian* with Gary Cooper in 1929.

Sound Westerns were a success after all, and studio technicians had to devise a more convenient means of filming outdoors. Fox even came up with a new revolutionary process called Grandeur, a 70mm process whereby the picture was twice the size of normal 35mm film and in widescreen.

Their first bold venture was to be another Raoul Walsh Western, *The Big Trail*, a film of epic proportions that told of a wagon train heading west. It would be bigger than the similar silent Western epic *The Covered Wagon*, said Walsh. "To play the lead, the train's scout, I wanted a young man with a certain aura that suggested the authentic American pioneer spirit. I knew that most of the established Western stars from the silent days were not only unrealistic, but they were too old. I was strolling around the Fox lot one day and as I walked by the property department, I saw this young feller come out — about six feet four inches in height. He walked over to a truck and picked up a big armchair and lifted it up over his head and carried it into the property department. So I went over and waited for him to come out and I asked him what he was doing.

"The young feller said, 'I work in the property department.'

"I said, 'Have you ever been in a picture?'

"He said, 'No, sir.'

"I said, 'How would you like to be in a picture?'

"The young feller said, 'Oh, I'd like it right well.'

"I said, 'Let your hair grow for a few weeks and come back to me.'

"So he came back a few weeks later and I got him into a buckskin and took a good silent test of him, and showed it to Winnie Sheehan, the Fox executive, and he said, 'That's a hell of a good-looking boy. Can he speak?'

"I said, 'Sure he can speak. He's a college boy.'

"And Sheehan said, 'All right, we'll sign

him up if you're willing to take a chance on him.'

"I said, 'I'm willing.'

"But they didn't like his name — Duke Morrison — and kept changing it around and called him Joe Doakes and Sidney Carlton and all those sorts of names. I had read a book about Mad Anthony Wayne, a Revolutionary War hero, and I thought this Wayne was a great character, so I said, 'Let's call him Anthony Wayne, or Mad Wayne, or whatever the hell you want to call him — but call him Wayne.' And someone suggested John Wayne. And that's how he got his name."

That's the story Raoul Walsh told. Of course, this story was being told to me in 1974, forty-one years after the event, by an eighty-seven-year-old master storyteller down a transatlantic phone line, and I suspect that there was a certain amount of poetic license taken. After all, Duke Morrison had already appeared in pictures and was already known at Fox.

Michael Wayne had a different version of how his father got his screen name: "He had an agent whose name, strange though it may seem, was also Morrison. And this guy said, 'Look, you've got to get rid of that Marion Morrison,' and my father said,

'What shall I call myself?' and he said, 'John Wayne.' ''

Michael could only have heard this story from his father, but the problem with this account is that Wayne had not been called Marion Morrison since he was a boy. Everyone knew him as Duke Morrison. That account also poses another question: Since Wayne was primarily a propman at Fox and only got a little work as an extra and an occasional minor role, would he have had an agent?

I'm inclined to believe the more romantic Walsh story, and I would assume that Wayne himself came up with the other version for the sole reason of not wanting to offend John Ford. As Walsh said, "Wayne was Ford's friend, and it's my belief that Ford felt that if anyone was going to discover this new star, it was going to be Ford. Instead, it was me, and Ford saw Duke's acceptance of doing *The Big Trail* and taking a star role under a director other than him, as well as one who created his new name, as an act of betrayal by Duke. And Duke was punished for it when Ford refused to speak to him for some years."

For the next five years, Wayne couldn't understand why Ford would never take or return his calls. In later life Wayne shrugged off the notion that Ford had done any more than put him to some kind of test. However, John Carradine, best known for his horror films but who also starred with Wayne in Ford's *Stagecoach*, believed the director was punishing Duke with his silence. On the creepy set of *House of Long Shadows* in London in 1982, Carradine stated, "Ford at his best was like a father, and at his worst he was a monster. He felt his actors and crew were his family — or rather that they belonged to him. He didn't take it at all well when Duke Morrison was reinvented as John Wayne by a director other than himself. I think that Ford had intended to gently ease Wayne into a career, to guide him, and when Wayne accepted Walsh's offer to star in *The Big Trail*, that was almost unpardonable to Ford. He didn't like it, and he showed it by refusing to talk to Duke for some years. This may sound disrespectful to Ford's memory, and believe me, I could respect him as a great filmmaker, but I suffered the same fate as Duke Wayne. Before *Stagecoach* I'd made a few films with Ford, but after that, for some reason, he ignored me for twenty years. So I can see that Ford would have shunned John Wayne just because he let another director turn him into a star."

Even before filming on *The Big Trail* began, the film was generating publicity, but not the kind that was wanted. The press and trade papers heralded their doubts about Wayne's ability based on his previous screen experiences. A reporter for *Hollywood Filmograph* wrote, "If he [Walsh] brings in a winner with Mr. Wayne, he will be entitled to a Carnegie Medal."

But Walsh had great faith in Duke and liked him enough to agree to Duke's request that his friend Ward Bond be given a part; he played just a small role as wagon driver.

Walsh recalled, "While I was out looking for locations, Sheehan and Sol Wurtzel, another Fox executive, had figured this boy should have some help. They sent for five prominent character actors from New York and surprised me with these fellows. Well they certainly did surprise me, because when I got a look at them I realized they had never seen the sunrise or the sunset, and knew I was going to have a hell of a time with them on location."

Screenwriters had not yet come to grips with creating intelligent dialogue for sound movies, and even though three names were credited with writing the dialogue — Jack Peabody, Marie Boyle, and Florence Postal — the script, Walsh said, "was lousy" when filming began in April 1930 outside Yuma, Arizona, where a frontier settlement had been built.

Said Walsh, "I told Duke to improvise much of his dialogue. In one of the opening scenes, Ian Keith was told to simply fire questions at Duke, who answered with whatever came to mind. His acting was instinctive, so that he became whatever and whoever he played. There is a lot of pride in the knowledge that I discovered a winner."

From the outset, Walsh had big problems to deal with. Walsh said, "When we got out on location, got started, and I called John, and I said, 'John, sit beside me when I'm directing these character actors from New York and you'll learn something from them.' Well, these prominent actors from the New York stage turned out to be heavy drinkers. The night before, a bootlegger got to them and in the morning they were pretty well oiled up for the scene. Not only did they scare the Indians that were sitting around, they scared the hawks and the crows that were in the trees, and I said, 'John, go over there and mingle with the

Indians. Pay no attention to them so-called actors.'

"I thought of renaming the film *The Big Drunk*. Duke and Ward Bond joined in with their drinking bouts and some mornings Wayne turned up in poor shape. He came down with a bad case of diarrhea and had to spend a week in bed."

Wayne recalled, "I was puking and crapping blood for a week, and lost eighteen pounds. I had to spend another two weeks recuperating."

Finally Walsh ran out of patience and threatened to replace him if he didn't pull himself together. Wayne returned to work, although he was still weak.

He had good cause to remember one particular scene in which he and Tully Marshall had to pass a jug back and forth. "Marshall had filled it with bootleg whisky. When I took my first slug, I nearly choked. You can bet I called him every kind of an old bastard."

Leading lady Marguerite Churchill remembered Wayne as "nothing but a drunk." Walsh said, "Duke learned to cut back on his drinking while filming progressed. Marguerite Churchill even developed a bit of a crush on Duke, and played him classical music on a windup Victrola phonograph. They had a brief fling, and I suggested he break it off. On-set romances too often lead to emotional disasters. Besides, he was still courting Josephine."

After Yuma, the company moved to Sacramento for the river scenes, but still the script was in poor shape. Said Walsh, "We had new pages of dialogue being written each day but I encouraged Wayne to continue ad-libbing most of his lines. It was a long, hard location, and those damned New York actors were constantly complaining. But not Duke. I could see he was enjoying the whole experience.

"My worry was that we had far too much talking and not enough action. We moved on to St. George in Utah and by then we had more footage than we needed of the wagon train fording rivers, toiling through rugged canyons, and crawling over mountains. I decided we needed something that would really bring home to the audience how the pioneers put their lives on the line during the migrations west. So I decided in St. George we would lower several wagons and horses and steers down the canyon.

"I scribbled some lines for Duke and told him to use them or just ad-lib as he directed the lowering of the wagons, which was really a dangerous scene. I watched young Duke and thought how well he was doing because he seemed to actually be there and not just making a motion picture. When we were lowering the last wagon, the rope slipped and the wagon hung lopsided enough to heighten the suspense, and there was Duke shouting orders like it was real because now the danger really was real. Then the wagon fell and crashed to the canyon floor. I held my breath hoping I'd caught it all on camera — and I had. And through it all, Duke was waving his arms and shouting orders. I think he really enjoyed the adventure of it all."

The next stop was Jackson Hole, Wyoming, by the shores of Jackson Lake in the Grand Tetons. Then it was back to California, to Sequoia National Park, and finally the location shooting wound up in Moise, Montana, for the buffalo stampede. With all outdoor shooting finished, the company returned to the Fox studio for interiors, and after ten weeks of production, the film was finally wrapped.

"We finally struggled through the picture. John was very attentive, very good. He was a nice boy to work with and I felt pleased that I had discovered the world's greatest box-office star. I also discovered a great American."

Filming *The Big Trail* proved to be an ordeal for Walsh, who admitted, "I went into it unprepared for the difficulties I would face. Apart from my drunken actors, I had to shoot several different versions of the film — one in 70mm Grandeur, another in conventional 35mm, and another version with German actors for foreign markets."

According to at least two books, *Starring John Wayne* by Gene Fernett, and *The Western: The Aurum Film Encyclopedia* by Phil Hardy, the 70mm version ran 158 minutes, while the 35mm version ran 125 minutes, which is the running time all other sources give for *The Big Trail.*

The 70mm version of the film was premiered in October 1930, at Grauman's Chinese Theatre, and was hailed as a momentous event in Hollywood, drawing praise from critics. Mordaunt Hall of the *New York Times* wrote, "The scenes in this picture are a testimonial to the progress of motion-picture work. Mr. Wayne acquits himself with no little distinction. His performance is pleasingly natural."

The Fox studio needed *The Big Trail* to be a success. Wayne was sent on a promotional tour to make personal appearances, and the studio publicists were busy making up false details about Wayne's life. They said that he was a veteran of the Great War, a former Texas Ranger, and an all-American football player. He tried to set the record straight, but the damage had been done as columnists published some of the earliest myths about John Wayne. Over time he managed to correct most of those.

As the promotional tour for *The Big Trail* rolled on, the young actor began to believe that he was going to become a big movie star. But the Wall Street crash in 1929 had affected every business in America, including the movie industry. *The Big Trail* had to be a success.

When the film went on release throughout America in November 1930, virtually every movie theatre showed the inferior 35mm 4x3 version because they simply couldn't afford to install the equipment needed to show the widescreen version.

The worst happened; the film bombed in America, although it did do well in Europe where filmgoers probably saw versions featuring actors other than Wayne and the New York actors. William Fox went bankrupt, the studio went into receivership, and contracts were either not renewed, or were dropped altogether. The studio only just about survived, thanks mainly to the success of its Shirley Temple films.

Wayne told me, "I'd been counting on *The Big Trail* to make me a star, not because I wanted the fame, but because I wanted the financial security so I could marry Josephine. You know, I was sure I'd set the world on fire, and it was hard for a young feller like me to realize the truth — that I hadn't set the world on fire, and I was totally unprepared to handle the consequences if *The Big Trail* had been a success and launched me as a star. What I did learn was that this picture-making business was a damn fine business, and I was proud to be a part of it — always have been."

It is almost impossible to critically assess *The Big Trail* today. It is certainly a physically impressive film, but it has dated badly, which is not surprising, considering it was made in 1930.

John Wayne's performance comes across as wooden and awkward. He had not yet affected his drawl or his famous walk, and against the likes of Gary Cooper, who had been so effective in *The Virginian*, or Warner Baxter who was so good in *In Old Arizona*, Wayne was no threat as a major star.

The failure of *The Big Trail* made studios wary of making big-budget Westerns and, with the exception of RKO's *Cimarron* in 1930, Westerns were relegated to only B-picture status for a number of years.

4

Happy Trails,
Unhappy Wedlock

It is generally assumed that after the failure of *The Big Trail*, Wayne went straight into B Westerns, but this is not so. Fox kept him on and starred him in *Girls Demand Excitement*, again with Marguerite Churchill. It was made on the cheap, with Wayne playing the captain of a college men's basketball team who find themselves up against the girls' team.

"I really hated making that film," said Wayne. "It had no substance to it and was a big comedown after the adventure I'd had on *The Big Trail*. The studio really only threw the picture together to give work to a group of young actresses it had under contract that they didn't know how to use. So the film was created for them, so my part was pretty lousy.

"One day I met Will Rogers, the biggest star at Fox, who saw I was pretty despondent and he asked what the matter was. I told him, 'I'm making a terrible movie,' and he said, 'But you're working, aren't you? Just keep it up.' That was the best advice I ever got; just keep working and learning, however bad the picture — and that's what I did, and boy, I made some lousy pictures!"

Girls Demand Excitement, released in 1931, was as poor as Wayne had feared, and he knew he was bad in it. "I began to wonder then if I had a future as an actor," he said. Fox gave him one more chance in *Three Girls Lost*, in which he costarred with his friend Loretta Young, who said, "I'd made a number of films and Duke was still new to it. I didn't really know how to help him with his acting; I was still trying to learn to do it. But I encouraged him and told him not to give up. I told him that if he could make a real go at it, he'd be able to marry Josephine and live happily ever after. I was married to Grant Withers, and he and Duke became great friends. Grant and I were only married for a year; it was a big mistake. Duke said to me, 'What was that about happily ever after?' But Duke and I stayed friends, and Grant and I managed to stay on friendly terms. That was in large part due to Duke, who'd say, 'Now then, you two, what's the beef? We're all friends.' He hadn't experienced divorce then — and when he did, he still saw no reason why he and his ex-wife couldn't be friends."

But it was the end of the line for Wayne at Fox. The studio did not take up the option of keeping him on for another year, and he was suddenly out of work.

There was a man who could have helped save Wayne's career at the time, and that was John Ford. But Ford chose not to. He had not yet forgiven Duke.

The Saenz family still disapproved of Duke, having heard rumors of his drunken carousing and womanizing. Despite his brief affair with Marguerite Churchill, he never was what his friend Paul Fix called "a mainstream womanizer."

When I spoke to Fix by telephone in 1979, he explained, "Duke would occasionally stray, but he always felt so guilty about cheating on Josephine, he usually broke it off as quick as he could. He just wasn't immoral enough to . . . let's say 'put it about,' the way a lot of Hollywood leading men did. As for his drinking, yeah, he liked his liquor, and he enjoyed it mostly in the company of his male friends.

Josephine disapproved of both his friends and his drinking. I didn't think they were well matched, but Duke was in love, for Christ's sake."

Loretta Young told me, "Jo and Duke were madly in love with each other, but they were poles apart in society. She came from a sophisticated and cultured background, while he was a former homesteader who had changed from being a shy, awkward, and anxious young man into a fun-loving man's man. What he saw in Josephine was an exotic beauty whom he could respect, and he hoped that some of her sophistication would rub off on him. They were desperate to get married, but those plans had to be put on hold when he found himself out of work."

Just as depression was setting in, he was put under contract at Columbia Pictures, a studio in a far healthier state than Fox, run by the tough Harry Cohn. As well as producing A-list quality films, Columbia also ran a production line of action-packed B pictures, and Cohn thought Wayne might be ideal as a star of some of the B movies. Wayne recalled, "My first Columbia picture [in 1931] was *Men Are Like That*, playing a soldier who breaks up with his girlfriend, played by an actress called

Laura LaPlante. You probably never heard of her. [I had, but I didn't want to interrupt the Duke in full flow.] She very sensibly retired from pictures shortly after *Men Are Like That.*

"During filming, I was summoned to Cohn's office where he accused me of playing around with his new girlfriend, a young actress he had under contract who will remain nameless. I told him I didn't know what he was talking about, but he pounded the desk with his fist and yelled, 'You keep your goddamn fly buttoned at my studio.'

"After that he always talked to me like I was little more than a mangy dog — or worse, like a rat that had crawled out of the fucking sewer. It was no wonder so many of his contract players loathed him. You just couldn't communicate with the son of a bitch.

"He then humiliated me in my second picture for that studio — a film called *Deceiver* in which the star of the picture, who was Ian Keith, ends up getting murdered. Before the director could get a shot of his dead body, Ian Keith had to return to New York, and so I was told to stand in — or rather lie down — as Keith's body. I just knew that was an order that had come down from Cohn to humiliate me because I knew damn well that a professional extra would have normally been used for that kind of work."

Having been chastised, Wayne was put to better use in the 1931 Western *The Range Feud*, second-billed to star Buck Jones. But in his next picture, *Maker of Men*, Wayne was way down in the cast list as a college football player.

Wayne made two more films at Columbia in 1932, both of them Tim McCoy Westerns, *Texas Cyclone* and *Two-Fisted Law*. By the time the latter film was on release, Wayne was out of work again.

"Cohn dropped me as soon as he could, and he began putting the word about Hollywood that I was a rebel and a drunkard. Well, maybe I was a bit of both from time to time. But I never got drunk when I was working. For a whole year nobody in Hollywood would touch me because of that bastard Cohn, and that's why I've never worked at Columbia. Never have, never will.

"For a while I thought about giving up acting altogether and take up prizefighting, which I was really too old for by then. I also considered going back to the University of Southern California to finish my law degree." He knew that going back to college would have put his plan to marry Josephine on hold for even longer.

At last he was offered a small part at Paramount in *Lady and Gent* in 1932, a film about prizefighting in which Wayne had a major supporting role as a fighter. Then Warner Bros., one of Hollywood's biggest studios, gave him a contract to star in six Westerns, with the freedom to work elsewhere, and a fee of $1,500 a picture.

In quick succession he made the first three, *Ride Him, Cowboy*; *The Big Stampede*; and *Haunted Gold*, and in every one John Wayne was top-billed. But they were all B pictures which ran for less than an hour, which meant that Wayne was merely a B actor. Of them, he says, "Those films offered me regular work and an opportunity to learn my craft." He played different characters but they were all called John — only the surname altered from film to film — and he rode "Duke, the Miracle Horse."

All the Warner Bros. Westerns were produced by Leon Schlesinger who later became better known as the producer of the early "Looney Tunes" and "Merrie Melodies" cartoons made by Warner Bros. "I later thought Leon's cartoons were better than the horse operas he put me in," said

Wayne. "Those Westerns I made at Warner Bros. were remakes of old Ken Maynard films, and all the big scenes like cattle herds and Indian attacks were taken straight from the original Maynard films. So I had to dress up to look like Ken Maynard because a lot of the old footage they inserted had shots of Maynard in the distance. I really hated that."

In just two years since *The Big Trail*, Duke had improved considerably as an actor and was making efforts to develop his own style. In its review of *The Big Stampede*, the *Motion Picture Herald* said, "John Wayne's drawl and deliberate style of movement are fitted to effect a likable picture, made-to-order for theatres that draw upon folk from and near the so-called open spaces."

By now Wayne had an agent, Al Kingston, who was approached by Nat Levine, head of Mascot Pictures, one of Hollywood's so-called "Poverty Row" studios which churned out cheap action pictures, to offer Wayne the starring role in three serials, *Shadow of the Eagle*, *The Hurricane Express*, and *The Three Musketeers*. As Warner Bros. were not yet ready to shoot the remaining three John Wayne Westerns, Kingston made a deal with Levine, with

Wayne earning $100 a week, half of what he had been paid at Columbia and Warners.

One of the greatest assets Mascot had was Yakima Canutt. He was not only one of the best stuntmen in the business, but he was an adequate actor when it came to playing heavies. His real name was Enos Edward Canutt and he was born in Colfax, Washington, near the town of Yakima. He was a ranch hand from boyhood, and at the age of seventeen, he joined a Wild West show and went on to become a world rodeo champion under the name Yakima Canutt — he called himself that after a newspaper described him as "The Cowboy From Yakima." From the early 1920s, he was appearing in films, usually playing a cowboy and always performing his own stunts. He virtually invented stunt work for Westerns and eventually went on, during the 1950s and 1960s, to become the greatest director of action sequences in the history of motion pictures, especially after creating and directing the most exciting moments from the famed chariot race in the 1959 version of *Ben-Hur*.

Nat Levine demanded hair-raising action all shot on a skintight budget to be completed in twenty-one days, and Canutt worked closely with the writers to help develop the story lines and action.

On the first day of filming for *Shadow of the Eagle*, Levine picked Wayne up at four in the morning and they drove out to the location in the Antelope Valley. En route Levine told Wayne the story line, such as it was. The plot hung on the antics of a traveling carnival in which Wayne would play the stunt flier who delivers many thrills and spills and finally reveals the true identity of the heavy known as the Eagle.

Arriving at the location, Wayne met the director Ford Beebe, his costars, and Yakima Canutt. Canutt told me, "My job was to beef up the action and double Wayne in the more dangerous shots, and to also play one of the villains alongside my friend Bud Osborne. I'd not met Wayne before but Bud had worked with him a number of times. I asked Bud what kind of fellow Wayne was, and he said, 'Yak, you'll love him. He's a great guy, and when it comes to ribbing, he'll hold his own — even with you.' I had a reputation as a bit of a practical joker.

"On the first day of shooting, Bud introduced Wayne to me, and he was very friendly; said that he was glad I was going to double for him because he'd heard a great deal about me. He seemed to know all about my achievements in rodeo as well as my stunt work.

"I decided to test Bud's claim that Wayne could take some ribbing, and on the second day I told Bud to tell Wayne that I was a spy for Nat Levine. When Bud told him, I was standing nearby, making notes in a little book. I saw Wayne look over to me, see what I was doing, and then he shook his head in disbelief.

"A bit later I went over to him and asked how everything was going. He just looked at me and said nothing. I took out a pack of cigarettes and offered him one. He gave me a real dirty look and said, 'No, thanks,' and walked away.

"After keeping this up for the first week I got Bud and another actor to take Wayne behind the set for a drink. I came walking around the corner just as Wayne was taking a slug, and he saw me looking at my watch and making a note in my little book. That was all he could take, and he blew his top. I ran away as fast as I could, and as soon as I could I got Bud to tell Wayne that it had all been a joke. Wayne just burst out laughing even though the gag was at his expense. He later told me, 'I'm glad it was just a gag, Yak, but you've left yourself wide open.' After that we were always trying to outgag each other, and there was never a dull moment when we were together in a picture."

Filming *Shadow of the Eagle* proved arduous. Each of the twelve episodes had more action than plot in them, and each episode had to end on a cliff-hanger. Athletic ability was more important than acting skills, with only one day in the week off, and no time for any kind of formal lunch break. One night they worked until midnight, after which most of the company, including Wayne and Canutt, decided to bed down in the desert for the night rather than go back to Los Angeles.

Wayne, sitting by a fire, was drinking whisky from a bottle. Canutt sauntered over and crouched beside him. Both men were too tired to talk. Wayne just handed Canutt the bottle, and between them they finished off the contents. It was the moment, Canutt said, when they became lifelong friends.

Between them, Wayne and Canutt take credit for inventing the technique of realistic screen fighting. "You look at other films of the period or earlier, and you see these guys bashing away at each other's shoulder," said Canutt, "and it never looked real. What Wayne and I did was develop a way of standing at a certain angle to the camera and throwing punches to the face, just missing but looking to the camera like the fist had made contact. In fact, I would say that no one has ever been able to make a screen fistfight look as good as Wayne, even when he was older."

When they finished *Shadow of the Eagle*, they went straight to work on the next twelve-episode serial, *The Hurricane Express*, a contemporary drama about a rivalry between a railway and an air-transport line, allowing for plenty of action on trains, airplanes, and cars.

With hardly a break, Wayne went back to Warner Bros. to make two more Westerns for them, *The Telegraph Trail* and *Somewhere in Sonora*. Among the cast of *Somewhere in Sonora* was Paul Fix, who would become Wayne's close friend, unofficial drama coach, and a regular in many of Wayne's films.

Wayne next found himself in the Mojave Desert filming his third Mascot serial, a supposedly updated version of Dumas's *The Three Musketeers* in which the French foreign legion are pitted against the marauding Arabs. One of the stars was Noah Beery Jr. who told me in 1979, "Duke was a great guy to be with and work with. He was always on the set on time. And it was a difficult picture to make. We filmed in the Mojave Desert where it got to one hundred and twenty degrees during the day. We had two directors [Armand Schaefer and Colbert Clark] each shooting different scenes, and Duke was going from one to the other. We never had much dialogue to say because it was virtually all action, but I believe it was on those Mascot serials that Duke really began to get a sense of how to work in front of a camera, and how to move."

John Wayne said of his Mascot experience, "We didn't have a hell of a lot of dialogue, and we didn't fool around with retakes. Usually it was the first take we printed. Even though there wasn't much dialogue, I had to learn my lines quickly, and I've always been able to memorize lines quickly. I learned how to do stunts too, and whenever I could I'd do my own stunts."

The first two Mascot serials were released toward the end of 1932, and the third early in 1933. Along with the Westerns Wayne made at Warner Bros., the serials were delighting a young audience to whom John Wayne had fast become a screen hero, and to them he was already a star.

There was a brief respite from action films when Warner Bros. cast Wayne in the minor role of the manager of a department store in *Baby Face* in 1933. The film starred Barbara Stanwyck as a woman who finds her way to success in business by using her charms on the men she meets on the way up. Wayne was one of those she met, and he was on screen for all of two minutes.

Then he accepted a leading role in a minor film, *His Private Secretary*, for a minor studio, Showmen's Pictures. He played a rich man's son who can't take his mind off girls long enough to make a success in his father's business. Evelyn Knapp played the granddaughter of a church minister who finally makes him see the error of his ways and reunites him with his father. The film remains one of Wayne's least known and has hardly been seen since its release in June 1933.

He was soon back in the saddle, riding Duke the Miracle Horse in *The Man from Monterey*, the last of the six B Westerns he made for Warner Bros. He was quickly snapped up in the spring of 1933 by Lone Star Westerns which made only B Westerns for another Poverty Row studio, Monogram. "For any actor trying to get on in the business, working at Monogram was not a good career move," said Wayne. "Most of the contract players there may have had regular work, but they generally didn't move up from there into the major studios — they went down, and that's the direction I thought I was headed."

Wayne may not have been in the same league as the really big movie stars at the major studios, but when it came to B Westerns, he was one of the most popular cowboy stars.

He started out at Lone Star as Singin' Sandy Saunders, the singing cowboy, in *Riders of Destiny*. It was something that would haunt Wayne for the rest of his life as the subject of his singing role would often be brought up. "I was just so fucking embarrassed by it all. Strumming a guitar I couldn't play and miming to a voice which was provided by a real singer made me feel like a fucking pansy. After that experience, I refused to be Singin' Sandy again."

From then on, at Monogram at least, he played straight, rootin' tootin' nonsinging gunmen on the side of good in sixteen Westerns for that studio. But Wayne also added a new dimension to the stereotypical screen hero in a cowboy hat. He said, "All the screen cowboys behaved like real gentlemen. They didn't drink, they didn't smoke. When they knocked the bad guy down, they always stood with their fists up, waiting for the heavy to get back on his feet. I decided I was going to drag the bad guy to his feet and keep hitting him. And if the heavy hit me with a rose, I'd hit him back with a chair.

"I learned that as a kid from watching the Westerns Harry Carey made with John Ford. He had realism, he was a real man, and I decided that's what my screen cowboy would be like."

Yakima Canutt, who worked regularly on the Monogram films, told me, "A guy called Paul Malvern produced all the Lone Star Westerns. A really nice guy too. He said he'd been reading dime novels since he was a kid, and a lot of the plots for those films came from the novels he read. He reckoned he had about a hundred of these stories in his head."

Wayne recalled, "The plots weren't really that important. There wasn't time to develop character or some long story line. The emphasis was on action, and plenty of it, no matter what. Come hail, rain, sun, hell, or high water, you had to make those films in six days. If the wind blew, the microphone picked it up and nobody could hear the dialogue, so if any talking had to be done, it was usually done indoors. Out of doors, dialogue was kept to a bare minimum. The main thing was, finish the film and don't go over budget. Those films cost around $30,000 to $40,000 to make, which was low enough for the studio to make a profit. I was earning $5,000 a week, and I was working *every* week, so I thought I was doing all right."

With the security that came with his contract at Monogram, Wayne was finally able to marry Josephine on 24 June 1933, in Loretta Young's garden in Bel Air. Josephine would have preferred to marry in church because she was a Catholic, but Wayne was not, so a civil but elegant ceremony was held at Young's Hollywood home. Wayne's best man was his brother Robert. Over recent years, Duke had grown closer to the brother he had resented in childhood.

The Waynes moved into a small furnished apartment on Orange Grove Avenue, just outside Hollywood. Josephine kept herself occupied with charity work while Duke made one Western after another over the next two years. Robert N. Bradbury, the father of Duke's old friend from Glendale, Bob, directed most of them. And since most of the films featured Yakima Canutt, whose friendship with Wayne grew stronger, they often rehearsed their stunts on their own. They also continued to play practical jokes when they got the chance.

Canutt told me of one such joke: "There was one picture we did; there were so many I can't remember which one — they were all kind of the same, but I had to double him by riding up to a hotel, catch hold of a rope, and swing up onto a balcony and go through the window. I needed enough speed so that the momentum would carry me up onto the balcony, but the horse kept slowing down. So I got a willow switch which I used on the horse's rear quarters to liven him up, and I did the stunt in one go.

"There was quite a gathering of spectators, and Wayne called to them, saying, 'Folks, when you see this picture, remember that it's not John Wayne whipping that horse!'

"I said, 'Yes, folks, and when you see the picture, remember that it's not John Wayne doing the dangerous stunt either.'"

There was a formula for all the Monogram Lone Star Westerns which was summed up in a review in the *Motion Picture Herald* for the 1934 *Blue Steel*: "The active and athletic John Wayne, star of Monogram's Lone Star Westerns, disports himself with his accustomed knock-down-and-drag-out ease, on and off his handsome white horse, as once again he does battle with the villains of the western mountains. A fast, active Western motion picture. Of Wayne's popularity there can be little question, and a certain quota of Western fans can be relied upon to respond to the call of the Wayne name on the theatre marquee."

The same trade journal noted in its review of 1935 for *The Lawless Frontier*, "A formula Western, this appears acceptable material in the regular-run theatre for the weekend action position. In the lead is John Wayne, screen cowboy with considerable popularity among the Western action fans."

That popularity was making good money for the studio and gave Wayne the muscle to ask — and get — a new contract and a bigger salary. The work was exhausting and Wayne felt he deserved as much money as he could get. He said, "I became more and more interested in learning the whole business of making pictures. I wanted to really learn my profession, but it wasn't easy making those cheap Westerns. I went in and out of each one so quickly that I didn't even know their titles. To play a cowboy you needed a good hat, a good pair of boots, and you had to be able to ride a horse. But I wanted to learn more than that.

"One of the most satisfying things about that time was the camaraderie of the cowboys who worked on those films. They were real cowboys, not actors. They'd been forced off the range by the depression and had migrated to Hollywood looking for work in pictures. The last of the big cattle drives were over. These cowboys were the last. Working in pictures together, they found some kind of solace in just being with each other. I liked being with them, and really respected them. I listened to their stories and kind of absorbed their culture.

"In the evenings, I spent my time with them playing poker. There was always somebody who'd bring along a guitar or a banjo, and we'd all sit around the fire singing with the stars shining bright above us. Great times."

Canutt also remembered those times. He said, "Wayne really thrived on working with the cowboys. He never pretended he was a real cowboy, just a screen cowboy, but he picked up on what those men were like, and he'd find ways of bringing those things out in his pictures. That's partly why Wayne was so realistic as a cowboy.

"I felt that John identified with the cowboys because they just weren't comfortable with the idea of home life, and John was feeling that way too. He hadn't been married long, but he had trouble relating to women. He was inclined to put them on a pedestal. The cowboy needed to be free to roam and be with his own kind. Josephine was a wonderful woman who was kind and gentle, but from what I could see, she didn't respect John's profession and she gave him hell over it sometimes. John wanted to work, and work well, and he buried himself in his work. He found the emotional support he needed among the cowboys.

"He liked the stuntmen too. We did a film called *'Neath the Arizona Skies*. I was the villain as usual. You know, Wayne could do a better fight scene in those days than many of the stuntmen, so we worked together on our own. John and I were so competitive and eager to top whatever stunt or fight scene we'd done before that I always thought we could have both been in real danger if we weren't good friends.

"There was a scene in that film where I make a getaway on one of those little motored handcars that railroads used when making repairs to the tracks. But I was also supposed to double John when his character makes a flying mount on his horse and races over the hill to intercept me. The script called for his character, which I would be playing as the stunt double, to gallop alongside the handcar and leap from the horse onto the car and then we'd fight while it was tearing along. For me it was pretty routine, but for anyone who wasn't a stuntman it was dangerous.

"When we were setting the scene up, the producer Paul Malvern realized they didn't have another stuntman to double me in my part while I doubled John, and the director Harry Fraser was trying to figure out how we were going to do it. We had some cowboys on the set but none of them were big enough to double either John or me. Suddenly I noticed John giving me a cheeky look and I knew what he was thinking. I said, 'Which one are you gonna do?' and he said, 'Give me your wardrobe.'

"So I doubled John and John doubled me, and we did the fight on the car, and then we changed costumes so Fraser could get the close-ups of us. We stayed in our own costumes as John knocked me off the car and then he leaped onto me and we carried on the fight until he won, which he always did! So he was a great stuntman, but often the producer didn't want his star getting hurt, so often I doubled John and another stuntman doubled me.

"In another film, which I forget the title of — they were all alike — I was going to double John as he rode fast down a hill and toward the camera and out of shot in close-up. But the cameraman said that if I rode into close-up they would see it wasn't John, so John said he'd do it, and they let him. I told him to bring the horse over the top of the hill at speed, but to be sure he checked the horse just before hitting the bottom of the hill where the ground leveled off.

"John came over that hill really fast and raced down the steep slope, but he didn't check the horse — that is, he didn't pull the horse back up as he hit the level ground. I just held my breath as he hit the level ground because I knew that horse couldn't collect himself. He fell and sent

97

John flying and turning through the air and it was a really spectacular fall. He must have hurt himself, but I just hollered, 'Get on the horse and ride out,' and he rolled to his feet as the horse got up, and he jumped back on and rode out past the camera. It was a sensational shot and they used it in the picture. As John got off the horse, he said, 'I heard you holler "get on him and ride out," and that I did.'

"I said, 'You sure did, and you're lucky you didn't kill yourself.' "

It was no wonder that when Wayne got home, all he wanted to do was relax with a few drinks and put his feet up. Josephine, however, had always enjoyed a good social life and she often told Duke as he walked in through the door that they were expected at Loretta Young's for dinner that evening, or at some church function she was involved with. Many times she had to attend those functions on her own as Wayne was often away on location.

"I have to admit," said Wayne, "that my marriage to Josephine, who was a really fine woman, and still is, just didn't have a solid foundation from the start. By the time we married, I felt that the romance had gone out of our lives and we saw each other more out of habit. She was very strong in her Catholic faith, but I grew more opposed to the idea of any kind of organized religion. And while I worked hard to strive for something better in my profession, Josephine just became more impatient."

Nevertheless, in 1934, their first child, Michael, was born. His arrival did little to strengthen his parents' marriage. Loretta Young, who was Michael's godmother, recalled, "They were too incompatible to make it work, although they did try. But they were arguing so much, and as time went on, the arguments became more bitter."

In 1935 they had a daughter, baptized Antonia Maria, but they always called her Toni.

Still the couple drifted further apart, and while Wayne tried to be a loving father, he was spending too much time, during his rare moments when he wasn't working, in the company of his male friends.

5

Enter Ringo

There was more behind Ford's failure to return any of Wayne's calls since 1930 than mere punishment. Ford often disappeared on air-reconnaissance missions and, unknown to anyone else in the film industry except his editor Leon Sedlitz, used his Hollywood facilities for editing his intelligence films.

Ford had bought a 110-foot yacht in 1934 and had it overhauled, making it into one of the most beautiful yachts on the West Coast. He called it the *Araner* and, in between films, Ford would cruise from California to Acapulco after being briefed by Captain Zacharias. American authorities were still allowing Japanese shrimp boats into San Pedro at Long Beach harbor, and Ford's job was to look out for any shrimp boats commanded by Japanese naval officers in disguise.

Ford was given a commission as a lieutenant commander in the Naval Reserve as well as a commendation from the commander of the Eleventh Naval District for his initiative in securing information.

Perhaps because he felt justifiably proud of his secret achievements, he decided it was time to forgive John Wayne. It was during one summer's day in 1935 when Wayne happened to be in a coastal bar that he received a message from Ford inviting him aboard his yacht anchored just offshore. Wayne was taken by small boat to the *Araner* and arrived to find the main saloon filled with people. Ford simply said, "Hi, Duke, sit down." About an hour later Ford announced that the shore boat would take his guests back to land, but to Wayne he said, "Duke, can you stay for dinner?" There was never an explanation from Ford, or an apology; it was as though they had never been estranged. Wayne recalled, "There began a series of Sunday afternoons on board the *Araner* where we'd read books, have dinner, and play cards. Most of the time Pappy didn't drink when he was on his yacht, so whenever I awoke on a Sunday morning with a hangover, I'd have a shot of tequila which cleared my head, and I'd head off to the *Araner*. None of this helped my failing marriage; I guess I was running away from my problems. We'd often spend up to three weeks on board on fishing trips, so I was away from home far too much.

"Some of these fishing trips were secret intelligence missions which myself and Ward Bond found ourselves caught up in, and we were happy to do so. For years Pappy kept his pre–Second World War naval activities a secret, which meant that Ward and me also had to keep silent."

When Wayne was later criticized for not enlisting when America entered the Second World War, and while he and his studio were giving out the various reasons why he could not join up, Wayne could not reveal that he had, in fact, assisted Ford in gathering intelligence for the navy leading up to the outbreak of war.

When not on his yacht, Ford would hold court at the Hollywood Athletic Club where their leader would spend evenings after a hard day's work relaxing in the steam rooms and listening to writers pitch their ideas to him over a drink, or several.

He would be joined by Wayne, Ward Bond, writer Dudley Nichols, Preston Foster, Johnny Weissmuller, and other actors, directors, and producers who formed themselves into a club called "The Young Men's Purity Total Abstinence and Snooker Pool Association."

Wayne laughed as he recalled, "The club had its own charter, which stated that our sole purpose was to promulgate the cause of alcoholism, and that would-be applicants must be a career-oriented or, at least, gutter-oriented drunkard. Our slogan was 'Jews but no dues,' and we elected the steam-room attendant, Buck Buchanan, described in our charter as 'the distinguished Afro-American,' as our president. I tell ya, we had some fun."

Despite Wayne's reconciliation with Ford, the director made no effort to further Wayne's career, and Duke continued making B Westerns. In his hotel suite in London (where he had come to perform *Clarence Darrow* in 1976) Henry Fonda told me, "There's no doubt in my mind that Ford could have helped Duke anytime he wanted. But he didn't. He let him suffer in those B Westerns for years. I liked Ford an awful lot at the start, but our friendship went kind of sour and I knew that he could be real mean. He wanted power over the people who worked for him. That's why he kept the same family of actors and crew on every picture, and if you broke any of his rules, you didn't work for him again, or for a long time. Duke had broken some rule by making *The Big Trail* and Ford finally forgave him, but he didn't give Duke a good part in one of his films for years. He could have done it anytime, and I call that mean-spirited."

Although a number of people were of the opinion that Ford treated Wayne badly, Wayne never said an unkind word about the Coach. His loyalty to Ford was extraordinary. Next to Ford, Wayne's best friends were Ward Bond, Grant Withers, Paul Fix, and Yakima Canutt. "I was probably closer to Yak in those days because we worked daily together on those cheap Lone Star Westerns," said Duke.

Canutt admitted that he found it difficult to distinguish one film from another. But he had good reason to remember one particular picture in 1935 called *Paradise Canyon*. He recalled, "I played a character called Curly, which was kind of ironic because I had, by then, developed a bald spot. Wayne and I had a fight scene, and it was really a tough scene.

"During this fight scene, I had to flip John's character over my head, so for this I doubled him, and another stuntman doubled me. I ended up crashing through a table and sitting on the floor with my back to the camera. When they ran the picture the bald spot was very noticeable, and I got a real chewing out from John and from Paul Malvern, who was the producer. We couldn't afford to reshoot it, so it went out as it was.

"Well, John, who still had all his hair then, didn't let up about my bald spot, so I decided to get my own back and I got a lady in New York to write a fan to me, and when it arrived, I got Malvern and John together, and I read them the letter which said, 'Dear Mr. Canutt, I saw *Paradise Canyon* with you and John Wayne. It was a good picture and you did some fine work. But why doesn't the producer find you a younger man than John Wayne who must be getting old because I noticed that he is getting a bald spot.'

"John looked at the letter and at the postmark on the envelope and saw that it was authentic, but I think he guessed it was a setup, and he said to me, 'Yak, you're gonna have to watch that damn bald spot if you're gonna double me.'

"He got his own back on the next picture where John is fighting me and some others in a saloon. He knocks down one of the guys, and then I swing at him, and he steps to one side and knocks me through the glass of the front window. It's all being shot in one take, and I have to tumble onto the sidewalk, get up, and run for my horse. Suddenly John leaps through the broken window, over the hitch rail, and makes a flying football tackle on me. I tell you, I've never been turned over so many times so fast. He got up and said, 'That's for the letter from your "fan" in New York!' He'd paid me back."

Working with Canutt taught Wayne a great deal about acting. Wayne was often quoted as saying, "I learned to react, not to act." But he told me, "I never said that. What I may have said was — and this is what I believe about acting — is that you can't just stand there and act when you've got your lines to say. You have to react when an actor says his lines to you. Learning to react was all part of the acting process, not all of it.

"I kind of learned that from watching Yak, and not because he was any good at it! He was the greatest stuntman ever, but he was a worse actor than I was. When I started, I knew I was no actor. I had to invent myself. It was a deliberate attempt to create 'John Wayne screen actor.' So I started to speak with a drawl, I squinted, and I tried to find a way of moving which would suggest that I wasn't looking for trouble but was always ready for it. It was a hit-or-miss project I set myself, but slowly it all began to come together.

"I'd watch other actors. I noticed that when Yak had to show anger, he'd grimace, raise his voice, and kinda snarl. But when Yak was in real danger, he reacted differently. There were a few times when I saw Yak heading for a real fight with some rough types who'd challenge him, just to show how tough they were. Yak would get this half-humorous look in his eyes, and he'd talk very straight and direct at the guy looking for a fight. You'd get the feeling that there was a steel spring inside of him just waiting to be released. I told him about it and said he ought to react with real attitude rather than put on a grimace and snarl. But he just didn't get it — but I did. That's what I learned from Yak; how to react in a real way."

He also learned a great deal from Paul Fix who appeared with Wayne in 1935 in Monogram's *The Desert Trail*. Fix told me, "Duke was bright and you could teach him, and he'd quickly learn. He had trouble with the physical side of acting, like how to move and what to do with your hands. He said he hated watching himself on the screen because he always looked so stiff. I told him to try pointing his toes into the ground as he walked, and when he did that, his shoulders and hips sort of swung. He practiced that walk until it looked so graceful on the screen that I told him he had to watch his films so he could see what he was doing. I told him, 'You can't learn what to do if you don't watch yourself on the screen.' And in a short time he had that distinctive rolling walk down perfect."

In 1935 Mascot, Consolidated Film Laboratories — which was run by Herbert J. Yates — and Monogram, along with its Lone Star Productions, were merged into one new company, Republic Pictures. Yates, who had no knowledge or experience of filmmaking, was head of the new company, and as Wayne would later say, "He was a nice enough guy but he had no taste." The filmmaking side of the business was left to Nat Levine as head of production.

As with the Monogram Lone Star Westerns, the films Wayne made for Republic had little to differentiate them. "Between April and September each year, we worked like hell to make our quota of pictures," said Wayne. "We had to make them on schedule because they were all sold in advance as a package to exhibitors. In the winter months we had time off to recover, and then come April, it was back in the saddle again."

By this time Wayne was beginning to formulate his philosophy of what it meant to be an American, based very much upon the myths which came out of the Westerns. He viewed life much as his screen persona did, believing that the American way of life was based on tough but firm individualism, self-sufficiency, and the need to stand up for yourself, even if it resulted in violence.

And he had become almost addicted to work. As Noah Beery Jr. told me, "He lived to work. If he wasn't working, he wasn't happy." And yet he knew he was getting stuck in a rut as a B-Western cowboy star. It didn't help when he was made to play the part of another singing cowboy in his first film at Republic, *Westward Ho*, in 1935. Wayne refused to sing — or rather to mime to another man's singing voice — in any more films.

By now Wayne had a new agent, Charles Feldman, one of the most powerful agents in Hollywood. He got Yates to agree to a new contract for Wayne whereby Duke could be loaned to other studios. When

Wayne heard that Cecil B. DeMille was going to make *The Plainsman*, an epic adventure featuring the exploits of Wild Bill Hickok, Buffalo Bill, and Calamity Jane, he asked to be considered for the role of Hickok.

"My agent, who was Charles Feldman, called DeMille and an appointment was arranged for me to meet the great director," Duke recalled. "Well, me and Charlie turned up on time but we were sitting for an hour outside of DeMille's office before the great director emerged, only to announce, 'I'm going to lunch.'

"I got up and Charlie thought I was going to hit him — maybe I was — and he said, 'Mr. DeMille, you asked John Wayne to come over for an interview.'

"DeMille said, 'Oh yes, so I did.' So we went into his office, and he said to me, 'You were in *The Big Trail*, weren't you? I saw it and you did just fine. But a lot of water has gone under the bridge since then.' That was DeMille's way of turning me down. To him I was now just a minor star of mere B Westerns."

Determined to improve his screen techniques, Wayne, with the help of people like Paul Fix, learned to deepen the timbre of his voice. "He worked hard on improving his delivery," said Fix. "He paid attention to the character actors he sometimes got to work with, he listened closely to what the directors wanted, he learned how to handle small comedic moments, and he paid attention to all aspects of filmmaking."

At home, life was still troubled. Said Paul Fix, "Josie really tried to make a gentleman of Duke and to make him become a Catholic. He just wanted to be accepted for what he was. He really wanted to love Josie, but it just wasn't working. I noticed that around her he really watched his Ps and Qs. But around his friends he was funny, boisterous, he could swear all he liked, and he just seemed so much more comfortable."

In 1936, Trem Carr, who had produced some of Duke's films at Republic, left the studio to work at Universal, and he took Wayne with him. Universal, a major studio that made minor action films of their own, signed Wayne to a six-picture deal. He made the films virtually back-to-back in 1936 and 1937 — and not one of them was a Western. They were all made just as quickly but not as cheaply as the Republic pictures. The budgets for the Universal pictures Wayne made were as much as $500,000.

The first, *The Sea Spoilers*, was an action film in which Wayne was a U.S. Coast Guard commander outwitting smugglers who have kidnapped his sweetheart, played by Nan Grey. Next he was in *Conflict*, playing a lumberjack who turns to prize-fighting, and *California Straight Ahead*, as the owner of a convoy of trucks in competition with a train for delivery of aviation parts.

I Cover the War was one of the more ambitious films at Universal. Wayne played a newsreel cameraman caught up in a tribal war in the desert, and the studio came up with 150 extras as the British cavalry and 400 extras as Arab tribesmen.

In *Idol of the Crowds* he was a professional hockey player who turns down bribes to throw the game; and in *Adventure's End* he was a pearl diver aboard a whaling ship on which the first mate leads a mutiny. But the Universal pictures didn't do well commercially, costing too much to make a profit from the market they were aimed at.

He was back riding the range again in 1937, this time at Paramount, in *Born to the West*. Then it was back to Republic to become part of a series of films featuring "The Three Mesquiteers," a trio of heroes supposedly modeled on *The Three Musketeers* of Dumas. This trio, however, were cowboys in stetsons and fighting with six-guns. Despite the Western setting, the series was set in the 1930s and featured automobiles and airplanes.

A number of Mesquiteer films had already been made, featuring Ray Corrigan, Robert Livingston, and Max Terhune, but because of ongoing tension between Corrigan and Livingston, Wayne was brought in to replace Livingston. He made the first four in the series back-to-back — *Pals of the Saddle, Overland Stage Raiders, Santa Fe Stampede,* and *Red River Range.*

They were all directed by George Sherman, who told me, "Those films were awful, and it certainly wasn't Duke's fault. They were just based on a simple formula. Wayne was the romantic hero whose love life was generally the cause of the trouble the Mesquiteers found themselves in. Terhune was the so-called comedian, and Corrigan was the cowboy who never fell in love!

"Duke had replaced Livingston to ease the tension on the set, but Corrigan, who was a big star in B Westerns, resented Duke. So they were not happy films to make. Duke hated them because he knew that Republic were intent on keeping him a minor star while they had bigger plans for Corrigan. You know, in Hollywood, it's true that nobody knows anything, because Duke went on to become the biggest movie star of all time, and Corrigan retired into obscurity in the 1950s.

"Those films were bread and butter for me and Duke, but for *Overland Stage Raiders* we had Louise Brooks as the leading lady, and she was a big star in the silent days. She felt that making that film was a real comedown for her. She was no longer in demand and very unhappy about the way her career had gone. But when I introduced her to Wayne, she was really impressed by him."

Louise Brooks would later say about Wayne, "Looking up at him I thought, this is no actor but the hero of all mythology miraculously brought to life." She said that Wayne was what Henry James defined as the greatest of all works of art — "a purely beautiful being."

Overland Stage Raiders was Brooks's last film; she retired after it was completed in two weeks. Wayne was not ready to retire, but he was still unhappy with his career, and he was even more unhappy at home. Sherman recalled, "Josephine just had no respect for her husband's profession and couldn't understand his frustrations." But despite the rift in his marriage, somehow he and Josephine refused to admit defeat, and in 1938 she was pregnant again; she gave birth to Patrick in July 1939. But only shortly after Duke was able to announce he was to be a father again, his own father, Clyde Morrison, died of a heart attack. Wayne loved his father and, remembering how generous Clyde had always been, Wayne hoped to emulate him by supporting Clyde's widow, which he did throughout the rest of her life.

With his father gone, Wayne looked ever more to John Ford as a substitute father. John Carradine said, "I think Ford loved the idea that Wayne would look to him for all the things he would have needed from his own father, and Ford really made the most of that. It seemed to me that Ford felt he owned Wayne and that Wayne owed him. But from the time Duke starred in *The Big Trail*, Ford didn't lift a hand to help him. He sort of kept him in his place until he really needed John Wayne."

It was in 1938 that John Ford really needed John Wayne.

In 1937 John Ford had become interested in a short story called "Stagecoach to Lordsburg" by Ernest Haycox. It had been published in *Collier's* magazine the previous year, and he and screenwriter Dudley Nichols went to work turning it into a screenplay, calling it *Stagecoach*. The result was something quite unique for the time: they had taken a basic Western tale about a stagecoach making a perilous journey across New Mexico and fending off Apaches, and filled it with fully rounded, three-dimensional characters. Most Westerns up to that time had been the typical John Wayne good guys in white hats versus bad guys in black hats. Seven years earlier Raoul Walsh had tried to transform the Western into a more adult and artistic form with *The Big Trail* and failed.

Among the characters that included a corrupt banker, a mild-mannered whisky peddler, a prostitute with a heart of gold, a cavalry officer's pregnant and delicate wife, a Southern gambler with few scruples, a sheriff whose sense of duty did not blind him to true justice, and the stagecoach driver who provided the comedy relief, there was a new kind of hero. He was the Ringo Kid. He was dangerous, he was wanted by the law, and he was out to

116

avenge the murder of his brother. In fact, the Ringo Kid was cleverly disguised by Dudley Nichols as an outlaw, but he turns out to be the hero. The audience of the day would not have known for sure which shade of gray Ringo's hat would turn out to be.

A few major Westerns were being made at the big studios, such as *Jesse James* with Tyrone Power, but mostly they were not interested in investing in prestige Westerns. Ford touted *Stagecoach* to every major studio in Hollywood, and every one of them turned him down. It just so happened that independent producer Walter Wanger was looking for a film property to make for United Artists. Wanger was something of a maverick of his day, so Ford took his script to Wanger, who read it, liked it, and took it to United Artists. Like all the major studios, United Artists (which was not a studio but a company that financed the works of independent producers like Wanger) initially balked at the idea of making a Western.

But Wanger persuaded them, partly by agreeing to limit the budget to a modest $392,000. This meant that most of the budget would be spent on the spectacular action that would be shot on location, while the cast, the director, and the writer would all be paid minimal fees. Ford's fee, for instance, would be $50,000, which, although a respectable amount, could not compare to the $100,000 plus 12 percent of the profits he had received from Fox for *The Hurricane* in 1937.

In October of 1937, Wanger was able to give Ford the green light on *Stagecoach* and they began putting together a cast of character actors who were not superstars but who would each bring their previous screen and stage experience to the project to flesh out the well-rounded characters. They chose George Bancroft as the sheriff, John Carradine as the gambler, Thomas Mitchell as the drunken doctor, Donald Meek as the whisky peddler, Andy Devine as the driver, Louise Platt as the officer's wife, and Claire Trevor as the prostitute.

Wanger had notions of casting Gary Cooper as the Ringo Kid, but the tight budget meant they couldn't afford him. Ford claimed he didn't want Cooper anyway.

Years later, Pilar Wayne (Wayne's third wife) asked Ford why he had waited so long before ever offering Duke a major role. She recounts in her book that Ford's reply was, "He wasn't ready. He needed to develop his skills as an actor — and more than that, I wanted him to lose his boyish looks, so he'd have some pain written across his face to offset the innocence."

But John Carradine told me, "I promise you, if Cooper had said he'd do the film for the paltry fee Wayne got, Ford would have jumped up and down with glee. He knew he needed John Wayne because Wayne was known as a screen cowboy, and Ford also knew that by this time, Wayne had really learned his business. He could act well, and his name would attract an audience who had followed him through his years at Monogram and Republic. So it was good commercial sense to cast Wayne, and a good artistic choice too."

Certainly, Ford's explanation to Pilar Wayne doesn't ring true. Ford needed an actor who was a convincing cowboy; someone who had a following; someone who would not demand a high salary (Wayne's fee was $3,700 as opposed to $10,000 for Andy Devine, $12,000 for Thomas Mitchell, and $15,000 for Claire Trevor. Only John Carradine was paid less, at $3,666). That person was John Wayne.

Having it in mind at some point to cast John Wayne as Ringo, Ford knew it was going to be difficult to persuade Wanger.

In fact, Wanger went ahead and tested Bruce Cabot, whose only real claim to fame to date was as the impresario in *King Kong*, which meant he would come cheap and the public would know his name. But his test was a failure, much to the relief of Ford, who still intended to cast Wayne in the part.

Ford had recently wound up work on two pictures, *Four Men and a Prayer* and *Submarine Patrol*, and he set about preproduction on *Stagecoach* over the next year. During the summer of 1938, John Wayne was aboard the *Araner* for the weekend when Ford handed him the script for *Stagecoach*. Wayne read through it and was impressed. Compared to the cheap cowboy pictures he'd been making, this one had real class. Ford asked him if he had anyone in mind who could play Ringo, and Wayne, who had been impressed by Lloyd Nolan in the 1936 Western *The Texas Rangers*, replied, "Why don't you get Lloyd Nolan?"

"You idiot," said Ford. "Don't you think you could play it?"

Because Ford had never bothered to give Wayne a role since his minor appearance in *Salute*, it didn't even occur to Wayne that Ford would have wanted him for a leading role in such a prestigious picture. Unfortunately, Ford did not have the final say in who played Ringo. It was down to Walter Wanger to decide.

When I spoke to Claire Trevor by telephone in 1979, shortly following Wayne's death, she recalled, "Wanger made Duke test for the part. I already had the part of Dallas, and we had a very well-written intimate scene together, so I did the scene with Duke, and although he was a little nervous and perhaps even a bit wooden, you might say, he did well enough to persuade Wanger to take the gamble and give him the part. Besides, Wanger knew that Jack Ford was just the kind of tough director who could get a good performance out of anyone."

Wayne's agent, Charles Feldman, immediately recognized that *Stagecoach* could only enhance Wayne's career and he persuaded Herb Yates to loan Duke to Walter Wanger and United Artists. "I don't think Yates knew what this film could do for me," said Wayne.

Filming began in October 1938 in Monument Valley, on the Utah-Arizona state line. Most of the footage Ford needed in Monument Valley was simply as a backdrop to the drama. It had a unique form of its own, with monolithic-type mountains.

It also came complete with its own Navajo Indians whose reservation was on this land. The valley had never been filmed before, and Ford needed permission from the Navajos to use it. In return, he gave them work in the film, although it couldn't be said that he allowed them to distinguish themselves, for, in that era, the Native American was always the arch enemy of the white man.

Yakima Canutt recalled, "Although Wayne was a B Western star trying to make his mark in an A film, he had experience that John Ford recognized and respected, and when Wayne urged Ford to give me the job of handling all the stunt work, Mr. Ford gave me a call. When I met Mr. Ford for the first time in his office, he said, 'Well, Enos, how are you?' Enos is my real name, and nobody ever used it, so I said to Mr. Ford, 'I see that Duke has given you all the inside dope on me.' Mr. Ford said, 'He has, and he's said so much about you that you're going to find it tough to live up to it all.'

"A lot of the stuff you see Wayne do in the film would normally be done by a stuntman. But Duke said, 'If Yak says I can do it, I'll do it.' Many think that the famous scene in which the Indians chase the stagecoach was shot in Monument Valley, but it wasn't. Just about before Christmas we moved to Victorville in California to shoot the chase scene on a dry lake. We needed very flat ground for that scene, and the dry lake provided it.

"While we were shooting the chase scene, Walter Wanger arrived to watch, and was horrified to see Wayne climbing up onto the top of the charging stagecoach. Mr. Wanger asked Mr. Ford why he was risking their new star's life on something a stuntman could easily do. When Wayne heard about the complaint, he went over to Mr. Wanger to tell him that he had been doing dangerous stunts for years and that I had taught him exactly how to do this particular stunt."

Canutt also helped Wayne rehearse. "When we were shooting in Monument Valley, we were staying at a small guest cabin which we shared. Mr. Ford was treating Duke like the greenest tenderfoot. I think every actor in the film was giving him help, and so was I. At night we'd go over his lines for the next day in our room, and we'd do them again and again. I always thought he was giving a good performance, but Mr. Ford never let up on him."

Claire Trevor said, "I think Ford knew

exactly what kind of performance he would get from Duke, and how he would get it — which was basically to bully him and humiliate him. He'd grab Duke by the chin to hold his head still and yell, 'Don't you know you don't act with your head — you act with your eyes. Keep your goddamn head still.' "

John Carradine remembered, "Jack Ford really lay into Duke Wayne. He'd yell at him, 'You dumb bastard, I should have got Gary Cooper. Can't you walk like a man instead of a goddamn fairy?' I know Claire felt sorry for Duke and gave him help. I just thought Ford was a sadist and just wanted to make sure that everyone knew who was in charge. The thing was, he treated Wayne like a newcomer, but he'd been making films for ten years or more. He'd learned his trade all right."

But the bullying and cajoling that Ford dealt out made Wayne feel that the years he spent at Monogram and Republic developing his own style of movement had come to nothing. He'd later say that he realized Ford was simply pushing him to give his very best: "He sometimes got me so goddamn angry and so ashamed, that I wanted to murder the old son of a bitch."

Wayne laughed when he said this,

adding, "And he got me so scared to death that I was going to fail that I went to my friend Paul Fix and said, 'You gotta help me. Jack's gonna push me too far and I'm gonna deck him, and that'll be the end of my career in movies.' So unknown to Pappy, Paul would come over to my house at night and he'd help me. He taught me how to say my lines in a natural way and with sincerity.

"There were a lot of moments in the film when I had nothing to say. All I had to do was react to them. I knew that reacting naturally was important, but until *Stagecoach* I hadn't realized just how important it is for a screen actor. You have to make it seem that you're hearing all those words for the first time. All that crap about reacting and not acting; let me tell you something. Here's my technique, and it's oversimplified, but when you talk, talk low, talk as little as possible, and say it with sincerity.

"One day Pappy said, 'Where's that big oaf I cast as the Kid? I got some goddamn actor playing the part. Where'd he come from?' He may have rode me hard, and he always did, but he was an absolute artist. He did what he had to to get what he needed, and he knew that the one thing that would make me do the job well was if I was scared enough to think I'd go back to being a B-Western actor; I wouldn't say B-Western star because you couldn't be a real star in those films. And I sure wanted to be someone. I wanted to be good in *Stagecoach*, and goddamn it, I think I was."

Filming stopped briefly for Christmas, and then continued again at Kerne River for the scene where the stagecoach had to cross the deep river, the horses swimming and dragging the floating stagecoach kept aloft by attached logs. Canutt recalled, "Mr. Ford was despondent about the scene because his wranglers had told him that it was impossible to do. But I told Mr. Ford, 'It can be done and I think it will look terrific.'

"He said, 'Can you do it?'

"And I said, 'Yes.'

"I had four hollow logs made, two to go each side of the stagecoach. Real logs wouldn't have worked. They needed to be hollow and have air in to keep them afloat. I also knew that the horses would never manage to pull the coach across as they'd have enough trouble swimming, so I just attached an underwater cable to the tongue of the coach, and the other end of the cable ran through a pulley out of camera shot. Using that cable, we dragged the coach across and it stayed afloat, and it looked just like it was supposed to, as though the swimming horses were dragging it across. I drove it across myself to test it with seven stuntmen inside, and it was perfect.

"Mr. Ford wanted to know if it would work if Andy Devine drove the coach himself, and I said, 'No problem. All he's got to do is hold the reins.' So we put Duke and Claire and the rest of the principals in the coach, and took the reins, and we did the scene. Mr. Ford said to me after, 'Thank you for not drowning my actors.' I told him, 'That's what you pay me for.' "

Ford still didn't ease up on Wayne, as John Carradine remembered. "Duke was watching some rushes with Ford, and there was a scene shot against back projection of Andy Devine driving the stagecoach. Ford said to Duke, 'What do you think of the scene?' and Duke said, 'Well, I think it looks phony because the reins are too loose.'

"Ford took Wayne back to the set and said, 'Now tell Andy what you told me,' and before Duke could utter a word, Ford went on, 'Tell him that he looks phony up there driving the stage.' Duke tried to explain to Andy and he even apologized, but the damage had been done and from then on, there was friction between Andy and Duke.

"I read somewhere that Ford claimed he did it to juice the pair of them up a bit, but I really wonder what was going on inside Ford's head. After all, Andy's character was supposed to like Ringo. There wasn't supposed to be any tension between the characters."

The unit finally moved back to Hollywood to film in Republic Studio's Western street, and on soundstages at the Samuel Goldwyn Studio, where a mock-up of the stagecoach was created on a soundstage. Virtually all the scenes requiring dialogue inside and on top of the coach were shot in the studio, where the actors performed in the mock-up of the stagecoach against back projection.

There were also a few interior scenes, which required Wayne to deliver some of his most important dialogue, usually with Claire Trevor, who recalled, "By this time Ford had eased up on Duke and even gave him gentle praise from time to time. I think Duke and I had a chemistry that really came across on film. We liked each other in real life and became great friends, but the on-screen chemistry was all-important. Some people thought we must have been having an affair, but that wasn't so. Duke liked dark, Latin types, and I was blond. Not his type at all. And he was in love with Josephine."

When filming was completed, Ford decided he needed to reshoot one single shot. It was the first shot of Wayne in the film in which the camera tracks into a close-up of the Ringo Kid, swinging and cocking his Winchester and yelling, "Hold it!"

Claire Trevor said, "Ford told me he decided to reshoot Duke's opening shot because by then, after all the punishment he'd put Wayne through, Duke had exactly the look of pain with the innocence underneath which would establish the Ringo Kid."

Whether or not Ford did actually refilm Wayne's opening shot is a question nobody has been able to answer for me. In one way it is a superb entrance for Wayne into the film, with the camera tracking into a close-up of him. But the shot is flawed. For one thing, it would have looked much better had it been filmed on location in Monument Valley, but it was filmed in the studio. It therefore lacks realism, which is probably why the tracking shot is intercut with a location shot of the stagecoach, to make it seem as though it were filmed at the same time. It is also technically weak because the camera goes out of focus. It would seem to make sense that if Ford had gone to the trouble of refilming that moment, he would have done it again after viewing the rushes. After all, to refilm one actor against a projected background was not expensive to do.

Stagecoach was not supposed to turn Wayne into a major star. "Ford had never intended that the Ringo Kid establish Wayne as a box-office draw," said John Carradine. "The film had an ensemble cast and of all of us actors who rode that stagecoach, Wayne had the least lines of dialogue. And yet he dominated the film back in 1939, and he still dominates it today."

John Ford may have honed some of the rough edges around Wayne as a screen actor but, by 1939 — after making sixty films in little more than ten years — John Wayne was a seasoned performer. The fact that he outshone the rest of the ensemble cast was partly due to an accident in the writing that made Ringo, the smallest of the film's principal parts, the pivotal role, and also to the star quality and convincing performance that came from John Wayne.

6

B Pictures and Politics

Curiously, while the public liked Wayne as Ringo, neither the industry nor the critics seemed particularly impressed. Still under contract to Republic, Wayne returned there to make four more — and final — Mesquiteer movies in quick succession before *Stagecoach* was previewed at the Fox Westwood Theatre on 2 February 1939 with an audience mainly made up of students from nearby UCLA. It was a tough venue to preview a Western simply because the audience was made up mainly of academically inclined young people, but they loved it. Michael Wayne said, "My father gave two tickets to a couple of executives from Republic and, for some reason, they were not enthusiastic. Perhaps they feared they would lose their star."

However, Canutt said, "I don't think the Republic executives were afraid, because I don't think they recognized what had been achieved."

The film opened at Radio City Music Hall in New York on 2 March 1939 to reviews which had the highest praise for the director while the principal cast en masse was largely considered merely a support to Ford's grand design — and little was said about someone they obviously considered a B Western star. Frank Nugent wrote in the *New York Times*, "Here, in a sentence, is a movie of the grand old school, a genuine rib-thumper, and a beautiful sight to see. . . . [The actors] have all done nobly by a noble horse opera, but none so nobly as its director."

Life magazine said, ". . . its rhythm mounts from the slow, steady roll of stagecoach wheels to the accelerated fury of flight from Indians with all the accumulative majesty of a great symphony."

And *Variety* thought, "Directorially, production is John Ford in peak form, sustaining interest and suspense throughout, and presenting exceptional characterizations. Picture is a display of photographic grandeur. . . .The running fight between the stagecoach passengers and the Apaches has been given thrilling and realistic presentation by Ford."

Stagecoach was nominated for six Oscars — for Best Picture, Direction, Supporting Actor (Thomas Mitchell), Photography, Art Direction, and Editing. It received only one, for Thomas Mitchell. The Best Picture that year was *Gone with the Wind* which won nine other awards, although, curiously, the Academy failed to nominate Thomas Mitchell for his supporting role in *Gone with the Wind*. One gets the feeling that his Oscar for *Stagecoach* was, perhaps, a token award for a film that was smaller and less bombastic than *Gone with the Wind* and yet was, in every way, artistically as good (some would say it was better).

Curiously, according to author Phil Hardy in his *The Western: The Aurum Film Encyclopedia*, *Variety*'s list of All-Time Western Champs does not include *Stagecoach*. Hardy wrote, "It was impossible to arrive at an accurate figure for *Stagecoach*, but research indicates it was not quite as financially successful as its huge reputation suggests."

In fact, according to the *Motion Picture Herald*'s Top Ten Moneymaking Western Stars poll of 1939, John Wayne came in at number nine, below the likes of Buck Jones, Roy Rogers, William Boyd and, at number one, Gene Autry. Even "The

Three Mesquiteers" came in at six, suggesting that *Stagecoach* was not an immediate success. It seems that it has only gained classic status over the years. In fact, in 1936 Wayne had been listed at number seven in the poll, so the 1939 list suggested that his popularity as a Western star had, in fact, dropped.

Biographers of Wayne claim that *Stagecoach* made him a star, but this was not the case. He certainly did not make a great impression with the major studios as none of them attempted to buy his contract from Republic. And there is no evidence to suppose that Republic immediately realized that they had a potential gold mine in their hands.

John Carradine said, "MGM or Warner Bros. should have been breaking down the doors at Republic to get Wayne, but they didn't."

Adding to the myth that *Stagecoach* had made Wayne into a big star is a story that tells how Harry Carey's wife Olive asked Duke, "What will you do now that you're a big star?" And he replied, "I might do something like *The White Company*" (a tale of English knighthood and chivalry).

Olive Carey gave him the benefit of her advice. "The people have told you how they like you. You must give them what they want, not what you want."

This conversation did take place, but it was much later, when Wayne had actually become a star. Wayne said that because of Olive Carey's advice, he did his best to make the films he felt his fans wanted.

There was at least one important film-maker who recognized that Wayne was star material, even though he had turned Wayne down in 1936, and that was Cecil B. DeMille. He sent one of his assistants to offer Wayne the starring role in his big-scale Western, *Northwest Mounted Police*. For a long time after, Wayne regretted his response, in which he echoed DeMille's earlier words of rejection when Wayne wanted the role of Hickok in *The Plainsman*. He said, "Just tell Mr. DeMille too much water has flowed under the bridge for me to want that role."

It was a huge mistake, Wayne realized, because a DeMille picture would have brought him major stardom much sooner.

The first of the final batch of Mesquiteers films, *The Night Riders*, was released in April 1939, a month after *Stagecoach*. Then came *Three Texas Steers* followed by *Wyoming Outlaw* in the summer of 1939.

Film historians and biographers have noted that because of the success of *Stagecoach*, more people than usual went to see the Mesquiteers Westerns. But that was not the case, as shown in the 1939 Western stars poll which indicated that more people saw "The Three Mesquiteers" series of films than saw *Stagecoach*. However, Americans were certainly beginning to visualize John Wayne as someone who represented the American way of life. It came at a time when turmoil was just beginning to brew in America for various reasons.

The fourth and final Mesquiteers film, *New Frontier*, was released in September 1939, virtually coinciding with the outbreak of the war in Europe. America was split between the majority who believed America should stay out of the war, and those few who felt their country should join the European Allies in their fight against Nazi aggression.

For several years prior to the war, Hollywood had been divided over the virtues and vices of Hitler's Nazi vision for Germany and Mussolini's Fascist vision for Italy. Some influential figures in Hollywood actually admired the style of what they described as Europe's "strong men." Harry Cohn, head of Columbia, was one of them. His studio made a documentary called *Mussolini Speaks*, which was supported by an advertising campaign that asked the question, "Is this what America needs?" Il Duce was so delighted with it, he invited Cohn to Italy to be decorated and presented with an autographed photograph of Mussolini which hung on Cohn's office wall until America joined in the war.

Few in Hollywood admired Hitler, though, as many of the studios were run by Jews who took Hitler's anti-Semitic views — and actions — far more seriously than many of the world's governments did. A group sprang up called the Hollywood Anti-Nazi League, which included Eddie Cantor who was known as a liberal, and a number of Hollywood leftists, such as writer-producer-director Herbert Biberman. Its chairman was screenwriter Donald Ogden Stewart who was also a leading Communist Party organizer. The league boycotted goods from Nazi Germany, organized mass rallies, and produced both a newspaper and a weekly radio show to get its points across.

In some quarters of America, people were beginning to become concerned about Communism. Pockets of Communists were certainly evident in America and, as far back as 1934, a list had been published in America of suspected Communist sympathizers, drawn up by an extreme rightist, Elizabeth Dilling, in a booklet called The Red Network. Among the suspects were lawyer Clarence Darrow and even Eleanor Roosevelt. Although the booklet was endorsed by William Randolph Hearst, it had little immediate effect as few people took Dilling's list of suspects seriously.

In 1937 an article in the *Screen Guild Magazine* noted, "We're up to our necks in politics and morality just now." In response, Communist organizer Donald Ogden Stewart assured the magazine's readers that he had personally attended virtually all of the so-called radical meetings and benefits. He stated that "99.44 percent of Hollywood is sleeping peacefully in its options" and that most people in the film industry were not "the least interested in anything political that does not concern their own studio or the abolition of the state and federal income tax."

Wayne remembered that Donald Ogden Stewart was someone who was extremely active in spreading Communism in Hollywood.

There were a number of political groups

that sprang up in Hollywood between 1935 and 1939, including the Motion Picture Democratic Committee and the Motion Picture Artists Committee to the Joint Anti-Fascist Refugee Committee. Filmmakers and actors hosted fund-raising events for the various organizations they supported. Herbert Biberman and actors Melvyn Douglas and Edward G. Robinson drew up a petition, modeled on the Declaration of Independence, asking Americans to put pressure on President Roosevelt to boycott all goods from Germany. Fifty-six other celebrities signed the petition, including Henry Fonda, Joan Crawford, Bette Davis, Don Ameche, Myrna Loy, George Brent, and Alice Faye.

The most politically active of Hollywood's artists were the screenwriters, and more than half of them were estimated to belong to radical leftist organizations. Wayne said, "Screenwriters, who were often the best educated people in Hollywood, generally thought themselves intellectually superior to mere actors, producers, directors, and studio executives. Many of them belonged to an alliance of liberals and Communists."

But that alliance began to crack following the Nazi-Soviet Pact in August

1939. Liberals and anti-Fascists turned away from their Communist partners who, under orders from Stalin, justified the pact in September by arguing that the war in Europe was an "imperialist war" that was of no concern to Socialists and Communists. Lending support and, indeed, leading the campaign to keep America out of the war was the American Communist Party.

There was further political upheaval in 1939 when the House Un-American Activities Committee, chaired by Martin Dies, arrived in California to investigate Communist influence and infiltration of the film industry. Studios told their contracted actors to cooperate with Congress, and the likes of Humphrey Bogart, Frederic March, James Cagney, and many others were forced to go before the Dies Committee to state that they were not Communists.

Critics of John Wayne's politics (and the role he would later play during the McCarthy era) point out that his name did not appear on the petition to boycott Nazi goods, nor did he speak out against Communism during 1939 and 1940 during the Dies Committee investigation.

But John Wayne was not considered by

his peers to be a major star, still appearing, as he was, in minor B films, and would not have been thought important enough to be invited to participate. Besides which, Wayne was not the liberal most of those involved in the anti-Nazi petition claimed to be.

Henry Fonda, who did consider himself a liberal, recalled, "John Ford and I would often talk politics, but Duke didn't express his convictions. I know that he called himself a liberal but I think he was already drifting to the right, and as he loved Ford, I think he didn't want to cross swords with him. I understand that because Jimmy [Stewart] and I fell out over a difference of politics. Jimmy was to the right and I was to the left, and when we realized our friendship was being destroyed by politics, we made up and decided never to discuss politics again. I don't know if Duke was beginning to shift to the right at that time, but back in the 1930s, John Ford was a dedicated liberal Democrat, and that was far too left for the John Wayne of later years. I always wondered about that."

Wayne must have known about Ford's interest in the Spanish Civil War of 1936, when Ford donated a great deal of money to the Loyalists, who were largely made up of Republicans, Socialists, and Communists, in their war against the Francisco Franco regime. The Loyalists had a great deal of support outside Spain from American and European liberals and from the Soviet Union. Supporting Franco were the Germans and Italians who wanted to turn Spain into a Fascist state.

To most, it was a war between Communism and Fascism. Ford's grandson, Dan, wrote in his biography of John Ford that his grandfather declared, "Politically I am a definite socialist Democrat — always left. I have watched the Russian experiment with great interest. Like the French Commune, I am afraid it might lead to another Bonaparte." That, in essence, took Ford off the hook of Communism, but it was still a far cry from the conservative that John Wayne would eventually become.

But during the 1930s, Wayne had not properly formulated his political beliefs. He, like Ford, saw himself as a liberal: "I was young and willing to listen to all sides of the argument. I just kept most of my thoughts to myself. I was just someone — an American — who worked hard for a living: I just happened to be an actor. I was still too busy trying to make a real name for myself to worry about being any kind of influence for any particular party. At some point [in 1938] I did join a number of Hollywood liberals in supporting a Democratic state senator, [Culbert L.] Olsen, and I guess that's when I really started to think about politics. I realized within a short time that the Democrats didn't stand for the same things I did, so I began to drift to the right. When it comes down to it, my family came from Winterset which was in a largely Republican state, and I guess I may have sprouted upward with Republican blood coursing through me, and as a grown man I found I was more comfortable with Republicanism."

Wayne's views grew partly from his membership of the only organization he belonged to, the Screen Actors Guild which, essentially, maintained conservative views and concerned itself chiefly with salaries, contractual rights, and general working conditions. His political leanings to the right were further strengthened by his friendship with Ward Bond who was a true ultraconservative, and who also avoided political confrontation with John Ford. As Fonda realized, Wayne loved Ford too much to get into political arguments with him, especially as he knew that Ford was a patriotic American.

Wayne was certainly not as blind to the political activities in Hollywood as some of his critics have suggested, citing his failure to support Dies. He told me, "It was back in 1937 when I realized something was happening in this business I love so much, and I knew it was not good. Communists were moving in on the business; they hid in the guise of anti-Fascism, but I saw that they were hoaxing a lot of decent men and women on basic humanitarian grounds. Like many others, I didn't believe that someone like Eleanor Roosevelt was a Communist, or a great many others named but, when I was on the executive board of the Screen Actors Guild, I did notice just a few of the members claiming they were for the little man, but they did nothing to help the little man. They were just trying to stir up dissension between actors and extras with producers and directors.

"I knew that Commies were setting up their party all right, because I heard so much leftist crap among the people I worked with, some of it from my own friends. And I often heard writers in particular talk about Russia being the hope of the world. I had nothing against the Russian people. It's Communism I'm against. In the late 1930s and in the 1940s it was a threat to our great country and to every other country that believed in freedom. And anyone who didn't believe that the Communists in America, and in our industry, weren't being sponsored by Joseph Stalin was nuts. And we all know now what kind of a man Stalin was. Hitler and Stalin were the two sides of the same coin. They both exterminated masses of their own people. So did Mao [Tse-tung] after his Communist reign in China started."

Paul Fix told me that Wayne was a firm Republican by the late 1930s. "He didn't talk too much about his politics, but every now and again he'd say something about the 'lousy pinkos' in the [film] business and that something should be done to get rid of them."

George Sherman remembered that "Wayne found his own way to begin expounding his growing philosophy and sense of patriotism through his films. When we did *Wyoming Outlaw*, he wanted a couple of lines written so that when Ray Corrigan said, 'You know, there used to be a time when being an American meant something,' Wayne replied, 'It still does. It stands for freedom and fair play.' "

Wayne became discouraged with the material Republic Studios was giving him after the quality of *Stagecoach*, although he could now afford to buy a Spanish-style house on Highland Avenue. His career received a slight lift when the studio RKO gave him the lead in *Allegheny Uprising* in which Wayne donned Davy Crockett–style buckskins and raccoon hat as a frontiersman opposing the British occupation just prior to the War of Independence.

As his leading lady, RKO cast Claire Trevor in the hope that they would produce the same *Stagecoach* kind of chemistry. It was, at least, recognition from a modest studio that Wayne might be star material, but the choice of bigger star Claire Trevor was as much a matter of insurance as the fact that Trevor was a fine actress. Claire recalled, "For six weeks we all lived — cast and crew — men and women — on location in tents, and throughout Duke was a delight. Contrary to popular belief, he remained sober while he was actually working, having learned that particular lesson from John Ford. He drank only at night before dinner when filming was over, and he refrained from overindulging. At midday lunch and evening meals we all gathered together — except for George Sanders [who costarred as the tyrannical captain of the British soldiers against whom Wayne leads a minor rebellion]. Mr. Sanders failed to make himself popular with the rest of us, snubbing us at mealtimes and keeping to himself.

"One day he said, 'Of course, the colonial Yankees had been a bunch of fairies.' That was enough to make Duke furious. He lunged at him and he would have really hurt him if several men hadn't held him back. Of course, we would all have liked to see Duke teach him a lesson, but when you're working together, you have to be professional and get on, and after that Duke and Sanders were professional enough, but no one liked Sanders. I think he thought the film was anti-British because the script made the British out to be the bad guys."

Wayne insisted that the film was not anti-British. "That's all history," he said. "What I wanted to say in the film was that Americans needed to be prepared to defend their freedom. That was the theme of many of my films, and it's no accident I chose those themes."

The material was not up to the standard of *Stagecoach*, but the film did well enough when released in the autumn of 1939 to make a healthy profit. Herbert Yates might have had the foresight to realize that John Wayne was on his way up, but he put Wayne straight into *Three Faces West*, a rather gloomy tale of a group of dust bowl farmers during the Great Depression who migrate to Oregon. Once more Wayne was able to expound his philosophy in the script, saying, "America was the land of the free for the Austrian refugees fleeing from Nazi persecution. In America they found salvation." Unfortunately, the message in the film was largely lost among its scenes of dull melodrama.

This time Wayne had a new leading lady, Norwegian actress Sigrid Gurie. A rather feisty woman, she proved an attractive proposition for Wayne, who had a brief affair with her during filming.

Ford, by now, should have been casting Wayne in star parts, but once more it was up to Raoul Walsh to step in. Walsh said, "I had a good story, *Dark Command*, based on a book by W. R. Burnett, which had been fashioned into a good screenplay by Grover Jones and F. Hugh Herbert. It was a fictionalized story of Quantrill's Raiders, telling how a cowboy opposes the murderous and guerrilla tactics of politician Will Cantrell. The story had political overtones that both Duke and I believed in — that America had to sacrifice whatever it took to maintain its freedom."

Herb Yates, known for his thrifty ways of filmmaking, was persuaded by Walsh to make *Dark Command* a big-scale historical Western which, with a budget of $700,000, was Republic's most expensive film to date. Yates insisted that Claire Trevor be cast as Wayne's romantic interest once again, and even paid the going rate for the loan of Walter Pidgeon, to play Cantrell, from MGM.

Wayne enjoyed making *Dark Command* and when it was released it made a good profit — enough to persuade Republic to reissue it just four years later when it again did well.

But Wayne was still just a B-picture player at a B-picture studio, in nothing like the same league as Clark Gable, James Cagney, or Errol Flynn. He was, nonetheless, the biggest star at Republic, and that was enough to inspire Herbert Yates to attempt bigger-budget films with their biggest star.

7

Dietrich and DeMille

At last Ford cast Wayne in one of his films, *The Long Voyage Home*, produced by Walter Wanger in 1940 and based on a one-act play by Eugene O'Neill. Wayne played an innocent and naïve Swedish member of a gang of merchant seamen whose ship, the *Glencairn*, leaves Baltimore for London carrying a cargo of dynamite.

Ford hired Danish actress Osa Massen, under contract to Wanger, to coach Wayne with his Swedish accent. Wayne recalled, "The night before I went to work for the first day on *The Long Voyage Home*, I had worked until midnight finishing *Dark Command* at Republic. That was quite a switch, playing a gentle Swede when the night before I'd been knocking the hell out of someone and jumping on a horse."

Why Ford chose a Dane to coach Wayne only Ford knows, but they spent weeks going over lines. Wayne lists the role as being among his favorite and yet when you watch the film closely you realize that, although his performance is outstanding, he somehow gives the illusion of being better than he was, probably because he managed a moderately good accent.

Robert Parish, who often edited for Ford, asked Ford how he got such a good performance from Wayne. Ford answered, "Count the times Wayne talks. That's the answer. Don't let him talk unless you have something that needs to be said."

Wanger feared the film would prove to be too highbrow for audiences, but to his surprise and delight the preview in October 1940 went very well. The film opened in New York to good business, and good reviews. Bosley Crowther thought it "one of the most honest pictures ever placed upon the screen." It was generally regarded as one of the best films released in 1940 and was nominated for five Oscars, including Best Picture. Unfortunately, it won none, but it has somehow continued to maintain a high regard among critics. Years later influential critic Pauline Kael called it "one of the finest of all movies to deal with life at sea."

After *The Long Voyage Home* it would be

another five years before Ford would use Wayne again. It seems Ford had a new favorite actor, Henry Fonda, who worked with Ford in *Young Mr. Lincoln, Drums Along the Mohawk* (both 1939), and *The Grapes of Wrath* (1940).

Henry Fonda told me, "Duke Wayne loved Ford, and I'm sure that from time to time, Ford loved Duke. But Ford was just so jealous when Raoul Walsh beefed up Duke's career after *Stagecoach* [with *Dark Command*]. It was just unforgivable, and I know that Ford made him pay for it by letting him stew in films that really kept Duke out of the so-called A-list of stars for a long time. Duke was still part of the Ford clan and we all went on fishing trips together."

John Wayne was just popular enough in 1940 for Universal to invite him over and offer him a role opposite Marlene Dietrich in *Seven Sinners*. He would be second-billed to Dietrich, a far bigger star, although her career was in a decline, and Universal felt that the increasing popularity of Wayne would help her career as much as her popularity would help his. He would play a naval officer on a South Seas island where, in the Seven Sinners Café, he would meet and fall for a honky-tonk singer, played by Dietrich.

The first time Dietrich saw Wayne was in the Universal commissary one noon. She was immediately attracted to him and sent word that she wanted a meeting with him — in her dressing room. She locked the door and said, "I wonder what time it is?" Before Wayne could check his watch, she raised her skirt and revealed a watch attached to her black garter. "It's very early, darling," she told him. "We have plenty of time." They spent that time making love.

Henry Hathaway recollected, "Duke's affair with Dietrich was the worst-kept secret in Hollywood. They would appear in public together at Hollywood nightspots, and she even went with him to football games and prizefights. And she took a great interest in his career and later took much of the credit for making him the star he became."

Dietrich introduced Wayne to her business manager, Bo Roos, and persuaded Duke to hire Roos to manage his finances. Duke didn't know it then, but it was one of the worst decisions of his life. She then got Roos to urge Charles Feldman, Wayne's agent, to renegotiate his contract with Republic. The result was that Yates agreed to give Wayne 10 percent of the gross takings from his films. Dietrich also taught Wayne that the only way to get on in the business was to be totally single-minded about his career.

Years later, Dietrich virtually dismissed Wayne as an actor and a lover, calling him an "ungifted amateur" in her memoirs. She said, "Unknown, penniless, he begged me to help him. I can't really say he was my 'partner,' since his performance was kept within very strict bounds — he spoke his lines and that was all. I helped as best I could." Production on *Seven Sinners* ran over budget, and was a week behind schedule, but it proved a big success when released in the autumn of 1940.

Wayne finished *Seven Sinners* late one Saturday night, took Sunday off to be with Josephine and his family, and started work at Paramount on Monday for *The Shepherd of the Hills*, directed by Henry Hathaway and costarring Wayne's boyhood screen hero, Harry Carey. It was an ambitious film, shot in Technicolor, in which Wayne played a hotheaded character living in the mountains who vows to kill the man he believes wrecked his mother's life and cast a shadow over his own since birth — his father. He meets a stranger, played by Carey, who is known as the Shepherd of the Hills by mountain folk because of his many kindnesses to them. The stranger, Wayne discovers, is his father.

During filming on location at Big Bear, Marlene Dietrich stayed at a hotel by the lake to be close to Duke. Henry Hathaway told me, "I didn't like having her around because her ardor sometimes made him late, which was unlike Duke. One morning he came rushing in and hit a corner and turned over his station wagon."

Hathaway would become one of Wayne's closest friends, and one of his favorite directors. Like Ford, Hathaway was tough and didn't think twice about bawling anyone out on the set if they didn't do their job properly. He said of Wayne, "Duke was never an actor. By that, I mean he had to do everything real. There wasn't anything in Duke that would allow him to pretend he was something. He couldn't be French, he couldn't have an accent, he couldn't be Olivier. Whatever he was called to do in the script, he did. It wasn't a question of acting, it was a question of reality."

Wayne enjoyed making the film, and told me, "It was a great thrill for me to work with Harry Carey, and the way Hathaway shot and edited it, it was easily one of the finest pictures I've ever seen. But the studio took all the suspense out of the picture by reediting it and having me told that Carey was my father."

Wayne went back to Republic to make two minor films in quick succession, *A Man Betrayed*, which was a contemporary drama in which he played a lawyer, and *Lady from Louisiana*, in which he again played a lawyer but this time in old Mississippi.

Despite Wayne's marital problems, in December 1940, Josephine gave birth to Melinda. Duke confided to Paul Fix that he was spending most evenings at Dietrich's house, pouring out his marital problems. Said Fix, "Duke was caught up in this incredible love affair with Marlene who really beguiled him with her vast experience as a lover. She introduced Duke to erotic pleasures he never knew existed. I said, 'Duke, you gotta choose between being a husband and being Marlene's toy because as sure as hell, she's gonna dump you sooner or later.' He'd say, 'I know! I know! I was telling Marlene what a wonderful, religious woman and a great mother Josephine is, but our sex life is virtually nonexistent. Four times in ten years. That's why we got four great kids.' I told Duke he was an idiot. He said, 'I know! I know!' So he knew all right."

A Man Betrayed and *Lady from Louisiana* were both released early in 1941, before *The Shepherd of the Hills*, which came out in the summer of 1941. None of these films did much to further Wayne's career and, in 1941, he was back on the Republic lot making *Lady for a Night* with Joan Blondell. Once more it was set in Mississippi, but for Wayne it was an attempt at light comedy, which he enjoyed.

In April 1941, Wayne received another offer from Cecil B. DeMille, and this time Wayne was wise enough not to turn it down. The film was *Reap the Wild Wind* and, accepting an invitation to come to DeMille's office, Wayne duly turned up and listened to the legendary director outline the character of Jack Martin, a sea captain who loses a ship when it is wrecked on the Key West shoals. As the story progresses, Martin tries to clear his name with the help of a lawyer, Steve Tolliver, and Loxi Claiborne, the owner of a Key West salvage schooner. There follow fights with pirates and a tug of love between Jack and Steve for Loxi. When Jack mistakenly believes Steve has double-crossed him, he purposely wrecks a steamboat and at his trial one of Jack's rivals says that his sweetheart died in the wreck. Jack and Steve don divers' suits and search the wreck where Steve discovers the dead girl's scarf, evidence that could send Jack to the gallows. The climax of the film had not been properly worked out, but somehow Jack would die while saving Steve's life.

DeMille announced that Ray Milland, under contract to Paramount where the film was to be made, would be playing Steve Tolliver and that Paulette Goddard would play Loxi. Wayne, knowing that Milland as a Paramount star would get top billing, told DeMille, "The only reason you're calling me over here is to make Ray Milland look like a man."

DeMille smiled and told Wayne that he had considered Errol Flynn, George Brent, and Fred MacMurray to play Jack, but had decided that he, Wayne, was the better casting, and he asked Duke to trust him.

As outlined by DeMille, it was a complex story with a complex character, which appealed to Wayne. But when he got the script, he was not so impressed, and dictated a letter to his agent to send to DeMille, telling him he was "disappointed in the lack of color and character in Jack Martin." However, he said that he recalled the picture of Martin that DeMille had painted in his office, "so I disregard the play of the character as painted by the writers." He wrote that when Steve enters the story, Jack becomes negative in all the scenes that involve the three principal characters, so Wayne suggested that Jack should be made "an individualist played boldly and impulsively instead of being played as a plodding dullard." This, he said, would develop Jack into a great character without distracting from Steve or Loxi.

He went on to describe Steve's character as "the suave, eloquent, mental type," and that Jack should be "brusque and sure of himself in all physical situations because of the station of life that he has reached at a youthful age." He added that Jack, while not a mental giant and a little short on logic, must have a definite sense of humor to "see him through two or three melodramatic situations that arise."

Jesse Lasky Jr., one of the film's writers, recalled DeMille reading the letter to him and to fellow writers Alan LeMay and Charles Bennett, when I interviewed him at his Mayfair home in 1978. "We all thought, 'Oh, oh! This is going to make DeMille explode, being told by a B cowboy star what to do with a script DeMille had already approved.' But instead he blew up at us, saying, 'If an actor can see what's wrong and work it out, why couldn't you?'

"What I came to realize about John Wayne when I met him was that he wasn't the dullard we had imagined him to be. He had read enough screenplays to know what was right and wrong with them. He was, of course, concerned with his image, but he showed great intelligence in his perception, and he also knew he was playing second fiddle to Ray Milland. Even at his studio, Republic, he had gained enough star muscle to put some weight behind some of the awful scripts they were giving him. Mr. DeMille came to admire Wayne very much."

Reap the Wild Wind, at a budget of $2 million, was the biggest film Wayne had ever made, and he was paid $25,000 for the eleven weeks it would take to shoot all his scenes. There were many scenes he was not needed for, and the entire production took four months to complete.

"Toward the end of filming," said Jesse Lasky Jr., "someone came up with the idea of having Wayne and Milland attacked by a giant squid. It would attack Milland and Wayne would die saving him. DeMille loved the idea and so he got his special effects team to create this giant squid."

In 1972, on the set of *The House in Nightmare Park*, Ray Milland recalled, "Wayne and I spent hours in Paramount's large water tank fighting this giant squid. The creature was an amazing piece of work. It was made of bright red sponge rubber and was operated by electric motors so it could lash out with its thirty-foot-long tentacles. While we were underwater, DeMille directed us through telephone wires attached to our diving helmets. It was a difficult scene to do because the squid wouldn't always do what DeMille wanted it to do, but somehow it all worked out and looked marvelous on the screen."

Although Wayne had worked for Ford and Hathaway, two directors with a tendency to chew their actors out, he found DeMille's handling of some of the actors far too dictatorial. He particularly resented the way DeMille would almost reduce Paulette Goddard to tears. "Wayne was one of the few actors DeMille never yelled at," said Jesse Lasky Jr. "DeMille liked Wayne so much that he invited him to join him for lunch each day, which was an honor for any actor. I think DeMille knew that John Wayne was going to become a very important star in Hollywood."

Ray Milland looked back, "During *Reap the Wild Wind*, I got on very well with Wayne, partly, I think, because when we were working underwater, we had only each other to rely on and it cemented our camaraderie. Sadly, our friendship didn't last."

When I pressed him to tell me why their friendship was short lived, he said, "It was over a woman."

Pressed a little more, he said, "Just a few months before Pearl Harbor, we went to Mexico City with Ward Bond, Fred MacMurray, and Bo Roos. We were there for two reasons: one, to explore the possibility of buying a movie studio there and, two, to get drunk. The second goal we achieved with far greater success than the first.

"There was a particular lady there, a rather voluptuous Mexican woman called Esperanza Baur Diaz Ceballos. She was a beautiful actress and someone I cared to call upon whenever I was in Mexico. I made the mistake of introducing Wayne to her, and they got — well — friendly and I got mad! End of story."

Esperanza was nicknamed Chata, which, translated literally from the Spanish, means "pug nose," but in Mexico it was a term of endearment, being a version of "sweetie" or "cutie." Her background has always been something of a mystery. Paul Fix said, "She was no film star. At best she was an extra, and at worst she was a prostitute."

All Wayne cared about was that she was beautiful, sultry, fiery, and she could match him drink for drink. "She was uninhibited in every way," said Fix, "but most of all in bed. I think Duke found her more exciting than even Dietrich, and that's saying something. Unfortunately, he mistook excitement for love. And they had so much in common, they seemed a good match. Josephine was a great woman, but she and Duke never were a good match."

Wayne returned to Hollywood and was recalled to Universal for *The Spoilers*, again with Marlene Dietrich, whose ardor for Duke had finally cooled, and Randolph Scott. It was a story set in the Yukon at the time of the Klondike gold rush that had been filmed a number of times during the days of silent films. It had been remade with sound in 1930, and was now being re-

made again in what would be its most famous version. Its highlight was a brutal
and lengthy fistfight between Wayne and
Scott. The two actors did most of their
own stunts, despite problems Wayne was
beginning to experience with his back,
which had become weakened over the
years by him doing too many of his own
stunts.

Then something happened that threatened any future success Wayne was
counting on. The Japanese bombed Pearl
Harbor on 7 December 1941, and America
entered the Second World War.

8

The War Years

It was now early in 1942, and Wayne was in a dilemma. Many Americans were enlisting to fight in the war, including a number of actors, film directors, and cameramen. The controversy over why Wayne did not enlist has never subsided. His critics have always maintained that none of his excuses for staying at home and building his career while Americans were fighting and dying for their country held up in the light of his purported patriotism.

The subject of Hollywood actors enlisting in the Second World War needs to be put into perspective. Most of the people from Hollywood who joined up were filmmakers, like John Huston and William Wyler. They risked their lives to record the war on film and were often in the battle lines. John Ford did likewise, capturing on film the battle of Midway.

It is true that a number of actors enlisted, but very few of them actually saw combat. They were considered too valuable to lose in war. Most of them were kept out of harm's way. Their jobs were often in intelligence or in boosting morale among the enlisted men, and very rarely did they go into danger zones. Very often, it was all a matter of propaganda concocted between the major studios and the American military.

James Stewart was an exception. He joined the air force and risked his life in thirty bombing raids, rising to the rank of colonel and emerging as a brigadier general. Clark Gable enlisted in the army air force in a state of grief after he lost his wife Carole Lombard in an airplane crash during a tour to raise war bonds. His job, like the Hollywood directors', was to film actual combat, and this he did from American bombers in action, earning himself the rank of major.

Because Wayne had four children, he was exempt from the draft, but that wouldn't have prevented him from enlisting if he'd volunteered. So why did he stay out of uniform? Wayne insisted that he did try to enlist but was rejected because he was unfit due to the old shoulder injury, a chronic inner-ear problem from working underwater for so long when making *Reap the Wild Wind*, and a bad back from doing so many of his own stunts.

Another reason given was that Herbert Yates, knowing that *Reap the Wild Wind* was going to make Wayne a bigger star at his studio — in fact, the *only* big star at his studio — refused to release him from his contract. All the other stars who enlisted had to have approval from their studios.

Henry Hathaway, who was never one for diplomacy, said, "Frankly, I think the excuse that he didn't enlist because of a shoulder injury was a story the studio put out to justify their own reasons for keeping Wayne to his contract and preventing him from enlisting. I think, knowing Duke as I have for a long time, he would have enlisted if he were able."

George Sherman said, "It frustrated Duke like hell that he couldn't join up. Despite his screen image of being a tough guy who couldn't be beaten in a fistfight, he was, by 1941, in pretty bad shape. There were times around 1939 when we were working and he'd do a stunt and really hurt himself. His back had taken so much beating that he suffered for many years, but he never complained about it and still insisted on doing many of his own stunts. In the end, I was one of a number of people who said to him that he could serve his country best by making films to boost public morale. And that's what he did. But I know he felt tremendous guilt about not serving. It's plagued him all his life."

To try to feel useful, Wayne became an air-raid warden in Los Angeles alongside Ward Bond. But that didn't ease his conscience because Los Angeles was never bombed. While John Ford was away in service, Wayne and Bond made regular visits to the Ford house to keep Mary company.

In March 1942, *Reap the Wild Wind* opened to good reviews and even better business. The film was, in Hollywood terms, a blockbuster, and although Wayne was billed second after Ray Milland, it was enough to inspire Wayne to write to DeMille, saying, "My appearance in *Reap the Wild Wind* was the highlight of my career."

Shortly after *The Spoilers* was released in April 1942, Wayne and Josephine finally separated and he moved in for a while with Paul Fix. Said Fix, "It was very painful for Duke to leave his kids. He felt terribly guilty about not being there for them that I think it nearly killed him, he drank so much to ease the pain."

When the separation was made public, Wayne told reporters, "I didn't really do anything wrong except stay away from home too much maybe. I was working so damn hard, and I thought I was doing the right thing then. Jo and I just drifted apart."

Wayne was back at Republic making another Western, *In Old California*. He played a pharmacist and based his character on his father. It was a big-budget film by Republic's standards, but it offered little excitement, and Wayne's enthusiasm for the film was minimal. It didn't help that he wanted to bring Chata to Hollywood and he was pressing Yates to give her a screen test.

The next film, however, was to be a landmark in Wayne's career. *Flying Tigers* was the tale of the American Volunteer Group, or the Flying Tigers, fighting for China's freedom in the war with Japan. It was a semifictional account about General Claire Chennault's famous Second World War flying squadron, and its spectacular flying scenes offered thrills and spills in plenty.

It also offered a touching love story between Wayne and British actress Anna Lee.

When I was able to speak to her by telephone in 1979, she said, "I first saw Duke in *Stagecoach* in England and I fell madly in love with him. So getting to play opposite him was just lovely. But he was a man's man, not a woman's man, and being blond, I wasn't his type. He liked dark, Latin women as you can tell from the women he married.

"We were shooting a scene where we're dancing together, and during rehearsal he asked me if I was a Republican. I didn't know what a Republican was and thought he said 'publican' which, of course, in Britain is someone who owns a pub. So I answered, 'No, but I'm very fond of beer.' That made him laugh, and we became good friends, and every now and then he made sure I got a part in his films."

Flying Tigers presented a new John Wayne to the cinemagoing public, especially to the Americans. The film's director David Miller, talking to me in 1979, said, "He was a believable World War Two hero. When you saw Wayne on-screen, you caught his sense of patriotism and sincerity. But I know it frustrated him being a hero on screen only and not in real life. One time he said, 'Jesus, David, what are people gonna think when they see me winning the war against the Japs when they know I'm a fake?'

"I said, 'You're not a fake, Duke. You're the real thing. You act with your heart, you give your character honesty and sincerity, and you're going to make Americans feel safer if they can believe that there are men like you fighting the enemy. So stop beating yourself up.' When we finished work on that film, I joined up and so did the producer [Edmund Grainger] and I think that only made Duke feel worse."

Somehow, during 1942, Wayne found time to return to Mexico to see Chata. But his trip across the border had to be short because in July he was back in front of the cameras in another Second World War picture, *Reunion in France*, filmed at MGM. He was second lead to one of Metro's top stars, Joan Crawford, who played a wealthy French socialite who befriends a wounded American pilot.

Jules Dassin directed, and it was produced by Joseph L. Mankiewicz. When I visited Mankiewicz on the set of *Sleuth*, which he was directing at Pinewood Studios in 1971, he told me, "Louis B. Mayer [head of MGM] would only make films that had an unreal quality to them. They had to have glamour, not grit, and even in the hands of Jules Dassin, it turned out to be a most unremarkable film in which Crawford was too glamorous, while Wayne had little interest in the material and it showed. He wanted to be a star, and of course, the emphasis was on Crawford.

"They had a strange working relationship. Crawford usually fell in love with her leading men, and this was no exception. But Wayne found her approach too aggressive and he was one Hollywood actor who refused to fall under her spell. Besides, he was in love with that Mexican woman."

Way down in the cast list in an early film in her career was Ava Gardner. One day at her London home in 1979, shortly after hearing the news of Wayne's death, she told me, "I thought Duke was a handsome man, and it was funny to see Crawford almost falling over herself to make herself available to him, but he was so sort of 'Gee, ma'am, I'm not that kinda guy,' and she was furious. She said to me, 'He was happy to fuck Marlene Dietrich. What's she got that I don't?' I was only a minor star at Metro and if I'd told her my answer — which was 'class' — I'd have been out on my ass before I knew it.

"Duke was such a charming man, he was too tame for me, so I wouldn't have made a play for him. I guess I went for bad boys which is why I fell for Francis [Sinatra]. Duke and Francis didn't get on for years."

Although *Reunion in France* was not well received by either critics or the public, it was another opportunity for Wayne to express his patriotism in time of war.

Wayne managed to fit in one more film before the end of 1942, *Pittsburgh*, again with Marlene Dietrich and Randolph Scott, and again at Universal. The story mainly centered on Wayne and Scott as two coal miners, Pittsburgh Markham and Cash Evans, respectively. Pittsburgh is driven by ambition to work his way to the top, causing a rift with his friend Cash, but after Pearl Harbor, the two patch things up and together they make a considerable contribution to the war effort and earn a citation of merit from the government. Dietrich was there merely to create some romantic tension. The moral of the story was that every American had a part to play in supporting the war effort, and it enhanced Wayne's patriotic screen persona.

Paul Fix, who had a supporting role, continued to help Wayne improve his techniques. "Duke had developed a wonderful expression where he'd furrow his eyebrow," said Fix. "Watch any John Wayne film and you'll see it. It was very effective, but I could see that Duke was tending to over-use it. Because directors don't care much for actors giving help to other actors, Duke and I devised a set of signals, and when I saw Duke arching his brow once too often, I'd make a signal to tell him not to do it this time. I also urged him to take to the stage in local theatres, but he shied away from that."

Because Wayne's contract with Republic allowed him to accept offers from other studios, he signed a six-picture deal with RKO. His first picture for them, *A Lady Takes a Chance*, offered a change of pace for Wayne at the beginning of 1943. He was second-billed to Jean Arthur in a light comedy about a New York band clerk (Arthur) who takes a bus west and meets a rodeo star (Wayne). It proved very popular at a time when life for everyone was grim. And it proved too that Wayne had a flair for light comedy.

Away from the studios, Wayne was trying to find a way to be a father to his four children. He visited them when he could, and he even socialized with Josephine. But when he brought up the topic of divorce, Josephine would not give way due to her strict Catholic beliefs.

It was around this time that Wayne brought Chata to Hollywood. "I was just one of his friends who told him he was making a big mistake," said Paul Fix. "She was great fun for him, but not someone to settle down with. You just knew she was trouble. John Ford told him he was out of his mind, but Duke told him to mind his own business, so Ford did and for the next few years Ford didn't speak to Duke."

Wayne moved out of Paul Fix's house and into a penthouse apartment at the Château Marmont on Sunset Boulevard with Chata. Paul Fix cautioned him to keep a low profile to avoid a scandal.

Said Fix, "He was like a different person. It was like he was telling everyone, 'I'm a big star now and can do what I like with whom I like.' But he wasn't a big star yet, and the whole thing really upset Josephine. I know that Mary Ford and Barbara Milland [Ray Milland's wife] rallied round Josephine and they openly criticized Duke for his behavior. I think his conceit was partly an outlet for his guilt at not being in the services, and he was letting himself live it up with Chata also as a way of drowning his sorrows over not being able to enlist."

At Republic, Herbert Yates knew he had a potential scandal on his hands, which was rare for his studio. The bigger studios had people whose primary jobs were to clean up scandals, but Republic had never needed anyone to fit that job description. Wayne was his biggest star and he had to protect his investment. He had already prevented Wayne from enlisting, and now he had to do something to keep the affair with Chata under wraps.

He also faced another problem, as Paul Fix explained. "Duke was getting really desperate to enlist and so he wrote to John Ford who was working with his own field photographic unit for the navy. He wanted to know if he could work in Ford's outfit, or if Ford could get him into the marines. Wayne hated asking favors, but he was desperate. Ford was mad at him over the thing with Chata, and he didn't even bother replying himself. I was sure Ford could have got Duke into his outfit if he'd wanted, but he was punishing Duke. Instead, Duke got a letter from a naval official saying that Ford's unit in the navy was full but he could enlist in the army's photographic unit. Duke received the forms and began filling them out. That really put the wind up old Yates."

Herbert Yates was not about to lose his most valuable asset. His solution to quell the potential scandal of Wayne's affair with Chata, and to prevent him from sending in his enlistment forms, was to wave his contract in front of him and send him off to Utah to film a Western, *War of the Wildcats* (or *In Old Oklahoma*). Paul Fix, who was also in the film, said, "Yates kept Duke happy by giving Chata a screen test and putting her under contract. But he never gave her any work. Meanwhile, he kept Duke away from her by making a Western in Utah. Chata stayed in Hollywood making screen tests for films she'd never make."

War of the Wildcats was so successful that it was the only Republic picture to break into the golden list of top-grossing films of 1943. It also got good reviews, with the *New York Times* saying that Wayne "is as convincing as a knockout punch." It should have been enough to have the bigger studios making him offers, but that didn't happen.

His next picture for Republic was the flag-waving war picture, *The Fighting Seabees*. He played a construction engineer who becomes an officer in the navy whose mission is to lead the newly formed Seabees in their construction work on a Pacific island under attack by the Japanese.

Paul Fix reminisced, "We shot much of the film at a camp near San Diego. Duke often spent evenings away from Chata, drinking with off-duty marines. There was a song he liked which the marines sang in North Africa — 'Dirty Gertie from Bizerte.' At times Duke drank a little too much, and a marine would occasionally pick a fight with him. He didn't always win, and the [film's] director [Edward Ludwig] ended up banning Duke from going there for the duration of filming."

When filming was completed in October 1943, Wayne began pressing Josephine for a divorce again, and this time she relented, knowing her marriage was well and truly beyond saving. She filed for divorce on 30 October 1943. Paul Fix recalled, "He was relieved but also full of guilt. He never did get over that feeling."

In December, accepting that he would never be able to enlist, Wayne set out on a tour of the South Pacific and Australia, meeting and entertaining the troops. But his job was not just as an entertainer. Paul Fix remembered, "Duke was over the moon when he got a secret commission from John Ford's own commander [William J. 'Wild Bill'] Donovan in the OSS to use the tour to collect information about the officers and men serving in the South Pacific. In particular, he had to make a personal assessment of General MacArthur who apparently seemed to be interfering or disrupting Donovan's work in the Pacific. Duke tried to get to meet MacArthur, but it seems he got wise to Duke's mission and avoided meeting him under any circumstances. Duke made his report as best he could, and Donovan sent him a certificate of commendation, although it was sent to Ford's house. Duke got pretty mad when he received a plaque saying he had served in the OSS because John Ford had it made out of copper — his way of putting Duke down. So Duke never even bothered to pick up the certificate. He felt he had done his duty, and Ford snubbed him anyway. Ford could be really cruel that way."

While Wayne was in the South Pacific, *The Fighting Seabees* was released in January 1944 and was a box-office hit. Wayne was firmly established as the embodiment of the American fighting man in uniform. The American public didn't care if he never actually fought in the war. They had their spirits lifted by the sight of Wayne killing the enemy.

Of his tour of the Pacific, Wayne said, "It became obvious to me that I could accomplish more by entertaining the troops and boosting their morale than I might have done if I'd been allowed to enlist. To them I was America. A lot of those guys had taken their sweethearts to the Saturday matinee and held hands through a John Wayne Western."

When Wayne returned from his tour, he held a press conference to tell Americans to boost the troops' morale with plenty of letters, snapshots, radios, and cigars. To celebrate his homecoming from the war zone, Republic arranged for a photo shoot of Duke and his four children for *Screen Guide*, but there was no mention that he was no longer living at home and trying for a divorce.

"Duke was anxious to get back to the troops," said Fix, "because of the plans to invade Europe, but Yates saw to it he didn't go. He filed for a 2-A deferment for Duke." (A 2-A deferment meant "deferred in support of national health, safety, or interest.") Wayne was officially grounded and would never be able to do more for the war effort. "Although he did his best," said Fix, "he always felt like a fraud for not getting in uniform, but that was never his fault, despite what some have said."

In 1944 Wayne purchased a bungalow on Tyrone Street in Van Nuys, in the San Fernando Valley, just a short drive from the Republic studio. It was a modest home by Hollywood standards, with one large bedroom, a good-sized lounge, a dining room, a large bathroom, and two smaller rooms. Duke and Chata moved in, and from time to time Chata's mother, Mrs. Ceballos, came to stay.

Paul Fix described the situation as such: "Duke liked Chata's mother in the beginning. She could put a fair bit of alcohol away too. But she kept coming to stay, and each stay got longer. Duke didn't mind at first. The only problem was, Chata's mother didn't speak much English, and Duke only knew a little Spanish. She was actually quite a beautiful woman, and she was only just a little less than ten years Duke's senior, which I think made him feel uncomfortable.

"Chata was great for Duke, but it should only have been a short-term relationship. I tried to tell Duke that she was the kind of girl who liked to party. Others tried to tell him too: Ward Bond, Bo Roos, John Ford — they all said the same thing. But Duke was so happy, he wouldn't listen. I think he wanted to enjoy that feeling of happiness, because when it came down to it, it helped to numb the guilt he felt about leaving Jo and the kids."

That summer, Wayne was back at RKO for a Western, *Tall in the Saddle*. It was based on a magazine story he had read and he got Paul Fix to write a draft screenplay. "Duke had decided it was time to get more control over his films, and he formed a good working relationship with the film's producer, Robert Fellows. He had a say in the casting, the script, everything, because he was already determined that he was going to produce his own films in the future."

Today *Tall in the Saddle* is regarded as a minor classic, with Wayne as a woman-hating ranch foreman who falls for a fiery cattle owner, played by Ella Raines. Fix was also in the cast, as was Ward Bond. Before work on the film began, a meeting was arranged for Wayne, Fix, and Bond to meet Raines at a restaurant across the street from RKO. By telephone in 1979, Ella Raines recalled, "I adored Duke. I remember walking into the restaurant with Paul Fix where Duke and Ward Bond were waiting, and I heard Duke say to Bond,

'Shall I use four-letter words in front of her?' Anyway, we had lunch, and Duke let loose a four-letter word here and there, and I didn't mind a bit, so we got on really well. After lunch, we were on our way back to the studio to begin work and I heard Duke whisper to Bond, 'I'll be goddamned if she doesn't walk like Arly.' Arly was the character I was to play. My part wasn't the stereotype Western woman in a long frock. I wore a cowboy hat and trousers, and that gave me a sort of butch look. The costume was actually uncomfortable, but it made me look the part as Duke and the director [Edwin Marin] wanted it. Actually, it was the first time I felt that I was not well liked by a director. Maybe he didn't like to see a woman act like a man. Duke was very protective of me and let the director know he was to treat me with respect.

"One evening when we'd finished filming, I was leaving the studio when I noticed two large women waiting for me in a car. They followed me as I drove home and I managed to lose them. They did the same for the next three evenings and I took different routes home each night, managing to lose them. I started getting worried about this and told Duke. He said, 'Oh my God, don't you know that they're lesbians?' Now believe it or not, I'd never heard the word and I asked Duke, 'What's a lesbian?' And he told me. I said, 'Oh my God! They think I'm one.' Duke said, 'I'll deal with it.'

"The next evening Duke and Ward Bond were right behind me as I left the studio. They went over to the two women, said something to them, and I never saw them again!

"Duke was very patient with me, except on one occasion. I had taken riding lessons and had ridden Blackie, the horse I was to ride in the film, quite a few times, and I felt like Blackie and I had become good friends. So I told Duke and the director I was okay on a horse. We were shooting a scene where we ride along on horseback, delivering our dialogue. We rehearsed it a few times and rode at the same speed as the camera truck. When we came to shoot the scene, a bell rang which was the signal for the camera operator. Blackie just took off and I was so embarrassed.

"Duke just smiled as I regained control of Blackie and rode back to him. The crew had to scrape out all the tire marks which ran for almost a mile so they wouldn't show when we shot the scene again. But when the bell rang for the second time,

Blackie took off again.

"This time Duke was clearly irritated and said, 'I thought you said you could ride that damn horse.'

"On the third take the same thing happened, and Duke got really mad. He said, 'I'll ride that blankety blank horse and you ride mine.' So we changed horses, everything was prepared to go again, and when the bell rang, Blackie took off with Duke trying to get control of it. He was furious now and swearing at the horse. Then the trainer came over and said, 'I forgot to tell you. Blackie is a former racehorse. He thinks the bell is the start of a race.'

"Well, that made Duke laugh and it was decided not to use the bell again."

Before the film's release in September 1944, Wayne received news which delighted him. With much of the American military forcing the Germans back in Europe, the forces were short of men for the impending assault on Guam and Saipan in the South Pacific. All 2-A deferments had been canceled and Wayne was issued with a 1-A, which meant "available for military service."

Paul Fix said, "Duke was all for it, but Republic stepped in again and got their attorneys to file an appeal against Duke's 1-A, claiming he was more important to the war effort through his film work than actual service. The studio won and Duke was re-issued with the 2-A. It broke his heart. Anyone who says Duke purposely avoided enlisting doesn't know what they're talking about."

9

Cold War in Hollywood

In November 1944, the divorce case went to court. Because Californian laws required a specific reason for divorce, Josephine, with Duke's agreement, charged him with "extreme cruelty . . . causing physical and mental suffering."

Wayne had already agreed on a settlement with Josephine, giving her custody of their four children, the house, the car, one hundred thousand dollars in securities, insurance, and 20 percent of his gross earnings. Wayne also arranged to put two hundred dollars a month into a trust fund for each of his children.

On 29 November 1944, the divorce was granted, although it would take another year before it was made final. Publicly, Josephine said that the divorce was "a purely civil action in no way affecting the moral status of a marriage."

In other words, she still regarded herself as Mrs. John Wayne and, although she never gave him any trouble, she insisted that she was his only legal wife. Paul Fix said, "She taught her children that she was their father's only legal wife, and I think Michael in particular had trouble accepting Duke's later marriages and the children he had with Pilar."

Of his divorce from Josephine, Wayne said, "It was the stupidest damn thing I ever did in my life. She was a woman whose weaknesses were outweighed by her strengths. Not only did I desert the first woman I ever loved, but I also left my four children."

His guilt over all this, especially over his children, haunted him all his life. Paul Fix said, "He was convinced Michael never forgave him. I think it's true that Michael, of all the children, judged him more harshly than the others, and it took a long time for Michael to respect his father again."

All Michael would say when I asked him about his feelings for his father was, "I love my father, and I always will."

Wayne was wearing a Stetson once more for Republic's *Flame of the Barbary Coast* early in 1945. Yates poured $600,000 into the production, a large sum for a Republic picture. Fix, who was also in the film, said, "He got on with his work, knowing his time had passed for getting into the war. He shouldn't be criticized for that. But it did mean that throughout filming he was in a mean mood and apt to lose his temper more quickly than usual, although you'd never know it from watching the picture.

"When anything went wrong, Duke got mad. He hated holdups and just wanted to get on with the job which he took very seriously. He had by then developed the policy that making pictures was a business and that films should make money. But he also approached films as a craft and [maintained] that an actor should be honest about his characterization and retain a level of emotion through sheer hard work, no matter how many times shooting was interrupted. That was another reason he got mad when someone screwed up. He believed everyone should be as professional as he was — and by God, he was professional.

"He was also overly generous. Whenever one of the cowboys in his pictures was broke, Duke would always lend them a few hundred dollars. He never asked for the money back. He was too generous. He was just like his father and that I respect."

When *Flame of the Barbary Coast* was released in May 1945, it received favorable reviews. The *New York Times* summed up the image of Wayne when it said, "John Wayne is perfectly cast. That is, he gambles, fights, woos, and rides with consummate ease if not histrionic aplomb."

He did get into uniform late in 1944, but it was for another war picture, *Back to Bataan*, which costarred Anthony Quinn and Paul Fix. Wayne's good friend Robert Fellows produced, and the director was Edward Dmytryk, a gifted filmmaker who was later named as a Communist, as was the film's writer, Ben Barzman. Quinn told me when I interviewed him on the set of *The Greek Tycoon* at Elstree Studios in 1977, "That was the cause of some problems while we were shooting the picture. Duke knew that Barzman and Dmytryk were far to the left, and when Fellows introduced Duke to Barzman, Duke said without a smile, 'I'm Duke to my friends.' He paused, and then added, 'Also to the people I work with.'

"We had a technical adviser on the set, Colonel George S. Clarke, assigned by the army to the picture. He was one of the last

Americans to leave the Philippines [in 1942] and was a very conservative soldier — someone Duke respected. There were some unfortunate moments when Dmytryk said some things to Clarke which were certainly not of a conservative nature; I never heard those things myself. But I heard that Duke was furious when he found out and he confronted Dmytryk and said, 'Are you a Communist?' Dmytryk said he wasn't."

John Wayne remembered the incident. He said, "I asked Dmytryk outright: 'Are you a Commie?' He said, 'If the masses' — emphasis on *masses* — 'of the American people want Communism, I think it'd be good for our country.' Well, to me, the word 'masses' is not a term generally used in Western countries, and I just knew he was a Commie. But we had a film to make, and I got on with my job."

Dmytryk remembered their relationship somewhat differently when I interviewed him. He said, "John Wayne was an amazing man who worked really hard. Sometimes, when the sun shone, Wayne, some extras, and myself played kickball during lunch breaks. Duke could throw his body around like a lightweight gymnast. When it rained, which it did often during filming,

Duke and Tony Quinn killed time by playing Chinese poker.

"When we started filming I think Wayne knew, through channels, that I was a Communist, but I didn't know that he knew. We got along well and even attended the same affairs thrown by Bo Roos, who was our mutual business manager."

Wayne's memories of making *Back to Bataan* were decidedly bitter. "Ben Barzman was another like Dmytryk. I had to work with these people, but I felt the time was coming when we'd have to do something about it. Thank God there were some good people in it, like Paul Fix and Tony Quinn." Paul Fix recalled, "It was a difficult film to make because Duke was working with what he called a 'lefty screenwriter' and a 'lefty director.' Try and imagine John Wayne working with them. It was explosive. Somehow we got through it.

"We were making the film toward the end of the war, with the Russians pressing the Germans on one front, and the rest of the Allies on the other. One day Barzman said to Duke, 'You shouldn't keep damning the Russian people. Without them we'd be losing the war.'

"This didn't impress Duke who told him, 'It isn't the Russian people I have a problem with. It's Communism. And let's not forget that the Russians are only our allies now because the Nazis invaded Russia even though Stalin was happy enough to sign a peace pact with Hitler at the beginning of the war. But I tell you this, when the war is over, it's Stalin's Communist state that will be the biggest threat to us.'

"Ben Barzman said, 'Talk like that is the very thing that causes wars. The Russians will be our friends.'

"To which Duke said, 'They'll be *your* friends.' "

As one of Wayne's closest friends, Yakima Canutt was privy to his concerns about Communists. Wayne also confided to him that Communists were trying to intimidate him. In London, in 1976, Canutt told me, "John stood for what we like to think of as good old American freedom. He was becoming more hostile toward the Communists in the business, and he got criticized a lot for his politics later on. But Wayne was standing up for what was right, and he knew it, because when he was making *Back to Bataan*, he had some cross words with the director Eddie Dmytryk and the writer Ben Barzman about their suspected Communist affiliation, and someone in the Communist Party didn't like it all. I'm sure neither Dmytryk nor Barzman knew about this, but Wayne received an anonymous letter from someone in the party telling him he'd better watch out.

"When Wayne told me about this letter, I said, 'Sounds to me like you better watch out.' He said, 'No goddamn Commie's gonna frighten me.' I said, 'Duke, why don't you let me look into this? See if I can find out who's behind all this?' He just said, 'Nah! It probably won't come to anything.' So I let it rest."

Just the year before, in 1944, a number of conservative-thinking people in Hollywood, led by director Sam Wood, got together and organized the Motion Picture Alliance for the Preservation of American Ideals which was intent on running the Communists out of the business. Many prominent people signed up for it, including Walt Disney, some of the most important executives at Metro-Goldwyn-Mayer, Hedda Hopper, and a good many actors, including Wayne's friend Ward Bond.

Critics of Wayne and the part he would play in the alliance are quick to point out that he was not a member of the alliance before 1947, and that he had distanced himself from the cold war in Hollywood as much as he had supposedly done from the Second World War.

Wayne told me, "I didn't sign up to the alliance at first because I'm a man who generally likes to beat his own drum. I was speaking out against Communism in my own way. At Ward Bond's urging, I did some unofficial work for the alliance, working sort of undercover, you might say."

This is borne out by an incident in 1945 when director Frank Capra was about to start filming *It's a Wonderful Life*. When I interviewed Capra in 1980, he said, "I was approached by a member of my cast, Ward Bond, who asked me if I'd checked with John Wayne about the suitability of an actress, Anne Revere, whom I was thinking about casting. I didn't see that it was any of Wayne's business and I called him, reminded him that he'd stayed home getting rich during World War Two, and telling him that he could go to hell. I didn't care. I didn't give a shit who was a Communist or who wasn't. I heard that Wayne was so mad, he said, 'I'd like to take that little dago son of a bitch and tear him into a million pieces and throw him into the ocean and watch him float back to Italy.' It was an ugly time in Hollywood. Years later we nearly worked together, but it didn't work out."

Although Duke had not signed up with the alliance, he was urged by Ward Bond to attend a few meetings, and at one of them he was treated as a guest speaker. But there was a problem.

Wayne told me, "[Screenwriter and producer] James McGuinness, who was a personal friend and a dedicated conservative, wanted me to give a speech, but he had written the whole speech for me. Well, I don't do other people's speeches, and I told him that if he wanted me to get up and talk, I'd give my own speech. Besides, I told him that I'd not come to the meeting as an actor but as an American because I believed in what they were doing. So the speech I was supposed to give was given to Ward Bond."

Although Wayne was not an official member of the alliance, it had become well-known around Hollywood that he was speaking out against Communism and calling it "a crime, not a means of government." He backed up his claim by citing the atrocities that were being committed by Stalin.

Yakima Canutt remembered, "The Communists in Hollywood that were being given full support by the Stalinists were really gunning for Wayne. Why they singled him out, I don't know for sure, but my guess is that they thought him an easier target than anyone who was a part of a great body like the Motion Picture Alliance. Duke kind of stood alone.

"Sometime after he got that threatening letter, he got a phone call at his office at Republic and was told to keep his 'big fat mouth shut, or it would be shut for good.' When he told me this, I said, 'Look, Duke, I've got the best undercover men in Hollywood. Nobody but the actors and the directors know the stuntmen in the business, and I'm damn sure these threats don't come from actors or directors. Let me put some of my best stuntmen about to see if we can ferret out who these people really are, before something happens to you.'

"He was very reluctant, but he said, 'It won't do any harm, I guess. But, Christ, let's keep this thing quiet.'

"So that's what I did. I had stuntmen going about asking questions and posing as leftists who wanted to know more about the Communist party. But it wasn't easy and there were no quick results."

★ ★ ★

In February 1945, Wayne began work on *They Were Expendable,* John Ford's tribute to the men in the PT boats (small, armed American craft) during the early months of the Pacific war. Produced at MGM and backed by the navy, it was all about sacrifice and duty. Wayne was given only a secondary role to play, with the principal part of Lieutenant John Brickley — based on Lieutenant John Bulkley, who commanded the PT boats — going to Robert Montgomery.

"That was a slap in the face for Duke," said Paul Fix. "Montgomery was not exactly a leading man, but he had served in the navy and been awarded a Bronze Star, so to Ford, who'd spent most of the war years at the front, he was a real war hero. But to Ford, Duke was not. But Duke never complained. He was just delighted to be working with Ford again."

Wayne admitted he did all he could to build up his own part. He said, "I managed to persuade Pappy to expand the emotional range of my character, and he liked my ideas enough so that I had some really fine scenes, including my idea that my character should make an attempt to remain behind with his men."

Donna Reed was the film's leading lady, providing Wayne with the film's only romantic moments. In 1979, she told me, "I really liked working with Duke. I don't think it was easy for him to play second fiddle to Robert Montgomery, but he did it to please Ford. I'd heard all the stories about how Ford could be really mean, almost sadistic, to his actors, and I saw how he treated Bob [Montgomery] with respect, while he gave Duke a hard time. He'd say things like, 'Haven't you learned anything about acting yet?' and I'd stand back and wait for Duke to explode. But he never did. He just said, 'Sorry, Coach, I'll do it better in the next take.'

"In one scene Ford didn't like the way Duke was saluting. He said, 'You don't have the faintest idea how to salute, do you, you clumsy so-and-so? That's because you never joined up. You just stayed at home and made money from lousy pictures while your countrymen were giving their lives.' And he kept on about this, really putting Duke down who said nothing in his own defense, until, finally, Bob stepped in and shouted at Ford, saying, 'You don't ever talk to Duke like that. You should be ashamed of yourself.' Ford just sat there, stunned into silence, and I think he did feel ashamed. In fact, I'm sure he was crying. Duke went over to him, patted his back, and said, 'That's okay, Coach. You just want to make this film the best it can be.'

"But there were also moments when you could feel the camaraderie between Ford and Wayne, and they'd share little jokes, often at someone else's expense, usually Ward Bond's. You could tell that Duke really loved Ford, and I think Ford loved Duke. Ford just didn't know how to show it. Duke generally kept quiet and did his best."

Wayne recalled a scene in which he did lose his temper: "We were shooting a scene where my boat is strafed by an airplane. A special effects guy was shooting ball bearings at my boat but he had forgotten to replace the windshield with a nonbreakable one made of Plexiglas. It was real fucking glass, and it went flying into my face. I picked up a hammer and went after the man, and Ford leaped up and said, 'No you don't. He's part of my fucking crew.' I yelled back, 'Your fucking crew, goddamn it. They're my fucking eyes.' I was lucky not to have been seriously hurt.

"Toward the end of filming, Pappy fell badly and fractured the upper end of his tibia and was put in traction for two weeks. By then I felt I knew enough about moviemaking, and I expected Ford to ask me to direct the final scenes. But he didn't. He asked Bob Montgomery."

Donna Reed said, "Duke was really disappointed not to be asked to take over the direction. I think Ford was putting him in his place. I've never seen such loyalty as Duke showed a man who seemed to take delight in humiliating him."

Wayne had two war films released in succession. The first was *Back to Bataan* in May 1945, just three months before the end of the war. It was a box-office success. Then *They Were Expendable* in November, when the war was over, by which time people no longer wanted to see films about the war, and despite the reputation the film has gained as a classic, it did poor business.

It was time for a change in Hollywood.

In September 1945, Wayne signed a new nonexclusive contract with Republic. Under this new contract, he would make seven pictures and would receive 10 percent of the gross profits with a guaranteed minimum. He also had a contract with RKO for several pictures and, in all, he stood to make more than a million dollars a year, more than he had ever earned.

"The most important thing for me was that I would be able to produce some of my own films," he said. The first under this contract, however, was not a John Wayne production, although he did exert far more control over it than he'd ever had before.

The film was a run-of-the-mill Western called *Dakota*. At Wayne's insistence, there were roles for Ward Bond, Paul Fix, and Grant Withers. And he insisted that second-unit direction be put in the hands of Yakima Canutt. "Yates humored Duke by allowing him to approve the casting," said Paul Fix, "but it was not unconditional. Herbert Yates had a new girlfriend, a Czechoslovakian actress called Vera Hruba Ralston, and she was to be Duke's leading lady. He didn't want her, but he had no choice."

"Vera was attractive," said Wayne, "and she never pushed her weight around just because she was about to marry Yates. As a human being, she was okay. But she was no actress."

Paul Fix said, "The film began well enough, but it soon became clear that Duke was dissatisfied with Vera's performance. Duke was also learning to flex his muscles and the director Joseph Kane was not having everything his own way. Halfway through production, Duke got a message that his son Michael had fallen off a cliff at a summer camp and had hurt his back badly. The doctors assured Duke that Michael would recover, but he was in a state for the rest of filming, although you'd never know it from the film. That's the kind of pro Duke is. Anyway, it was a pretty lousy film. It did okay, I think, by Republic's standards, but nobody was interested in seeing Vera Ralston except Herbert Yates."

Dakota made it to the screens in November 1945, just before *They Were Expendable* opened, and it proved enough of a diversion from the memories of war to make a profit.

Next came a comedy in the manner of *It Happened One Night*, starring the leading lady from that film, Claudette Colbert. *Without Reservations* saw Colbert as an authoress whose latest book is about to be made into a film. The search is on for the star of the film, and on a train she meets Wayne and Don DeFore, both marines returning home from the war. She immediately realizes that Wayne is perfect to play the hero of her book, and sets about wooing him for the sole purpose of getting him to agree to make the film.

Neither Wayne nor Colbert wanted to make the film. Wayne told me, "I was a little hesitant about making a light comedy without any of the action scenes my audience expected. So I almost chickened out. I think Claudette didn't want to make it because she thought it was too much like *It Happened One Night,* and perhaps she didn't think I was as good at comedy as Gable was in that film.

"The producer was Jesse L. Lasky, and he was convinced we would be able to make a success of it. So Claudette and I insisted on an outstanding director to make sure it would be good, and he got Mervyn LeRoy. I knew Mervyn and liked him, although we'd never worked together, and I thought I'd like to do a movie with him, and he convinced me I should try light comedy. He said I did a lot of light comedy in my films, so why not do it for a whole movie. Claudette was convinced by Mervyn, and so we did it."

Probably, the fee of $68,000 being offered to Wayne also helped change his mind. He said, "I liked that picture. I always felt I had a good sense of comedy timing, and that film gave me the chance to prove it. Claudette was a joy to work with, and we had a lot of laughs, although some said she was getting a little too old at forty-five to be playing those kind of parts. But she still looked good, and she knew how to get the most from the script.

"Mervyn LeRoy was a good director. Claudette knew the script wasn't the best ever, and she tried to make some suggestions to Mervyn, but he wasn't having any of that and told her, 'I'll make the decisions about what to change in the script.' Now people say I'm a chauvinist, but Mervyn said, 'I'm not letting any woman tell me what to do.' That makes him sound a bit cold and unpleasant, which he really wasn't. He was trying to get on and shoot the film within the tight schedule he had. RKO wasn't the biggest company, not like Metro or Paramount, so there was no time for any of that film-star stuff. And the more she made suggestions, the more irritable he got.

"He'd get mad when she bumped into props and lights, but I think her eyesight was not so good and she wasn't going to wear glasses while filming. And she kept insisting that Mervyn should film only her left profile because she said her left profile was better than her right. LeRoy wasn't having any of that and said, 'Goddamn it, you look good on both sides.' It turned out to be RKO's biggest picture of 1946."

Wayne had to accept second billing to Colbert, an indication that he still had not become a major movie star.

10

A New Bad Marriage

On 17 January 1946, Wayne married Chata at the Unity Presbyterian Church in Long Beach. There was just a small gathering of family and friends present, including Ward Bond who was best man, Olive Carey who was matron of honor, Herbert Yates who gave the bride away, and Duke's mother, Molly, who hosted the reception at the California Country Club.

Hollywood's two most influential columnists, Louella Parsons and Hedda Hopper, made their reports on the nuptials, both having agreed to sanitize some of the details for public consumption. Hopper wrote that Wayne had met "the comely Mexican actress" just a few months before the wedding and they had enjoyed a whirlwind romance. Parsons wrote something similar, and added, "It is doubtful if she will continue her movie career after becoming Mrs. Wayne."

Of course, there was no movie career either to continue or retire from.

In the early summer of 1946, Duke got an unusual offer from director Howard Hawks, who had set up his own company and had made a deal with United Artists to make a film based on the Borden Chase story "The Chisholm Trail." It was going to be an epic Western by the name of *Red River* with a budget of $2 million.

Hawks had wanted Gary Cooper to take the starring role, that of Thomas Dunson, an aging cattle baron. Set against the first cattle drive along the Chisholm Trail, the story would be a complex psychological account of the enmity that comes between Dunson and his surrogate son, Matthew Garth, culminating in a ferocious fight between the two.

Howard Hawks told me in 1974 over the phone how he came to cast Wayne as Dunson. "Cooper didn't want to do it. He thought that Dunson's ruthless nature didn't suit his screen image. It was Charles Feldman, Duke's agent, who convinced me that Duke would be ideal for the part.

"I never showed Wayne the screenplay. I just told him the story and he thought it was one of the best he'd ever heard, but he said, 'I don't want to play an old man.'

"I said, 'Duke, you're going to be one pretty soon, so why not get some practice?'

"He said, 'How the hell am I gonna play one?'

"I was about fifty then, so I said, 'Just watch me getting up. That's the way to play it.' "

Wayne accepted, thinking that this might be an opportunity for him to try his hand at character roles; he feared that his days as a leading man might soon be over.

To play Matthew Garth, Hawks chose Montgomery Clift, a student from the Actor's Studio in New York who'd never been before the cameras. Wayne had never heard of Clift, and met him for the first time in Hawks's office. "I thought he was very odd," said Wayne. "He wouldn't look me in the eye. I didn't know what he was talking about, and he was six inches shorter than me. I just didn't think he had a chance against me. Shows how much I knew then!"

Principal photography began in September 1946, in a desolate area just east of Tucson in Arizona. Howard Hawks recalled, "Wayne said to me, 'Howard, this is not going to work.'

"I said, 'Why's that, Duke?'

"He said, 'That kid isn't going to stand up to me.'

"I said, 'Well, why don't we make the first scene.'

"So the first scene we shot was alongside a wagon. Wayne was talking tough, and Clift had a coffee cup, and he had it up to his face all the time. He never changed expression or anything. After the scene, we did another, and then Duke said, 'I watched that kid the whole time. I think you're right. He can hold his own. But one thing still bothers me; I don't think he can keep up with me in a fight. We're supposed to have a fight.'

"I said, 'Duke, I couldn't keep up with you in a fight. But if I got a lucky chance and you fall down and I kick you in the jaw, that would be quite a fight and I think I'd have a good chance.'

"He said, 'Okay, let's do that,' and so we had Monty kick him in the jaw.

"We took three or four days to do that scene and make Monty look good enough to be against Wayne because he didn't know how to punch or move when we rehearsed. My arms got sore from showing Monty how to throw a punch. I think we made a good fight scene."

It was the first time Hawks had worked

with Wayne, and he was obviously impressed with his choice of star. Hawks said,
"There's a scene where Wayne has to make
that walk through the cattle. Well, you
didn't have to tell Wayne how to do that;
he just knew. He took his horse right up to
the herd, and then he walked through
them. The cattle would get in his way and
he just shoved 'em and kept on walking.
He never stopped.

"We had a story, written by Borden
Chase, who turned in the first draft of the
script. But I had Charles Schnee with me
and we rewrote as we went along. I don't
really read scripts and shoot them. I just go
out and make scenes. Monty had to learn
about film technique — my technique,
anyway. He was so intense and studied the
script because he wanted to be word perfect. I said, 'Monty, you don't have to
study lines. You don't have to have them
exact.'

"I called Duke over, and I said to Monty,
'Give us a situation from the story,' so he
did, and then Duke and I just played the
scene, improvising as we went, and Clift
said, 'I'll be goddamned. You didn't even
know what scene I was going to pick.'

"See, Wayne never read a script that I
had. He'd say, 'What am I supposed to do

in this?' and I'd say, 'You're supposed to give the impression of this and that.' And he'd say, 'Okay.' He'd never learn lines before I talked to him, because he said that threw him off. He could memorize two pages of dialogue in three or four minutes, and then he just goes and does it. He's the easiest person I ever worked with because he doesn't discuss it and try to fine-tune it; he just goes and does it without squawking.

"I had not planned to make Wayne the heavy. It was just a good part that resembled the story of the King Ranch, a man who was there at the beginning and built one of the greatest ranches in the world. Wayne took that part and made him the heavy and also made him sympathetic. That's what Wayne did with the part.

"What you get from Wayne is authority. He looks like he belongs in Western gear. You also get a personality that has so much power that he just blows anybody else who's in the same scene off the screen if they can't match him. We were lucky because Monty, although he had a different approach to acting, was able to match him. But it was Wayne who dominated that film, as he always does."

Red River cost nearly $2 million, the biggest film Wayne had made so far. After three months of filming, *Red River* was completed at the Goldwyn studios just before Christmas.

Wayne loved working with Hawks, calling him "the best director" he'd ever worked with alongside of Ford. He said, "He gave actors the feeling that they were really a creative part of the process in any scene. He let actors come up with ideas, then he'd go away and write them into the script. Pappy would never have allowed that, but his way of working was so different.

"Howard would sometimes give an actor lines without telling the other actors in the scene, and that way he got actors to respond naturally. He liked spontaneity. He never had anything written in stone.

"He told me, 'Duke, if you can make three good scenes in this picture without annoying the audience, you'll be okay for the rest of the time.' So every now and then, I'd say, 'Is this one of those scenes?' His usual reply was, 'This is a scene where you get it over with as quickly as you can and don't annoy the audience.'"

Without a doubt, Wayne had given his finest performance to date in *Red River*, and it was also the best film he had made so far. It is flawed, however, by two things: the first is the awful score composed by Dimitri Tiomkin which had a male chorus break into a terrible song every time the herd was moved on.

The second, and most unforgivable, was the ending which had Wayne and Clift, having just tried to kill each other in a ferocious fight, sit side by side grinning inanely up at Joanne Dru who tells them off. The film would have had a stunning and classic ending if Clift had shot Wayne dead.

But Howard Hawks would not accept that as a valid criticism, telling me, "I don't believe in making pictures where a picture ends with the death of one of the protagonists. The ending we had was the only one you could have with those characters and their relationships."

I'm only one of many, it turns out, who has aimed that same criticism at the film.

Red River was held up for release through problems that have never been made totally clear. One account says that Howard Hughes sued Hawks for stealing the climactic fight scene from *The Outlaw*. Hawks started directing *The Outlaw* but walked out early in production over "artistic differences" with Hughes, and

Hughes had finished the picture himself. To satisfy Hughes, Hawks had his editor cut and recut the fight scene, overlaying it with new dialogue, until Hughes was satisfied with the finished product. Hughes, it was said, was just getting even with Hawks.

Wayne had another version for the holdup: "I filed a suit against the backers because they'd promised me $75,000 plus a percentage of the profits, but they didn't even come up with the $75,000. So I asked that the defendant be restrained from distributing the film until they paid up."

Hawks told me, "I actually withheld *Red River* from release for about a year because I thought the people running United Artists were a bunch of cheats." He didn't elaborate further, and the film did not get released until July 1948.

Chata complained that Duke was spending too much time working as he was busy setting up his own production, *Angel and the Badman*. For the first time, Wayne was producing his own film from a script written by a former journalist, James Edward Grant. He also acquired a secretary, Mary St. John, whom he had known for many years.

Grant had arrived in Hollywood a few

years before and established himself as a screenwriter with films such as *Boom Town* and *Johnny Eager*. "I liked his style of writing," Wayne told me. "He seemed able, better than any other screenwriter I knew, to write the kind of dialogue that suited me best. It was also an interesting story he'd come up with, something unconventional, something even Pappy wouldn't have done."

It was the story of a wounded gunman taken in by a family of Quakers. Although he has sworn to kill the man who murdered his foster father, the Quaker girl he falls in love with persuades him to hang up his guns. Ultimately, he must face the man he's been hunting, but the Quaker girl intervenes, and he hands her his gun. His father's killer is finally gunned down by the local marshal.

"I liked the twist in the story," said Wayne. "The audience expected me to kill the man, and they're surprised when I don't."

Grant persuaded Wayne to let him direct the film, and they spent much of 1946 in preproduction. Wayne cast Bruce Cabot, who would become a close friend of Duke's, as the father's killer. Harry Carey played the marshal, and in the role of the

Quaker girl was the delicately beautiful Gail Russell.

Wayne had developed the habit of getting up early in the morning, no matter how late into the night he had been working — or drinking. All day long he and Grant worked on every detail of the production, and Chata constantly complained that he was ignoring her. Filming began in April 1947.

"That was a big step for me, to produce," said Wayne. "But I felt that if anyone was going to give my career a kick up the rear, it would have to be me. I knew that the film was a modest one, and a good one to start with. But the pressures of producing and acting were more than I'd realized, and I have to admit I gave a tongue-lashing to just about everybody, which was more than was usual for me in those days. I found I was going around apologizing to everyone all the time, and thankfully, because they were my friends, they forgave me."

Chata accused him of having an affair with Gail Russell and he loudly denied the accusations. Wayne actually became very protective of Gail who was only twenty-two years old and had had a rough time in Hollywood since her debut in *Henry*

Aldrich Gets Glamour in 1942. Wayne had a glint in his eye when he said of her, "Gail was just such a beautiful young girl that some of those fucking sons of bitches at the studios had taken advantage of her. You know about the old casting couch? She'd been there a number of times. Well, it didn't happen with me. I gave her the part on her own merits. She was one person I never shouted at because I knew she was insecure. She had an anxiety problem, which I understood because I'd had that when I was just a kid. I felt all she needed was someone to show her some kindness. She didn't understand it at all because she thought that I was like everyone else and wanted to take advantage of her. I didn't have to say anything specific to show her she was wrong. I just did what I could to encourage her and give her advice, but I never made any advances on her, and that took her by surprise.

"One day Jimmy Grant said to me, 'You know she's got a real crush on you, don't you?' I said, 'Yeah, but that's only because she's not used to someone she's working for showing her real respect and kindness.' I made sure Gail knew I wasn't like that. But when she wanted to talk, when she needed a friendly ear, I made sure I was there for her. God rest her soul. She died in 1961 after a long battle with alcoholism. I sure loved that girl, but not in a romantic way. I know there were rumors, but I say fuck them that like to think sordid thoughts."

When the film wrapped, Wayne hosted a party for the cast and crew at Eaton's restaurant which was opposite the Republic studio. Duke finally relaxed and drank more than was usual. When the party ended early in the evening, some, including Wayne, decided to head for another bar. Duke drove Gail's car, but en route they lost sight of their friends, and the two of them ended up at a restaurant on the beach at Santa Monica.

They didn't arrive at Gail's home until it was almost midnight and Wayne apologized to Gail's mother for getting Gail home so late. He stayed for a while, chatting and drinking with Gail's mother and brother, and then he headed for home in a cab.

When he arrived home, he found he didn't have his key to the front door, so he had to break into his own home. He would later relate this incident in detail in court during his bitter divorce battle with Chata, claiming that she tried to kill him with a .45 automatic.

Wayne spent much of 1946 working with Grant on the post-production of *Angel and the Badman*. He came to realize that the strength of the film lay in its script and in the on-screen chemistry he had with Russell, but Grant's direction was too pedestrian for the unconventional story. Wayne said, "I finally had to tell Jimmy, 'Stick to writing. That's what you do best.' "

When work on *Angel and the Badman* was completed in December, Wayne took Chata on a belated honeymoon to Hawaii, along with James Edward Grant and his wife. It turned into the honeymoon from hell as Chata was still convinced Duke had had an affair with Gail Russell and that Grant had been an accomplice. The more she drank, the louder she got, and the more drunk and loud she got, the more Wayne tried to drown his own sorrows in whisky and tequila.

He was an emotional wreck when he and Chata returned home to find Mrs. Ceballos waiting for them. Paul Fix described the scene: "Chata's mother seemed to have moved in for good and that was too much for Duke. He told Chata that the bungalow was too small for the three of them, to which Chata said, 'Then buy me a bigger house.' That was the start of all their problems. Chata and her mother drank more than Duke, and he would come home and find them both drunk and arguing about something or other. They'd go shopping together and Duke would find they had spent a fortune in one afternoon. Duke was making a good living, but he wasn't earning the fortunes that other stars at bigger studios got.

"It was all made worse when Chata's mother convinced her that an actor and an actress must have real feelings for each other to be able to do love scenes, and so Chata would go crazy when she knew he was kissing his leading lady. He'd tell her, 'It's only a job.' By then I think he'd learned his lesson about having affairs with his leading ladies, and he was, as far as I knew, faithful to Chata in the early years they were together. He was really relieved every time Chata's mother finally left to go home to Mexico.

"When things were good between Duke and Chata, they were very good. They'd laugh and have a great time. But when things got bad . . . oh boy!

"One night they were at a party for an important Mexican businessman, and

Chata got so drunk, she was insulting everyone: Duke, the guests, and the important Mexican businessman. Duke said, 'It's time to go,' and she refused to leave. So like John Wayne in a movie, he scooped her up in his arms and carried her out to the car and dumped her on the seat. When he got in, she reached over and scratched his face, drawing blood. When he got her home, he locked her in the bedroom. He turned up the next day at his office at Republic with scratches on his face.

"It was a bad situation. A lot of us told Duke that she was bad for him. I think he knew that, but he felt he'd failed in his first marriage and didn't want another failed marriage, though God knows, it was never going to be a great success. He even had a heated argument with John Ford who finally said to Duke, 'Did you have to marry that whore?' "

Angel and the Badman was released in February 1947, but it was only moderately successful. Wayne was disappointed although he had learned a lot about producing his own films.

11

Stardom at Last

It was at Ford's house that Wayne first met Maureen O'Hara. The ever-delightful actress told me by telephone in 1974, "We had a tradition which somehow started. I had to sing as sweetly as I could, and then Duke had to sing, which he could actually do well. But John Ford always wanted Duke to sing to Mary [Ford's wife] off-key, which Ford, Mary, and everyone else thought hilarious."

Wayne and O'Hara liked each other instantly. "Maureen is not like most other women," said Wayne. "She didn't mind you using four-letter words around her, which I tend to do — often — and she didn't get all girly and dainty, and yet she is still totally feminine. She's like a guy almost."

O'Hara told me, "Duke said I was the greatest guy he'd ever met."

Wayne and O'Hara were to be teamed

for the first time in RKO's Technicolor adventure about rail construction in the Andes, *Tycoon*. Wayne recalled, "Some bright spark at RKO decided we were mismatched or something, and so they decided to put another actress [Laraine Day] in the part. Obviously someone at RKO didn't know dick."

Anthony Quinn, also in the cast, remembered, "We were going to shoot the film in Mexico, at Churubusco. Duke and I thought, hey, RKO are giving this special treatment, because the Mexican location would add some authenticity. But a week before we started shooting, they changed their minds and we made the film at Lone Pine. That was typical RKO."

Filming began in February 1947, beginning well but running into trouble when Day's new husband, Leo Durocher, manager of the Brooklyn Dodgers, began turning up on the set. "He didn't like to see his wife being held and kissed by John Wayne," said Quinn. "Every day, Durocher sat and watched, and when it got to a love scene, he glared at Duke, and I think Duke just thought, what the hell, I'm not going to get him all upset by being all over his wife, and so the love scenes lacked a certain passion. I said, 'Duke, don't worry about him. You're a pro. Do your job.' He said, 'Tony, I got enough problems in my own marriage without getting Laraine into any rift in hers. Let's just get this piece of shit over with.' Because that's what the film was — total shit.

"Duke told me, 'I think I may be getting past it to keep playing the romantic lead. I'm losing my goddamn hair, and I'm the wrong side of forty now.' I said, 'Duke, I've been in this business a long time now and I'm still playing the friend of the lead star, or the villain. What are you complaining about?'

"He said, 'Tony, I just don't think I'm ever going to last as a leading man for too much longer, and I'm never going to get another part like Ringo. That's why I want to produce, and I think I'm going to try directing when I get the chance. It won't be too long before my acting days are over.' Jesus, was he wrong."

But he wasn't wrong about *Tycoon*. It made a considerable loss.

Wayne had good reason to be concerned about his status as a leading man. When John Ford cast him in *Fort Apache*, he was given the secondary role of Captain Kirby York, while Henry Fonda was given the lead role of Lieutenant Colonel Thursday.

225

However, Wayne received $100,000 for his part, which was the same amount that both Henry Fonda and Shirley Temple, now a beautiful teenager, received.

Of course, Wayne was delighted to be working with Ford again, but he knew that Ford still didn't consider him good enough to play a complex character like Thursday, an ambitious, glory-seeking hero from the Civil War who was based on General Custer.

Wayne told me, "I could see the writing on the wall when Ford cast John Agar in the romantic role of Lieutenant O'Rourke, Hank Fonda in the lead role, and me just trying to make peace with the Indians."

Ford discouraged his actors from bringing their spouses on location, and Chata was furious that she could not join Duke in Monument Valley. John Agar, who played a major supporting role, said in 1979, "Duke told me that before he left for Monument Valley, Chata got very drunk and hurled all the verbal abuse she could think of, in both English and Spanish.

"With his troubles at home and his feeling that his career was still not going where he wanted it to go, I knew that he was getting despondent. I tried telling him, 'Hell, Duke, Pappy just put me in this part because I happen to be married to the leading lady [Shirley Temple]. I'd rather be playing your role. You're the one who makes peace with the Indians and then refuses to betray them as Hank Fonda does. You're the real hero.' But he wouldn't listen.

"When we began filming [in early summer 1947], John Ford gave me such a hard time. He said I was a lousy actor, and he just lay into me. I felt like the one who should give up, not Duke. Duke said to me, 'Don't worry. At the moment you're the whipping boy. Give him time, he'll get around to the rest of us.' Now Duke was Ford's old friend, and he rode Duke hard too, but I had the worst of it to start with.

"I was petrified of Ford who complained about my delivery, the way I rode my horse, everything I did. Wayne told me how badly Ford had treated him when they made *Stagecoach*, and he said, 'He's just trying to get a performance out of you.' I wasn't convinced."

By this time, Wayne had found that the best way for him to spend time with his children was to start bringing them to work with him. Michael, then still a teenager, was on the location in Monument Valley, assisting in any way he could. Michael said, "My father took a lot of heat from John Ford. But so did Henry Fonda who'd made a lot of films with Ford. One day Ford turned on Fonda and said some outrageous things, and when Ford had finished telling him what he thought, I saw Fonda turn and walk away with tears in his eyes.

"I think Ford resented me because I was a lot more aggressive than his own son, Pat, who was more laid back. So Ford was not too kind to me, but my father said to me, 'Your Uncle Jack loves you. I mean, look at the way he treats Ward Bond, and he loves Ward.'

"But there were some fun times too. In Monument Valley at night, you'd hear someone singing or an accordion floating on the night air. My father would play cards with Ford, and Dad thought I brought him luck at cards, so Ford said, 'Get that goddamn kid out of here.' So there are a lot of pleasant memories. But no matter how hard Ford was on my father, Dad just took it and didn't complain."

Agar recalled, "Ward Bond arrived in the valley by airplane, buzzing the set and wrecking a take. Ford just exploded, and Duke said to me, 'You can relax now.

Pappy's got his new whipping boy.' "

Wayne thought the world of Ward Bond: "Ward just had such an enormous ego, he thought he was irresistible to women and complained that he should have my role. He just had all the gall in the world and always spoke before he thought. But he was so thick-skinned that all the ridicule we threw at him just bounced off. His ego just left him wide open to practical jokes, so making fun of him was a favorite sport between Pappy and me. But we loved Ward, and he enjoyed being picked on because it made him the center of attention. Ward and I would purposely hurl sarcastic abuse at each other, just to make newcomers think we were on the verge of tearing each other apart. But it was all an act. We had great times; yes, sir."

Anna Lee had a part in the film and recalled: "I don't know if Ford did it on purpose, but he made Shirley Temple, Irene Rich, and me stand for ages in the hot sun on a balcony. We were wearing these tight, uncomfortable corsets and we could hardly breathe. Finally I fainted and woke up in John Wayne's arms, and he carried me down from the balcony. When Ford started teasing me about having a poor head for the sun, Duke told me, 'It's okay! That means he likes you!' "

Filming finished in August, and after Ford had finished post-production in October, Wayne, Bond, and Fonda joined him for a cruise on the *Araner* to Mexico where they fished, got drunk, and visited the hot spots along the coast. All of this simply added fuel to the fire in Duke's marriage.

When Howard Hawks decided to show John Ford a rough cut of *Red River*, Ford was surprised. Hawks told me, "When John Ford saw Duke in *Red River*, he said, 'I never knew that son of a bitch could act.' I thought it odd that he'd never considered Wayne a big enough star to carry a motion picture, despite the fact that he was doing just that at Republic. Now, suddenly, Ford decides that Wayne should be the star of his next film, *Three Godfathers*."

Three Godfathers was a Western fable based somewhat loosely on the Nativity story. Three outlaws on the run discover a dying woman with a baby. They promise the dying mother that they will save the baby and, after burying the woman, they head across the desert for New Jerusalem, Arizona. Only one man survives, saving the baby and giving himself up to the law.

In September 1947, Harry Carey died

after a long, agonizing battle with cancer. Ford was with him at the moment he died, and Wayne was in the next room taking care of Carey's son, Harry Jr., who had played small roles in *Red River* and *Pursued*.

Wayne recalled, "It was a terrible day for us all, but especially for Olive and Dobe [Harry Jr.'s nickname because his hair was the color of adobe brick]. I gave Dobe a drink of whisky but he turned it down. He told me that his father had told him, 'You will work for John Ford one day. Not till after I'm dead, but you will.'

"Harry Carey had made a lot of pictures with Ford in the silent days [twenty-five films, altogether], but they kinda drifted apart and I was sorry that Pappy never gave Harry a part in any of his films after sound came along. But I was glad I made a few pictures with him. He was my idol when I was a boy."

At Carey's wake, Ford told Olive Carey that he was going to remake *Three Godfathers* as a tribute to Harry, and he told Harry Jr. he was going to be in it, along with Wayne and Pedro Armendariz as the three outlaws. Ward Bond was to play the marshal who pursues them into the desert.

Ford told Harry Jr., "You're going to

hate me when this picture is over, but you're going to give a great performance."

Filming began in May 1948, in Death Valley. Ford had been right; Harry Jr. did come to hate the director who gave Carey the kind of treatment he had given Duke in *Stagecoach*. Wayne recalled, "I loved Pappy, but he could be a real son of a bitch. A number of times while filming *Three Godfathers*, he told Dobe to 'assume the position' and kicked him in the ass. I didn't think that was so bad, but a few times he told me to kick poor Dobe, and I felt really bad about that, but when Pappy gave an order, it was carried out."

Making *Three Godfathers* was, said Wayne, "damn hard." "One of the most difficult locations I ever worked on. We were out in the desert sun in soaring temperatures for much of the time. We'd work from eight in the morning until eleven, and then break for a four-hour lunch during the hottest part of the day when it was impossible to work. Then back to work again until around six in the evening. I drank gallons of water to try to keep from getting dehydrated, but my lips still cracked and I got terribly sunburned. That wasn't all makeup on my face.

"There was a scene where we had to

walk through a sandstorm, and we had two huge airplane propellers blowing the sand up around us. It got in your eyes, your mouth, up your nose, in your ears. It took days to film that fucking scene.

"Pappy was in his worst mood when we were in the desert, but after, when we returned to the studio at MGM, he lightened up and there was a bit more pleasure in the process.

"You'll recall that at the beginning of the film there's a shot of a cowboy who was dressed like Harry Carey riding to the crest of a hill and looking into the sunset. That was Cliff Lyons, a great stuntman. And Ford put over that shot the words, 'To the memory of Harry Carey. Bright Star of the Early Western Sky.' When Olive saw that, she just wept buckets. We all did."

As soon as Wayne finished on *Three Godfathers*, he went to work at Republic again, to make *Wake of the Red Witch*. "I think that was one time Duke would have liked a break because he was just so exhausted from making the Ford film, and he wanted to give Chata some time," said Paul Fix, "but Republic were waiting for him, and Chata was not at all happy about it."

Wake of the Red Witch was a sort of cross between *Reap the Wild Wind* and *Wuthering*

Heights, with Wayne purposely wrecking ships, losing the love of his life to another man, holding her in his arms when she dies, and then losing his life when he dives to the wreck of the *Red Witch*. It's even got a giant octopus.

Although Wayne did not produce *Wake of the Red Witch*, he still had the power to approve the casting, and he gave the role of ship's mate to Paul Fix, and the role of the girl he loves to Gail Russell. He also found a small role for Grant Withers. The film's director, Edward Ludwig, and the producer, Edmund Grainger, chose Gig Young to play Wayne's good-natured partner.

Gig Young told me in 1970, "It was one of those quick, relatively cheap action films Republic specialized in, although I think they thought they were making an epic by their standards. I didn't develop any great particular bond with Wayne as he was already surrounded by many of his friends like Fix and Withers, and of course Gail.

"Now Gail was absolutely perfect for that part because she had such a fragile quality. Well, she was fragile, very nervous, and unsure of herself, and I admired the way Wayne nurtured her and was very protective of her. I asked Paul Fix if there was anything going on between Wayne and Gail, and he said there wasn't. But I do know that Wayne's Mexican wife thought there was, and she gave Wayne hell about it."

As his marriage was falling apart, Duke's relationship with Josephine had improved, and he often stopped by at her house to see her and the children. He was impressed with the dignity she displayed. "She never criticized me for what had happened between us," Wayne said. "And she never made any attempt to make the children hate me. I came to realize that it was me who destroyed our marriage. I was much too selfish. But I believe I got along better with my children after the divorce. I wanted to do what was right by them."

Patrick Wayne recalled, "We were able to see our father a lot. We were really just crazy about him. He instilled in us all an appreciation for hard work and other good solid values which his own father had instilled in him."

Fort Apache opened in March 1948 and did well. Then came *Red River* in July which took a whopping $4.5 million at the domestic box office, a sizable sum for 1948. In fact, in 1983, an inflation-adjusted list based on *Variety's* All-Time

Western Champs put *Red River* at number eleven.

Three Godfathers and *Wake of the Red Witch* both followed in December, giving Wayne four films released in one year. They were all crowd pleasers but, of them all, it was *Red River* that really put John Wayne on the map. It took everyone in the business and the media by surprise. Ben Johnson, who had a small role in *Three Godfathers* and would become a regular in Wayne's films and a lifelong friend, remembered, "There was John Ford, putting Duke into secondary roles and telling him what a lousy actor he was, and all of a sudden, the critics were raving about Duke's performance in *Red River*. People were suddenly asking, why was it that John Wayne had been in the business for two decades and that instead of going into decline, he had suddenly become a major attraction?

"Ford suddenly comes up with the answer which he claims he knew all along. He said, 'Duke is the best actor in Hollywood, that's why.' He suddenly puts Duke into the starring role in *She Wore a Yellow Ribbon* which again proved that Duke was a really fine actor. I can tell you that the reason he had been so successful, and became even more successful, was because he was the hardest-working actor I ever knew. He worked damned hard to prove himself.

"But still, even with *Red River* he was being shunned by his peers. He should have been nominated for an Oscar, but he wasn't."

Johnson was right. Wayne had given a superb performance as Dunson — one of the best performances of his career — and his peers at the Academy of Motion Picture Arts and Sciences just would not admit it. But that would change.

Inspired by Wayne's performance as an older man in *Red River*, Ford cast him as Captain Brittles, a cavalry officer on the verge of retiring in *She Wore a Yellow Ribbon*.

Much of it was shot in Ford's beloved Monument Valley, and the cast was full of Ford regulars, including John Agar, Harry Carey Jr., and Victor McLaglen as the Irish sergeant, a role virtually reprised from *Fort Apache* (and one he would reprise again in *Rio Grande*).

The new boy, this time, was Ben Johnson, a real cowboy and a rodeo champion. Although he'd appeared in *Three*

Godfathers, he had a more prominent role in *She Wore a Yellow Ribbon.* Johnson said, "I think Ford chose me because I rode a horse better than just about anyone else, and that's pretty much what my role required me to do. I had no aspirations to be a great actor and I think Ford knew that because Wayne told me, 'Watch out, you'll be the new whipping boy,' but Ford treated me so well, it was a bit unnerving.

"I didn't really want to be a part of the Ford family, and when he invited me to play cards at night, which was a tradition on his films, I made sure I played so lousy that he never asked me again. But there was Duke Wayne playing cards every night — and Duke was a great cardplayer — but he had to lose so as not to upset the old man. Duke just did anything to keep Ford happy.

"What really impressed me about Duke was that he could stay up late at night, playing cards — and losing every hand — and drinking, but still he was up early every morning and knew not only all his lines, but everyone else's too."

Wayne enjoyed the challenge of playing a man of sixty, and told me, "For the first time, Pappy was treating me like an actor, and he showed me greater respect, which I appreciated. I felt like I'd worked hard and long to reach that stage of my career, having been thinking of giving it up. Really, Hawks and Ford saved my career. The only problem was, because I'd suddenly become so successful, a lot of those awful old B Westerns, including those Three Mesquiteers pictures, were being reissued, and people were getting a look at how awful I'd been in those early days.

"Ford had many methods of getting a performance out of an actor. He decided that in the scene where the men give me an engraved silver watch, I should take out a pair of spectacles and make quite a thing out of reading the inscription. He knew that my reaction would be simplistic and moving, that I'd give an emotional reaction rather than a studied response to the lines. It made me feel that I couldn't cope emotionally with that moment any more than Brittles could and would try to hide it, and when tears came to my eyes, it was for real.

"But there was one thing that disappointed me about the ending of *She Wore a Yellow Ribbon*, and it still disappoints me today. The picture should have ended just after the scene in which I'd run off with all the Indians' horses which prevented the war from happening. The scene I'm talking about is where I take out my watch and I say, 'Well, what time is it by my brand-new silver-dollar watch and chain? Three minutes after twelve. I've been a civilian for three minutes. Hard to believe.' And then I should have just rode away, and that should have been the end. That was the end in the script, but Pappy decided that at the last minute I'd get the job of Indian scout. I said, 'Oh, come on, Coach, that's a bullshit ending.' That didn't please him none, and he had to have it his way."

When released in July 1949, *She Wore a Yellow Ribbon* earned a domestic box office of $2.7 million, less than *Red River* but still a more-than-respectable amount. In fact, the 1983 inflation-adjusted list of the most successful Westerns put it at number thirty-three, way ahead of later films such as *The Outlaw Josey Wales*, *The Wild Bunch*, and *Hang 'Em High*.

Because of his association with RKO, Wayne was able to ask Howard Hughes, who now owned the studio, for a loan, and with it he purchased a house in Encino, set on a small hill in a five-acre estate. The house had twenty-four rooms, a swimming pool, and stables.

Encino was then a relatively underdeveloped area in the San Fernando Valley.

Around his estate, Wayne had erected a ten-foot-high brick wall with an electrically operated gate for added security. He hoped the luxury Chata now found herself living in would make life easier. It didn't. He said, "It finally dawned on me that Chata had married me for what I could do for her. That made me feel degraded. I felt used. I'd do anything for anyone, but they have to be upfront about it."

By this time, Wayne had committed himself fully to a new mission — the fight against Communism.

12

Wayne's Crusade for Freedom

On 12 March 1947, President Truman declared America's determination to take "immediate and resolute action" in support of any nation resisting Communist aggression. In what became known as the Truman Doctrine, he stated, "I believe that it must be the policy of the United States to support free peoples who are resisting attempted subjugation by armed minorities or outside pressures. I believe that we must assist free people to work out their own destinies in their own way."

That same year, John Wayne joined the Motion Picture Alliance for the Preservation of American Ideals. It was the year that President Harry S. Truman initiated a nationwide hunt for Communists. It was also the year the alliance invited the House Un-American Activities Committee to investigate Communism in the film industry.

A number of actors, directors, and writers were summoned to Washington to appear before the committee headed by J. Parnell Thomas. Ten names became prominent as suspected Communists — producer-director Herbert Biberman, Edward Dmytryk, producer-writer Adrian Scott, and screenwriters Alvah Bessie, Lester Cole, Ring Lardner Jr., John Howard Lawson, Albert Maltz, Samuel Ornitz, and Dalton Trumbo. All ten cited the First Amendment (and its protection of the right to free speech and association) and were held in contempt of Congress for their refusal to divulge their political affiliations, past or present. This group became known as the Hollywood Ten, although there were others who were named as either Communists or Communist sympathizers, and whose careers suffered because of it.

Some actually admitted to being former members of the Communist party, and those who named names were generally pardoned. Those who didn't found their careers cut short.

In 1948, the Hollywood Ten were summoned to Washington for trial and were subsequently imprisoned, not for being Communists, but for contempt. That was also the year Ward Bond and John Wayne were elected to the executive board of the Motion Picture Alliance.

Many in Hollywood denounced the Communist witch hunts, as they came to be known. A delegation headed for Washington, led by John Huston, Humphrey Bogart, and many other top names, to protest the treatment of the Hollywood Ten. But their protest had no impact. There were many inside and outside the alliance who believed that the Hollywood Ten got what they deserved.

In 1949 John Wayne was elected as president of the Motion Picture Alliance — a position he held for three consecutive terms — and he spoke out openly against Communism. He gave Senator Joseph McCarthy his full support in Congress's new investigation into Communism in the entertainment business.

He was now in a position that brought much criticism for his right-wing views. He told me, "I never felt I needed to apologize for my patriotism. I felt that if there were Communists in the business — and I knew there were — then they ought to go over to Russia and try enjoying freedom there."

He was openly critical of anything in the film business that he considered un-American. He denounced the film *All the King's*

Men which won the Oscar as Best Picture in 1949. He said the film "smeared the machinery of the country's government" and that it would "tear down people's faith in everything that they have been brought up to believe is important in the American way of life."

He had the full support of many including Ward Bond, stuntman Cliff Lyons, James Edward Grant, and Borden Chase. John Ford, however, tried to ease tensions in the industry by urging his ultra-conservative friends to moderate their words and deeds. But this was one order from Ford that Wayne was not going to obey.

"We were just good Americans," Wayne said, "and we demanded the right to speak our minds. After all, the Communists in Hollywood were speaking theirs. If you're in a fight, you must fight to win, and in those early years of the Cold War I strongly believed that our country's fundamental values were in jeopardy. I think that the Communists proved my point over the years."

He made his views clear at special Crusade for Freedom rallies organized by the alliance. In one public speech in 1949, he said, "The past ten years the disciples of dictatorship have had the most to say and have said it louder and more often. All over the world they [the Communists] pour their mouthings into the ears of the people, wearing down their resistance by repeated hammerings of half-truths. That's where our Crusade for Freedom comes in."

It just so happened that in America in 1949 there was a representative for Joseph Stalin who heard about John Wayne and his Crusade for Freedom against Communism.

In 1983, Orson Welles was enjoying telling me of events taking place in Russia during the summer of 1936 which, he insisted, would later have a direct effect on John Wayne. "There was a noted Russian screenwriter called Alexei Kapler who just happened to be a Jew. Now, Joseph Stalin hated Jews, but he tried his best to keep his hatred to himself, although those closest to him knew he was completely anti-Semitic. Stalin knew of the advantage propaganda could play in motion pictures, and he decided that a film must be made about Lenin.

"And so he invited Kapler to his dacha in Kuntsevo, and commissioned him to write the screenplay. Kapler was a Jew, but he was also one of the very best screenwriters in the Soviet Union. Stalin decided that Mikhail Romm, one of the most prominent of Soviet film directors, would direct the film. Stalin frequently discussed the script with Kapler and Romm, offering his own advice, which neither Kapler nor Romm was foolish enough to turn down.

"Kapler's script turned out to be far too long for one movie, so Stalin ordered him to turn it into two movies, with the titles *Lenin in October* (1937) and *Lenin in 1918* (1939). Now Stalin had a young daughter, Svetlana, who was only thirteen years old at the time, and she fell madly in love with Kapler, who was a handsome man of thirty-four. At first, Stalin did not notice Svetlana's infatuation with Kapler, but when he did, he accused Kapler of being a British spy and had him imprisoned in the Vorkuta camp."

I asked Welles what all this had to do with John Wayne, and he replied, "I am getting to that. Be patient." I quickly learned that when Welles was in full flow with a story, you didn't interrupt him. He continued, "In 1949 Stalin sent a film director, Sergei Gerasimov, to America to attend the Cultural and Scientific Conference for World Peace in New York. He was faithful to the party line, and was honored by Stalin by being appointed as head of all the studios producing documentaries, the sole purpose of which was to promote Stalinism. In his speech at the conference, Gerasimov denounced Hollywood films as being devoid of any moral standards.

"He also heard that an actor called John Wayne was publicly denouncing Stalin and the Communist party. He was also denouncing the newly created People's Republic of China and its leader Mao Tsetung.

"In 1949 there was a great deal of brouhaha in Moscow when Gerasimov returned to Moscow and brought to Stalin's ears the news that John Wayne was leading the war to crush Communism in America, and in the American motion picture industry. Wayne had been elected president of the Motion Picture Alliance for the Preservation of American Ideals, and its main objective was to fight all that was anti-American, and that meant Communism. Despite all the efforts of Soviet infiltrators, the Communists had failed to fully penetrate the American film industry, and people who had become sympathetic to the cause and those who had fully joined in the cause had been blacklisted by Hollywood. Some had even gone to jail.

"It is doubtful that Gerasimov intended that his report should produce the result it did, but Stalin decided on the spot that John Wayne had become one of the greatest of enemies to the Soviet Union.

"Many within the Soviet film industry, though they may not have seen a John Wayne film, or may not have even heard his name before, whispered that Stalin, the man who thought little of murdering his own people, had plotted to kill a major American movie star. Even in prison, word reached Kapler's ears that Stalin was going to send Wayne a warning that if he continued to urge the American people to wage war on Soviet Russia, he would die.

"There were ways and means of getting messages in and out of prison, and there were ways and means of filtering information to American agents working in the Soviet Union. Kapler was able to urge some of his Jewish friends in the Soviet film industry to warn American intelligence that Stalin was going to have a movie star called John Wayne assassinated.

"I do not know if the name John Wayne was already known to Joseph Stalin before 1949, but in 1949 he certainly came to know of the name. He came to hate it. He feared it. He felt that the name had become a major threat to him and his ideals. It was as though, in Stalin's warped mind, the Americans had invented some new secret weapon, more subtle than a nuclear bomb, but just as destructive to Stalin's ideals and his dreams of world domination.

"Stalin urged Mao Tse-tung to join him in his conspiracy, impressing upon him that John Wayne had become the greatest enemy of Communism. Mao had previously asked Stalin for help in establishing his regime in China, and Stalin had refused him. So Mao, who had his own agenda which was to bring destruction to the United States without taking his own country to war, told Stalin that he would only support the assassination of John Wayne if Stalin would make every effort to push America into a war. For all of Stalin's ranting about the corrupt West and his threats of nuclear war, Stalin had no wish to fight a war he did not believe he could win, but he gave Mao his promise, and the conspiracy was established. In doing so, both Stalin and Mao, the two most powerful Communist leaders in the world, were engaged in what we corrupt Americans would call 'the double-cross.'

"Soon after Stalin died [on Monday, 2 March 1953], those he had imprisoned were released, and among the many to be freed was Alexei Kapler. He told Sergei Bondarchuk all this, but Bondarchuk had already heard the rumor and did not believe it. So Kapler told Bondarchuk to ask Gerasimov, under whom Bondarchuk had studied filmmaking, to verify it. And Gerasimov told Bondarchuk how Stalin tried to kill John Wayne, Bondarchuk told it to me, and now I tell it to you."

Wayne got on with his life and, in May 1949, he signed a non-exclusive contract to make seven pictures over seven years for Warner Bros. As part of the agreement, Wayne would be allowed to produce his own films at the studio.

But first he returned to Republic to produce *The Fighting Kentuckian*. Set in 1819, it was the perfect vehicle for Wayne, playing a Kentucky rifleman trying to protect French officers, who have taken refuge in Alabama, from illegal eviction. It had plenty of rousing action, especially in the climactic battle, and some fine moments of comedy, much of it supplied by Oliver Hardy.

Paul Fix, who played one of the heavies, said, "Poor Duke really had a rough time with Herbert Yates over that one. Yates was insisting that Wayne use Vera Ralston again, and he said, 'Damn it, Herbert, I know you love the gal, but she just can't act.' Well, there was an almighty argument, but Yates won because all he had to do was wave Duke's contract in his face and say, 'You wanna produce this picture or not?' And Duke wanted to get the film made because he was trying to persuade Yates into letting him make *The Alamo* at Republic. He had also reached the stage where he wanted to work off his contract at Republic, so he had to cast Vera, who was a really nice lady, but, boy, she was just a disaster.

"Duke said to me, 'Never mind. Nobody's gonna remember Vera in the film because all they're gonna remember is Oliver Hardy and me doing our comedy scenes, and they'll remember the battle, but they won't remember Vera because she'll soon be forgotten.' And he was right — sort of. People remember Vera because she was in Duke's films and because she was a disaster."

Wayne told me, "I was always mad at Yates when he made me use Vera in that film because I think we lost the chance to have one damn fine picture."

Producing and acting in the film took its

toll on Wayne. Now in his forties, he was less agile and could do fewer stunts. He found a good stuntman in Chuck Roberson who doubled Wayne for the first time in *The Fighting Kentuckian*, and remained his stunt double for the rest of Wayne's life. Duke also gave Roberson small speaking roles in many of his films.

Wayne's next at Republic turned out to be the biggest film — and probably the most successful — that studio ever made. It was *Sands of Iwo Jima*. The producer of the film, Edmund Grainger, had not originally thought to cast Wayne as the tough marine, Sergeant Stryker. Herbert Yates had agreed to make the film for $200,000, but Grainger argued that it would cost more to make the film as realistic as he hoped it would be. He went to his own father, Jim Grainger, who was head of sales at Republic, and got him to put pressure on Yates who finally caved in and put the budget at $1 million — but only if Edmund Grainger would cast John Wayne in the star role.

At first, Wayne was unsure about the film: "People had had enough of the war, and I felt that maybe they weren't ready for another war picture. But this one had class. It was written by Harry Brown, and I had Jimmy Grant come in and tweak it here and there, and the director, Allan Dwan, was a fine director. In fact, after Ford and Hawks, I'd probably place Hathaway and Dwan as the best directors I ever worked with."

Wayne was also encouraged to do the film because he was paid a handsome $180,000 plus 10 percent of the profits. But he admitted that he got far more from that film than the money.

"The role itself was such a good one — a great one for me. The picture was made with much more realism than many other war films, and Grainger had managed to get real marines to play marines, so there was none of the phoniness you sometimes get with extras trying to play soldiers."

Wayne prepared for his role by spending time at Camp Pendleton, talking to marines, especially the sergeants. John Agar, who was in the film, recalled, "The role of Sergeant Stryker was perfect for Duke. I think that had a lot to do with the way James Grant rewrote much of his dialogue and helped develop the character into someone with real dimension to it. Our director, Allan Dwan, really got the best from Duke, which is why he was Oscar nominated for the first time."

Filming took place in San Diego, and Wayne took Chata with him in the hope being near him would make her happy. But he spent so much time filming, she was almost always on her own. John Agar remembered, "When Duke spent an evening with Chata, they just ended up arguing, so he avoided being with her, and most evenings he and I wound up at a bar at the marine base at Oceanside and stayed until it closed.

"Some of the young actors in the film, including me, tried to match Duke drink for drink, but he took particular delight in outdrinking all of us. I don't know how he did it. In the morning we'd all turn up all hungover, and Duke would just be fresh and eager to work. Allan Dwan decided to teach us a lesson and had a real drill sergeant put us through our paces. We never stayed up later than ten o'clock after that, even though Duke did. He just didn't want to be alone with his wife."

Released in December 1949, the film was a huge hit, and Wayne received an Oscar nomination as Best Actor. But as good as he was as Stryker, it didn't compare to the superior performances he gave in *Red River* and *She Wore a Yellow Ribbon*. Nevertheless, Duke was thrilled to be recognized at last by his peers and, as far as the cinema-going public was concerned, the role of Stryker only enhanced his patriotic image even more.

It also enhanced his commercial image, with *Sands of Iwo Jima* coming in eighth position in *Variety*'s 1950 list of top moneymakers.

Wayne was keen to express his political beliefs — or at least his anti-Communism — on screen, a view he shared with Howard Hughes. And so in 1949 Wayne made one of the oddest films of his entire career, *Jet Pilot*. Janet Leigh played a Soviet pilot who pretends to defect to America where Wayne, as a colonel in the U.S. Air Force, takes her under his wing. They fall in love, she takes him back to the Soviet Union, and then they escape back to the freedom of America.

"That is without doubt one of the worst films I ever made," said Wayne. "The script was too silly to get the message across, and to make things worse, the director Josef von Sternberg insisted on making us rehearse over and over, and he kept making remarks which I didn't take kindly to. I'd take them from Pappy, but not from him. I was ready to punch the son of a bitch in the mouth, but Janet kept calming me down.

"As for Hughes, he was obsessed with filming hours and hours of jets flying, and he spent the next eight years doing that. That's why the film didn't get a release until 1957. The final budget was something like four million. It was just too stupid for words."

As much as Wayne liked Howard Hughes, he realized that film-making was not Hughes's greatest talent. By 1950, Wayne had learned just about all there was to know about films, and he looked forward to producing and directing his long-cherished dream, *The Alamo*. After he completed his work on *Jet Pilot*, Duke took Chata to Central America where, apart from getting into constant arguments with his wife, he was making a tentative search for possible locations to shoot The Alamo.

There had been a time when Wayne had to feel continually grateful to John Ford, but in 1950 Ford had to be grateful to Wayne. Ford had a pet project called *The Quiet Man* which he was developing.

Wayne went to Herbert Yates and persuaded him that allowing the great John Ford to make *The Quiet Man* at Republic would add much prestige to the studio.

Ford wanted to make *The Quiet Man* in color, and on location in Ireland, which would prove expensive. Yates agreed on the condition that Ford first make a film along the lines of *Fort Apache* and *She Wore a Yellow Ribbon*. So Ford came up with *Rio Grande*, a relative quickie shot in black and white to save costs, in the summer of 1950 in Moab, Utah.

For the first time Wayne was paired with Maureen O'Hara but the usual company was in evidence, such as Harry Carey Jr., Victor McLaglen, Ben Johnson, and Grant Withers. There was also Ken Curtis, a singer who had become a star of B Westerns of the 1940s.

"Ford liked having songs in his films," said Curtis, "so I got the job. I don't think he thought I was a great actor because my part was pretty much restricted to singing and serenading Wayne and O'Hara." Curtis would become a member of Ford's stock company.

Wayne brought twelve-year-old Patrick to the location and Ford gave him a small role and a few lines of dialogue to deliver. When I interviewed Patrick at Pinewood, where he was making *The People That Time Forgot* in 1976, he told me, "That was a special time for me. I was on location with my dad, and I had him all to myself because I was the only one of the four kids to be on location with him. John Ford was my godfather, and I was the apple of his eye. Ford wasn't so nice to my older brother Michael, but I could do no wrong."

Rio Grande would, like Ford's other cavalry pictures, become highly regarded as a classic, but it gave film historians and critics the wrong idea that Ford had planned a trilogy of cavalry films. Ford was not as enthusiastic about this project as he had been about the previous two cavalry pictures. Ben Johnson noted, "It seemed to me that Ford wasn't taking the film as seriously as he normally did. He seemed to be sort of easier to work with. Not much shouting and abuse. Except for one time when I made a comment to Dobe that there'd been a lot of shooting going on that day, but not many Indians had bitten the dust.

"Ford said, 'What did you say?'

"I said, 'I was just talking to Dobe, Mr. Ford.'

"He said, 'I know that, but what did you say?'

"And again I said, 'I was talking to Dobe.'

"Now he started to get nasty, and he

said, 'Hey, stupid, I asked you a question.'

"Well, I wasn't taking that from anyone, not even from Ford, and I got up and left, and as I passed Ford, I whispered to him what he could do with his damn picture. I could see Duke and Maureen with their jaws dropping to the ground. It wasn't too smart of me, I guess.

"Ford told Dobe to come and get me and bring me back, but I didn't feel too happy about it. I thought I was in for a roasting, but Ford didn't mention the incident again. He even joked with me for the remainder of the filming, and I thought everything was okay between us. But it wasn't. He didn't use me again or talk to me for years after that. That was John Ford for you. Ken Curtis, a really great guy, kind of took my place. But I worked with Duke a lot."

Although it seemed a regular cavalry-and-Indians-type film, *Rio Grande* was actually a political statement, a fact I would have remained oblivious to had Wayne not enlightened me. "*Rio Grande* was written by James McGuiness as a metaphor for the invasion of South Korea by North Korean Communist forces. In *Rio Grande* it's the Apaches who come across the border to make their attacks, and then go back over

the border where the cavalry weren't supposed to go. But Lieutenant Colonel York,
the part I played, knew he had to lead his
men across the border to save the lives of
innocents. In Korea the Communists were
making their raids into South Korea and
then going back to the North. Well, I felt
that our forces should have gone after
them, and that's what York did in *Rio
Grande* — and it was the right thing to do."

Wayne loved working with Maureen
O'Hara. "She is a woman who speaks her
mind," said Wayne, "and that impressed
me, despite my old-fashioned chauvinistic
ways! She is feminine and beautiful, but
there is something about her that makes
her more like a man. It's her stubbornness
and her willingness to stand up to anyone
— even Jack Ford."

O'Hara and Wayne enjoyed a mutual respect and fondness for each other. Said
Maureen O'Hara, "There was a chemistry
between us that you don't get very often. It
comes along only now and again. Spencer
Tracy and Katharine Hepburn had it. So
did William Powell and Myrna Loy. Duke
was tall and strong, and I was tall and
strong. When we quarreled on screen, it
was a battle between two equals, which is a
rare thing between a leading man and

leading lady on the screen. I always like to think that the audience enjoyed imagining what it was like when we made up."

When I interviewed Patrick Wayne, he said, "John Ford saw himself as the same kind of man as my father — I think that's who he really wanted to be. He saw himself as a Western character and identified strongly with that sort of role, which was my father. Maureen O'Hara was the perfect mate for my father — on screen, that is — and so she must therefore be the perfect mate for Ford."

In fact, John Wayne also saw himself more and more as the kind of character he was getting to play. He said, "For years I've played the kind of man I'd like to have been."

As Charlton Heston noted when I interviewed him in 1979 in his suite at The Dorchester hotel in London, "Wayne's greatest achievement may have been creating John Wayne. The character he played, the character he invented, was the American persona of the man who is hard and believes in doing right and will do it against all the odds."

From my observations and from what I was told by those who knew him best, Wayne was as close to the kind of man he'd been playing for years as any actor could ever get. After all, how many actors could play the part of the all-American patriot fighting the evils of Communism and fight that same evil in real life while it was preparing to fight back? How many actors would have been prepared to put their lives on the line for what they believed?

Duke was well aware that the lines between his screen self and his real self were often blurred. "Whatever part I'm playing, whether it's a cowboy or a sergeant in the marines, or a cop, I always have to be John Wayne and living through the experience. You know, the hardest thing to do in a scene is nothing — or seem to do nothing, because doing nothing requires extreme discipline. You see, there are critics who say that I'm just natural on the screen, but nobody can be natural on the screen. If you are, you'll drop the scene. The audience will ignore you. The trick is making every nuance minimal. One look that works is better than twenty lines of dialogue. I know what the critics think — that I can't act — but it seems nobody likes my acting but the people.

"What is a good actor anyway? You might say that a good actor can play all kinds of parts, like Olivier can. Well, my roles are all tailored to fit me — or rather to fit John Wayne. All I do is sell sincerity, and I've been selling the hell out of that ever since I started — or at least, since I learned that lesson. You know, I'm an investment in a motion picture, and I've got to protect that investment. If I don't, the people will stop coming to see me and producers won't hire me because I can't sell their films."

He was certainly doing all right selling films in 1950 when he topped the list of the top ten box-office stars of that year. He would stay in the top ten for the next twenty years.

13

Quiet in Ireland

In the autumn of 1950, Wayne returned to Warner Bros. to make *Operation Pacific*, a Second World War adventure in which he played the captain of a submarine. His leading lady was Patricia Neal and she had very few happy memories of making that film when she spoke to me in 1979.

"I don't know why, but I just didn't really warm to Duke when we first worked together, and he didn't really warm to me. I think it had a lot to do with the fact that he was going through marital problems at the time and so he was not exactly good humored at the time. He could even be a bully and was at odds with the director [George Wagner]. He also gave the publicity man a bad time; he was gay and just seemed to draw Duke's wrath at every turn."

Wayne, oddly enough, had more pleasant

memories: "Patricia was in love with Gary Cooper, and Coop was often on the set as a visitor, and I got to like him an awful lot. We became good friends."

He knew the film wasn't particularly good, though. "You hope every film you make will be great, and the reality is that it ain't gonna happen. So you do your best and hope to come out of it with your dignity intact. But the film made money, which is all the studio cared about anyway."

For much of the first half of 1951, Wayne was busy as a producer. He had become interested in *The Bullfighter and the Lady*, which was based on the early career of film director and former bullfighter Budd Boetticher. Yates agreed to back the production with a modest budget.

Together, Wayne and Boetticher, who would direct, chose their cast which included Robert Stack, Gilbert Roland, and Katy Jurado. Filming took place in Mexico in a small village called Xayai. It did not start well. Over a transatlantic line in 1974, Budd Boetticher said, "Duke decided he'd be there on the first day of shooting, which I didn't think would be a problem, but on the first shot, he walked in front of the camera and grabbed Robert Stack and said, 'Jesus Christ, Bob, if you're gonna say the line, say it with some balls.' He almost scared Bob to death. Six times he walked in front of the camera, and after the sixth time I called him aside and said, 'Duke, do you think you could direct this picture better than I can?' With Duke, you have to let him know who's the boss on the set. We went back and Duke confessed to the cast and crew that he'd been scolded by me and that I'd said, 'One of us has to go home.' He told everybody, 'I'm leaving tonight and won't see you until the end of the picture.'

"He was true to his word. But he left me with Jimmy Grant who was an alcoholic. He disappeared for a week in Mexico City and was living in a whorehouse where he was supposed to be fixing the script. He finally turned up with a script that was so awful, I never used it. I didn't rewrite the script. I just shot it from my own treatment.

"Duke returned on the day we wrapped, and we had a party. He consumed half a bottle of tequila and a full bottle, which he gave to me. We locked arms and began drinking. Duke was so drunk he fell off a veranda into a bush.

"Chata was with him, and we all went to a bullfight together. Then Jimmy Grant turned up with eleven whores. Chata turned to Duke and said, 'If you even smile at those girls, I'm going to hit you.'

"Duke worked with me on editing the film and at the end of the week we'd get drunk. We'd call each other around one in the afternoon the next day and try to remember where we'd been the previous night. Duke wasn't an alcoholic, but he was a Saturday-night drunk. He'd work his ass off all week, and on Saturday he'd get drunk.

"During the postproduction, we frequently disagreed as producers and directors often do. He'd have his group of people with him, and when he and I disagreed, he'd walk away, and his group would all follow him. He'd turn around to say something to me and find I wasn't there among his group, and he'd get furious. His people would always agree with everything he said, but I would tell him if it was full of crap.

"He could be a real bastard, but he could also be a wonderful guy, depending on what his attitude was that day. There was no middle road with him. He either thought you the greatest guy in the world or the biggest son of a bitch. There wasn't a mean streak in his body, and when he had to say something to someone that would hurt them, which he had to do on occasions when someone didn't do their job right, it hurt him too. He would really fret when he did those things. And if he realized he was wrong, he'd apologize."

Wayne's next movie, *Flying Leathernecks*, took him back to RKO, where Howard Hughes had a high regard for him. The feeling was mutual, even though Wayne could not understand Hughes's obsession with continuing to film miles of footage of planes in flight for *Jet Pilot*. But a measure of how much Hughes thought of Wayne was the fee he paid him — $3,000,000, then the highest salary ever paid to an actor for a single picture.

Duke was a pilot again in a decent war film directed by Nicholas Ray and scripted by James Edward Grant. It was a standard war film, with Wayne as the tough officer who had to make difficult decisions that put the lives of his men on the line. Robert Ryan played a subordinate officer who disagrees with a fateful decision Wayne makes, but in the end Ryan learns that making decisions in time of war is not as easy as he thought.

In the summer of 1951, Wayne was off

to Ireland with John Ford and his company to make *The Quiet Man*. Included in that company was Maureen O'Hara, teamed with Wayne for the second time. She told me, "Pappy had had the story, which had been published in the *Saturday Evening Post* [in 1933], certainly since 1944 when he told Duke and myself that he wanted us to star in the picture."

The original story had been written by Maurice Walsh, and turned into a screenplay by Richard Llewellyn, but the original draft proved to be too political, so Ford had Frank Nugent rewrite it as a love story. Wayne played Sean Thornton, a former boxer who returns from America to his homeland of Ireland to settle in the village of Innisfree. There he falls for the charms of fiery Mary Kate, played by Maureen O'Hara.

When they shot the scene when Sean first kisses Mary Kate, Maureen had to take a swipe at Wayne, and for some reason, Maureen felt she had good reason to really try to land one on Wayne's chin. She said, "I got so mad at Duke that I felt ready to kill him, so I hauled off with all my strength and socked him in the jaw. He saw it coming and put his hand up, and my hand came off the tip of his fingers and made contact with his jaw and cracked a bone in my wrist. But I didn't cry out. I just hid my hand in the red skirt I was wearing, but the pain was just dreadful. After we shot the scene, Duke said, 'Let me see your hand. You nearly broke my jaw!' I said, 'That's what I was trying to do.' I had to go to the hospital, but it wasn't too serious.

"It all became very competitive on the set, which I think was encouraged by Pappy because he really wanted the sparks to fly between Duke and myself. Duke had his gang like Ward Bond and John Ford, and I had my gang of Irish actors. We had that long scene where Duke had to drag me across the countryside, and we filmed part of it on the golf course of Ashford castle where the grass was kept short by sheep grazing on it. So the field was covered in sheep manure. There was Duke's gang kicking more and more manure along the path he had to drag me, and my gang would go in and kick it out. But Duke's gang won, and he dragged me on my stomach through that sheep manure, and it just *stank!*"

Wayne recalled, "Maureen and I rehearsed the whole of that scene without Pappy knowing because he wanted it all to be done spontaneously. But we planned the whole thing meticulously, so when we came to a bush, Maureen would lose a shoe, and at another spot she would go down on her butt and put the shoe back on. And then she'd get up and take a swing at me and I would turn and kick her in the rear end. It was all planned and rehearsed, and then after we filmed it, Pappy said, 'When things aren't rehearsed and they're spontaneous, you see how wonderful they are?'

"You know, *The Quiet Man* was a simple enough story, but that was a goddamn hard script for me. For the first nine reels I was playing straight man to all those wonderful characters that people like Ward Bond (as Father Lonergan), Barry Fitzgerald (Michaeleen Flynn), and Victor McLaglen (Will Danaher, Mary Kate's brother) got to play, and that's really hard.

"Ireland was just a beautiful place to be, and most evenings after work, I went fishing with Ward Bond. A little later we'd go up the river where there was a waterfall, and then I'd go back to Ashford castle where we were staying, and I'd play gin rummy with Pappy who'd been out walking up the river with Maureen and the other women. Victor would sit in a high-backed chair by the fire and fall asleep. It was like a holiday, except we had to work in the daytime. And I was able to have all four of my children with me for a while, and Pappy used them all in one little scene."

Maureen recalled, "Duke had such a great relationship with his children. He was wonderful with his boys. Michael, being the oldest, had to keep the other three in line. The youngest of the four was Melinda, who would hide from Michael when he came looking for them to send them to bed, and she'd run up to me and say, 'Hide me,' and I'd hide her."

Chata had also arrived in Ireland, and it fell to Maureen to try to keep her happy while Wayne was working. "When I had a day off," she said, "I'd take Chata to see the sights. There were monuments, old monasteries, castles — we got on well together. But I could see that she and Duke weren't happy."

Victor McLaglen's son, Andrew, was assistant director on the picture. I interviewed him at Pinewood Studios while he was working on *North Sea Hijack* in 1978 and he recalled, "Duke had an afternoon off and went to a local pub. It was the only time he drank while making that picture, and he drank too much. That evening I went with Jack Ford to look for Duke, and we walked into that pub, and Duke was as drunk as I've ever seen him. I mean, he was falling-down drunk. Jack told him, 'We were just checking that you're okay,' and we left him to it. That night around twelve, I took some milk and a sandwich up to Duke, and he had just the worst-ever hangover. But by the morning he was perfectly okay."

Maureen had her memories of the idyllic location. "I used to lie out in the long grass along with my makeup man and hairdresser."

Most people's memories seemed to indicate that making *The Quiet Man* was easy and always fun. But, according to Wayne, that was not the case. "It was all wonderful stuff Pappy was getting on film, but when Herbert Yates saw it, he complained that the countryside looked too green and that the humor was too Irish, and he was so afraid that the film was not going to be commercial. He began ordering Pappy to cut costs. He got on a plane and came over to Ireland to see what Pappy was spending his money on.

"Actually, Pappy wouldn't admit it, but he didn't know if he had a good picture or not, and he had quarreled with his son Pat who was directing second unit, and he was so worried he developed a stomach problem. He asked me to take over, which I loved doing because I was definitely of the mind that I wanted to become a director. I was already in discussions with Herbert Yates about *The Alamo*, which I was going to direct come hell or high water. I got to direct a scene where Maureen walked up from the beach, and when Yates saw it, I said, 'You see, I know how to direct.' The son of a bitch said, 'Maureen O'Hara walking up from the beach is not the same as filming the battle of the Alamo.'

"I always said he had no taste, and I was right. I knew where to put the camera and I knew how to work with the lighting cameraman, and all there was to know. It doesn't matter if you're directing a small scene or a big scene, you still have to know where to put the goddamn camera. But Yates knew nothing about filmmaking. He got me so damn mad, I got Ward Bond to climb up a tall tower with me with a piece of slate with the words 'Fuck Herb Yates' scratched on it.

"Anyway, Pappy got well and came back and took over again, and I was just an actor again. But I was still able to have some input. Pappy didn't usually like his actors giving him ideas about how to do scenes, but there was one scene which I felt was not right as written. Sean and Mary Kate have just got married, but on the wedding night, Mary Kate locks Sean out of the bedroom. In the script, Sean picked up his boxing gloves and just felt sorry for himself. I said to Pappy, 'Look, Coach, Sean wouldn't do that. He'd stand up to Mary Kate. She's his wife. He'd kick the door down. He'd say, "There'll be no locked doors between us, Mary Kate Thornton." He wouldn't just leave her in there.' Well, this made Pappy a little annoyed, but he had a word with Frank Nugent, who agreed with me. So that's how we shot it. It's one of my favorite moments in the film."

While the tempestuous love scenes are memorable, *The Quiet Man* is perhaps best remembered for the epic fistfight between Sean and Mary Kate's brother Will. Wayne told me, "I was no youngster at forty-five, but Victor McLaglen was almost seventy, and he said, 'Don't you worry about me, youngster' — he called *me* 'youngster.' He said, 'I can still give you a good whopping if I had to.' Pappy, who'd say or do anything to get his actors to play the scene as well as they could, said, 'You're getting too old, Victor, for that sort of talk. *Young* Wayne here will still be fresh when the scene's over, but you'll be flat on your back from exhaustion.' Victor — who wasn't Irish at all but a Londoner — said, 'We'll see about that, you Irish son of a bitch.' And sure enough, when we did the fight, which took endless hours and days of rehearsing and shooting, Victor never let up. When Pappy called 'Cut!' for the last time on that sequence, Victor was still standing.

"I went up to him and said, 'You did all right for an old Cockney.'

"He said right back at me, 'And you did okay for an old Yank.' He was almost thirty years my senior, and he was calling *me* old! I loved Victor. He never gave up. Kept right on working till he died [in 1959]."

Following the climactic fight, Sean takes Mary Kate home, but not before she whispers something in his ear, to which Sean registers tremendous shock. I asked Wayne what it was that Mary Kate was supposed to have whispered. He said, "That, my friend, is a trade secret. No, it really is. Pappy told Maureen what to say to me, and believe me, coming from the lips of a lady, it was *shocking*. Pappy wanted me to look shocked, and the look on my face was *real*. When Pappy told Maureen what to say, *she* was shocked and said, 'I can't say *that*.' He said, 'You can and you *will*.' So she said it, and it worked. But Pappy swore us both to secrecy."

When I tried to get Maureen to tell me what she'd whispered, she replied, "There was a deal between Duke, Ford, and myself that we would never divulge what I'd whispered. No one but we three ever knew."

When filming ended in August, Wayne returned to Hollywood in what he called "a really good fucking mood because I knew we'd made a great picture." "I was in high spirits, and I went to see Robert Fellows, my partner in our own production company, and together we went to talk over *The Alamo* with Yates. It turned into a real battle of words, although I'd have liked to . . . ! Anyway, the long and the short of it was that Yates wasn't going to let me make *The Alamo* at Republic. Fortunately, *The Quiet Man* fulfilled the contract I had with Yates at the time, and when he said, 'I'd still like us to work together. How about signing a new contract,' I said, 'You know where you can put your contract. I'll never work *here* again.' And I didn't. And within a few years, Republic was little more than a TV production company. I know it sounds like sour grapes, and really, I was fond of the studio. We'd grown up together. I'd had success and I made a fair bit of money. Yates was starring me in pictures when other bigger studios would only let me either star in a minor film, or play second lead in a bigger film. But I was sore at Yates, not just because he wouldn't let me make *The Alamo* but because having told me that I couldn't film the story of the Alamo, he went and filmed the story anyway — a picture called *The Last Command*. It was a big-budget picture for Republic, but not as big as the film I had planned."

Wayne never did work at Republic again. When *The Quiet Man* was released in August 1952, it was a great success and enhanced Wayne's reputation as a major movie star.

As well as having his troubles with Yates, Wayne also had his domestic problems to deal with. Paul Fix told me, "Chata had been with him on *The Quiet Man*, but she was just always mad at Duke for one reason or another. So shortly after they got back home, they separated and she went back to Mexico. At first Duke was relieved, but he began to miss her. We all tried to tell him he was better off without her."

Early in 1952 Wayne and Robert Fellows formally sealed their partnership and set about preparing to film *Big Jim McLain* for Warner Bros. It was a contemporary thriller that had as its heavies Communists, with Wayne and James Arness playing investigators exposing a Communist spy ring in Hawaii.

The screenplay had been written by Richard English and Eric Taylor, but Wayne brought in James Edward Grant to fashion the dialogue to Wayne's own particular style.

To direct *Big Jim McLain*, Wayne and Fellows hired Edward Ludwig who had directed *The Fighting Seabees*. Andrew V. McLaglen was assistant director. "Duke believed in what the film had to say," McLaglen told me. "Warner Bros. was concerned because the film would show witnesses refusing to answer questions in the hearing room of the House Un-American Activities Committee. They didn't want the scene to be offensive, so Jimmy Grant revised the script and Warner Bros. were happy with it."

Said Wayne: "Even J. Edgar Hoover had me and the film investigated. He sent agents to Hawaii to check us out. He thought we were playing FBI agents and he wanted to know how the FBI would come across. But when the agents found out we weren't playing FBI but House Un-American Activities investigators, they left us alone.

"It was a difficult time for me. The film was getting criticism from the do-good leftists before we'd finished filming, and at the same time my second marriage was coming to an end."

By the time filming began in Hawaii, Chata had returned for an attempted reconciliation. But after a fight at a party on Waikiki Beach, Chata returned to their Encino home and filed for divorce. When filming was completed, Wayne returned to Los Angeles and rented a house for himself. Paul Fix said, "Duke blamed himself for the failure of his second marriage. He just kept saying it was his fault because he devoted too much time to business and not enough with Chata. All his friends told him the same: that nothing he could have done would have made Chata happy. But again he was full of guilt."

When *Big Jim McLain* opened, the reviews were disastrous. Critics damned the film as little more than Wayne's own crass anti-Communist propaganda.

"I got a lot of flack over that picture from the left-wing liberals in Hollywood and the left-wing press," Wayne told me. "They figured that it was just all part of the so-called hysteria that was going on in Hollywood about Communists."

It might have seemed a good time for Wayne to go public about the Communist threat to his life, because the very people the press thought he was being hysterical about had already made their first attempt to kill him.

14

Assassins

"American Intelligence was pretty smart to discover Russian agents had arrived in America," Yakima Canutt told me. "FBI agents had infiltrated a lot of Communist groups — and I mean groups of real hardliners who were sponsored by Stalin and who played host to the agents Russia sent over. They had nothing to do with the film industry. The Communists in the business were just trying to follow a policy that they believed in, although they were naïve to do so.

"The FBI were able to discover the time and place, which was at Wayne's office at Warner Bros., where he and Jimmy Grant would be working on the script [for *Big Jim McLain*]. The KGB agents would be masquerading as FBI agents. John had decided to set up a 'sting' for his would-be-assassins.

"The FBI agents were prepared to be

with John and Jimmy when the KGB turned up. Wayne prepared for the FBI's arrival by telling the guard at the studio gate that he was expecting two agents, so they were able to drive straight in and up to John's office. They spent the rest of the day and into the evening waiting for KGB to turn up. No one knew how the Russians would get to John's office.

"The FBI agents said they'd have to make a report back to J. Edgar Hoover. John said, 'Just so long as it's all hushed up.' Years later, we all found out Hoover had his famous 'secret files.'

"John told them that he and Jimmy would scare 'the living shit' out of the Russians and he worked out with Grant how they would take them to a remote beach John had in mind. I mean, this was literally scripted, written by James Grant. They'd have guns armed with blanks, and John and Jimmy would act out an execution on them. After that the FBI could do what they liked. Well, the agents thought this was just a great idea.

"John had them hide out in another room. It was dark when the two Russian agents turned up. I suppose they were KGB. They spoke with perfect American accents and had FBI badges and were able to convince the guard on the gate that they needed to see Wayne because his life was in danger. When the guard phoned through to John's office, he told the guard to let them in, and then he told the FBI agents to be ready.

"When the Russians came into John's office, the FBI agents came into the room and held them at gunpoint. Then they got into cars and drove up the coast until they came to the place where John planned to carry out the mock execution. He told me, 'I just wanted them commies to know they didn't scare me.' "

And that's how John Wayne and James Grant came to be on a remote beach late into the evening, with guns aimed at the heads of two KGB agents, kneeling on the sand, and thinking their time was up.

Canutt told me, "Wayne later learned that those Russian agents were so afraid of going back to Russia that they happily began working for our side, and they were able to provide a lot of useful information. John thought he was safe after that. But a bit later, I learned from my own network of undercover guys — my stuntmen — that the danger wasn't over."

Wayne immersed himself in his work,

heading for Mexico City with Robert Fellows as the producers of *Plunder in the Sun*, which starred Glenn Ford. Then he returned to Los Angeles for the opening of *Big Jim McLain* in August 1952.

Wayne continued to keep himself busy, scouting locations for *The Alamo* outside Hollywood. Rising costs were forcing many film-makers to work outside the United States where nonunion labor was cheap. Late in the summer of 1952 he and a friend, Ernie Saftig, arrived in Peru, partly to make some investments, partly to see if it was a viable location for *The Alamo*, and partly as a vacation.

There Duke met Richard Weldy, who worked for Pan American Grace Airways and who also conducted trips up the Amazon. Weldy's estranged wife, Pilar Palette, was a Peruvian former air stewardess who'd become an actress and was filming her second film, *Green Hell*.

There was no animosity between Pilar and Weldy, who by this time had another woman in his life, and he flew Wayne into the Peruvian jungle where *Green Hell* was being filmed. They arrived just as Pilar was doing a scene where she danced barefoot around a fire. When the scene was over, the director introduced Pilar to Wayne.

She wrote, "He was the handsomest man I had ever seen."

That evening, the Peruvian film director threw a party in honor of Wayne on the patio of a hotel cantina. When Pilar arrived, Wayne stood up and asked her to sit with him. She knew that Wayne was a big film star in America, but she was not sure she had ever seen any of his films. Finally she said, "You were wonderful in *For Whom the Bell Tolls*."

Wayne smiled and replied, "You're thinking of my good friend, Gary Cooper."

He asked her if she saw many pictures, and she replied she rarely went to the movies. He asked her if she liked Westerns, and she said she didn't.

Paul Fix told me, "Duke was smitten by Pilar, not just because of her incredible beauty, but because she liked him for who he was in real life, not because he was a film star."

When the party was over, Duke said good-bye to Pilar, and they both assumed they would never see each other again. Wayne continued his tour of South America, returning to Los Angeles in September where, said Paul Fix, "Chata told him that she needed a new life so she could marry someone she loved. Obviously she didn't love Duke anymore. There must have been someone else in her life."

Both Duke and Chata filed for divorce, but she beat him to the court by thirty minutes. There she accused Wayne of physical and mental cruelty, and of having an affair with Gail Russell.

"There were mutual charges," said Fix, "each charging the other with infidelity and too much hard liquor."

Even as the impending divorce was hitting the headlines and causing a scandal, Wayne was filming *Trouble Along the Way* at Warner Bros. "The title says a lot about what was going on at that time," Melville Shavelson told me when I interviewed him by telephone in 1979. Shavelson was producing the film from his own screenplay. Michael Curtiz was directing the film which was not at all a typical Wayne movie. Duke played an alcoholic football coach who finds himself persuaded by Father Burke, played endearingly by Charles Coburn, to coach the football team at a run-down college. The film concentrates largely on Wayne's attempts to maintain custody of the young daughter he adores, played by Sherry Jackson, and he finds he is being investigated by a probation officer in the form of Donna Reed, who told me,

"Duke Wayne had a lot of problems in his life when we worked together. Just as we started the picture, he and his wife both filed for divorce. His wife charged him with physical and mental cruelty. I don't know what went on in their marriage, and I didn't pry. All I know is Duke was on time and knew all his lines. He was a real pro, and it's always rewarding to work with someone as professional as that. I couldn't say that we became particularly close friends. Besides which, he had a new lady in his life, Pilar. She, it seems, turned up in Hollywood to dub a film she had made into English, and she and Duke had already met in Peru, so they started seeing each other. So on the one hand he had his wife causing him misery in a divorce battle, and on the other, he had Pilar making life more pleasant for him. But his problems did spill over into the production at times."

Melville Shavelson confirmed: "Wayne was going through his divorce and he was having an affair with Pilar. His wife hired a detective to follow him to try and catch him with Pilar, and one day Duke got hold of the detective and shook him. Then Wayne disappeared for a week and we had to shut down the picture until he came back.

"I liked Wayne — we later made *Cast a Giant Shadow* as a joint production. In the main, he is one of the kindest and most sensible of men. But he wasn't happy with the script I had written with Jack Rose. He insisted that James Grant do a rewrite. He said Grant had a good feel for Wayne's style of dialogue. Frankly, I hated Grant's script, and we ended up with two scripts, one which we used for Wayne's scenes, the other we used when he wasn't in the scenes. The trouble is, one day he turned up when he wasn't supposed to and found we were using the original script. He was furious and grabbed me, and to be grabbed by a guy who stands over six feet and is running the goddamn picture was pretty terrifying. After that we used Grant's script. But for a long time after that Wayne and I never spoke.

"Somehow we managed to make up for some of the time lost when Wayne went missing and finished just three days over schedule [in November 1952]."

Trouble Along the Way is actually an endearing and amusing film, with Wayne proving he could handle romance, drama, and light comedy without resorting to hitting or killing anyone. But the film was a disappointment for Shavelson, who said,

"The picture never made any money [when released in March 1953] because people didn't want to see John Wayne in something other than a Western or an action picture."

Pilar was only supposed to stay in Hollywood for a month. But when she fell in love with Duke, she stayed forever. "Duke and Pilar were very discreet," said Paul Fix. "They'd go out to little restaurants where the other film stars never went, which meant that reporters never went there either, and so they were able to be together without anyone noticing them."

Fix was among the cast of Wayne-Fellows's next production, *Island in the Sky*, again at Warner Bros. Wayne played a pilot who has to land his troubled airplane in a snowy uncharted landscape. In freezing temperatures and occasional blizzards, he has to keep his crew together while a seemingly futile search goes on for them.

Much of the film was shot on location early in 1953, under the direction of William Wellman. On Wayne's recommendation, I was able to telephone Wellman in 1974, and he told me, "I'd signed a contract with Wayne's corporate setup for six pictures, three of them with Wayne, and three with whomever we got. The first story they had bought was Ernest Gann's *Island in the Sky* and they sent it to me to read. It was wonderful. So Ernie and I worked on the script together. It was a true story, and every one of the characters were real characters. There was a plane down and the rescuers left everything — their wives, their kids — and they went up there and found them. They gave up everything to find their pals, and that was fliers."

Wayne numbered Wellman among his favorite directors. "He's just a wonderful old son of a bitch. He had a metal plate in his head from some accident, and all the actors we had would never get into an argument with him. And they certainly wouldn't get into a fight with him because they were afraid they'd kill him."

Lloyd Nolan, who was also in the film — and whom I was able to talk to in 1979 — said, "Duke Wayne really respected Wellman. He didn't always respect his directors, as I discovered the more I got to know him. There's a handful of names I can give that Duke respected, and they would be Wellman, Ford, Hathaway, and Hawks. I'm sure there are others, but those he definitely always deferred to."

Paul Fix recalled, "When Duke wasn't

on location, he'd head back to Hollywood to be with Pilar. It seemed that finally Duke had found a real soul mate. She even agreed to give up her career as an actress for him. Then she discovered she was pregnant, and this threatened to cause a major scandal for Duke. Pilar was a Catholic and she had already committed a sin in the eyes of her Church, but it was really awful for her when she decided to have the pregnancy terminated. This was all happening while Duke's lawyers were getting ready for battle in the courts."

There was a temporary alimony hearing in July 1953, at which Chata accused Wayne of twenty-two acts of physical cruelty, claiming that Wayne had "clobbered" her and asking for an order restraining Duke. Wayne swore that he never once struck Chata, but had held her back at arm's length whenever she charged at him in a drunken rage. He countered with thirty-one charges against her. Outside the courthouse, one girl waved a giant sign which read: JOHN WAYNE, YOU CAN CLOBBER ME ANYTIME YOU WANT.

The court awarded Chata a temporary settlement of $1,100 a month. Wayne was relieved to be out of court and on his way to Mexico to film *Hondo*, a Western for

Warner Bros. produced by Wayne-Fellows Productions and directed by John Farrow who had directed *Plunder in the Sun*. The cast included some of Duke's favorite actors and friends: Ward Bond, James Arness, and Paul Fix.

Wayne played Hondo Lane, a U.S. Cavalry scout who discovers a lonely ranch where Angie Lowe, deserted by her husband, lives with her son Johnny. Despite Hondo's warning that she and her son are in danger from Apaches, she refuses to leave her home. As well as providing plenty of action, the film also concentrated on characterization and the growing romantic relationship between the homely Angie and the tall, handsome Hondo.

Paul Fix said that Duke didn't want a pretty young thing to play Angie. "He wanted a woman with a more hardened look, but still sort of handsome — not ugly. Duke's agent, Charles Feldman, also represented Geraldine Page who was a successful actress on the New York stage. Robert Fellows offered her the part without testing her.

"Duke was dismayed when he first saw her. She had bad teeth, so the first thing Fellows did was send her to a dentist who worked on her for three days. There was another problem Duke quickly noticed when he began working with her. She had a rather bad aroma. I think it was her way, as a New York stage actress, of getting into the part of a realistic frontierswoman.

"When it came to a love scene, Duke said, 'Jesus Christ, I'm afraid I might puke.'

"Then John Ford decided to show up uninvited, and he took one look at Geraldine and told Farrow, 'Nobody's going to believe that John Wayne is in love with such a homely woman.' So Farrow had some of her dialogue rewritten so she would say, 'I know I'm a homely woman.' I felt this was unfair because she was the very type of woman they had wanted, but because John Ford had spoken, Duke duly obeyed. I sometimes wish he'd stood up to Ford more. It wasn't even Ford's film.

"James Edward Grant revised the original script drastically, and they shot it in 3-D, a process requiring two cameras mounted side by side which was very cumbersome to use. It really wore down Duke's patience. He hadn't made a Western in quite a while, and he got pretty sore in the saddle. He told me, 'I'd be glad if I never saw another horse again.'

"Although the film was being directed by

John Farrow, Duke maintained very tight control over the filming. He *wanted* to direct — that I know — but he felt he wasn't ready to do so until he was ready to make *The Alamo*. A lot of people criticized Duke for not always letting his directors do their job without interference, but Duke knew that if any film of his bombed, especially if it was one he produced, the blame would be laid at his feet. It was only a really influential director like Hawks or Ford who would get the blame. Otherwise, it would be Duke's failure, and I think that he wanted to make sure that if the film was going to fail, it would fail on his terms, because he'd be big enough not to blame the director for his own failings."

After Wayne died in 1979, I was able to talk to Geraldine Page, who either didn't know about the criticism that was leveled at her, or was generous enough to shrug it off, because she had a considerable amount of praise for Wayne.

She recalled her experience of making *Hondo* and working with Duke: "There were many times when the 3-D cameras broke down and we had nothing else to do while they were being fixed but to sit in the baking Mexican sun and talk politics. I was used to the liberal politics of New York, but here I sat with these three men [Wayne, Bond, and Farrow] and listened with growing horror to their right-wing political views. There was nowhere for me to escape so I sat there, and the more I listened, the more I noticed a difference between them.

"John Wayne, for instance, would talk very sensibly about his views, while I found Mr. Farrow quite illogical, and Ward Bond was just a bully in his approach. When Duke said something that made sense, Farrow would take what Duke had said and turn it into whatever his own horrifying view was.

"By the time we'd finished the film and I had heard several of their conversations, I realized all three men were reactionaries and not activists at all. But Duke was a reactionary for all sorts of non-reactionary reasons. I came to the conclusion that if John Wayne was transplanted out of this circle of people that were around him all the time, he would be the most antireactionary force for good and decency. I didn't agree with a lot of what he believed in, but he was very protective of his country. And you have to respect that.

"The biggest problem with working with Duke was that he was grumpy a lot of the time and would snap at anyone. Every morning he would just scream and destroy somebody, like the time he lost his temper with Lee Aaker who played my son, Johnny. Lee was just a kid and he made mistakes in several scenes, blowing his lines or opening a door at the wrong time, and Wayne would stalk around the set saying, 'What are we going to do about that goddamn kid?'

"Then Wayne would calm down and apologize, but poor Lee became quite terrified.

"But Duke never yelled at me. If he got bad tempered or hungover, he'd get sarcastic to me about New York and Stanislavsky. There were times when I was on the point of saying that I'd had enough and telling him what to do with his cowboy picture when he'd suddenly calm down and say, 'Aw, Geraldine, you're not mad at the old Duke, are you?' And I'd say, 'No,' and when I'd get back to my hotel I'd say to myself, 'I'm so stupid. I'm the same as all the others. I get taken in by that charm. That tremendous charm.' In a funny way, I just loved him. He was John Wayne, on screen and off.

"When he was charming, he was *charming*. And for that reason, I loved him.

Everyone did. They'd all do anything for him, because even when he lost his temper, he would later tell you how sorry he was. He didn't like hurting anyone. He wasn't like John Ford. If Wayne was cruel at times, he didn't do it for effect. He was just under so much pressure. But you knew where you stood with him because he hated hypocrisy. And he was so loyal to the people who worked for him.

"One evening, it was getting late, and we were shooting a scene in a dried-up lake when a terrible storm blew in. Mr. Farrow and Mr. Fellows were quick to get the American cast and crew out of the lake bed before it flooded, but they left the Mexican crew to clear all the equipment. By the middle of the night all the Americans were tucked up nice and warm in the motel, and Duke started worrying about the Mexicans because they were camped outside and were cold and wet. So Duke got the caterer up out of bed and they made sandwiches and took them out to the Mexicans with coffee and tequila, and Duke spent the rest of the night outside with them, eating, drinking, and telling stories. He was just wonderful that way. He had great leadership qualities which is why people just revered him. He had loyalty to those who were loyal to him.

"He loved to swear. Oh, the colorful language! And he was fond of jokes. He would always listen to someone who had a joke to tell, and he had the most spontaneous, warmest, most wonderful laugh.

"And with the boots and the hat he was suddenly seven feet tall. He looked like he was a part of the landscape."

There were other problems to deal with during the making of *Hondo* that had nothing to do with the film. Yakima Canutt, who did not work on the picture, said to me, "Do you know the story about detectives sent by Chata to Camargo where John was filming *Hondo*?" I didn't, so Canutt explained: "When the local police found out that there were strangers asking questions about Wayne, they asked John if he wanted these characters 'taken care of' — which meant permanent disposal, if you know what I mean. John told them, 'Just lock them up for a while, and then make them leave the country.' The story was true, but not all the investigators were working for Chata. I learned from my own undercover boys that some of the investigators were Communists out to get Wayne. This time they were not Russians, but American citizens.

"I got in touch with John and told him that there were Communists heading his way, and *those* were the men the police were ready and able to dispose of. When Duke told the police to make sure they left the country, he didn't just mean they should get them out of Mexico. He meant they should be sent to Russia. And that's what the police did, rounding up these guys and getting them on a plane for Russia at gunpoint.

"Duke said to me, 'I guess this Khrushchev fellow still wants me out of the way.' [Stalin had died earlier in 1953.]

"I said, 'I'm not so sure. My guy who got me this tip says that the American Commies are making their own decisions. All the same, you better expect more trouble sometime.'"

With secret detectives, Communist assassins, Chata's accusations of cruelty, and trouble with the 3-D cameras all plaguing Wayne while he was making *Hondo*, it's a wonder the picture turned out to be as good as it was.

Costing around $3 million to make, *Hondo* took in $4.1 million in domestic sales alone when it was released quickly in November 1953, probably making at least as much overseas. The rush to get it edited, scored, and released was an attempt to cash in on the popularity for 3-D. Unfortunately, the gimmick was already losing its appeal and, after just a week into its release, *Hondo*'s 3-D version was withdrawn, and the "flat" version went nationwide. Its popularity proved that a good piece of cinematic storytelling didn't need gimmicks to be successful.

There was one more indication of the film's quality which came as a complete shock to Wayne. Andrew McLaglen told me, "Duke always said that Geraldine [Page] may have been great on Broadway but she didn't know a damn thing about movies. Well, you can imagine his surprise when I called him a few months after the film came out and told him that Geraldine had been nominated for an Academy Award for her performance in *Hondo*. There was just silence on the other end of the line. Duke just couldn't understand it."

15

From the Mighty to the Mongols

In October 1953, the divorce trial finally got under way. Paul Fix, there to give Wayne moral support, told me, "It got very nasty. Chata told the court that Duke was every kind of awful man — a drunk, violent, unfaithful.

"Duke told the court he often returned home to find Chata and her mother lying drunk on a bed. He also claimed that Chata once threatened to kill him, and related the events of the night he came home after the *Angel and the Badman* wrap and how Chata tried to kill him."

Wayne told the court that following the wrap party at the studio, he returned home at 1:30 A.M. "My wife refused to let me in. I could hear her and her mother talking about me loudly. I rang the bell but they wouldn't open the door. Then I broke a glass panel, reached in, and opened it myself. Chata and her mother, they came charging out. Chata had a .45 in her hand. She and her mother were fighting over it."

Under oath, Chata said that she had thought a burglar was breaking in which is why she came running out with a gun.

Wayne refuted this version, saying that Chata had been hysterical and demanded to know if he had been to a motel with Gail Russell. Accusing him of infidelity, she aimed the gun at him and threatened to fire.

Wayne's attorney asked him if there had been any affair with Russell, to which Wayne replied emphatically, "Absolutely not," insisting that he and Miss Russell had only ever shared a friendship.

Wayne, who always insisted that honesty was a virtue he demanded of himself and from others, was not entirely honest in his testimony. According to Budd Boetticher, "On the stand Duke told how one night he and Esperanza had been at my house for a party, and sometime after midnight all the guests decided to drive to a restaurant which was not far from where I lived. Chata was very drunk and refused to go, so I told Duke and my wife to go on ahead and that I would try and sort Chata out. Finally I threw her over my shoulder and we arrived fifteen, maybe twenty minutes later. But Duke told the court that we'd been alone for *two hours.* I was furious.

"When we left the court, I said to Duke, 'That was a despicable thing you did. It wasn't two hours. You know damn well it was only fifteen or twenty minutes. Look what you made it look like. Why do this to me?' And he said, 'You didn't want me to lose the case, did you?' "

The trial suddenly ended after three days when the lawyers persuaded their clients to settle. The judge granted them an uncommon divorce, unique to California law, whereby neither party would concede to the other's charges, and the divorce would not become final for one whole year. Wayne agreed to give Chata $150,000, pay off all her current debts, and pay $50,000 per annum for the next six years. But he got to keep the Encino estate.

Paul Fix said, "That divorce trial took it out of Duke. He came away from it exhausted. And he still felt guilty. He felt even worse when he heard that Chata died a year later from a heart attack. She'd been living in Mexico City and after her mother died, she became a recluse and just drank herself to death. She was only thirty-eight. Believe me, Duke didn't feel happy about that at all. He felt responsible."

While the divorce trial had been in session, Pilar had gone to Mexico City, making sure she didn't accidentally step into any spotlight and give Chata any more ammunition. Duke joined her and they traveled to Acapulco where he rented a house with a view of the ocean. They went waterskiing, scuba diving, and sailing. It was just the kind of relaxation Duke needed. Then they returned to Los Angeles and Pilar moved in with Duke into the Encino home.

Said Paul Fix, "Duke would have married Pilar in an instant, but he had to wait a year when his divorce would become final."

As Andrew V. McLaglen said, "Duke was always a one-woman man. When he fell in love with a woman, he had to marry her."

Wayne had been waiting to hear from RKO where he still had one more picture to make. Howard Hughes had a project in mind but was being very vague about it. Whatever it was, Hughes kept delaying it but insisted that Duke should not undertake any other assignment until the RKO project had been completed. But Wayne was not the kind of person to sit around, waiting for something to happen, so he went on to his next Wayne-Fellows production, *The High and the Mighty*, to be directed by William Wellman.

It was about an airplane in trouble and became the basis for many of the disaster movies of the 1970s. The script delved into the backgrounds of the various passengers and crew, leading to the moment when one of the engines catches fire and the pilot becomes too hysterical to keep control of the plane, forcing the heroic copilot to take over. After a perilous journey, the copilot manages to bring the plane safely down.

William Wellman loved anything to do with aviation, and was wildly enthusiastic about making *The High and the Mighty*, even before it was written. He told me, "When Ernie Gann and I were writing the screenplay for *Island in the Sky*, one day Ernie said, 'Look, Bill, I want to tell you a story, just for fun so we can take our minds off this job for a while. It's a thing I call *The High and the Mighty*. I haven't written it yet but I can tell it to you.' So he told me the story and I said, 'Stay right here and I'll make you the quickest sale you've ever had in your life.' I called Wayne and his partner, Fellows, and I said, 'It's Bill here.

I've got to come over so don't go away. I've got the greatest story to tell you that you've ever heard in your life.'

"I went down there full of enthusiasm and I told them the story. I said, 'That's what's going to be our next picture with you playing it, Duke.' Duke said, 'No, we'll get Spencer Tracy to play it.' I said, 'That's okay, Tracy will be great.' They said, 'What does Ernie want for it?' I said, 'Fifty-five thousand dollars.' I sure as hell didn't know what he wanted. But then I said, 'And he wants at least five or ten percent of the profits.' Duke said, 'Okay, we'll pay him fifty thousand and he can have ten percent of the profit.' So I went back to Ernie and told him what Wayne was going to pay him. He'd never had such a quick and lucrative sale. So that's how *The High and the Mighty* got started.

"We tried to get some big-name stars like Joan Crawford, Barbara Stanwyck, and Ida Lupino but they all turned me down because they didn't feel the parts being offered were big enough. The thing with *The High and the Mighty* is that it's an ensemble piece. So I said to Wayne, 'To hell with the big stars. If we can get Spencer Tracy to play the copilot, which is the only big part, we'll get good character actors for the rest of the cast.' So we got Robert Stack as the pilot, people like Claire Trevor, Phil Harris, Jan Sterling, Laraine Day, Robert Newton, David Brian. Spencer Tracy read it and thought it was lousy and said he wouldn't do it. So Wayne had to do it, and Wayne thinks that he wasn't good in it."

Andrew McLaglen, who was assistant director on the film, had a slightly different story for Tracy's refusal to do the film. He told me, "Bill Wellman was the best-prepared director I'd ever met, but he also had a reputation for browbeating his actors. He got Tracy to read the script, and they had lunch and shook hands on a deal. But then Tracy's friends who'd worked with Wellman told him that he was in for an ego-bruising ride, so Tracy pulled out, telling Wellman that the script was lousy."

I asked Wellman why Wayne hadn't liked his own performance, and he replied: "Wayne didn't think he was good when we were making it, and he *still* doesn't think it's any good. I said to him, 'What the hell: you mean to tell me you don't think you were good in that?' He said, 'Well, it never had any love story.' I said, 'It had the greatest love story that had ever been written. The audience never saw your wife or your kids. All they saw was a half-burned-up little toy bear you carry with you, and you're a lonesome, attractive, wonderful man. Everybody visualized a beautiful woman and a lovely kid and a wonderful guy that could only ever love that one woman. You couldn't ask for a better love story.' Oh, we used to argue like hell. He still thinks it's lousy, and I think he's crazy."

Claire Trevor was delighted to be working with Wayne again. Although she wasn't as big a star as a Crawford or a Bette Davis, she was a highly regarded character actress who'd won the Oscar as Best Supporting Actress in *Key Largo* in 1948. And with Wayne having to step into Tracy's role, there was suddenly a lot of marquee power in having the names John Wayne and Claire Trevor together again. Trevor said, "It was wonderful working with Duke again. He had become such a fine performer as well as an important person in Hollywood since we had last worked together. He was so ambitious. He was so dedicated to his work. He always wanted to win. He was a perfectionist.

"It was the first time I'd met Pilar. She came to the set most days, and was very shy, but when you got to break through her shell, she was wonderful. You could see how much in love she and Duke were. He was a romantic. He liked women although he was much more at ease with men. But he was a very true man, very true to his marriage, very true to his wife.

"I came to realize that Pilar had had no formal education and she was very sensitive about that. She was actually very bright, very intelligent, but she was concerned that people would perceive her as being uneducated and therefore not very clever. Her command of English was not very good back then, and so she tended not to talk, which some people took as her being standoffish. She felt a little out of place, I think, and she didn't particularly enjoy the typical Hollywood life — you know, the parties, the events. She was a strong woman, but as a Peruvian living in America, speaking broken English, she suffered some anxiety. It was difficult for her to relate to or with Duke's Hollywood friends, but she became good friends with Duke's secretary, Mary St. John. She had to find herself in Hollywood, and that took some time."

During the 1950s television was developing quickly into a popular form of entertainment, giving cause for concern in the film industry as people began staying at home more. The industry was trying to find ways of enticing people back to the cinema by coming up with gimmicks that television couldn't hope to compete with. The only gimmick that turned into a cinematic format that remains to this day was the wide screen. Despite the failure of *The Big Trail* in 1930 and its use of wide-screen process, in 1953 Twentieth Century Fox introduced CinemaScope, and other studios began following suit. *The High and the Mighty* became Wayne's first CinemaScope film.

The CinemaScope format was especially effective in the aerial scenes of *The High and the Mighty* which were photographed by William H. Clothier. I was privileged to speak to Clothier twice — in 1974 and 1979. He told me, "It was Bill Wellman's idea to hire me. He loved anything and anyone to do with aviation. He'd been a pilot during the First World War with Layfayette Escadrille and only came out of the service because his plane was shot down and he broke his back. He got all sorts of awards — the Croix de Guerre and several other citations. When he was well again he became a stunt flier doing barnstorming and wing walking — that sort of thing. And I had served in the Army Air Corps in the Second World War, but before that I had done what he thought was pretty good work on the silent picture *Wings*, but I hadn't done a lot of work as a director of photography in Hollywood before the war. I'd worked a lot in Spain and Mexico, and then after the war I returned to Hollywood and was lucky to get work. Bill Wellman, or 'Wild Bill,' as he's known, thought I could do a good job for him shooting the aerial photography."

Clothier, in time, would become Wayne's favorite director of photography, working on many of his films. Said Clothier, "I had an immediate rapport with Duke. There was something about the guy I liked. He carried his authority well, and he used it, but he was never cruel or harsh. And if he liked you, and the work you did, well, you were likely to be with him for the rest of his or your life."

Although Wayne and Fellows were the producers of *The High and the Mighty*, Duke was not able to wield the kind of authority and control over the production that he had exercised over *Hondo*. Said William Wellman, "I only had one row with Duke on *The High and the Mighty*. He suddenly wanted to become a director and began giving orders. I told him, in front of the entire cast, 'Look, if you come back here behind the camera and do my job, you're going to be just as ridiculous as I would be if I were in your place in front of the camera with that screwy voice of yours and that fairy walk and trying to be Duke Wayne.' He never tried to direct my film again."

When *The High and the Mighty* wrapped toward the end of 1953, the film at RKO still wasn't ready. There was also another matter to deal with. In January 1954, Robert Fellows and John Wayne agreed to dissolve their partnership. William Wellman said, "Robert Fellows got involved with one of his secretaries and he told his wife Eleanor that he wanted to leave her. So Eleanor went to Duke and asked him to talk some sense into her husband. He was very uncomfortable about that and told her it was none of his business, but she kept up the pressure until he agreed to mediate in a meeting between Robert and Eleanor. Well, it all went downhill and turned into a shouting match until Duke stood up and said, 'This is something you've got to settle yourselves,' and he walked out.

"Fellows decided he needed to liquidate

his assets because of the impending divorce, and he asked Duke to buy him out, and Duke obliged."

All Wayne would say was, "Robert was a good friend of mine but he didn't quite do the job. Anyway, I wanted the company to have a proper name, and this was a good chance to have something other than 'A Wayne-Fellows Production' on the marquee, or 'A John Wayne Production.' I didn't care too much if audiences knew whether I'd produced the film or not. The only thing that mattered to them was whether I was in it."

He needed a name for his company and for a while he called it the Fifth Corporation. Michael Wayne came up with a better suggestion. He told me, "I suggested 'Batjak,' spelled B – a – t – j – a – k, which was the name of the shipping company in *Wake of the Red Witch*. JW [Michael always called his father JW] liked the name, but one of the legal secretaries who was examining the documents thought that there was a typo in the word 'Batjak.' She wondered if it should be 'Batjack,' so she called Robert Fellows and said, 'Is there a "c" missing from the company title?' And he said, 'No "c." ' But she thought he meant, 'No, "c." ' So she typed it 'Batjac.' When the document was prepared, the mistake was noticed, but JW said, 'I liked it better with a "k" but leave it as it is. It's no big deal.' "

While most big stars were still under exclusive contracts to major studios, Wayne was among a small number of stars who were not tied to any single studio. Although this gave him considerable freedom, it also caused complications and frustrations. Wayne said, "It was, overall, a damn fine way for an actor to work because you were not tied down to any one studio. But just after I finished *The High and the Mighty*, I was caught between two studios. On the one hand, there was RKO where Howard Hughes didn't have his next picture ready for me, which should have been in January [1954] and they were now saying it would be February. And on the other, I had Warner Bros. who were waiting for me to make another picture for them but I couldn't until I'd made the RKO picture — whatever that was. Howard hadn't told me what it was.

"I liked Howard a lot, but his delay was really getting me into deep fucking water. I wrote a frank letter to Howard, telling him how at the other studios and for my own company, I didn't work on a picture for more than eight to sometimes ten weeks overall *and* I got paid top terms for this. At RKO, I was giving up six months of my time for a fraction of the money the other studios paid me. That didn't have much impact on Howard, who was not going to be rushed — and I *still* didn't know what this project was he had in mind for me.

"Then I started getting letters from an attorney at Warner Bros. telling me that I was in breach of contract and how they'd bent over backward to accommodate me in my obligations to RKO. I was fucking mad, and I wrote to Howard and told him that it was *his* studio's responsibility to have scripts ready for me on the dates he had promised.

"I *still* don't know to this day what Howard had in mind for me, but I had a meeting at RKO at an office in which Dick Powell was ensconced and I saw a treatment lying around for something called *The Conqueror*. I took a cursory look at it and thought, 'This might be interesting.' I kind of liked it. Thought it would be something different, playing Genghis Khan. It was just like a Western only with different costumes. Turned out Dick Powell was going to direct it, so I told him that I'd like to do *The Conqueror*. I kind of took him by surprise and he said, 'Are you serious?' I said, 'Sure, why not?' So he said, 'Okay,' and we shook hands on it.

"What I didn't know was that the full screenplay had been written [by Oscar Millard] for Marlon Brando, and it had a certain kind of style to it which would have been fine for Brando, but for *me?* I thought, 'Oh, shit!' Turned out that Fox wouldn't let Brando do it. So I guess Dick Powell thought that John Wayne might just pull in the crowds. My big mistake was, I didn't actually read the script until we got to our location in Utah. I'd got used to getting interested in pictures from listening to the directors tell the story; Hawks could do that, so could Ford and so could Wellman. I had all this terrible dialogue which I'm not convinced even Brando could have handled.

"I got on the phone to Oscar Millard and said, 'You gotta do something with this dialogue. I can't say those lines.' He said, 'You should have said so before. I can't rewrite the entire script now.' You see, even John Wayne makes mistakes. And that was one of my biggest.

"For a start, Dick Powell had never directed before, but I figured every new director needs their first one to cut their teeth on. And he was such a nice guy that when I could see that he really was over his head, I tried to be helpful without coming on too strong, which, I admit, I have a habit of doing. I just barge right in there, 'Hold it a minute; you're telling me you're putting the camera *there?*' That's what I'm like. But on this picture I had enough to contend with trying to get to grips with that goddamn dialogue. So we had a less-than-talented director who just happened to be a terrific guy, and we had a script that was written for Brando but was being spoken by Duke Wayne. And it was just a fucking disaster."

Despite all that, Wayne went about his work with a considerable amount of enthusiasm, as described by Lee Van Cleef, who was in the picture. When I interviewed him in Ireland, where he was filming *The Hard Way* in 1978, he told me, "I never did become one of Wayne's in crowd, but it was hard not to like him. It was obvious that he was out of his depth as Genghis Khan. I mean, he was no Omar Sharif. He was Hondo and the Ringo Kid. But he was never less than professional, although he was clearly unhappy with some of the decisions that Dick Powell made. The thing is,

when he complained about something —
and he never did it belligerently — he was
always right. He knew as much about making movies as anyone. He was in trouble
because of the part and because of the director. But to give Powell his due, no director could have pulled that one off.

"We shot that picture near St. George in
Utah where the temperature got to around
one hundred and twenty degrees. I think
we were up there for around six weeks.
Wayne's beautiful wife came out there to
be with him, which didn't please our
leading lady Susan Hayward at all. Susan
had kind of fallen for Wayne, and when
Pilar arrived I could see that Susan was
kind of jealous. Not that there was anything going on between Wayne and Hayward.

"I think Susan really had a thing for
Wayne. She just wasn't used to her leading
men rejecting her. But he was never frank
with her in an unkind way. He could have
said, 'Look, I'm not interested so leave me
alone.' He just treated her with his usual
courtesy, and you could see she kind of
liked that. But she couldn't understand
why he didn't want to jump into the sack
with her.

"You probably heard about the number

of people who died from cancer who were involved with that film. Where we were filming was about one hundred and forty miles from the site in Nevada where they were testing the atom bomb. We were right in the path of the nuclear fallout. I heard that a lot of people living in that area had some form of cancer, but we didn't know it then.

"There's a place called Snow Canyon which has a lot of dunes. A spectacular place. We filmed a number of scenes, mainly the battles, so there were a lot of extras as well as crew involved. It turns out that a lot of radioactive dust blew into that canyon, and I remember that a lot of the actors, extras, and crew got covered in that dust. We had to have our mouths and eyes cleaned out with water; we were covered in it. There were more than two hundred people working on that picture, and around half of them came down with cancer. Wayne had lung cancer and then stomach cancer, Susan Hayward had a brain tumor as well as cancer of the skin, uterus, and breast. Pedro Armendariz had cancer of the kidneys and larynx, Agnes Moorehead died from uterine cancer and Dick Powell died from lung cancer. I was lucky. So far I'm okay."

That was what Van Cleef told me in 1980. He never suffered from cancer, and died from a heart attack in 1989.

The subject of cancer was, at times, a difficult one for Wayne to discuss. At the time I met him in 1974, he had recovered from lung cancer in 1964 against the odds. He was cagey about his opinion that his lung cancer was brought on by working in Utah on *The Conqueror*, and made a point of defending the testing of nuclear bombs. "All I can tell you is that I smoked — and I smoked too much. So did Dick Powell, so did Susan Hayward, so did Pedro [Armendariz], and I guess you could say that in those days at least fifty percent of people smoked, probably more, and those who did smoke and didn't get cancer were lucky.

"As for testing nuclear weapons, we had to. Russia had developed its own atom bomb and when Stalin was alive he was mad enough to threaten the Western world with nuclear war. It became a stalemate, and that's what has kept peace in the world. Both the Korean War and the Vietnam War could easily have escalated into the Third World War and you and I wouldn't be sitting here having a pleasant time. It's that fear of nuclear war that has created stability, such as it is, in the world.

"But, contrary to what people might think, I'm no politician, and I'm no military strategist. I make movies, and when I have something to say, I say it through my pictures."

I asked him what the message was in *The Conqueror*. He said, "The message is, don't make an ass of yourself by trying to play parts you're not suited to. But I didn't learn that lesson. I still manage to make an ass of myself every now and then."

Filming *The Conqueror* ended in August 1954 but, like Hughes's *Jet Pilot*, it was withheld from distribution while Hughes endlessly tinkered with it, reediting it again and again, and still ending up with a dreadful picture that remained an embarrassment to Wayne.

16

The Bloody Battle of Burbank

In September 1954, Wayne was finally able to keep Jack Warner happy by making *The Sea Chase*, produced and directed by John Farrow. Wayne played an anti-Nazi German sea captain (minus any German accent) who, upon hearing the news that the Second World War has erupted, tries to get his ship from Australia back to Germany with the intention of helping to overthrow Hitler. While in Australia, he takes on an unexpected passenger in the guise of Lana Turner who turns out to be a German spy. Although Wayne does not support the Nazis, his ship is nevertheless chased all the way home by the British and, in between bouts of action, Wayne and Turner fall for each other. Although it was not one of Wayne's own productions, he had considerable muscle now even at the big studios, and he was able to secure roles for his friends Paul Fix and

James Arness. He also persuaded Warner Bros. to hire director of photography William H. Clothier, and stuntman Cliff Lyons as second-unit director.

Among the male-dominated cast was Claude Akins who, like Lee Van Cleef, was one of those American actors who worked regularly in action films, especially Westerns, and was bound to turn up in one or two of Wayne's films.

During a visit to London in 1980, when I was able to interview him, Akins told me, "I didn't really connect with Wayne. But I liked him. There wasn't really much to dislike. I guess I didn't seek his approval, which some actors would do because it was well-known that he liked to have his pals in his films and if you clicked with Duke, you knew you'd always be working. But I was doing okay anyway. So our relationship was cordial, professional, sometimes we had laughs, but I didn't try to break into his circle, and he didn't invite me. I think that's the way it should be because if you become dependent on one major movie star for work, if that star falls, you go down with him. I didn't know John Wayne was going to become such a legend, but even if I did, I would have still been the same."

Paul Fix recalled, "We shot that film in Hawaii. Pilar came with him and they lived in a house which Warner Bros. provided. They were happy times for Duke and Pilar. They got to Hawaii early to make a holiday of it. I think Duke wanted to make sure Pilar got some enjoyment out of his location work, and they went scuba diving, which wasn't such a good idea because it gave Duke an ear infection. He'd suffered with that ear since the DeMille picture. He was in so much pain when filming began that he was on strong painkillers. You'd see this glazed look come over his eyes from the medication, and his ear was so swollen that for several days John Farrow could only shoot him from his good side. But he got on with his job and didn't let it stop him working, no matter how much pain he was in. He'd only go and lie down in between takes, and then when he was called, he'd be back. That infection started in September, and he was still in pain two months later."

Making *The Sea Chase* was not a happy experience for Wayne, and not just because of his ear infection. Said Wayne, "We had two writers [John Twist and James Warner Bellah] with us in Hawaii while John Farrow and myself tried to get the script

326

into shape because what they were giving us just wasn't that good. And it never finished up very good.

"It didn't help that Lana Turner took an instant disliking to our director. And she didn't much like the rest of the cast. In fact, she didn't much like *anything*. That's not good for someone like me because it tends to throw me into the position of becoming defensive of all the things that *I* didn't like about the film.

"She led a troubled life and drank a lot. I might have had some sympathy for her but she'd usually turn up late in the morning with a hangover. In fact, for the first five days she didn't turn up for three of them, and that's enough to lose my sympathy vote. In fact, John Farrow decided he'd had enough and fired her. She came running to me and asked *me* to help her. I told her straight. I said, 'You've not behaved in a professional manner.' I could see the tears welling up, and that was enough to tug at my old heartstrings, and I said, 'I'd be willing to give you another chance. I'll talk to John.' And he gave her back her part. She cut back on her drinking and turned up on time, more or less, after that."

"Lana Turner was stunning," Paul Fix

remembered, "but she seemed so insecure about her own talent and probably the script that she compensated by becoming obsessed with her looks. I mean, talk about vanity. That was because she came from MGM where actresses like her were *supposed* to look glamorous all the time. So when Duke had a love scene with her, she'd say, 'Don't touch my hair.' Or 'Don't smudge my makeup.' Duke said — not to her — 'How am I supposed to make love to a woman who won't let me touch her?' He had to make sure that when he held her, his hands didn't go near her hair and when he kissed her, he couldn't make it look too passionate because he might ruin her makeup. So the love scenes in that film look so false."

The unit returned to Hollywood to film at the Warner Bros. studio in December. The Encino house was still undergoing alterations, but over the festive season many of Duke's friends dropped in on the Waynes, including John Ford, Andrew McLaglen, Grant Withers, Yakima Canutt, James Edward Grant, and many others — all men.

Canutt recalled, "I sensed that Pilar was not always happy about the constant stream of visitors, although she was always kind and courteous. But I know she treasured her time alone with John, and it seemed she never had much time alone with him."

The Sea Chase was released in May 1955, to poor reviews but moderately good business. People still wanted to see a John Wayne picture.

By the mid-1950s television was trying to seduce many of the cinema's biggest stars, and Wayne was among them. CBS, one of the biggest TV production companies, offered him the lead as Marshal Matt Dillon in the Western series *Gunsmoke*. He turned them down: "The men who ran the theatres relied on the big movie stars to keep them in business, and I wasn't going to let them down because they'd given me a pretty good life. Batjac had an actor under contract, James Arness. A good actor, but I felt he was never going to become a star in films. But I figured he could do well on television, so I told CBS they could offer him the part, and if he accepted, I'd release him from his contract. So they cast him, and he not only made that show something special, it also turned him into a major TV star."

The first film to be made under the

Batjac banner was called *Blood Alley*, another swipe at Communism, this time aimed directly at the Chinese. The story centered on the attempts by 180 villagers to flee from Red China into Hong Kong on an old steamer, captained by an American merchant seaman. Wild Bill Wellman was directing, and the screenplay was by A. S. Fleischman from his own novel. Wayne told me, "I'd really wanted Humphrey Bogart to play the part [of the captain], and for Betty [Lauren Bacall] to play the leading lady. I figured that was a sure-fire way to help make the picture a commercial success, and Jack Warner, who was putting up much of the money, thought so too. Well, Betty said okay, but Bogie wanted more than we could afford to pay him. So I asked Bob Mitchum to play the role and he agreed. It seemed a good idea because Wellman had given Mitchum his big break in the lead role in *The Story of G.I. Joe* [in 1945].

"We'd already spent a fortune constructing a Chinese village near San Rafael in California. When Wellman started shooting at the beginning of the year [1955], I took Pilar to New York for a holiday. But on the third day into production Wellman called me and said he couldn't work with Bob. Bill said Bob was drinking a lot and causing all kinds of hell. I said, 'Give Bob a chance. Try to work things out. We can't afford any holdups.' A week or so later I got another call from Bill who said he'd had enough and told me to fire Mitchum. That was a goddamn situation to be put in because every day Wellman didn't get anything on film was losing us money, so I had to let Bob go and, rather than waste more valuable time looking for another actor to take his place, I played the part myself. But I wasn't happy about it."

Wellman gave me his version of events: "Mitchum was drinking and raising hell and continually sleeping through his wake-up calls, upsetting everyone in cast and crew. I phoned Duke and told him that I couldn't work with Mitchum. Duke said there was a lot of money riding on the film, which I understood, and he wanted me to try and work with Mitchum, so I tried, but it was hopeless. I called Duke again and said, 'It's either Mitchum or me. Either you take the part, or I'm off the picture.' So Duke fired Mitchum and took over the role."

But Mitchum had a very different story to tell when I interviewed him, sitting outside of a London pub while he was taking a liquid lunch break on *The Big Sleep* in 1977: "I wasn't fired from *Blood Alley* because I was drinking. Wellman didn't want me on the picture in the first place because I had politely refused to appear on *This Is Your Life* when they did Wellman. I simply didn't have the time to come on the show, and when Wellman found out he was determined, after Duke cast me in *Blood Alley*, to find a way to get rid of me. He rode me so much I finally said, 'I've had it' and left. Wellman gave his story to Duke, and then I told Duke the *real* reason why I was off the picture, and we remained friends. When we later made *El Dorado* [in 1967] we had the time of our lives working together."

It was mid-January when Wayne took over Mitchum's part, and filming went relatively smoothly until, as Duke put it, "I hurt my back doing my own stunts and had to lie in a fucking hospital bed for a few days while Bill filmed around me. I've always hated hospitals, and more than that I hated the idea that I was beginning to get too old to do all my own stunts."

"I liked Duke Wayne a lot," Lauren Bacall told me. "I somehow expected him to be rather cold and intimidating. I also thought we would clash because he was very right wing and had supported the House Un-American Activities Committee. Bogie and I and John Huston had led a group we called the Committee for the First Amendment which opposed the investigations — or rather, we opposed the way the investigations were being carried out. So I was very surprised when I found Duke to be a very warm person, very friendly and amiable. After Bogie was diagnosed with cancer, Duke, who really didn't know Bogie at all, was among the first people to send his best wishes."

In March the unit moved to the Warner Bros. Burbank studio for interior scenes. John Ford was already having discussions with Warners about *The Searchers* with Wayne in the starring role. Duke recalled, "Jack Warner was enthusiastic about a John Ford–John Wayne Western, but when Ford told him it would cost nearly $4 million to make, Warner nearly burst a blood vessel and wanted to back out. Pappy was not in the best of health back then. He'd had something of a breakdown while making *Mister Roberts* and really wasn't up to bartering with Jack Warner. So I wrote to Warner and said that if he didn't agree to Ford's terms, I'd terminate my relationship with Warner Bros. So Jack Warner agreed. Anyway, I was pretty damn mad with the way Warner had treated Pappy, so I decided I'd end my relationship with Warner Bros. anyway. After *The Searchers*, it was a long time before I went to work at that studio again."

After filming on *Blood Alley* finally wound up in June 1955, Duke received disturbing news. Yakima Canutt told me, "I called Duke and told him that one of my guys, Cliff Lyons, who was one of the best stuntmen in the business, had been very successful at infiltrating the most hard-core group of Communists in Los Angeles. It had taken a lot of time for Cliff to win their trust. They thought he was just a cowboy on the rodeo circuit who was disenchanted with the American government and wanted to do something about it. I only chose those I could really trust because we were not doing this in cahoots with the FBI or any official government agency. We didn't know who we could trust, and we didn't want anything to jeopardize our plan and put Duke's life at risk.

"Most of the Communist groups around Hollywood were just people in the picture business who believed they were doing the right thing. They didn't know about the

Stalinists who had nothing to do with our industry. But the people Cliff had infiltrated were the truly dangerous people, not the Hollywood Ten. These guys were Stalinists who were brainwashed to believe they were the true government of America in waiting. I didn't know it then, but Khrushchev had rescinded the decision to kill Duke, but these people were part of a schism that still believed that true Communism was Stalinism.

"Cliff had spent months meeting with these people — just a small group of about ten or so — in a large room at the back of what I think was a printing company. It was in Burbank, not far from the Warner studios. They didn't know his real occupation. Cliff said to me, 'You know, Yak, I've never considered myself an actor, but I gave an award-winning performance.'

"They'd heard that Duke had made another anti-Communist film [*Blood Alley*] and they'd decided they were going to finish what Stalin had started. They'd tried before when Duke was in Mexico making *Hondo*, so this time they were going to get him in his own home. As soon as I learned this, I got really frightened for Duke and Pilar, especially when Cliff told me this was going to happen that night.

"I called John and told him to be armed and ready, just in case. He said, 'They so much as show their little pinkies, I'll blow them all to kingdom come.' I said, 'Look, John, I think we can stop them, but what if we can't?' He said, 'I've got enough guns to arm the Seventh Cavalry.' I said, 'John, the Seventh Cavalry were wiped out at Little Big Horn.' He said, 'You'd better make sure they don't get here.'

"Cliff helped me round up our most trusted stunt guys who were all cowboys, and we went to the Communist meeting place. Cliff went inside because he had to. We were armed with handguns, just in case, but we hoped we wouldn't have to use them as gunfire would certainly bring the police. We had to arm ourselves because Cliff said *they* would have guns, but we hoped to surprise them and jump them before any shots were fired.

"Cliff had made sure the door was open for us, and we crept in, and when they saw us, they all sort of froze. They just didn't know what was happening. But we went straight into action and we just lay into them. There was an almighty fight. Unfortunately for the Communists, my guys knew how to fight for real. Chairs and tables went everywhere. The Communists were just no match for us. One Communist picked up a chair, and tried to hit me with it, but I just stepped aside, took the chair and hit *him* with it. Our main concern was to disarm those men as quickly as possible, and one or two of them were able to draw their guns. But they were too slow for my guys who were on to them quickly and just beating the hell out of them. Not a shot was fired.

"After giving them a good beating, we drew our guns. When they realized Cliff wasn't one of them after all, some of them called him all kinds of a bastard, so we gave those guys the biggest beating. There was a lot of blood spilled, and I reckon it was lucky nobody got killed. I always think of it as the Bloody Battle of Burbank. Then I said, 'Okay, fellers, you like your precious Stalin so much, you can join him.' They took that to mean we were going to kill them, and a couple of them began pleading for their lives, saying they had families and so on. So I said, 'No one's gonna die if you do as we say.'

"Then I told them what we had planned for them. We'd bought them all tickets on the next flight to Russia. I told the couple of guys who said they had families that they could call them when they got to

Russia and arrange for them to join them there.

"We bundled them into several of our own cars and drove them to the airport, and we made sure they boarded their plane and watched them fly off into the night. Then I called Duke and told him what had happened, but I told him I'd keep my boys on the lookout in case there were any more Communist cells thinking of trying the same thing. Fortunately, as time passed, it all went very quiet. I think we must have driven out the most dangerous Communists in Hollywood. As far as I know, the cops never knew what we'd done, nor the intelligence guys. We kept it a secret. What we didn't know was that Mao Tse-tung was gonna later try the same thing, so for a long time Duke thought it was all over. He's lucky he's still alive."

17

Searching for the Darkness

Wayne had barely finished work on *Blood Alley* in June when he began making *The Searchers*. He was glad to be back with John Ford in Monument Valley.

"I really looked forward to that picture. I was back with the Coach and I was playing a role that I felt could be the best I'd had since *She Wore a Yellow Ribbon*, or even *Red River*. It was also something new for me in the story's format. It was a saga that took place over a number of years."

The Searchers saw Wayne in the darkest role of his entire career. As Ethan Edwards, he sets out with Martin, who is half Indian, played superbly by Jeffrey Hunter, to look for his two nieces, Lucy and Debbie, who have been taken by Apaches. The Indians had also killed Ethan's brother and his wife, and so the film was not only about the search for the two girls, but was also a mission of vengeance.

The film featured several scenes that gave Wayne a depth and a dimension he'd never shown before. As the film winds its way through the years, during which they discover Lucy has been raped and murdered by her abductors, Ethan becomes less like the usual John Wayne hero, taking on a dark persona driven by his dogged determination which in turn is driven by his complete hatred for Indians. Neither Martin nor the audience realizes that Ethan has come to the conclusion that when they find Debbie, he is going to kill her because she will have become an Indian.

In a scene that has become a classic moment in cinema history, Ethan, on horseback, chases Debbie who flees on foot. He corners her and grabs her, and it is the moment the audience expects him to kill her. Then, suddenly, he cradles her in his arms and says, "Let's go home, Debbie."

"A lot of people ask me why Ethan had become so hell-bent on killing Debbie and then, at the final moment, takes her home," Wayne said to me. "Pappy was clever because he hinted, and so did I, that Ethan had had an affair with his brother's wife. But we didn't spell it out. It was for the audience to figure out. So Ethan's thirst for vengeance wasn't just for killing his brother, but also for killing the woman Ethan had loved. When Ethan picks up Debbie at the end, I had to think, what's going through his mind as he looks into her face? I guess he saw in her eyes the woman he'd loved. That was enough to overcome his hatred. Wow! That was a terrific moment. And a great part for me to have the opportunity to play."

Many actors who worked on that film were impressed, and some even quite shocked, to see Wayne giving a performance so different from anything he had done before. Ken Curtis told me, "Duke was usually pretty laid back when he was working. He usually found time to play practical jokes, and he loved to laugh if someone told him a joke, but when we were making *The Searchers* he wasn't quite so loose. He just didn't seem as relaxed. I thought at first it was because he was expecting John Ford to lay into him like he usually did, and sure enough Ford found opportunities to say things that would needle Duke. But then I came to realize that wasn't why Duke was so pensive. It was simply his concentration on the part. Dobe Carey said to me, 'Did you notice the look in Duke's eyes in that scene we did?' I asked him what he meant, because I'd not been there to see it, and he said, 'When I looked at him, he had the coldest, meanest eyes I'd ever seen. I've never seen Duke like that before.' And that was because Duke was, I felt, reaching down deep inside himself into some dark corner he'd never gone before. Now *that's* a mark of how good an actor he was. Anyone who says Duke always played himself — and I've even heard Duke say it — should take a look at *The Searchers*, and they'll see John Wayne with a whole new dimension to his character."

Wayne told me the secret of how he found that dark place he'd reach down to for his performance as Ethan. "I just thought of the Apaches not as Indians but as the Communists who'd been trying to kill me. I thought, What if the Commies were the ones who had done this? What if they had managed to burn down my home and kill my family? You see, I can be a method actor too."

Since Wayne himself had not given me any details of the attempts on his life at his home but had mentioned that it was Yakima Canutt he owed his life to, I asked Canutt if the attempt had any bearing on

Wayne's portrayal of Ethan. He said, "Why, of course Duke was thinking of the Apaches as the Communists who'd tried to kill him. He was so goddamn mad and full of rage when I told him we'd put all the Communists we could round up on a plane for Russia. He was spitting mad. He said — though I'm sure he didn't mean it literally — but he said, 'You should have called me and I'd have come over and shown those sons of bitches what it means to threaten *my* life, *my* home, *my* wife.' I saw the look in his eyes that I later saw in Ethan's in *The Searchers*. He should have won the Oscar, but he didn't even get nominated."

To play Debbie, Ford had to choose two actresses, one for the younger Debbie in the early scenes, and one to play the older Debbie. He decided to cast former child actress Natalie Wood, then aged just sixteen, to play the older Debbie. It just so happened that Natalie had a little sister, Lana, aged nine and perfect to play the younger Debbie, so Ford cast Lana as well.

After Wayne's death, I was able to interview Natalie Wood who recalled for me her time making *The Searchers*. "We all had to live on location. There was me, my mother, and my sister Lana, and we all lived at a trading post outside Flagstaff. I had a room to myself and Lana and my mother shared another room.

"Every night we would hear the local Navajos singing, and I'd look out of my window and I'd see the campfires they'd built. When Lana heard the singing, she got scared and was convinced the Indians were going to attack us. I kept explaining to her that that sort of thing didn't happen anymore.

"We were smack in the middle of the desert with nothing but sand for miles. During the day it got extremely hot, and we would break for a long lunch and get under shade when the sun was at its height. There were snakes and scorpions, and one day Ward Bond was bitten by a scorpion. I watched them draining the poison from the bite, and I actually felt faint at the sight of it. I was always on the lookout for scorpions after that.

"John Wayne was a giant to me, and when he picked me up in that scene near the end of the picture, he was able to lift me as though I were a doll. It was pretty frightening because he had this look of hatred and I thought that he could easily crush me. But then there would be an almost indefinable gentleness that would come over him as he cradled me and said, 'Let's go home.' Everyone had always told me, 'John Wayne's no actor. He always plays the same part.' I can tell you, Mr. Wayne was a very fine actor. He said to me, 'When I pick you up, I may seem a little rough, but I'll be as gentle as I can be.' I said, 'You must pick me up without worrying about that or you might not give the performance you need to portray.' He smiled and said, 'Well, little lady, you're a real professional, that's for sure.'

"There was one little Navajo child. A baby really, just two years old, I think. She came down with a serious case of pneumonia. They needed to get her to a hospital urgently. Duke had his own airplane on location, and he had his pilot fly the girl to the hospital. Otherwise she might have died. The Navajos gave him a new name for his deed. They called him The Man with the Big Eagle.

"Duke's son Patrick had a part in the film. He was really handsome. Didn't look a lot like his father, I thought. Duke had a real rugged kind of handsomeness, but Patrick, who was the same age as me, had a really boyish face. Just my type. I had a deep crush on him."

I had interviewed Pat Wayne in 1976,

four years before I met Natalie Wood, so I had to guess who Pat was talking about when he said, "I had a friend who was my age on *The Searchers*. A very pretty girl, a really nice girl, so making the film was great fun for me during the day as well as at night."

The very last scene in the film was shot through an open door, looking out on the desert from inside the house where Debbie is delivered to family friends, played by Olive Carey and John Qualen. They all enter the house, including Jeffrey Hunter as Martin, and only Wayne remains outside, which was Ford's way of showing that Ethan had always been, and would always be, an outsider.

Wayne told me, "I wanted to end the film with something that would mean something to Olive Carey. Harry Carey used to have a way of reaching across his chest with his right hand and taking hold of his left arm by the elbow. So as I stood looking in through the door, I did just that, and I could see Olive standing out of camera, tears just rolling down her cheeks. And I turned and walked away as the door closed."

The Searchers remains Ford's finest film, and it is certainly one of the greatest Westerns of all time. As for Wayne's performance, he was never better, before or since.

Pilar had been on location with Duke, and by her own account, she seems to have enjoyed the experience. By the time the film wrapped in August 1955, she was pregnant. The Waynes returned to their Encino home and, for a change, Duke had time to spend with Pilar before rushing into another picture. But all too frequently they were not often alone. Duke's male friends were forever visiting, and it was the same old crowd as usual, and the same amount of drinking went on. Paul Fix recalled, "Pilar is a wonderful woman, but she really felt outside it all when people like Ward Bond and John Ford came by to talk and drink. I'd like to think I didn't make myself a nuisance, and kept my visits to a minimum. One day I noticed he seemed . . . less than enthusiastic about Pilar's pregnancy. I said to Duke, 'Aren't you looking forward to the birth of your new child?'

"He replied, 'I'm thinking I'm too old to start a new family.'

"I said, 'Duke, you wait till you see your new baby. You'll change your tune.'

"And he did. When Aissa was born, he

told me, 'You were right. Having a baby around the house has made me feel young again. And this time I'm going to make sure I'm a good father.' He said that because he was convinced that Michael and some of his other children had never forgiven him for leaving their mother.

"Aissa was born on 31 March 1956.

"He just went gaga over her, but he told me his other children resented his new family. I said to him, 'Duke, look, why don't you talk to them about it? Make them understand how you feel.' But he just couldn't stand to face any kind of confrontation with them. I think there was always a certain distance between Duke's first and second family. He tried his best to bring them together. But he was afraid of upsetting them in any way. When his eldest daughter, Toni, found out Pilar was pregnant, she said to her father, 'How could you?' Duke said, 'Don't blame me. *She's* the one who's having the baby.'

"When I heard this, I told Duke, 'How can you say that?' He said, 'It was the first thing that came into my head. Oh Jesus, I shouldn't have said it.' "

Claire Trevor recalled, "Duke adored all his children. He took them everywhere with him. He loved them all with a passion.

I never saw him show favoritism. He was always hugging and kissing them. But when Aissa was a baby, I sensed there was some jealousy there among the older four."

Trying to be a good father to all his children, including those yet to be born, became an obsession with Wayne.

Blood Alley had turned out to be the disappointment Duke had expected when it was released in October 1955. The critics, especially the left-wing press, slated it, but it still managed to make a profit. "All I ever cared about," said Wayne, "was that the public liked my pictures."

He liked to pretend that what the critics said didn't matter to him, but it did. He read every review of every one of his films, and when they were lacking in praise, he would swear under his breath, and then say, "Oh, who the hell cares what *they* think?"

Just before Aissa was born, *The Conqueror* finally made it to the screens. The critics panned it, or as Duke would put it, "They *crucified* it — and me. And in that instance, they were right."

None of the reviews made any difference to the success of the film. It earned a whopping $12 million worldwide, outgrossing both *Blood Alley* and *The Sea Chase*, much to Wayne's amazement. "*The Conqueror* is one of the worst films I ever made, and it was a massive success. I think it was only because epic films were in vogue at the time, and although I thought the film was a sort of Mongolian Western, it was a historical epic, and I guess people liked those films. I began to wonder if they'd like Westerns anymore."

His faith in Westerns was restored when *The Searchers* was released to good reviews and good business in March 1956. But as good as the reviews were, there was little to suggest that the film would become a classic, except from the *Hollywood Reporter* which called it "undoubtedly the greatest Western ever made." *Variety* was not so enthusiastic, saying, "Despite its many assets, there is a feeling that *The Searchers* could have been so much more."

Nevertheless, the film took a respectable $4.9 million in America and Canada, and its success around the world would have, at least, doubled that figure. Its place in *Variety*'s 1983 All-Time Western Champs is at sixty-two, but rises to seventeenth position with its figure adjusted for inflation, meaning that if released in 1983 and seen by the same amount of people, its domestic figure would have been more than $24 million, and its worldwide takings as much as $48 million.

As far as work was concerned, Wayne was at the top of his profession, but his family life was proving ever more complicated. Three weeks after Aissa was born, his oldest daughter, Toni, invited her father to her wedding to Don LaCava, the son of film director Gregory LaCava. To Duke's dismay, the invitation did not include Pilar. He still avoided confrontation with any of his first four children.

"Can you imagine how that made Pilar feel?" Paul Fix asked me. "I always felt that was the beginning of the troubles which beset Duke's third marriage. I think that maybe some of his children, especially Toni, still felt that Josephine was her father's real and only wife. Toni, and the other three, had had a Catholic upbringing, and Toni was married in a Catholic church [in May 1956]. The reception after was at the Beverly Hills Hotel, hosted by both Josephine and Duke. Now Duke and Josephine had maintained good relations, but to cut out Pilar like that . . . ! Well, I personally thought it was a disgrace."

Wayne went to work for Ford again in

the summer of 1956, in *The Wings of Eagles*, the story of screenwriter Frank "Spig" Wead who had written Ford's *Air Mail* (1932) and *They Were Expendable* (1945). Wead had previously been a pioneer in naval aviation, but had fallen down a flight of stairs and broken his neck, bringing his aviation career to an abrupt and sad end. He began writing aviation stories for magazines, which caught the attention of John Ford, and the two became good friends.

Wayne was cast as Wead, and he was reunited with Maureen O'Hara as his wife. Also in the cast were Ken Curtis, Dan Dailey, and Ward Bond, who played film director John Dodge, who was clearly modeled on Ford.

Ken Curtis told me, "It wasn't a film that Ford really wanted to make. It was MGM's idea, and when Ford told them he didn't want to do it, they said they'd get another director, and Ford decided that he didn't want anyone else making a film about the friend he loved so much, so he said he'd do it. And he decided that if he was going to make a film about a man he loved, he might as well get another man he loved to play Wead, and that was Duke."

I was fortunate enough to interview Dan Dailey by phone in 1997. Sadly, he died the following year. He recalled for me: "It was a difficult role for Duke because he felt he had an obligation to play Frank Wead with honesty and dignity. That's why when he's into the scenes where he plays Wead as an older man, for the first time ever, Duke removed his toupee and revealed his thinning hair to the public. But the funny thing was, he was so good in the part that nobody noticed he was showing his naturally balding pate.

"The film began with some comic moments, and Duke and I had some good laughs. But always Duke was worried that he might be too frivolous. But I think we got the balance just right. The story of Frank Wead was such a tragedy that you couldn't just go straight into a heavy, dramatic film. Besides, those moments where Wead crashed a plane into a swimming pool, which was hilarious on screen, all happened. The film moved from comedy and action to drama and tragedy. I think it's a most underrated film."

Maureen O'Hara also found herself faced with the pressure of portraying a real-life character. "Wead's marriage to Minnie was strained," said O'Hara, "and she became a drunk. We shot scenes where I had to play her drunk, which was a vital part of the story. All very dramatic and truthful, and I thought I was bloody good in those scenes, and so did John Ford and so did Duke. But when we finished the film, Wead's children saw it and objected to the scenes that showed their mother was a drunk, and those scenes were all cut out. I think the film suffered because of that."

Wayne was also disappointed with the way it turned out. "I don't think the Spig Wead film was bad. I just don't think it was what the public expected. The title was wrong. It sounded like I was in another war picture, shooting down Japanese planes or something. Pappy tried to persuade the studio to change the title but they rejected that idea. They decided they were going to sell the film as a John Wayne's–back-at-war picture, which it wasn't. It was a biography of someone both Pappy and I thought the world of. The public didn't really know who Spig Wead was, so we wanted to tell them who he was. But the studio didn't make that clear.

"There were some studio executives who complained to Pappy that the picture had too many laughs. Pappy wrote to me and said, 'How can a picture have too many laughs?' I never did work much at MGM. Thinking back, I realize why."

Wayne was working on one film after another and, in November 1956, he began preproduction work on *Legend of the Lost*.

"Duke should have slowed down," said Loretta Young, whose own career had considerably slackened off by then. She remained a close friend of Duke's, yet she never imposed on him to give her work, happy as she was working for various charities. She continued, "He told me he had to keep working before 'the well dried up,' as he put it. He also needed to earn as much as he could as quickly as he could to put toward *The Alamo*. But his work was gradually breaking down his marriage, brick by brick."

Henry Hathaway, who would direct *Legend of the Lost*, had written the original story about three people — two men and a woman — who head off into the Sahara Desert in search of a lost city and the treasures it is rumored to contain. He told me, "The film was a coproduction between Batjac, United Artists, and an Italian company called Dear Films. It was a really complicated setup with too many fingers in the pie. We had a screenplay by Ben Hecht which wasn't really good enough, so we had another writer, Robert Presnell Jr., have a go.

"When I told Wayne about the story, we didn't have a script, but he loved the idea, which is why he wanted Batjac involved. But when we got our first draft of the screenplay by Hecht, we knew it wasn't good enough. Even so, we began making deals left, right, and center.

"Duke wanted Sophia Loren in the picture so we'd have plenty of sex appeal, and we chose another Italian, Rossano Brazzi, a good but uninteresting actor who had become an international star in *South Pacific*. So with Loren, Brazzi, and Wayne, I had my three characters. And that's pretty much all I wanted in the film — just these three people. But Wayne wanted more to it, so we added the early scenes involving a bazaar and crowds, and I felt it all got too messy.

"Wayne went to United Artists to sell them on the idea, and they couldn't make up their minds, so Duke told them, 'Look, I'm giving you John Wayne, Sophia Loren, and Rossano Brazzi, for Christ's sake. What more do you want?' Finally they agreed to come in with us.

"We started filming in January [1957] in a village called Ghadames which was smack in the middle of the Sahara. We shot there and in the desert for two months, and then we moved to Cinecitta Studios in Rome for twelve weeks. Filming in Italy was part of the deal we made with Dear Films. And all the time we were trying to rewrite the screenplay to make it work. When we were in the Sahara everything — actors, crew, equipment — had to travel by plane and camel. It was a relief to get to the studio in Italy. But in the end it was just a fiasco."

In an interview I conducted with Rossano Brazzi in a London street, while he was filming *The Final Conflict*, he told me, "I kept asking myself, 'Why am I doing this?' It was like working in hell. The village we were living in at the start of production was unbelievably primitive. I didn't know such places could exist in this century. There was no telephone. No radio. No contact with civilization.

"We stayed in what was supposedly a motel. You think in the Sahara you'd be hot all the time, but at night it got bitter cold, and this motel had no heating, so you either froze or went to bed. Only Sophia had any kind of heating — a space heater, which some of the film crew installed for her. And it nearly killed her.

"It used up all the oxygen in her room and filled it with deadly carbon monoxide.

For several nights she said she had terrible nightmares, but all the time she was being asphyxiated until one night she nearly suffocated to death. It was only because she fell out of bed that she was able to rouse herself. She said that by the time she had crawled to the door, struggling for breath, she was almost comatose. She fell into the corridor just as I was coming by. I managed to find a doctor who used mouth-to-mouth on her, gave her injections of what I think was adrenaline. He brought her around, but he said that she would have died if I hadn't found her.

"When John Wayne found out, he was furious but he didn't know who to be angry at. He felt terrible that Sophia had nearly died, and it didn't help that Henry Hathaway's biggest concern was how they would have replaced her if she'd died. I could see that Wayne would like to have punched his director, but he held his temper and calmed down. It was a matter of humanity versus commerce. I will give Wayne his due; he was more concerned for Sophia than for the film.

"Sophia's main problem at that time was her difficulty with the English language. She learned her lines first in Italian and had them translated into English, and she was able to deliver her lines perfectly well. She was still pretty raw back then and hadn't had a lot of acting experience, but she was doing well, I thought. And the thing she most certainly did have, which was what I'd wanted from her, was tremendous sex appeal. I thought she did, but Henry didn't."

Henry Hathaway said frankly if ungallantly, "I was disappointed with Sophia. She had tremendous beauty, but she was so one-dimensional. There was no depth to her acting. I always thought she was overrated."

Despite the problems, filming wound up more or less on schedule at the end of March 1957. "It was a long, hard shoot," said Wayne, "and after all that it wasn't much of a picture."

18

Duke Meets Nikita

Wayne had three films released in 1957, the first being *The Wings of Eagles* in January. In September Howard Hughes's production of *Jet Pilot* finally saw the light of day. Audiences, unaware the film had been made several years earlier, were baffled at how young Wayne suddenly looked, and they, and the critics, found the anti-Communist story far too much like a comic book to take seriously, which didn't help Wayne's cause against Communism or his box-office appeal. The film was an expensive flop and was quickly withdrawn.

Wayne's third film of 1957 was *Legend of the Lost*, in December, and its success along with that of *The Wings of Eagles* put John Wayne in second place in the top ten American box-office stars of 1957. It must have delighted Twentieth Century Fox, for when they signed him in 1957 to make three films, they guaranteed him a fee of $2 million for all three films upon their completion. The first under this agreement was *The Barbarian and the Geisha*, directed by John Huston.

Despite my respect and admiration for Huston, for whom I worked on and off over several years, as well as my admiration for Wayne, I never could understand Huston's reason for casting Wayne. So I asked him why while I was working for him in London in 1974, and he told me. "I felt that Wayne was the right actor to play Townsend. He had proved he could act in *Red River* and *The Searchers*, and I wanted to tap into that talent. I saw Wayne as a giant form among the tiny people who existed in the exotic world of Japan in the 1880s. I thought, Who better to symbolize the big and awkward country that was the United States back then? I was sure Wayne was the right choice. I made a terrible mistake.

"I had no idea that Wayne would have any kind of vanity. But he kept saying, 'My best profile is on the right,' so I shot his left profile whenever I could. A film should be a partnership between director and actor. But we were at odds almost from the beginning."

Having some knowledge of both men and their work, it didn't surprise me that the combination of Huston and Wayne was a disaster in the making. As Wayne told me, "I just couldn't connect with Huston, though God knows I tried. The script was being rewritten with new pages each day. He'd promised me he'd get a decent script together, but he never did. We had no god-damn plot. I'd go up to his room and ask what we were going to be shooting in the morning, and he'd say 'Duke, just look at that view. Isn't it magnificent?' I'd say, 'Yeah, great. But what are we doing to-morrow?' I could never get a straight an-swer.

"After just a few days of filming, I real-ized that I was just a character in Huston's idea of a narrated tapestry. There seemed to be no real exploration of the character of Townsend. I guess Huston thought it was enough to say that Townsend was like John Wayne, and so he just put me through a series of admittedly beautifully shot scenes, but with no substance. I told him that there were all sorts of things we could do to make the story about *people*, and not just a series of moving photographs. But he thought his images were more important than his characters."

Playing Townsend's interpreter was Sam Jaffe, whom I interviewed by telephone in 1981. He was an incredible ninety-one years old then and still working up until his death in 1984. He said, "It was obvious from the start that Huston and Wayne were not going to work well together. It didn't help that we never had a completed script when we started the film, and we were having to learn new lines every day. I could see Huston was trying to make a beautiful film, and you couldn't fault him for the way he shot it. But Wayne had a point too. He couldn't get inside the head of Townsend, and Huston wasn't giving him anything to go by. So Wayne just played Wayne in a top hat. There was nothing else he could do. Wayne told me that he relied on people like John Ford and Howard Hawks to push him into giving a performance that was not just another John Wayne role. Huston just didn't want to do that. Perhaps with another actor, Huston might have been able to get the picture he wanted. They both cared about the picture, make no mistake. But they thought they were making two different pictures."

Huston told me a story about a near catastrophe which occurred during filming.

His disdain for Wayne showed. "We nearly had a disaster when we were shooting the scene where Townsend sets fire to a village infected with cholera. Then he took the dead bodies and put them on boats and set fire to them. We had a barge which was some forty feet long which was supposed to be full of these bodies. We set fire to it and launched it. We had a line attached but the line somehow broke and the barge drifted free. We got some fine shots of it, but the problem was that a wind blew up and drove it into some fishing boats anchored in a small cove. The boats caught fire, some exploded because they were driven by fuel. It started a riot as the local fishermen and the villagers attacked the Japanese crewmen I had. A lot of people were knocked unconscious and thank God no one was killed."

When I told Wayne that Huston had told me this story, Duke gave his version of events: "When I saw the riot begin, I ran down to the docks and began waving my hands and shouting for everyone to calm down. The rioters saw me and I guess they liked John Wayne enough to stop the riot. I promised all the fishermen that I would make good their losses out of my own pocket if the studio wouldn't. Well, when

Huston saw and heard this, he just walked away and never said a word. He couldn't bear the fact that he'd goofed badly and that I was the one who handled the situation."

It would seem that Huston's dislike of Wayne intensified after filming was completed. "I finished all the work on film — all the editing, the sound, the music — and I left for Africa to start work on *The Roots of Heaven*," said Huston. "Behind my back, Wayne took over because he pulled a lot more weight at Fox than I did, and he made a lot of changes, even adding new scenes and reshooting some scenes. By the time he'd finished with it, it was no longer the picture I shot. It was just a mess. Just a John Wayne film without the cowboys and the Indians."

Wayne defended his actions, saying, "I tried to work with Huston, but he just kept saying, 'Don't worry. It will all come together.' Well, it sure as hell didn't. When I saw it, it was just what I'd thought it would be; a rich tapestry with people in the foreground. So I said, 'To hell with this. If Huston wants to go off to Africa and leave his film a shambles, *I'm* going to do something about it.' But it was unsalvageable. I hated that goddamn picture. Huston has made a few good films, but I think he's greatly overrated."

Apart from his difficulties with Huston, Wayne had other more domestic problems to cope with. Pilar had arrived in Japan to spend Christmas with Duke, but she remained uneasy about leaving Aissa back home. It didn't help that Duke was in a bad mood because of his problems with Huston, and his mood caused tension between him and Pilar. Before the film wrapped, she persuaded Duke to let her go home.

Shortly after she returned to Los Angeles, their Encino home caught fire in the night. Pilar managed to grab Aissa from her crib and escape the flames, although Pilar received slight burns to an arm. The whole of the second floor was gutted and the downstairs badly damaged by smoke and water.

A few days later, Duke arrived home, the film finally finished, and he rented a house while renovations began on the Encino home. "Duke was shaken by what could have happened," said Paul Fix. "It was an experience that seemed to stir up the deepest, darkest emotions in both Duke and Pilar, and Pilar suddenly told Duke she wanted a divorce. She said she couldn't bear Duke's long absences from home, and she just couldn't cope with the kind of life a wife of John Wayne was expected to lead. She had become an insomniac and was taking pills to make her sleep. That was a damn sad thing. So they lived apart for a bit, but they loved each other so much they decided they had to try and make their marriage work. He was so damn relieved when she moved back in with him. And he'd missed Aissa. For a time there his life was so bleak. He got to drinking a lot more than usual and he seemed to lose interest in work. Then she came back and he was happy. But things were never really great between them."

The Barbarian and the Geisha was Wayne's only major film released in 1958 (in September), and that year turned out to be the only one between 1949 and 1969 when he was not one of America's top ten box-office draws.

Just as Duke and Pilar were making an attempt to patch up their marriage, Wayne had to leave in May 1958, for Old Tucson in Arizona to work with Howard Hawks on *Rio Bravo*. Pilar stayed at home to supervise the renovations to the Encino house.

Rio Bravo gave Wayne his best role since *The Searchers*, playing John T. Chance, the sheriff of border town Rio Bravo who arrests Joe Burdette (Claude Akins) for murder. Joe's older brother Nathan (John Russell), the most powerful rancher on the border, has his men surround the town to prevent Chance from taking Joe to the U.S. marshal and to stop any help getting in. Chance shuns help and has to rely on his new drunken deputy, Dude (Dean Martin); a crippled old deputy, Stumpy (Walter Brennan); and a young gunfighter, Colorado (singer Ricky Nelson). Trapped in Rio Bravo is stagecoach passenger Feathers (Angie Dickinson), who becomes Chance's romantic interest. A final showdown is inevitable.

Hawks said, "I made *Rio Bravo* because I didn't like *High Noon*. Neither did Duke. I didn't think a good town marshal was going to run around town like a chicken with his head cut off asking everyone to help. And who saves him? His Quaker wife. That isn't my idea of a good Western. I said that a good marshal would turn around and say to someone, 'How good are you? Are you good enough to take the best man they've got?' And the fellow would say, 'No,' so the marshal would say, 'Then I'll just have to take care of you.' And that scene was in *Rio Bravo*. It was the exact opposite of *High Noon*."

Wayne, who had also disliked *High Noon* and wanted *Rio Bravo* to tell the same kind of story "the American way," was Hawks's first and only choice for the role of Chance.

"I just don't see how you can make a good Western without Wayne," Hawks told me, which I thought was an overstatement, considering he was talking about a period between 1958 and the late 1960s when good Westerns were made without Wayne (*The Big Country*, *The Magnificent Seven*, *Man of the West*, just to name a few) but a John Wayne Western was almost a genre of its own. Hawks continued: "Whenever you get John Wayne in your picture, you better find someone good for him to buck up to. In *Rio Bravo* we had Dean Martin. Having two good actors like that means that the dialogue and the events that take place between them are easy to work out. I start off with a script, but it will always change. When an actor has a particular quirk, I'll rewrite the script to bring those quirks in. It's not so much rewriting as just saying the same thing with different words. The other thing I do is go straight into the scene and film it without rehearsal, because what you often get is so spontaneous, it works better than doing take after take.

"I always feel that there are about thirty plots in all, and they've all been done. If you can think of a new way to tell a plot, that's fine. My only criteria is that I like to start a picture with a dramatic sequence and then find the place in the story where we start to get some laughs out of it.

"I like to let the characters tell the story for you, and don't worry about the plot. Movements come from characterization. Dean was a great drinker in real life and we had him play a drunk in *Rio Bravo*. We saw Wayne watching his old friend Dean get rehabilitated. And just as he's getting better, someone tells him, 'You stink,' so we catch him taking a bath. I like that kind of storytelling. The characters dictate the way the story develops. If the audience don't find the characters interesting, they won't care how clever the story is. But when they like the characters, they'll just enjoy watching to see what happens to them. Almost all the men in my pictures have gone through some troubles and then they have to be straightened out.

"Dean was fun to work with. All you had to do was tell him something. There's a scene where Dean has a hangover, and when we first shot it, he didn't look like he was suffering. So I said to him, 'I knew a guy with a hangover who'd pound his leg trying to hurt himself to try and get some feeling back into it.' And Dean said, 'Yeah, I know the kind of guy,' and we went on and did the scene with no rehearsal, and he did a damn good job.

"When you have people like Wayne and Martin, you don't always have to stick to the script. You can tell them some bit of business, and they'll ad-lib it, and if it works I stop there. I don't like to do retakes."

For twenty-six-year-old Angie Dickinson, *Rio Bravo* was a big break after a run of mediocre films. "The luckiest thing that happened to me was to do *Rio Bravo*, and to do it with Duke," she told me later. "Duke was a real man. And I mean a *real* man. He was like it on screen and off. I was still new to movies, and Duke really helped me a lot. We had some long scenes together. Much longer than Duke is used to. So he was working harder than ever to get through those scenes and keep his concentration. It didn't matter if the words didn't come out the way they were written. He'd say the lines the way he thought his character would say them. I loved Duke.

And he enjoyed working for Howard Hawks. He never argued with him. He just did whatever Howard told him to do. He trusted Hawks."

Wayne enthused, "We were damned lucky to have Angie Dickinson. She had beauty, sex appeal, and brains. And she was one of the best actresses I ever worked with. There was none of that 'Don't mess my hair or makeup,' or 'I'm late because I had to get my hair just right.' She was there on time, she knew what was needed, and she did the job as good as any actress.

"I've worked with Maureen O'Hara a few times and she's like the female equivalent of me. She could rough me up and I could rough her up. I liked working with Gail Russell because she had such a fragile quality which played in contrast to my characters. And with Angie you had someone who was not the female equivalent of me, nor was she fragile, but she was a real woman who could be tough and gentle and sexy, and she didn't have to rough me up to get her way with me. She was the kind of woman in *Rio Bravo* you just couldn't resist."

When Bud Boetticher visited the set, he recalled: "John Wayne had a powerful presence and he was so perfect in cowboy boots and a cowboy hat that what he did kind of rubbed off on the other actors if they weren't careful. They were doing a scene in a saloon, and he had some lines with Claude Akins, and they were halfway through it and Akins said his line which was, 'So what are you gonna do now?' Wayne came back without a beat and said, 'Well, the first thing I'm gonna do is change the tone of my voice if all you assholes are going to talk just like me.' It was really funny to hear the other actors starting to talk like Duke and they didn't even realize it."

Released in February 1959, *Rio Bravo* was an immediate hit, earning $5.7 million domestically and around $12 million worldwide.

There are many stories about John Wayne which, for various and often good reasons, are sanitized. Such was the story of how Wayne came face-to-face with the leader of the Soviet Union in 1958. The idea that Duke Wayne and Nikita Khrushchev could make for good drinking buddies stretches the imagination, but that was the story put out in 1958, and it was the one Wayne told me in 1974.

"President Dwight Eisenhower invited

Nikita Khrushchev to the United States [in September 1958]. The president sent me word that Khrushchev wanted to meet me. Seems that he had seen many of my films which he pirated across the Iron Curtain and had dubbed into Russian just for his own pleasure. When I got word from the president that the Soviet leader wanted to meet me, I accepted because I certainly didn't want to embarrass the president.

"I guess I was curious to know what a Communist leader was like. I knew he was not another Stalin who was a goddamn monster, but these people were still enemies to freedom. Although it hadn't happened yet, Khrushchev was the guy who sent all those nuclear missiles to Cuba and aimed them at us. And yet the guy I met didn't seem the type to want to blow up any country, but that's what he was always threatening to do. So anyway, we met up at a function thrown by Spyros Skouras who was the president of Twentieth Century Fox, and we talked a while through interpreters, but it was about as private a conversation as two people can have with another person standing there interpreting everything and surrounded by film and political bigwigs, not to mention the security agents all over the place.

"We decided to make the conversation more private by going to a private bar — with the interpreter — and Khrushchev said to me, 'I am told that you like to drink and that you can hold your liquor.' I said, 'That is right.' He said that he also liked a drink and could hold his liquor, and I said, 'I had heard as much.' We went on to compare the virtues of Russian vodka and Mexican tequila, and then we matched each other drink for drink. If he hadn't been a Communist, the man might have impressed me. But even though he was no Stalin, he was still a Communist, and I'll tell what's bad about that. Khrushchev said something with a big smile on his face and laughed, and I was smiling as I said to the interpreter, 'What did he say?' The interpreter said, 'He is the leader of the biggest state in the world and will one day rule the whole world.' I laughed politely and said, still smiling, 'And I'm gonna knock him on his sorry fucking ass.' The interpreter said something and Khrushchev laughed, so I said, 'What did you tell him I said?' He said, 'I told him you would buy him a drink the day he rules America.' And then the guy said, 'We have to maintain diplomatic relations here.' So I just laughed and raised my glass.

"Three months later he sent me a large crate stamped with Russian letters CCCP [USSR]. Mary, my secretary, was uncertain about opening it, but I said, 'Hell, Mary, open it up. It's too damn big to be a bomb.' So we opened it with a crowbar and inside were several cases of top-quality bottles of Russian vodka and a note which read, 'Duke, Merry Christmas, Nikita.' I reciprocated by sending him a couple of cases of Sauza Conmemorativo Tequila, and wrote a note saying 'To Nikita. Thanks. Duke.'

"Bearing in mind that the Communists were still our greatest enemy, I felt that it would be great if all conflicts could be settled that way. Of course, that's idealistic bullshit, but it's kind of a nice thought. Anyway, it was a good piece of propaganda for the press."

But Wayne didn't tell me the real reason why he decided to meet Khrushchev and what they really talked about — apart from the virtues of alcohol. When I told Yakima Canutt in 1976 that Duke had related his meeting with Khrushchev to me, Canutt explained, "Duke called me and said, 'What do you think? Khrushchev wants to meet me. Says he liked my pictures.' I said, 'Maybe he does. I think it's worth seeing him — if only to ask him face-to-face why he is trying to kill you.' Duke said, 'That's just what I was thinking.'

"So when Duke met Khrushchev, once he got over the formalities and was able to speak to him in private, he asked him outright why he was trying the hell to kill him. And Khrushchev apparently looked very grim and said, 'That was the decision of Stalin during his last five mad years. When Stalin died, I rescinded the order.' Duke said, 'Then how come after Stalin died some of your guys over here tried to bump me off?' Khrushchev said he knew nothing about it but that there had been a number of Communist cells around the world who refused to renounce Stalinism. He said that he had taken steps to remove those people.

"Duke was fascinated to hear about the machinations of Stalin's government and its secrets, and Duke was impressed with Khrushchev because he was trying to make the Soviet Union a country based on pure Communism and not Stalinism. Of course, Duke didn't think Communism was good in any form, and he told Khrushchev just that. So Khrushchev changed the conversation and brought up the subject of drinking.

"He warned Duke, though, that he should not let his guard down. He said that Mao Tse-tung was like Stalin and he kept trying to push the Soviet Union into a war with the West. Khrushchev told Duke that Mao was in on the conspiracy. Duke said that Khrushchev seemed concerned but he gave no guarantees.

"Duke finally said to him, 'Do you really watch my pictures?' and Khrushchev said, 'Yes, I especially like the ones about the U.S. Cavalry. They remind me of how the white Americans oppressed the true natives of America.' Duke said he wanted to punch Khrushchev in the mouth but thought better of it. Then Khrushchev said, 'Our Russian actors do not do a very good impression of you. Now I have heard you speak, I will try to imagine how you would say your lines.'

"Duke said he had to pretend he liked the leader of the Soviet Union because it suited the president's PR men to say that even John Wayne liked the president of the USSR. Duke didn't mind so long as it helped ease tensions between East and West. But, of course, it didn't help a damn."

I asked Canutt how the interpreter took the news that the Communists had been trying to kill Wayne. Canutt said, "John said that the interpreter told him *he* wouldn't be the one to tell the president that the Russians had been trying to kill John Wayne, and John told him, 'That's fine by me. Because if you did ever say it was discussed, I'll deny it, and I'm sure you won't get old Iron Curtain Pants here to back you up.' John had a way of putting things that made people do what he told them — *asked* them." It was especially important to Wayne that all of this was kept secret.

Also in 1958, Wayne made a surprise unbilled cameo in a Diana Dors comedy, *I Married a Woman*, in which he appeared in a film within a film. It was little more than a favor to RKO.

More importantly, in late October 1958, Wayne and Ford reunited to make *The Horse Soldiers*. Written and produced by John Lee Mahin in partnership with Martin Rackin, it was based on a true incident in the American Civil War. It wasn't a Western in the traditional sense but a historical film. And yet it was Ford and Wayne and columns of men in blue on horseback, giving its backers, the Mirisch brothers and United Artists, hopes of a picture to compare with the likes of *She Wore a Yellow Ribbon*, *Fort Apache*, and *Rio Grande*. But Civil War films were risky enterprises.

Over the phone in 1980, John Lee Mahin (who was giving me good advice about screenwriting) explained, "John Ford was an American Civil War buff and had wanted to make a Civil War picture for a long time. But that's the hardest kind of film to make in America. With the exception of *The Birth of a Nation* and *Gone with the Wind*, there has never really been a successful Civil War picture because somebody has to be the heavy and it's either going to be the Confederates or the Yankees. So *The Horse Soldiers* was a risky project because it was based on a historical event about a Union cavalry raid deep into Southern territory. Martin Rackin and I had read the book [by Harold Sinclair] and we decided to form our own production company and optioned the book for a year for one dollar. We wrote our screenplay and took it to Walter Mirisch, who agreed to put up three and a half million dollars if we could sign several bankable stars.

"We figured that the combination of John Ford and the cavalry was as good as a bankable star and he loved the idea. He wanted to cast John Wayne, which made the project even more viable, and we were able to interest William Holden, who was a top star then following his success in *The Bridge on the River Kwai*. So Mirisch went to United Artists and they came on board. Then Paramount, who had Holden under contract, tried to keep him off the film, and that resulted in a legal battle which we won.

"Ford knew the film would be difficult to bring off because of the problems all Civil War films have. He told Marty Rackin, 'You know where we should make this picture? Lourdes. It'll take a miracle to pull this picture off.' We actually shot in Louisiana."

John Ford wasn't totally satisfied with the script. According to William H. Clothier, the film's director of photography, "Ford liked the story but he said to me, 'If they think I'm gonna make their goddamn script, they're wrong. There are a lot of things in it I don't like.' He didn't like the ending which had the Union troops led by Wayne returning from their mission in triumph. Ford wanted an ending which reflected the pain of war. So he demanded they change the ending so it was more downbeat.

"It was a difficult picture to make all round. Pilar had become addicted to sleeping pills and Duke insisted she join him on location so he could keep an eye on her. Before they left home, she had run out of pills and after a day without them she got terrible withdrawal symptoms. Her doctor wanted to put her in a private sanatorium for people with drink and drug problems. But Duke wanted her in Louisiana and said he'd be with her as much as he could. So she arrived in Alexandria where we were based with little Aissa and a couple of maids.

"Ford was also battling alcoholism, and he was on the wagon, and he was especially bad tempered. And because he couldn't drink, he ordered Duke and Bill [Holden] not to drink. But Bill ignored him. He never turned up late for work, though, and he was never drunk on the set."

William Holden hadn't worked with Ford before, and he swore he never would again after *The Horse Soldiers*. During an interview I conducted with him in London on location for *Damien: Omen II*, he said, "Ford treated Duke badly because Ford was on the wagon and he took it out on Duke and wouldn't let him have a drink.

He also told me I couldn't drink. So I found myself lodgings in Shreveport where Ford couldn't stop me having a drink after work.

"I liked Duke a lot. I wasn't sure how we'd get on, but he was a really nice guy. But I was pretty disgusted with the way Ford treated him. Ford would yell at him and treat him like he was a newcomer. I said to Duke, 'Why do you let that old bastard treat you like that?' He said, 'Aw, Bill, that's just his way of making sure I give him a good performance.' I said, 'Duke, you've been at this longer than *me*. You got nominated for an Oscar, didn't you?' He said, 'Yeah!' I said, 'And what film was that for?' Of course I knew the answer. *Sands of Iwo Jima*. I said to Duke, 'Did Ford get a good performance out of you for *that*?' He said, 'Ford didn't direct *Iwo Jima*.' I said, 'That's what I mean.' But Duke would just do anything for Ford, and I admired his loyalty. But I wasn't having Ford talk to *me* that way. I told him. I said, 'Jack, I'll sweat blood to give you a good performance, but if you ever talk to me that way you talk to Duke, I'll walk off and I won't come back.' Ford said, 'Oh Bill, I don't need to force a good performance out of you. I saw *Sunset Boulevard*. You're twice the actor Duke is. He *needs* me to bully him.' I couldn't believe it. I never worked for Ford again. I never worked with Duke again, either, but that's just because nothing came along that suited us both.

"Marty Rackin and I felt sorry for Duke, who really wanted to have a drink. So Marty and I came up with a plan to get him away from Ford for a whole day. Marty told Ford that Duke's teeth looked off color in the early rushes and they needed to be cleaned. We made an appointment for Duke with a dentist in Shreveport, drove him there so he could have his teeth cleaned, and then we spent the day drinking."

Clothier recalled, "When Ford found out, he was furious. He went into one of the worst tantrums I've ever seen. You'd think Duke had broken all Ten Commandments. Ford would go sneaking into Duke's room looking for bottles."

Anna Lee, who had become one of Duke's regular players since first costarring with him in *Flying Tigers*, was aware of the problems Pilar was having trying to go without sleeping tablets. She said, "Duke had promised her he'd be with her all the time, but it was impossible for him to keep his promise because he had to work so much. During the first week she spent in Louisiana, she had hallucinations and was in just a terrible state because she was basically going cold turkey. She just went through hell. She got so bad she slashed her wrists with a razor blade. Duke's secretary, Mary St. John, found her and called for an ambulance. That's when Duke realized he couldn't keep her on location and that she needed professional help. A doctor patched her wrists, and Duke hired two nurses and a plane to fly her back to Encino, where she went straight to the hospital and she was able to get proper treatment for her drug addiction."

Clothier, who had become a confidant to Wayne, said, "Duke took it very hard to think that he couldn't be there for her. He blamed himself for her addiction to sleeping pills and for her suicide attempt. He blamed himself for all of it. He knew he had to get on with the film and he did, but I knew that he needed to be able to have a drink when he wanted, so I told him he could hide a bottle in my room. Ford never knew."

For most of the time, filming on *The Horse Soldiers* went well. Holden told me,

"I thought we were getting some good stuff on film. I liked the edge Duke and I had to play. I was a doctor who hated war and blamed people like the character Wayne played for all the miseries war caused. And he was a soldier who hated doctors because they'd botched an operation on his wife and killed her. Wayne was criticized a lot because his voice wasn't always expressive. But when you saw his eyes, they told you everything. That's what impressed me about his performance in *Red River* and *The Searchers*, and I think he was better in those films than he was in *Sands of Iwo Jima*. But he never strayed too far away from the usual John Wayne persona in *The Horse Soldiers* because he knew that his audience wanted to see a John Wayne Western. But he got to show a bit of that dark side he'd had in *The Searchers*, and I think that some of that came from the distress that came from the problems he was having with Pilar, who was addicted to sleeping pills. He didn't want her to be treated by doctors at first — until she tried to kill herself.

"As an actor, I'd say that if I was playing his role, I'd use those demons to work for me in the part, and I think that he may have been doing that. We never discussed it. Often with Duke, he just learned his lines, got in front of the camera, and he was usually so good in the first take he didn't improve any with more takes. He didn't *need* more takes. That's what makes a good screen actor. I hated war, so it wasn't difficult for me to believe what I was saying. People may say Duke wasn't a method actor, but I'd say he had a method of his own."

On the subject of acting, Wayne said, "People like Brando and Clift talked a lot about method acting. Hell, I'd been doing that for years. I just don't make a point of explaining it to everyone. I just get on with it."

As location shooting in Louisiana neared an end, a terrible tragedy occurred which affected not only the film, but also Ford's state of mind. John Lee Mahin explained, "A guy called Fred Kennedy had a small part in the film. Ford used him in a lot of his pictures because he was also a stuntman. But he was almost fifty by this time, and he begged Ford to let him double for Bill Holden for a horse fall. Ford didn't want him to do it, but Kennedy said he needed the extra money which stunt guys would get for each gag they did. So Ford let him do it. Kennedy came off the horse and lay there. He'd broken his neck and was barely struggling to breathe. He died on the way to the hospital.

"That just broke Ford. He couldn't direct a thing after that, and we had a battle scene to shoot, and then there was supposed to be the scene where Wayne leads his men back home. Ford just wanted to get it over with and shot the battle on the bridge with no enthusiasm for it. It was an awful scene. The Confederates charged across the bridge and not one guy fell off his horse. It was a mess. We had to hastily write a scene which had Bill Holden staying behind with the wounded Union soldiers, knowing he'd be taken captive, while Wayne and the surviving Union soldiers ride off."

Wayne commented: "Pappy had been on the wagon, but after the accident, he began drinking again. We still had three more weeks of location shooting to be done, but Coach just lost the heart for it. I hated to see him like that. It damn well broke my heart. He suddenly canceled the remaining scenes and sent everyone home. I went back to Pilar, who was recovering well, and then three weeks later I got a call to go to the San Fernando Valley where Ford finished off the picture with the battle at the bridge all in one day. At the end of the day, he looked like such a broken man, I was convinced he'd never work again."

It was bad enough for Duke seeing Ford looking like a broken man, but there was worse news to come. Grant Withers, Wayne's friend of thirty years, had died. After battling with alcoholism for many years, Withers finally ended his misery by washing down an overdose of sleeping pills with vodka.

Although it had been twenty-seven years since Grant and Loretta Young had divorced, she was nevertheless upset when she got the news. She told me, "I was so glad to hear from Duke, who called to see how I was bearing up. Grant and I had been apart for many years, but I hated to see him going downhill for so long and finally take his own life. Duke thought the world of Grant, and I knew that he was just as upset about Grant's death, but Duke's only thought was for me.

"He knew I had become a practicing Catholic, and when I told him how despondent I felt, he said to me, 'Have you tried talking to the man upstairs?' I said that I'd had my faith tested severely and hadn't felt like praying. He just said, 'I think you ought to give it a try.' And I did. And I felt so much better."

Not too many months later, Loretta Young would be giving Duke the same kind of advice.

The Horse Soldiers was released in June 1959, and contrary to popular belief, it received some fine reviews. Arthur Knight wrote in the *Saturday Review*, "Its action scenes tingle with an excitement all too rare upon the screen these days. And the conflict between Marlowe and his surgeon major is projected with a surprisingly convincing intensity by John Wayne and William Holden. The script makes no effort to blunt the issues over which the war was fought, nor does it pretend that it was a glorious pastime."

Paul Beckley, of the *New York Herald Tribune*, thought it "a flying slash and gallop and essentially romantic race through one of the stirring cavalry episodes of the Civil War." Bosley Crowther wrote in the *New York Times*, "This is made supremely graphic and exciting by the touch of Mr. Ford and, what is more, some of it has the look of history seen through the mists of the years."

Some critics, especially in recent years, have thought it inferior to what they perceived to be Ford's "cavalry trilogy." *The Horse Soldiers*, of course, is not a cavalry picture but a Civil War film and, despite its anticlimactic ending, it succeeded in many areas, particularly in its depiction of the horrors (by 1959 standards) of war. It also featured good performances from Wayne, Holden, and Constance Towers and it somehow stands up well today, being far less dated than any of Ford's cavalry pictures, apart from the obligatory cavalry song over the main titles.

19

The Alamo

After at least ten years of preparation, Wayne was almost ready to make *The Alamo*. But before starting work on it, he broke one of his own rules and made a brief appearance on television. "It wasn't completely unconditional," he told me, "because it was as a favor to Pappy and Ward Bond. Ward was the star of the Western TV series *Wagon Train*, and Jack Ford was directing an episode, so he asked me to make a fleeting appearance as General Sherman. I was billed as Michael Morris, and I was on and off so fast people were left wondering if that had been John Wayne they'd seen."

Getting *The Alamo* off the ground had been a long, hard process. Wayne told me, "I went to every studio in town, tried calling in favors, reminded the studio heads how much money I'd made for them, but they all turned me down unless I got John Ford to direct. But this was *my* dream. I didn't want anyone else to direct it — not even my dear friend Jack Ford. United Artists only agreed to put up part of the money if I played a part, so I said I'd play Sam Houston, which was really a cameo kind of role. But they said I had to play a major role and said if I didn't play Davy Crockett, they wouldn't be interested. So, reluctantly, I played Crockett."

United Artists was only prepared to put up some of the $7.5 million needed if Wayne raised the rest. A million dollars alone went on constructing the Alamo mission on a piece of land at Bracketville in Texas, owned by millionaire rancher James T. "Happy" Shahan.

"There were no studio sets," Michael Wayne told me. "*The Alamo* was constructed in its entirety so we could film anywhere in it. All the rooms were designed so you could be outside, go through the door, and you were in a room designed so filming could take place. It was actually cheaper than renting space at a studio."

Duke elaborated: "I couldn't have done it all without the help of my son Michael, who was credited as assistant producer, but he did a helluva lot an actual producer would have done. I have so many people to thank for that picture, you'll just have to look down the cast and credits, and every one of them made a priceless contribution."

The Alamo told the story of how, in 1836, 185 Texans and volunteers from Kentucky under the leadership of Davy Crockett tried to defend a broken-down mission-turned-fortress against 5,000 Mexican troops led by the Mexican general Santa Anna. Commanding the makeshift garrison was Colonel Travis, whose sole mission was to halt the enemy long enough for General Sam Houston to raise an army to fight Santa Anna and bring about independence for Texas from Mexico. Second in command at the Alamo was Colonel James Bowie.

There were plenty of small roles for many of Duke's friends, such as Hank Warden, Olive Carey, and Wayne's regular stuntman Chuck Roberson. But getting the right actors for the principal roles didn't always prove easy, and Wayne was not always initially satisfied with what he got.

A good many actors in Hollywood received copies of the script by James Edward Grant, including Charlton Heston. "There seemed good reasons to me not to do the film," he told me. I wondered if one of them might be because it was being directed by John Wayne. He simply replied, "It might be."

Duke told me, "I wanted Charlton Heston to play Bowie. He could have played Travis. Either part. But he didn't want to do it. United Artists insisted on Richard Widmark. I thought he was wrong for the part. I was wrong. He was magnificent. We didn't always see eye to eye, but he was just great as Bowie.

"I could have cast a lot of American actors as Travis. There are two reasons why I chose Laurence Harvey. One is, a lot of American actors didn't want to be directed by John Wayne. The other reason is that Harvey is a hell of an actor. We were bringing a touch of British class to the picture. This was an actor of the British stage, and I admire those kind of actors. I was kind of jealous of Kirk [Douglas] when he announced he'd got Laurence Olivier and Peter Ustinov and Charles Laughton for *Spartacus*. Olivier could have played Travis with his eyes closed. Laughton would have been a little too large. But those are class actors, as you well know. And they gave the best performances in Kirk's film. So when I couldn't get a good American actor to play Travis, I thought, the hell with it, let's get some British class. And that's what we had in Laurence Harvey. And the critics were unkind about *him*. I mean, this was a guy who could play the part as an aristocrat, which Travis was. He could do a Texas accent that was just subtle enough not to sound fake. And when he had to be a son of a bitch, he could do it, and when he had to get the sympathy vote from the audience, he could do that. I think he gave a better performance than Chill Wills, and Chill got Oscar nominated and Harvey didn't."

I had the pleasure of meeting Laurence Harvey at a private function in 1972. He was clearly ill (sadly, he died the following year) but he spoke with energy and enthusiasm about *The Alamo* when I asked him about his experiences making it. He recalled his first meeting with Wayne: "It wasn't an audition. There was no actual screen test. When I first met Duke, he had John Ford with him. I think Ford muscled in on the auditions whether Duke liked it or not. Ford sat there with a big cigar, and I was trying to tell Duke about my extensive experience on the stage at Stratford and the Old Vic. He said, 'Don't give me all that horseshit about art. I'm up to my ass trying to get this picture together. Can you do a Texas accent?'

"So I said to Ford, 'Can I have a cigar?' He looked puzzled but he gave one to me, and I lit it, and as I puffed on it, I said with a soft Texas accent, 'But soft, what light through yonder window breaks. It is the east, and Juliet is the sun . . .' And I went on, and that just cracked Wayne up. Ford just grunted, 'We haven't got much time. Just sign him up.'

"You didn't see a lot of British actors getting to play Americans in American movies. I must have been one of the first."

To play the role of Smitty — who was actually based on a character called Deaf Smith because he *was* deaf — pop singer Frankie Avalon was chosen. "I knew we needed someone to bring in a young audience, especially someone who would appeal to teenage girls," Michael Wayne explained. "So I suggested we give the part to Frankie Avalon. Well, my father wasn't keen on *that* idea, but I convinced him, and we all agreed that Frankie did a good job."

With "nepotism running rife in my family," as Wayne put it, his son Patrick was cast as Captain James Butler Bonham. "We have a joke in the family," said Patrick. "We say that my father had looked forward to that picture for so long that when he started he was right for the Frankie Avalon part."

Ken Curtis, Duke's friend and a John Ford regular, got the crucial part of Captain Dickinson. Wayne needed a little girl to play Dickinson's daughter, Angelina Lisa. Duke said, "One morning I was watching Aissa playing on the living-room rug with a doll, and I noticed that her focus on the doll was intense. I knew I'd found my little Dickinson girl." Aissa received a fee of $250 a week which was deposited in her own personal savings account.

To play Sam Houston, Wayne asked Richard Boone, whom I interviewed in 1977 when he was in London filming *The Big Sleep*. He told me, "I thought the part of General Houston was a wonderful cameo role. The critics had a go at Jimmy Grant, but he wrote great dialogue — for *me*, anyway. Duke was kind of funny because he would have liked to have played Houston, and he'd say to me, 'I think Houston might have done this,' or 'Houston would have said it like this.' And I'd say, 'Duke, you hired me to act, not to listen to how you'd play the part. Now just tell me where to hit my marks.' And he'd go, 'You're damn right.' I respected Duke as an actor, and I came to respect him as a director because although he didn't always know the right words to use in directing you, he by God did the job and it was a helluva good job."

To play Flaca, a widow Crockett rescues and then falls for, Wayne chose Linda Cristal, a stunningly beautiful twenty-four-year-old actress from Mexico who had starred in a number of unimportant films in Mexico, Italy, and America. When I telephoned Linda Cristal in 1979 for my planned John Wayne tribute, she recalled enthusiastically, "One day I was approached by this tall man who said to me, 'I'm John Wayne,' and I'm looking up at him and, yes, it really was John Wayne. He said, 'I'm going to be making a picture called *The Alamo* and you're going to be my leading lady.' And I said, 'Thank you.' About two years passed and I got a phone call, and it was Duke, and he said, 'We're going to start filming, so can you come and play the part I promised you?'

"I was very young and Duke was in his fifties, and he was so terrified about our love scenes that he kept putting them off until he found a reason not to do them at all. So I never even got to kiss Duke Wayne, even though the characters we played loved each other very much.

"It was due to Duke casting me in *The Alamo* that I then got to do *Two Rode Together* with James Stewart and Richard Widmark, and which was directed by John Ford. And that eventually led to the television series *The High Chaparral*, which was the thing that really made me famous. So I owe it all to Duke."

One actor who chased a part but failed to get it was Sammy Davis Jr., who revealed this to me when I met him at a party in London thrown by Peter Lawford in 1974: "When I heard there was a part for a Negro in Duke's film, I managed to get a look at the script and I thought, 'Man, this Negro slave has been written with integrity and dignity.' Usually Negro slaves were portrayed as stereotypes, but this was different. It was unlike anything I'd done before. I wanted to take a chance and play a straight role instead of always being the song-and-dance comedian. So I personally asked Duke if he would consider me. He said, 'But this is the role of a slave. It's a straight part.' I said, 'I know. That's why I want to do it.' He said, 'Okay, let me think about it.'

"I'm pretty sure he was going to give me the part, but he had a lot of influential Texans investing in the film, and they didn't like the idea that I was seeing [Swedish actress] May Britt at the time. They disapproved of a man of color going out with a girl who was white. Duke was upfront with me about it. I respected him for being upfront, but I was damn disappointed not to get the gig."

Duke never considered anyone other than William H. Clothier to be his director of photography. One of their first discussions was about what format they would shoot *The Alamo* in. Clothier told me, "At that time, CinemaScope looked just awful because it distorted people. You couldn't get good close-ups without it looking like people had the mumps. But there were a number of good 70mm processes around then which not only eliminated the distortion but gave greater depth.

"So I was alarmed when Duke said he was thinking about shooting *The Alamo* in Cinerama, which I thought would be just a *terrible* mistake. In theory it sounded good, but as Henry Hathaway would tell you, the way the Cinerama camera worked, with three films running behind three lenses in a special camera, gave you all sorts of problems. The first was that you couldn't get any kind of close-ups. If you watch *How the West Was Won*, most of which Hathaway directed, and some of it John Ford directed, you don't see a single close-up. You can't get closer than a shot from the waist up. And you can't change lenses. But worst of all, you could see the joins."

The joins Hathaway was referring to were due to the giant picture being made up of three different films which ran through the Cinerama camera simultaneously, and were projected onto the giant, curved Cinerama screen. The process had been introduced in 1952, a year before CinemaScope, and the result was the first virtual reality cinema experience because it gave the audience a feeling it was moving with the camera.

Clothier recalled, "Duke thought the battle scenes would look tremendous in Cinerama. He was actually a little ahead of his time in his thinking because up until then, all the films shot in Cinerama were just travelogues. There hadn't been a dramatic film made in Cinerama.

"I said to Duke, 'If you shoot in Cinerama, you're going to have to also shoot a version in CinemaScope,' because only a few theatres in the world were equipped to show Cinerama. So you'd have to make a second version of the film shot in CinemaScope for general release, and then you had a film shot from a slightly different angle, and it would have the distortions, and, oh . . . I just had to talk him out of it.

"I said to Duke, 'Look, Michael Todd created Todd-AO as his version of Cinerama.' Todd-AO was meant to be a single-camera version of Cinerama, shot on 70mm film and intended to be shown on a big curved screen. Like Cinerama, the problem was that there were not enough theatres equipped with a big curved screen. But there were a lot of premier theatres with 70mm projectors, a big screen, and stereophonic sound, and any of them could show the film. Further, the 70mm negative could easily be transferred into ordinary 35mm anamorphic, or CinemaScope, prints. So we shot it in Todd-AO, and it was breathtaking. And thank God, Panavision refined the anamorphic process, so we didn't lose quality when it was transferred to 35mm."

Production costs quickly soared, with thousands of uniforms to be made, props to create, sets to build, and temporary housing erected for not only the principal actors and the supporting actors, but also for the two thousand extras. Before Wayne was able to roll a single foot of film, the United Artists money ran out. Determined not to cut his losses and see his dream dissolve into a financial fiasco, he mortgaged everything he had — his house, Batjac, all the family cars, anything and everything of value, announcing, "I have everything I own in this picture, except my necktie."

His desperate actions to keep the production solvent included persuading a consortium of Texas investors, which included wheeler-dealer Clint Murchison who would soon own the Dallas Cowboys, to invest in the film. The final cost of making *The Alamo* would come to $12 million.

Before principal photography began, Wayne decided to use the two thousand extras he had there to play the Mexican soldiers, and he filmed some of the opening shots of the final battle as the Mexicans begin to advance. Duke recalled, "For the beginning of the battle, when the Mexican army begins their advance, we had two thousand men who all had to begin moving at the same time, and to get it on film Bill Clothier had five Todd-AO cameras set up. He and I went to each camera to check the blocking of each shot, and we'd go over the fine details to make sure every cameraman knew what to do. He stayed in contact with each cameraman by walkie-talkie. I had various assistants among the extras to make sure their movements would be coordinated. It was like a military operation. Then when I gave the cue, the cameras all began rolling and the extras began their advance. It was the most awesome sight."

Finally, principal photography began in September 1959. Ken Curtis remembered, "Duke had a priest come on the set of the first day of filming to bless the production. I'm not sure why Duke decided to do that. I guess he felt making *The Alamo* was his kind of divine mission, and he might just as well get the good Lord on his side from the outset. It was actually an impressive moment when the priest said his prayer. If it were anyone but Duke, I would have said the prayer was a gimmick. But you didn't get gimmicks with Duke — especially not when it involved God."

Filming began with everyone in high spirits. The cast, crew, and extras lived largely on thick Texas steak. Wayne told the press, "I hope that seeing the battle of the Alamo will remind Americans that liberty and freedom don't come cheap. I hope our children will get a sense of our glorious past, and appreciate the struggle our ancestors made for the precious freedom we now enjoy — and sometimes take for granted."

It would take eighty-one days in all to film *The Alamo*. Many involved felt that Wayne had taken on too much. The stress upon him increased and he became quick to lose his temper. He lost thirty-five pounds and his cigarette habit increased from sixty to a hundred Camels a day. Not surprisingly, he developed a terrible smoker's cough.

The man who often eased the tension was Laurence Harvey. Wayne told me, "What I best remember about Harvey is when things got a bit tense — which they did, and often — he'd just crack us up by going into Shakespeare with a Texas accent. And talk about the show must go on. That scene where we're on the battlements and listening to Santa Anna's messenger, and Travis lights the cannon. When it fired, it recoiled — right over Harvey's foot. And he didn't even flinch. He knew it would ruin the take. When I said, 'Cut!' only then did he cry out in pain. Now *that's* a professional. He had that foot in plaster for weeks, and I had to keep his damaged foot out of shot."

Laurence Harvey had a wonderful time making *The Alamo*. He said, "It wasn't always fun, but it was never dull. John Wayne treated me very well. I found him to be most amiable, although as time went by his fuse burned ever shorter and quicker. But he never lost his temper with me. I think he thought I was *Sir* Larry Harvey because I came from the British theatre.

"I liked the part I had — Colonel William Barrett Travis. But there was quality in the script, at least as far as my part was concerned. It had many layers to it. And I liked working with Wayne, and I liked Richard Widmark, although things started a bit strained between Wayne and Widmark. But they sorted themselves out and got on with working together in, shall we say, a professional manner."

Stories have surfaced over the years that Wayne and Widmark supposedly got into a fight and had many heated arguments. But when I spoke to Widmark in 1979, he said, "We didn't start off too well, and so much has been made of our so-called feud that it's kind of gone down as Hollywood lore. The fact is, I thought Duke, who's a really nice man, was not an actor's director. He was great at working with William Clothier to get some good shots, both the action scenes and the intimate scenes. But he couldn't help actors. I already had an idea how I wanted to play Bowie, but Duke would show me what he wanted me to do, and it would have been Bowie as played by John Wayne. So we had some friction to start with. But we were both professionals. We had a job to do, and Duke had more than anybody else to do. I take my hat off to him. We needed to get on because we needed a certain chemistry on screen. Crockett and Bowie liked each other and we had to make the audience believe that. We had some nice scenes together, and once we'd made it clear where we both stood, we got on with the work, which is all that matters. And we had some good times. We laughed a lot."

Wayne's attempts to show his actors how to play their parts seems to be the only major criticism anyone involved in the film had. Said Ken Curtis, "Duke didn't know how to motivate an actor with just a word or two. He'd say, 'Do it this way.' If you watch the scene where Pat Wayne rides into the Alamo, gets off his horse, takes a drink, and throws the ladle away, he does it just the way his father would do it. He'd always say, 'Be graceful . . . like me, goddammit.' But I can't complain because it was just about the nicest part I've ever had."

Clothier had only praise for Wayne: "You know, one way or another Duke was getting the job done, and it was being done with quality. Duke didn't hog the movie. There are some wonderful scenes. Like when Bowie gets a message in his hat that his wife has died. Duke let Richard go with that scene. He put him in the foreground, and Duke stood back in the shadows while Laurence Harvey as Travis reprimands Bowie for receiving information. Widmark was superb in that scene, and so was Harvey. And Duke just stayed back and let the other actors have the scene, which is as it should be.

"Every morning Duke and I would get up early and have breakfast, and then we'd go out on the set or to a location, and we'd discuss and plan every shot we were going to use that day. Duke knew the entire script, and we were able to plan each shot, so when we began work with the cast and crew, we knew exactly what we were going to do. Duke would even tell me what kind of natural light he wanted, so we were able to plan which shots to start with to get the morning light, and which shots we'd do in the afternoon so the light would be right. He learned that from Ford. And he knew in his head what he wanted.

"I'd say the biggest problem he had was that during a take, he'd mouth the other actors' lines, like he was willing them to get it right first take. And I'd make a motion to him, and he'd suddenly realize what he'd been doing, and he'd get mad at himself.

"A week or two after we started, John Ford arrives on the set. He wasn't invited. He didn't ask if he could come down. He just turned up. Now, that would have been okay if he hadn't brought his director's chair with him and set it up next to me. He'd sit there watching Duke direct, and this intimidated Duke which didn't help his concentration. Ford would loudly say, 'Jesus Christ, Duke, that's not the way to do it.' Duke was very patient with Ford who began telling him how to make the film. Duke just didn't want to hurt the old man's feelings, but he said to me, 'He's gonna take over the whole goddamn picture. What the hell am I gonna do?'

"I said, 'I got an extra first cameraman and we got plenty of crew we can do without for a while. Give the old man a second unit.' Duke said, 'Bill, why didn't I think of that?' I said, 'Because you've got enough to think about.' "

Michael Wayne told me, "When JW decided Ford could direct a second unit, he gave *me* the job of watching over him. That was a pretty rough situation to be put in, trying to keep John Ford in line. My father said to me, 'Whatever you do, don't let him near any of the principal actors.' I said, 'Why me?' He said, 'You're not afraid of him.' Well, there were still some rough moments between Ford and myself because he'd keep asking if I could bring over Richard Widmark or Laurence Harvey, and I'd have to think of excuses for them not being available."

Clothier recalled, "Ford shot a lot of stuff, most of it expensive wastage, just because Duke didn't want to upset him. There are one or two moments in the film that Ford directed. Like the two guys who are always saying, 'Do it mean what I think it do?' 'It do.' Ford shot their death scene during the final battle, and that's in the film. But so much of what he shot wasn't used that he was furious at Duke. For a long time after, he was rough on Duke."

When the critics panned Wayne's direction, he didn't try to blame others but took it all on the chin. However, when he had someone like me who liked the film, he was free to share the credit. He told me, "I had sole credit as director but I couldn't have done it without Bill Clothier and Cliff Lyons [second-unit director]. I'd tell Bill what I wanted, and he got what I wanted. The critics think they know it all and write about how well I directed the big battle scene. But I left Cliff to direct that as second-unit director. So while he was directing the action, I was directing the principal actors in the scenes that were dialogue scenes, and Bill Clothier was correcting my mistakes. And then I worked with Stuart Gilmore on editing it all together, and Gilmore did a damn fine job. If you've got good stuff on film, the editor makes it all come together. He can even correct mistakes in the process. So I can't take all the credit for the battle scenes. Shows how much the critics know."

Ken Curtis recalled a scene from the film that was eventually cut: "There's a scene where Joan O'Brien, who played my wife, and I have to sing a song to our daughter, played by Duke's own daughter, Aissa. The song was called 'Tennessee Babe' and it was kind of too sentimental really. And then Aissa had a line which was 'We are three together' and I said, 'Always, honey.' Well, Duke told me that Aissa used to say that to him and Pilar, and he'd say, 'Always, honey.' But when he and Pilar separated, he'd think of Aissa as a little girl saying that line, and he'd just break down.

"Aissa had another scene which was cut, where she had to hide in a cart from the Mexican soldiers. Duke told her, 'This isn't real, sweetheart. Just remember, it's only make-believe. Men dressed as soldiers and holding guns are going to pull back the cover and find you under it.'

"Duke covered her over, and when he was ready he yelled, 'Action!' And the soldiers yanked back the cover and poor little Aissa found herself staring at several bayonets barely inches from her face which nobody had told her about. She gave an ear-piercing scream, and proving she had Wayne blood in her, she flew into a rage, yelling at her mother, the actors, the crew, everyone. But she knew better than to yell at her father.

"When it came to filming the battle scenes, it was amazing to see. I was up on the battlements, and everyone was in place inside the Alamo, and we watched these thousands of extras marching toward us. We opened fire, explosions were going off. Actors and extras were dropping dead on cue. The coverage that Duke and Bill Clothier got was amazing. Once we had all the master shots, we spent many days covering little episodes of the battle. Cliff Lyons directed second unit and he had the Mexican cavalry charging forward, and when explosions went off, all his riders and horses were trained to fall to the side. In the old days, they used trip wires which sent the horses toppling head over heels, and a lot of horses got maimed and killed. Cliff Lyons and his stuntmen and their horses were so well trained and well rehearsed, that even though there are some spectacular horse falls, not one animal got hurt. And I don't know of any stuntman who got seriously injured, which was a miracle because you often hear how on big pictures stuntmen get injured, and some are even killed."

Filming wrapped on 20 December 1959. After Christmas, Wayne immersed himself in the postproduction. An important part of this process was the composing and recording of the film's score.

"I never had any other thought than to ask Dimitri Tiomkin to compose the score," Wayne told me.

But what really persuaded Wayne was Tiomkin's score for *Rio Bravo*. I met

Tiomkin at a media bash for the London premiere of his production of *Tchaikovsky*, where he told me, "I used a piece of music in *Rio Bravo* called 'De Guello' which is composed for the trumpet and which the Mexicans played during the siege of the Alamo as a way of trying to make the defenders of the Alamo anxious. And in *Rio Bravo* the men who have the town surrounded play that music. I always thought it was a most beautiful piece of music and couldn't understand why it would upset anyone.

"John Wayne said to me, 'We have to have that music in *The Alamo*.' I said, 'It won't upset the defenders.' He said, 'I know, but can you find different ways to use it?' I said, 'Yes,' and I used it as a lament for the dead and dying Mexican soldiers, I used it as a piece of military music just before the battle, and I used it to glorify Crockett's death.

"It was the biggest picture I had worked on up till then, and it gave me the opportunity to really expand my repertoire. I already had a certain style, so people tell me, but *The Alamo* widened my horizons and gave me the reputation of being able to compose for epic films, which is just about all I went on to do after *The Alamo*."

Although I'm not an admirer of Tiomkin's music, *The Alamo* actually turned out to be a great, and arguably his finest, score, which proved that Wayne had an instinct for film music, something not all directors have.

There was not a single detail of *The Alamo* that Wayne bypassed. He said, "I put my heart and soul into that picture. It said everything I felt about my country, about freedom, and about dictatorships. It was seen by those to the left as a piece of propaganda, and hell it was, but it was also first and foremost a great story and a grand piece of entertainment."

But was it another way for him to express his views about Communism? He told me, "It was, in part. But it was more than that. I hoped it would convey to people all over the free world that they owed a debt to all men who gave their lives fighting for freedom. I hope that the battle of the Alamo will remind people everywhere that the price of freedom and liberty doesn't come cheap.

"I was always inspired by the story because I don't know of any other moment in American history which portrays the courage of men any better. It's the courage of those men that always moved me. Since then men — and women — have shown many great acts of courage in the face of adversity. But what for me was the defining moment when men put their lives before all else, was when Travis tells all the volunteers who are on their horses and ready to withdraw from a battle they know they can't win, that they can leave the Alamo without fear of criticism or shame. And every one of those volunteers got off their horses and stood behind Travis. It's a story for all the world, but it is a special story for the patriots of America."

In all his blazing patriotic glory, in May 1960, Wayne publicly criticized Sinatra for hiring screenwriter Albert Maltz, one of the Hollywood Ten, to write *The Execution of Private Slovik*. Based on a book by William Bradford Huie, it told the true story of the only American to be executed as a deserter during the Second World War. Wayne commented, "I disliked the book because it portrayed our military as the heavies. I never thought Sinatra was a Commie, but he hired a Commie to write a screenplay the Communists would have just loved.

"When I heard about it, I was so goddamn mad, I told a reporter, 'I wonder how Sinatra's crony, Senator John Kennedy, feels about Sinatra hiring such a man.' The whole thing became a minefield, especially when Hedda Hopper attacked him in her column — so did the Hearst Press. I heard that Kennedy put pressure on Frank, and he had to back down. And he sure as hell didn't like it. He ended up paying Maltz seventy-five thousand dollars *not* to write the goddamn thing.

"The next time I saw Frank was at a charity benefit, and he'd been drinking heavily. He walked up to me — and he's not exactly tall enough to see eye to eye with me — and he said, 'You seem to disagree with me.' I told him, 'Just take it easy, Frank. We can talk about this later.' And he said, 'I want to talk about it right *now!*' It's a good thing some of his friends pulled him away because I'd sure hate to have flattened him."

Sammy Davis Jr. recalled the incident: "There was a benefit for retarded children at the Moulin Rouge nightclub. Everyone who came had to pay a hundred dollars, and they had to come dressed in costume. Duke turned up as a cowboy, which didn't surprise anybody, and Frank came as a Red Indian, so that kind of put them at odds to begin with. It all started okay. Duke got up and sang 'Red River Valley.'

Frank did his 'The Lady Is a Tramp,' but later, after Frank had had a few drinks, he started annoying Duke and trying to pick a fight with him. And there are all these poor retarded kids watching, and they must've been thinking, 'Man, we're gonna see a cowboy and Injun fighting.' I thought Duke was going to deck Frank, but Frank got dragged away before he got hurt. Frank and Duke had a long-running feud."

Wayne explained, "For a long time, Frank and I never got along, not just because he's such a goddamn liberal, but because he always thought he was a gangster. I mean, he *was* a gangster. Who the hell doesn't know he's in with the Mafia?"

Carl Foreman was incensed by Wayne's actions to stop Sinatra making his film. At his London office in 1978, Foreman told me, "Wayne always boasted he'd run me out of Hollywood, and I decided it was payback time. I made a film called *The Victors*, which was an antidote to all the flag-waving films that glorified war — the kind Wayne had made for years. It was an antiwar film, and I wrote into it a scene where American GIs are forced to watch the only American deserter to be shot in the Second World War. The whole scene was played in the stark whiteness of the snow at Christmas, and on the soundtrack, over the whole scene, I put Sinatra singing 'Have Yourself a Merry Little Christmas.' That was my swipe at Wayne, and Sinatra loved it."

Wayne was aware of Foreman's "swipe," but disregarded it, saying, "*The Victors* was probably the most unsuccessful war film of the 1960s. Nobody went to see it."

Wayne continued postproduction on *The Alamo* until he finally had to accept he'd reached a point where he could no nothing more. He was ready, in May 1960, to begin work on his second picture for Twentieth Century Fox, *North to Alaska*. The comedy Western reunited Wayne with Henry Hathaway. "After *The Alamo*," Duke told me, "it was a relief not to have to do anything but remember my own lines."

Meanwhile, the publicity campaign for *The Alamo* got under way, run by Russell Birdwell, the man who had promoted, among others, *Gone with the Wind* and *The Outlaw*.

"I made a bad error of judgment over the publicity," Wayne said, blaming himself for what turned out to be one of the most infamous publicity campaigns in Hollywood history.

Ken Curtis said, "Duke's mistake was in

giving Birdwell a free hand. In fact, his mistake was in hiring Birdwell in the first place. Birdwell's greatest success was in selling Jane Russell's breasts [in *The Outlaw*]. But selling *The Alamo* was different. We all know Duke made the film as a patriotic statement, but that wasn't the angle to sell to the public. They wanted action, romance, comedy. They didn't want to be told that if they were patriots, they would see *The Alamo*, and that's what Birdwell's publicity campaign said. It was in poor taste, and it upset — well, not so much the public — it got the media's backs up. That's why I think the critics went for it in such a savage way, they were like hounds tearing a deer apart. They just didn't give the film a chance."

When *The Alamo* was premiered 24 October 1960, at the Woodlawn Theatre in San Antonio, the critics, as Ken Curtis said, did indeed go for it like a pack of hounds.

The most famous criticism of *The Alamo* came from *Newsweek*, which called it "the most lavish B picture ever made." *Time* was a little less cruel: "*The Alamo* is the biggest Western ever made. Wayne & Co. have not quite managed to make it the worst."

The *New Yorker* said that Wayne had "turned a splendid chapter of our past into sentimental and preposterous flapdoodle. Nothing in *The Alamo* is serious. Nothing is true. *The Alamo* is a model of distortion and vulgarization."

Variety thought the picture had "a good measure of mass appeal" but noted that "in spite of the painstaking attempts to explore the characters of the picture's three principal heroes, there is an absence of emotional feeling, of a sense of participation. With the rousing battle sequence at the climax, for which a goodly share of credit must go to second-unit director Cliff Lyons, the picture really commands rapt attention. It is as actor that Wayne functions under his own direction in his least successful capacity. Generally playing with one expression on his face, he seems at times to be acting like a man with $12 million on his conscience."

The most damning criticism came from the *Southern California Prompter* which, as Wayne had said, reviewed Duke's politics and not the film. "If [Wayne] is saying that what America needs is about ten million men with the courage and determination of Davy Crockett, Jim Bowie, and Colonel Travis, the point is well-taken. It may also occur to some that he is suggesting that the easy answer to today's complex problems is to pit this raw courage against Russia's ten million Santa Annas, the result of which may well be a worldwide Alamo and instead of a shrine we may have only a cosmic incinerator full of ashes. If this is what Wayne is proposing, the defenders of the Alamo were not only brave but smarter than those who speak for them. Their fate was extinction but this was not their purpose."

Over the years the film has gained greater acclaim, and I am at a loss to understand those who damned the film in 1960 (and those old boys who still insist on damning it today). I was not the only one. Laurence Harvey said, "The critics were most unkind about just about everything to do with the film, which I understand was something of a backlash against Wayne's politics. I mean, they absolutely tore him and the film apart. I couldn't understand why it was criticized so vehemently."

The screenplay by James Edward Grant has, at times, a simple poetry to it that gives the film an authentic feeling for what Travis describes as "cracker-barrel philosophy" and "homespun wisdom." Critics accused Grant's screenplay of being too "talky," but it is the dialogue that carefully establishes the characters.

Wayne gave me his response: "When we premiered the film, everyone said it was too long. I said, 'How can it be too long? It's not as long as *Gone with the Wind*, and that didn't have any action scenes in at all.' It was the fucking critics. The left-wing critics on the East Coast — they still had it in for me, and they didn't like the idea I was saying that freedom from dictatorship was bought with blood. They didn't like it that I was using the Alamo as a metaphor for America, and although I wanted to show the Mexicans with dignity, it was a warning against *anything* that stole our freedom, and yes, that included Communism.

"They didn't like that. They criticized my politics, not my film. So United Artists said, 'We gotta lose half an hour.' It broke my heart cutting so much out of my picture. But I know the people liked it. They still do. People still tell me they like it. That picture meant more to me — *means* more to me — than any other picture I made. Or will make."

Only recently have I been able to see Wayne's original 192-minute version, and among the scenes thrown out are some of the so-called "talky" scenes that explain the motivations of both Bowie and Travis. The film suffers for its cutting of some 30-odd minutes.

Wayne's performance has moments of exceptional emotion. His own style of minimal delivery coupled with Grant's often economical dialogue make for the most effective. Such a moment occurs in the scene in which Crockett sends Flaca, with whom he has only just fallen in love, away to safety. There is a look of deep despair in Crockett's eyes as the parson says, "You never pray, do you, Davy." Wayne almost turns from the camera as he replies in a low voice, as though he is trying not to show his heartbreak, "I never found the time." Those few words and Wayne's delivery tell a whole story.

Richard Widmark is excellent, Laurence Harvey is also good, and after the spectacular but ultimately tragic battle, the final scene of Mrs. Dickinson, her daughter Lisa, and their small Negro slave boy leaving the shattered mission brings a lump to the throat. Except for those with hard hearts.

Critics of the film have taken delight in stating that the film was not a financial success and lost money. Wayne was correct when he told me, "The critics always say it lost money. It only lost *me* money. United Artists did very well out of it. I sold all my shares in the picture to them to help pay off the debt I'd got myself in, and I ended up doing some work for them for free, so they were the ones who earned all the money.

"It cost 12 million dollars to make, and it took in almost 8 million dollars in America alone. It made at least as much again abroad. I make that at least 16 million dollars. I don't call that a box-office failure."

He was right. In *Variety*'s 1983 list of All-Time Western Champs, it reached twenty-fifth position, and in an inflation-adjusted list, it came out as being the tenth most successful Western up to that time.

United Artists knew there was still money to be made from it; it was reissued several years later and its box office continued to rise until it was number 117 on the 400 top-grossing films of all time up to 1970.

With poor reviews and initially slow business, Wayne was depressed. Then came worse news: Not long after the premiere of *The Alamo*, Ward Bond died from a massive heart attack at the age of fifty-five. Wayne was just two years younger than Bond, and he felt his own sense of mortality. At the funeral, Duke fought back his tears to deliver the eulogy.

Loretta Young recalled, "I would call Duke from time to time, and ask how he was. After Ward Bond died, he told me he felt as though he had a black cloud over him and he couldn't shake it off. I told him to try praying. The next time I talked to him, I asked how he was doing. He said, 'I took your advice. Somebody upstairs listened. It kind of lightened the load.' I was so glad about that."

Although he was hardly an old man, Wayne's fifty-three years felt heavier upon him than they should have. But the years of hard drinking, heavy smoking, and a losing battle with his weight made him look older and slowed him down. Fortunately, on-screen he merely appeared rugged.

20

Working Twenty Years
for Nothing

North to Alaska had been having its own
problems *before* filming on it began, and everybody fought hard to keep it all a secret
from Wayne.

Hathaway, who directed and produced
the film, told me, "When we began
shooting, we barely had any kind of a
script. For a long time, the project had
simply been a business deal made by agent
Charles Feldman with little more than the
title of *North to Alaska*. The title could
have meant anything. Feldman represented
me; the writers, John Lee Mahin and
Martin Rackin, Wayne; and a young
French actress, Capucine, who just happened to be Feldman's latest flame. So
Feldman went to Buddy Adler, who was
then head of production at Twentieth Century Fox, and through sheer tenacity talked
Adler into green-lighting *North to Alaska*

— although at that time I wasn't involved. Feldman had another director, Richard Fleischer, who'd done good work with Kirk Douglas on *The Vikings* and *20,000 Leagues Under the Sea*. So Fleischer was pretty hot in those days.

"Feldman's deal with Fox was that Mahin and Rackin would write the script for John Wayne to star in with Fleischer directing, and it would all be signed and sealed even before the writers got to work on the script.

"Feldman told Duke, who was still finishing off *The Alamo*, that the film had the green light, and typically of Duke, he didn't ask to see the script. If he had done, there would have been no script to show him. But from time to time he asked how the screenplay was progressing, and Feldman would always say, 'It's nearly finished.' I don't think Mahin and Rackin had even started writing it. They were still trying to come up with a story to fit the title.

"When Richard Fleischer found out there was no script, he pulled out and I took over. So I started badgering the writers to get the script finished because I knew that if we didn't have a finished screenplay to show Duke as soon as he was finished on *The Alamo*, he would pull out. Then we had a damn strike by the Writers Guild, so Mahin and Rackin couldn't finish the screenplay. Duke turned up for work and I had to explain that we would work on the screenplay as we went along. Somehow it turned out not to be a disaster."

John Lee Mahin told me, "Marty and I knew we had to have a story about gold prospecting, because there was no other reason for anyone to go north to Alaska. But we needed a plot. We decided to go for broad comedy and romance with a few fistfights and a gunfight or two here and there. It was all thrown together without much thought other than to get it finished. Then we had to go on strike because the union told us to and we didn't finish the script. But with what we had written, although we didn't realize it at the time, we were setting the pattern for most of the next half-dozen Wayne films, mixing comedy with action. Wayne had a style of comedy that was all his own, and it proved a winning formula."

They finally had a weak story line in which Wayne, a gold prospector in Alaska, agrees to go and collect his partner's sweetheart and bring her back. The problem is, his partner's fiancée is already married, so Wayne brings his partner back a beautiful French girl. Playing Wayne's partner was Stewart Granger, who said, "Henry Hathaway was a sheer bully. I'd never come across his kind before. I couldn't remember a bloody line in the first scene I had with Wayne because of the way Hathaway chewed me out while he also chewed on his cigar. The more I blew my lines, the more he'd growl and chew on his cigar and I just became so terrified that I lost all my confidence. I became terribly depressed. Duke just took it all in his stride. He said to me, 'Aw, that's just Henry's way.' I said, 'This is supposed to be a comedy and we're supposed to be having fun. But I just feel ill.' Duke said, 'You're not a kid anymore. You're a grown man. Pull yourself together. If you don't like the way Henry talks to you, stand up to him. Tell him whatever kind of bastard you think he is.'

"So I took Duke's advice. I finally said to Hathaway, 'You don't like what I'm doing? Fine. How's this then? I think you're a lousy director and I think that picture you made in the desert with Sophia Loren was the most ridiculous thing I'd ever . . .' I suddenly remembered that Duke was in that film, and there was silence. I could feel Hathaway's eyes on me, and I could feel Duke's eyes on me. Duke said, 'You were saying?' And Hathaway said, 'I think he was going to say that film with Sophia Loren was the most ridiculous movie he'd ever seen.' They were all deadpan, and I was sure I would be fired — or beaten up. Wayne jabbed a finger in my chest, and said, 'Is that what you were gonna say?' I decided to stand up to him and I straightened my back, jabbed him in the chest, and said defiantly, 'That is *exactly* what I was going to say.' And Duke jabbed me again and said, 'That is *exactly* what that film was.' He looked over at Hathaway, winked, and said, 'Right, Henry?' And Hathaway nodded, and Duke just started laughing so much, I was never so relieved in my life.

"But Hathaway still bullied me through that picture. Eventually I just ignored it and took every curse and bellow from him as direction. Thank God I was working with Duke on that picture. He made it fun."

Not having quite so much fun, though, was Capucine, who played the French girl Wayne brings back for his partner. When I interviewed her at Pinewood Studios where she was filming *Arabian Adventure*, she told me, "I wish I could say I liked John Wayne very much. But I didn't. I just happened to be someone who was in a John Wayne picture. He knew it, and he expected everyone else to know it. He was not the man I had expected. I was surprised he wore a toupee because he was losing his hair. And I thought he was supposed to be so tall, but he wore lifts in his boots."

Actually, the subject of the "lifts" had come up before, and Wayne himself explained: "I've often heard people accuse me of being shorter than I am and trying to look bigger by having big heels on my boots. Of course I had big heels when I was in a Western. Cowboys had big heels. But this picture [*Brannigan*] isn't a cowboy picture. Here, look at my shoes. Do you see any lifts?" I said I didn't. He said, "Do I seem short to you?" He didn't.

Wayne did have a word or two to say about his fellow actors from *North to Alaska*. "Granger had a great sense of humor and we had a good time — once he overcame his fear of Henry Hathaway. Capucine was . . . well, she was Charlie Feldman's girlfriend and he was trying to make her into an international star. But she was all wrong for the part. Our writers had to make the leading lady French because that's what Charlie wanted. It was a fun film to make and to watch, but — damn it, I hate bad-mouthing a lady — Capucine was not very good, and we'll leave it at that."

Filming ended in August, and Hathaway was set the Herculean task of editing it in time for its opening, set for early November. It was met with lukewarm reviews but excellent business. While the media and even some people in the film industry were trying to tell the public that *The Alamo* was a failure, *North to Alaska* suddenly confirmed Duke Wayne as a big box-office star.

Then came the broadcast of the episode of *Wagon Train* that Wayne appeared in. Wayne, Bond, and Ford had planned to watch it together and have a good laugh. But Ford was deep in his own depression, Bond was in his grave, and Wayne was struggling with his own demons. Besides losing Ward Bond, he found himself facing financial ruin due to his own personal losses over *The Alamo*. He desperately needed to work to try and rebuild his fortune, and that meant he was going to have to make as many films as he could in as short a time as possible.

Some in Hollywood blamed Wayne for his own misfortunes. Darryl F. Zanuck stated, "I have great affection for Duke Wayne, but what right has he to write, direct, and produce a motion picture?"

Wayne was incensed by Zanuck's comments. He said, "I couldn't believe that there was such a backlash even in the industry I loved. I don't know — maybe I was being blamed for the writers who went to jail for being in contempt.

"It seemed there were some who didn't agree with Zanuck when it was announced that we were nominated for Academy Awards in six categories. We got six nominations, including Best Picture, Best Score, Best Supporting Actor [for Chill Wills], Best Song, Best Photography. But the people who thought like Zanuck got the last word because we won only for Best Sound.

"There's been a lot said about the publicity campaign for the Academy Awards. A full-page ad was taken out by Chill Wills in the *Hollywood Reporter* on his own cognizance, with a picture of the men who played the defenders of the Alamo standing behind a superimposed picture of Wills. It was bad taste."

The caption on Wills's ad read, "We of *The Alamo* cast are praying harder than the real Texans prayed for their lives in the real Alamo for Chill Wills to win the Oscar. Cousin Chills's acting was great!" It was signed "Your Alamo cousins."

"He'd been given no authority to do that," said Duke. "And it caused a storm. I called him up and told him if I saw him soon, he'd better start running fast.

"There was a lot of jostling for the Oscars. There always has been, and there always will be. But the only film that gets criticized for its Oscar campaign is *The Alamo*. Why is that? And which film won Best Picture that year? *The Apartment*. A comedy about how funny it is to let your boss use your apartment to commit adultery. *The Alamo* was about courage, justice, and freedom. Sour grapes? You bet."

Wayne's financial problems turned out to be worse than he'd realized when, in 1960, while trying to salvage what he could to pay off his *Alamo* debts, he discovered that Bo Roos had made many bad investments which had lost Duke a fortune. "I'd been hearing people saying that Bo Roos had screwed them, but I thought they were joking. Then I started wondering about it, so I asked my secretary Mary to take a look at my file at Roos's office. It should have been packed with papers about my investments. But all Mary found were mortgage papers on property in Culver City and the Flamingo Hotel in Acapulco.

"So I met with Roos and I asked him how much money I had. He said, 'Well, there's not a lot of actual cash. It's all invested.' He was getting mighty nervous and I was smelling a rat, and I said, 'Just tell me how much I can raise.' He said, 'Give me a couple of weeks.'

"So a couple of weeks go by and I asked him again: 'How much am I worth?' He was really squirming. He said, 'It isn't that simple.' I lost my patience then and I slammed my fist on his desk and said, 'It's a simple question. I've given you a goddamn fortune over the years. Millions of dollars! Where is it, goddamn it?'

"Well, I could see him giving up his charade as he slumped into his chair and said, 'It's all gone.' That did it. I blew my top. I told him I was going to sue him for screwing me, and I went to my lawyer who had his accountants go over Roos's books with a fine-tooth comb. Finally my lawyer came to me and said, 'The guy isn't a cheat. He hasn't stolen anything from you.

It's just a case of complete incompetence.'
I said, 'Nobody's that stupid to lose that
much money.' He said, 'Bo Roos is.'

"I said, 'I want to sue the living shit out
of that son of a bitch.' The more I looked
into things, the more I found out what had
been happening to my money. It was going
into dry oil wells, cheap Mexican hotels for
which he paid top prices, a shrimp company that went bankrupt, and on top of
that were his own fees and expenses. I was
stupid enough to trust him and not ask
questions over twenty years. And I wasn't
the only one. A lot of people had trusted
him and lost money.

"Then we found out that many of his expenses were of a dubious nature. Nothing
illegal. But when he came to Japan when I
was making that Huston film, he was
spending my fortune on geisha girls.

"In the end it was pointless suing him
because he was broke. Besides, my lawyer
told me if we went to court, *I'd* be the one
looking like an idiot for letting Roos spend
my money without asking him where it was
going for the past twenty years. So I had to
let it go.

"But Roos cost me the first twenty years
of my career. I'd worked for twenty years
for nothing."

Wayne began to solve his financial problems by signing a non-exclusive contract with Paramount for ten pictures, guaranteeing him a fee of $600,000 per film.

John Ford would direct his first film under this contract, *The Man Who Shot Liberty Valance*, but first he had a commitment to make a third film for Twentieth Century Fox, which would be *The Comancheros*. Upon its completion, Wayne would receive a full $2 million from Fox as originally agreed upon.

Pilar, however, had more on her mind than her husband's obsession with making money. Claire Trevor, who remained a close friend of Duke's to the day he died, said, "Pilar had become pregnant, but she lost the baby. She was feeling isolated and she was suffering from depression and anxiety, so she went to Peru for a holiday. She didn't stay long, and came home to find Duke was too busy with sorting out his problems to realize she needed him. He loved her deeply and he showered affection on her, but affection wasn't what she needed the most. She needed to feel she was more than just Mrs. John Wayne. So she pulled herself together and started to help run a charity called SHARE which raises money for handicapped children.

That did the world of good for her, and she did so much good for others."

If *North to Alaska* provided Wayne with the style of comedy he would inject into virtually all of his work, *The Comancheros* established Wayne as the mature Western hero who could shoot straight, punch hard, and still deliver a comical quip in the process. He played a Texas ranger on the trail of a Confederate renegade who plans to establish a new Confederate empire in Mexico.

Wayne's director from "The Three Mesquiteers" series, George Sherman, produced the film with Michael Curtiz directing from James Edward Grant's screenplay. Filming began in June 1961, in Moab, Utah. Sherman told me, "We actually began filming earlier than I'd planned because John Ford wanted Duke to be in his next picture [*The Man Who Shot Liberty Valance*] which needed to start at the end of the summer. I later wished we'd held off until he'd finished *Liberty Valance* before embarking on *The Comancheros* because Michael Curtiz proved to be too old and ill to take on such an ambitious project, and I would have probably found another director or directed it myself."

Stuart Whitman costarred as a gambler who reluctantly helps Wayne. When I interviewed him at Elstree Studios where he was making *The Monster Club* in 1980, he told me, "Duke Wayne was a pure delight to work with. With *The Alamo* behind him, he was free to enjoy himself playing a role that came to him as easy as falling off a log. And when Michael Curtiz became too ill to direct, Duke kind of unofficially took over, and I think he enjoyed doing it because he knew he didn't have the whole film on his shoulders as he had with *The Alamo*.

"He had his family with him and he managed to get his son Pat an important part, and his little daughter Aissa was also in it, playing his granddaughter. In fact, a lot of the people who worked with him on *The Alamo* had roles.

"I liked the comic touches Duke put into his part. I played a gambler from Louisiana and had a French name. In the script, he was supposed to call me 'monsieur.' He pronounced it 'mon-sewer' each time, and that was typical of Duke's self-effacing approach to himself. He played the tough Texas ranger who was uncultured, and that allowed him to laugh at his own image."

Capturing the stark but beautiful backdrop of Moab on film was William H. Clothier, who said, "By now I had become Duke's regular director of photography, and that suited me just fine because he was making wonderful outdoors productions, and I enjoyed location work. Duke had followed John Ford's example of having about him an extended family who he knew he could work with, from actors to technicians. He carried a lot of power and while he was able to let the producer, George Sherman, do the worrying, Duke was able to enjoy himself.

"Michael Curtiz was unwell much of the time. He had cancer, and so Duke very gently began taking on some of the director's responsibilities without Curtiz really being aware of it. Duke didn't want to offend Curtiz. Before the picture was finished, Curtiz was too ill to work and Duke took over as director. He was glad he had me with him because we knew how to work together because we had a routine we'd established during *The Alamo*."

Providing some glamour among the dusty backdrops and the violence was Ina Balin. "John Wayne seemed very much at ease, although most of my scenes were with Stuart Whitman," she said when I talked to her about Duke on the telephone in 1979. "When I was offered the part in a John Wayne film, I thought at first I would be Duke's romantic interest. But when I read the script, I saw that he was playing the older man while the younger man [Whitman] was the one I fall for. He said, 'Thank God I don't have to do any love scenes in this. It's so much easier to knock a guy down than it is to play love scenes.'

"He told me I reminded him of his wife because I have dark looks and he said we looked alike. I took that as a compliment because his wife Pilar was a tremendously beautiful woman. In fact, the name of my character was Pilar, which I think was Jimmy Grant's way of paying tribute to Duke's wife."

In the small but significant part of a gun-runner was Lee Marvin. "That was my first picture with Duke," he told me. "I only had a few scenes, but it was fun because mainly we had to drink and get drunk together, and that we could both do really well. Duke said to me, 'I think there's a great part for you in *The Man Who Shot Liberty Valance*.' I said, 'Which part would that be?' He said, 'Liberty Valance.' I said, 'Who's the man who shot him?' He said, 'Me.' I said, 'Duke, if anyone's gonna shoot me, I can't think of anyone I'd rather be shot by.' And he was as good as his word."

Finishing *The Comancheros* in mid-July 1961, Wayne collected his $2 million from Fox. He also discovered that Pilar was pregnant. She had waited a while before telling him because, since the birth of Aissa, Pilar had suffered three heartbreaking miscarriages. This pregnancy seemed fine.

It was also time to go to work on *The Man Who Shot Liberty Valance* at Paramount. Pilar was of the opinion that he was working too hard and too often, and so was his agent Charles Feldman, who wrote to him, saying, "I am very concerned about you, Duke, and your not getting a holiday and working week after week practically for the past year."

On reflection, Duke had to agree: "I was scared to death that I would never have financial security again, and I put that before all else, even though I was doing it for the good of all my family. I lost sight of what's really important in life. And I've paid the price for it." He was referring to the fact that by 1974 he and Pilar had separated, something I was completely oblivious to at the time.

John Ford had agreed to cast Lee

Marvin as Liberty Valance, and Wayne was cast as tough rancher Tom Doniphon. But it was really only a secondary role. The real starring role, that of mild-mannered lawyer Ranse Stoddard, was given to James Stewart who had only recently worked for Ford — for the first time — on *Two Rode Together*.

The bulk of the film was told in flashback, with the film opening with Senator Stoddard and his wife, played by Vera Miles, arriving in Shinbone for the funeral of Doniphon. Stoddard had helped to bring law and order to the frontier town and became famous as the man who shot brutal gunman Liberty Valance. Stoddard proceeds to tell the truth about what really happened all those years ago and only toward the end of the film does he reveal that it was Doniphon who shot Liberty Valance. The local newspaper editor, played by Edmond O'Brien, decided not to run the story he has just heard, stating, "When the legend becomes fact, print the legend."

The Man Who Shot Liberty Valance is curiously highly rated as one of Ford's greatest Westerns, with critics reading all kinds of nuances into the film. They talk about its claustrophobic atmosphere, created by the film being virtually entirely shot on Paramount's soundstages, and how the black-and-white photography created a dark and oppressive mood. If John Ford wanted the critics to think that, he was simply being true to the credo in which he believed in real life: to only ever print the legend.

William Clothier told me, "There was one reason and one reason only why the film was shot in black and white and on Paramount's soundstages. Paramount was cutting costs. Otherwise we would have been in Monument Valley or Bracketville and we would have had color stock. Ford had to accept those terms or not make the film. He accepted the terms, but when the time came to start work on it, he had already lost interest. He was in a foul mood, creating tension on the set between actors, treating Duke worse than he ever did, just being a real son of a bitch."

John Wayne admitted it wasn't a happy experience. "I was just wandering around while Jimmy Stewart and Lee Marvin had all the good scenes. I was a background prop almost, doing little for the story but to be the one who shoots Valance and then keeps it secret so the townsfolk'll think it was Jimmy. I didn't mind playing second fiddle for a change, but I had nothing to go on. I'd ask Pappy and he'd . . . well, he was pretty unhappy the whole time, and he didn't have a lot of advice for me."

Lee Van Cleef, who played one of Liberty Valance's thugs, put it more bluntly. "Ford was a complete bastard to Wayne. He'd abuse him and swear at him and call him a 'goddamn lousy actor.' Ford just seemed intent on humiliating the guy who got him the job of making that film, because Paramount said that if he couldn't get Wayne, who had some contractual obligation to him, they wouldn't back the film. And that's probably why he treated Duke that way. He didn't want Duke to think he was doing *him* any favors.

"I had a nice moment with Duke. We never were friends, and we hadn't worked together much, but we had a scene where I had to draw on him and he would simply knock the gun out of my hand. Before filming the scene, he said to me, 'Can you draw that gun?' I said, 'I can draw this gun so fast you won't be able to clap your hands before I put it between your hands.' He said, 'I'd like to see you try that.' So we did it. We got Lee [Marvin] to count one, two, three, and he clapped his hands and I drew my gun, and I had the gun between his hands before he could bring them to-gether.

"He said, 'That's pretty damn good. How am I gonna knock the gun out of your hand if you're too fast?' I said, 'It's okay, Duke. I'll slow it down for you.' He laughed and said, 'That's right nice of you to help an old actor out.' That's the nicest memory I have of John Wayne."

When I interviewed James Stewart in London in 1980, he remembered the way Ford created tension between his actors: "For the scenes at the beginning and the end when we were all playing our parts older, Woody Strode had his black hair grayed up, and he was put into overalls and a hat. And Ford asked me what I thought of Woody's wardrobe, and I said, 'Well, it looks a bit Uncle Remus–like to me.' I im-mediately knew I'd made a mistake when Ford said, 'What's wrong with Uncle Remus?' And he starts yelling, 'Hey, Woody, Duke, everyone, come over here and have a look at Woody. One of the . . . *players* . . . seems to have some objection. One of the . . . *players* . . . here doesn't like Uncle Remus. As a matter of fact, I'm not at all sure he likes Negroes.' Well, that had tensions rising on the set for a while."

Woody Strode recalled that incident, and

one other: "I appreciated John Ford for giving me a really good part in *Sergeant Rutledge*, but I didn't like him too much, I'm afraid. He tried to make out that Jimmy Stewart was a racist, and Jimmy is one of the nicest men you'll ever meet anywhere in the world.

"But the most damage Ford did was to the friendship me and Duke Wayne might have had. He kept needling Duke about his failure to make it as a football player, and because I had been a professional player, Ford kept saying to Duke, 'Look at Woody. He's a *real* football player.' It's like he'd needle him about whatever reasons he had for not enlisting in the war by asking Jimmy, 'How many times did you risk your life over Germany, Jimmy?' And Jimmy would kind of go, 'Oh, shucks' or whatever, and Ford would say to Duke, 'How rich did you get while Jimmy was risking his life?'

"This really pissed Wayne off but he would never take it out on Ford. He ended up taking it out on me. We had one of the few outdoors scenes where we hightail it out to his ranch in a wagon. He's driving and I'm kneeling in the back of the wagon. Wayne was riding those horses so fast that he couldn't get them to stop. I reached up to grab the reins to help, and he swung and knocked me away.

"When the horses finally stopped, Wayne fell out of the wagon and jumped off ready for a fight. I was in great shape in those days and Wayne was just getting a little too old and a little too out of shape for a fight. But if he'd started on me, I would have flattened him. Ford knew it, and he called out, 'Woody, don't hit him. We need him.'

"Wayne calmed down, and I don't think it was because he was afraid of me. Ford gave us a few hours' break to cool off. Later Wayne said to me, 'We gotta work together. We both gotta be professionals.' But I blame Ford for all that trouble. He rode Wayne so hard, I thought he was going to go over the edge. What a miserable film to make."

For Lee Marvin, the film offered him his most important role so far, and he gave credit to Wayne for getting him the part. "Fortunately I have no trouble playing a mean son of a bitch! I often wished Duke and I had had the chance to make a film where we had either good opposing roles, where he's the good guy and I'm the vilest meanest bastard ever to walk God's green earth, or we played on the same side, like Burt Lancaster and me in *The Professionals*.

We had a lot in common. We're not only experts in getting completely and totally drunk, but we both have culture too. He found out that I enjoy reading and appreciate works of art and that I like history, and I found out he enjoyed reading history and biographies, and he read everything ever written by Winston Churchill. I said to him, 'You're not the illiterate, uneducated ignoramus you'd like people to think,' and he said, 'Neither are you.' I said, 'Let's keep it to ourselves or we'll ruin our image.' "

Before *The Man Who Shot Liberty Valance* wrapped in November, *The Comancheros* had been rushed through postproduction and released in October 1961, to good reviews and tremendous business. Wayne was on his way to becoming not only the archetypal American movie star and the definitive Hollywood cowboy, but he was in the process of becoming a movie legend.

Michael Wayne put it more simply when he said, "The cowboy is the hero of American folklore. My father has become the symbol of that cowboy."

21

Winning the West, the War, and Wild Africa

The work did not let up, and Wayne continued to push himself without a break. He was off to East Africa with Howard Hawks to make *Hatari*, a film about the adventures of the people who capture big game for the world's zoos.

Wayne was joined by German actor Hardy Kruger, comedian Red Buttons, Italian beauty Elsa Martinelli, old friend Bruce Cabot as an Indian, and a lot of wild animals.

The film had a very loose plot formulated by Leigh Brackett, but it was mostly a series of largely improvised set pieces highlighted by the scenes of Wayne and the other actors catching wild animals for *real*.

Hawks said, "Duke had the time of his life chasing those rhinos in the truck. He didn't have a stuntman; he did it all himself. One time the rhino got in closer than we wanted, and for a moment or two Duke was in trouble. It made for a great scene.

"You couldn't control the animals. We chased nine rhinos, filmed them all, and we caught four. I told Wayne and the other actors just to ad-lib their lines, to say whatever came to mind, and if we had to have them dub over the lines in the studio later, that would be okay. So those scenes of the animals being chased and caught have a real sense of danger and excitement about them because they really were dangerous and exciting."

When I telephoned Red Buttons in 1979 for his recollections of Wayne, he said, "I worked with Duke twice, in *The Longest Day* and *Hatari*. On *The Longest Day* we worked together maybe two days. On *Hatari* we were in Africa for four months. So when you're with someone in Africa for four months, you *better* get on with them. Duke was easy to get on with, and we had a lot of fun. One night we were outside playing cards. A leopard walks out of the bush. He's walking toward us. I said quietly, 'Duke, there's a leopard walking toward us.' He said, 'Buttons, see what he wants.' That was the Duke. He had a quick wit, and he was having such a good time on that film. It was a damn shame we had to finish it."

In January 1962, Duke flew to France to appear in *The Longest Day*, Darryl F. Zanuck's epic about the D-day landings. Duke worked just four days on the film which featured most of Hollywood's major stars of the day. "I wanted to do the film because I thought it was an important picture," Wayne told me. Then, with that lopsided grin of his, he added, "and I wanted Zanuck to pay for what he'd said about me directing *The Alamo*. He paid all right, to the tune of two hundred and fifty thousand dollars. He got his money's worth anyway."

Wayne also accepted another cameo role in another all-star epic, this one a Western, *How the West Was Won*. Filmed in the original Cinerama format, the title gave an apt description of what the film was about, as seen through the eyes of three generations of one family.

Bernard Smith had the daunting task of producing this project which was so big it had three directors: Henry Hathaway, George Marshall, and John Ford. In 1969 my boss at Cinerama, where I was still a humble messenger boy, put a call through to Bernard Smith in Hollywood especially

454

for me to talk about *How the West Was Won*. Smith told me, "We had three units working under three directors, each with his own cameraman and his own cast, although some of the actors had parts in more than one episode. Henry Hathaway had the biggest job, filming the pioneer and river scenes, the wagon train, and the railroad. George Marshall directed the sequence with the outlaws and the runaway train. John Ford had the small segment. I didn't think he was up to anything really big because he was getting old and ill, and so I offered him the Civil War episode. He pretended like he was doing us all a big favor by accepting it, but I knew he liked doing it because he was a real expert on the Civil War.

"It was a simple enough job. There was an opening sequence where the boy [George Peppard] goes off to war, the aftermath of the battle of Shiloh, and then the boy returning home as an officer to find his mother dead and buried. The battle sequence was taken from *Raintree County*.

"Ford said to me, 'I gotta have John Wayne.' I said, 'That's what Henry Hathaway said. Wayne can't play two roles.' Ford said, 'I'll talk to him. I guarantee he'll do my episode.' And he was right. Wayne did a small cameo as General Sherman. Hathaway said to me, 'It's a mistake. People wanna see Duke killing the bad guys. But all he's gonna be doing is talking.' As far as I know, no one complained."

Wayne gave me three good reasons why he did *How the West Was Won*. "The first is because Pappy wanted me to do it; the second is because the studios [MGM and Cinerama] would be making donations to St. John's Hospital in Santa Monica from the profits; and the third is because it gave me the chance to play a character part. I said to Pappy, 'Come on, Coach, convince the men in suits to let us make a whole damn film about Sherman and Grant. This is the best role I've had since *The Searchers*.'

"Pappy wanted everything to look right. Henry Morgan as Grant grew a beard and looked a lot like Grant. I had hair hanging down below my hat and a week's growth of beard because Sherman thought winning the war was more important than getting his hair cut and his face shaved. I didn't sting the studio like I did Zanuck. I got a standard five thousand dollars for a week's work, which is what every star on that picture got paid per week. That way they kept costs down and made more profits which was good for MGM and Cinerama, which means it was good for the business, and it was good for St. John's Hospital."

George Peppard had the film's biggest role, dominating the whole second act of the film. He began as the boy who goes to war and wound up as the marshal who shoots it out with the outlaws on a runaway train. "I got to work with all three of the film's directors," he told me. "Duke Wayne said to me, 'I've been in this business almost forty years and I only worked with two of the film's directors — Hathaway and Ford. You've been in it for five minutes and you get to work with Ford, Hathaway, and Marshall. You'll learn more from this film than from any other you'll ever do.' And he was right.

"We were both in the Civil War episode, but I didn't actually have a scene to play with him. I just prevent an attempt on his life. But I watched him and I listened to everything Ford said, and I learned so much. Duke had only a couple of pages of dialogue, but he gave what I think is one of the best performances of his career. And the stupid fucking critics missed it. Not one picked up on it."

In February 1962, Pilar gave birth to John Ethan, adding to Duke's second family. Publicly, he was able to maintain the image of a father with his loving children all about him. But the image was not all it appeared to be. Aissa wrote that her father told her to regard her older siblings not as half brothers and half sisters, but as full brothers and sisters. She said that she never knew if their warmth toward her was real or merely a show put on to please their father. She said that although it was always cordial between them all, it was also "superficial." Because their father was not a man to share his true feelings and virtually discouraged others from ever doing so, Aissa never really knew, as a child, what Michael, Pat, Toni, and Melinda really thought of her.

Aissa believed that because of her father's stubborn refusal to manifest his true inner feelings in an unending attempt to maintain the image of a happy family, his torment and guilt often manifested itself in a rage that terrified all the children.

Wayne came close to spanking Aissa only once, and that was because she was speaking disrespectfully to her mother just as her father came into the room. He told

Aissa to go and sit outside and think about the spanking he was going to give her. When he stepped outside with a leather belt in his hand, she began to cry. He bent her over his lap and raised the belt, but was unable to go through with it. Instead, he stood her up and gave her a sound lecture on how she should never again speak to her mother that way.

Michael said that his father could be strict, "but that was because he just wanted you to do what was right. If you kept your nose clean, you didn't hear from him. He wasn't the kind of father who constantly preached at you, but if you did something wrong, the punishment was swift. He didn't have to hit us. He just sometimes gave a few taps with the belt, just to let you know you'd done something bad. Usually, he just reached for his belt and you knew you were in trouble, and that fear was punishment enough."

Aissa wrote that on the occasions when he did display a fit of anger at home, it was explosive but always short-lived. He invariably blamed himself for his sudden burst of temper, and he was always quick to apologize. Aissa came to suspect that Wayne's insecurities as a father forced him to get control of his temper and apologize with all the sincerity he could muster. She wrote that it was as though he was thinking, I've scared them and now they won't love me. She was sure he often asked himself, Did they ever love me?

When punishment was dealt out by Wayne the father, it was usually spontaneous and effective. George Sherman told me, "When Duke's eldest girl, Toni, was a teenager, he caught her smoking at the dinner table. He said to her, 'Do you like to smoke?' She said she did, so he said, 'That's good,' and he shoved it into her mouth. As far as he knew, that was the end of her smoking."

Wayne's concerns about being loved as a father increased during the 1960s. By 1974, nothing had obviously changed, although I was not aware just how insecure he was when he told me, "I love all my kids. I hope to God they love me as much as I love all of them." There was no doubt that he did truly love his children.

There must have been many answers to life's mysteries that were never cleared up for some, if not all, of his children. Like every child of a big movie star, Aissa missed out on a normal childhood. She lived a permanent existence within the ten-foot-high walls of the Encino estate. When she was young, she couldn't understand why she couldn't play outside the house. She was not allowed to go to sleep-over parties at friends' houses, and she was told not to even look at strangers, let alone talk to them. Her mother tried to impress upon her the real threat of kidnap, but as a youngster, all of this was lost on Aissa.

There was, of course, another security risk which Duke always kept to himself. The risk of assassination. Yakima Canutt told me, "Since Duke didn't get any help from Khrushchev, he managed to maintain a high level of security and yet also maintain a degree of normality — at least, it was normality by Hollywood's standards. No movie star's kids played in the street. But I think Duke was just that bit more security conscious and so his home became his own fortress — his own Alamo. Glad to say, he never suffered the same fate as those at the Alamo.

"But he was right not to become too complacent because the Communists didn't give up on him. There were still the Chinese and the North Vietnamese only too happy to see him dead."

The year 1962 was a fine one for Wayne. There hardly seemed to be a month that went by when he wasn't appearing somewhere in some film. *The Man Who Shot Liberty Valance* opened in April to reviews that were mixed, and business that was poor. Over the years the film has gained critical favor, but it hasn't improved with age. It looks like a B Western with its black-and-white photography and phony studio sets. It also had very long interior scenes and it seems more like a filmed play at times. It was certainly not a film for Wayne fans, and it did not appear on *Variety*'s 1983 list of All-Time Western Champs.

Hatari hit the screens in May, and despite lukewarm reviews, the public ate it up. It had Wayne, it had color, it had excitement, it had comedy, it had wild animals, it had everything but a plot, and the public didn't care about that. Today the film seems too long at 157 minutes but is still worth watching for its tremendously exciting action scenes, and for its Waynesque humor. It's also fun watching for the occasional ad-lib that makes you realize everyone involved was having fun. The film also produced an enduring little piece of music called "The Baby Elephant Walk" by the film's composer, Henry Mancini.

In October 1962, *The Longest Day* opened and saved Fox from bankruptcy after it lost millions making *Cleopatra*. Although only one of many stars — others included Robert Mitchum, Henry Fonda, Sean Connery, Kenneth More, Jeffrey Hunter, and Robert Wagner — Wayne still managed to stand out. He had become, in the public's perception, the epitome of the American fighting man, carrying his authority as easily as a general carries his gold stars. Despite the later success and brutal reality of *Saving Private Ryan*, *The Longest Day* remains an enthralling experience and arguably the greatest Second World War picture ever made.

How the West Was Won was also a huge success, despite the generally poor critical response when it opened in November 1962. It was a long-running hit in every city in the world where a theatre was equipped to show Cinerama. If the film is uneven, it's because the three directors had different styles, but it was a fabulous piece of entertainment which stands up even today as one of the most rousing horse operas filmed on an epic scale. It was such an eagerly anticipated cinematic event that in London, it broke all records for prebooked seats. In *Variety*'s 1983 All-Time Western

Champs, *How the West Was Won* was placed thirteenth, and in an inflation-adjusted list, it became the fifth-most-successful Western. Although Wayne did not have a major role to play in it, his box-office popularity helped to play a part in the film's huge success — and the film was enhanced by his brief but effective performance. The short Civil War episode was, as Peppard noted, "a trailer for what would have been the best Civil War film John Ford could have ever made, and possibly the best character performance Wayne could ever give."

22

Life Is a Circus

By 1962 Wayne's finances were already growing steadily healthier. Sadly, his physical state was not. He was coughing far more than was normal. "Pilar was growing more and more afraid for Duke's health," said Henry Hathaway, "and that put such a stress on Pilar, it just added to the strains already on them."

That year Wayne bought a 136-foot former minesweeper for $110,000, and called it the *Wild Goose*. "His boat was one of the great loves of his life," said Claire Trevor. "It became his sanctuary from the madness of life. He would take off with his family to the San Juan Islands in the Pacific or anywhere he felt like going. And he'd just have a great time fishing and reading."

The *Wild Goose* had an oak-paneled lounge with a wood-burning fireplace, a master suite, three guest staterooms, a poker table, and a bar, and a film projector and screen were installed, along with state-of-the-art navigation equipment. It was manned by a crew of eight whose company Duke always enjoyed.

While it was being modernized, Wayne went to Hawaii in the late summer of 1962 to make *Donovan's Reef*. Wayne told me he had no idea it would be his last film with John Ford who had been planning it for the past couple of years and had discussed it with Wayne on the set of *How the West Was Won*. Typically, Duke agreed to do the film mainly for Ford's sake, but it also provided Wayne with another film to work off his Paramount contract.

Lee Marvin played the part of an old enemy who turns up on Wayne's island, has a well-staged and funny fistfight with Duke, and does little else as though the screenwriters forgot he was there. "*Donovan's Reef* was one of those films that seemed like a good idea at the time," Lee told me. "Duke says to me, 'Let's go to Hawaii, make a film with John Ford, have lots of fun.' So I went, and ended up with nothing much to do but drink an awful lot, which I may say I did with great aplomb."

Wayne explained, "Jimmy Grant had

written the screenplay, and I was happy enough with it, but Pappy didn't like it and he got Frank Nugent to rewrite it. A lot of good stuff that would have involved Lee Marvin got lost in the rewrite."

Wayne was unhappy with the script, and with his part. But he would never admit he was unhappy with Ford. "I was just all wrong for the picture," he said, blaming himself for the film's flaws. "It needed a younger guy. I felt awkward at my age to be romancing a young woman."

Costar Cesar Romero, whom I interviewed by telephone in 1988, recalled, "Wayne loved John Ford and had so much respect for this great director that he did all he could to help Ford. And while Wayne was busy assisting Ford as well as playing his part, Lee Marvin had nothing to do but get drunk. One night he was so drunk at the Kawaii Hotel that he took off all his clothes and did a hula on the bar."

Dorothy Lamour played a small, inconsequential role. She had not worked for Ford since *The Hurricane* in 1937. "It was a difficult film because John Ford was getting old and he was ill, and he was just bad tempered all the time," she said. "One day on the set he insulted me, and I said that I wasn't having any of that and walked off.

Ford turned up at my dressing room and apologized, which wasn't like him at all. *That's* when I realized how ill he was. Duke took on some of the director's responsibilities like checking the rushes each day, and just making sure with the assistant director that everything was set up right. I could see the strain was getting to him, and sometimes he blew his top. But we all knew he was doing his best to help Ford."

Released in July 1963, *Donovan's Reef* had a ready-made audience, one which had enjoyed *North to Alaska*, *The Comancheros*, and *Hatari*, and who now looked upon the release of a John Wayne film as an event not to be missed. Despite its weaknesses, *Donovan's Reef* makes for an easy 109 minutes of comedy and romance, with an occasional brawl for good measure. And even though leading lady Elizabeth Allen was just twenty-eight, she played Wayne's love interest with the kind of feisty strength that was reminiscent of Maureen O'Hara. In fact, as Wayne told me, "I begged Ford to get Maureen for the part so I wouldn't look so foolish next to a young girl. He said, 'Are you going to be the one to tell Maureen she's perfect for the part because she's *old?*'"

Two weeks after finishing *Donovan's Reef*

in October, Wayne went to Arizona to make *McLintock!* And this time he made sure he had Maureen O'Hara as his leading lady.

This film was John Wayne's very own movie, made by Batjac for release by United Artists. Batjac had become more of a family business than ever before. Duke's son-in-law, Don LaCava, was working at the Batjac office, having taken over the management of Wayne's business investments. Michael had taken on the basic running of the company, and Duke's brother Bobby was kept on the payroll with various jobs on the production side.

The film lacked any solid story, with Wayne as McLintock negotiating on behalf of the Indians. But that subject took up only a small portion of the film. The rest was largely devoted to a series of episodes between Wayne and O'Hara in a thin plot that borrowed from both *The Taming of the Shrew* and *The Quiet Man*. But plot didn't matter. The film was fun for all concerned to make, and fun for audiences to watch.

William Clothier told me, "That was a lot of fun to work on. It was like working on a Ford film only without Ford — until Ford showed up like he did on *The Alamo*. Andy McLaglen was directing, and doing a fine job; we had a funny script by Jimmy Grant; John Wayne and Maureen O'Hara were having a ball working with each other. Patrick [Wayne] had a good supporting role. Michael was producing. We had Yvonne de Carlo in a part specially written for her as a favor by Duke because her husband was stuntman Bob Morgan who'd lost a leg on *How the West Was Won*; and there was Chill Wills and Bruce Cabot, and even Duke's old friend from college, Bob Steele, had a small role — it was like a Ford-family film. Maybe that's why he decided to turn up. Maybe he felt left out. He pushed Andy out of the way, walked up to me, and said, 'Okay Bill, let's go to work.'

"This was Duke's production, and this time he wasn't going to let Ford take over. Besides, I think Andy had a tough enough time having to cope with Duke trying to direct the film, let alone Ford. I think Andy was happy to let Duke devise the fight scenes because he did them as well as any stuntman."

The most memorable fight scene takes place in a mud hole. Wayne recalled, "The stuntmen started complaining that they wanted extra hazard pay to do the scene. I stood at the top of the hill with Maureen and said to the stunt guys, 'You white-livered chickenshits, it's as dangerous as diving into a swimming pool. Maureen and I will show you, won't we, Maureen?' Maureen looked like I'd just told her to jump off Niagara Falls and she said to Chuck Roberson, 'Why, that old bastard wants me to slide down that hill and into that mud pool. If you say it's safe, I'll do it, but not because that old bastard says I must.' And Chuck told her it was safe and that all she had to do was slide down on her ass and keep her head up. So she told the stuntmen, 'Duke's right. You *are* a bunch of chickens,' and with that I told everyone to get out of our way and down she went, and by God, she made that scene funny because the audience knew it was her. So, of course, that meant I *had* to do it, and down I went. It was a great scene. We had a lotta laughs, I tell ya."

Maureen didn't remember it being quite as much fun: "It took several days to film the mud-pool scene. We were filming it in November and the mud pool was so cold that each day they had to thaw the ice that formed over it. When I went down the slope and into that disgusting mess, the Indians were so thrilled they knelt down and bowed to me."

The film was made for less than $2 million. Duke was unable to collect his contracted salary of $700,000 because it went straight to United Artists to pay off part of the debt Batjac owed for *The Alamo*. A big success when it was released in November 1963, *McLintock!*, along with *Donovan's Reef*, put Wayne at number two in the top ten box-office stars.

When filming on *McLintock!* ended in January 1963, Duke took off in the *Wild Goose* with his family for some much needed rest. Then, in May, he reported to the Desilu studios to make a cameo appearance in George Stevens's epic about Christ, *The Greatest Story Ever Told*.

Much has been said about an appearance so brief. In the role of the centurion who accompanies Christ to Calvary, Wayne said, "I felt like a fraud but since United Artists were willing to pay me and then keep my salary to help pay off my debt to them, I thought, what the hell. They put me in this heavy Roman uniform and when I did the chin straps up I looked exactly like every other Roman soldier there. I figured that since they were using my name to bring in the customers, they ought at least to be able to see me, so I left my chin strap undone.

"I really was nothing more than an expensive extra. I had no lines to say, just like Sidney Poitier who they also got in at the last minute to play Simon of Cyrene. And there was Carroll Baker with no dialogue. We were all fucking extras. I only did two days' work."

The film's director George Stevens was savaged by the critics for, firstly, filming in Utah and, secondly, for having so many stars who appeared fleetingly. The biggest criticism of all was the casting of Wayne as a Roman soldier. Carroll Baker came to Stevens's defense when I interviewed her at her London home in 1979, telling me, "George wanted to film the whole thing in Israel. The movie industry begged him not to; to give the work to the people in Hollywood. It was expensive to make a film that big in Hollywood and would have been better and cheaper filmed in the Holy Land. Then they said the movie was running too far over budget, so they said, 'We've got to get some names in it,' and the only place was at the end. Everyone was in the last fifteen minutes; me, John Wayne, Sidney Poitier, Pat Boone."

Most of the all-star cast had good cameo roles to play, including Telly Savalas as Pontius Pilate. He was surprised to find one particular famous and unlikely name on his call sheet for the trial scene. He said, "I looked at the call sheet for the day and saw John Wayne's name. I thought, John Wayne? It's probably an extra with the same name.

"We worked all day, and I didn't see any sign of Wayne. Finally I said to George Stevens, 'Where's John Wayne?' He said, 'He's down there with Max [Von Sydow]. He's the soldier who's got Christ under arrest.' And I looked and there he was. I hadn't recognized him in that Roman gear, and he'd been there all day."

There is a famous but untrue story concerning Wayne's only line of dialogue in the Crucifixion scene, and this is the time to put the record straight. According to legend, Wayne said his line "Truly this was the Son of God" three times, none of them to Stevens's satisfaction. So Stevens said, "Can you give it a little more awe, Duke?" and Duke said, "Aw, this was truly the Son of God." Very funny. But not true.

When I interviewed Roddy McDowall on the set of *The Thief of Baghdad* at Shepperton Studios in 1977, he talked about his work on *The Greatest Story Ever Told*, in which he played the disciple Matthew, and about John Wayne's brief appearance as the centurion. Said McDowall,

"We shot the Crucifixion on a soundstage in the studio. It was a marvelous set. There was hardly any dialogue except between the actors playing the two thieves and Max as Jesus. I promise you, John Wayne as the centurion did not say a word. If you watch the film closely, when you hear his voice saying, 'Truly this was the Son of God,' you don't see his lips move, and that's because George Stevens had decided he wasn't going to let the audience hear Wayne. In fact, he shot the scenes of Jesus carrying his cross and the Crucifixion in such a way that you hardly knew it was John Wayne. George was embarrassed that he'd been made to bring in so many stars as extras. After filming, George decided he needed the centurion to say the line after all, and he got Wayne into a sound studio, and he wasn't in costume and he just had a microphone, and George asked him to deliver the line. Wayne told him, 'I can't do this.' George said, 'You're an actor, aren't you? That's what you've been trying to prove all these years.' And Wayne said, 'I've got nothing to react to, so if I screw this up, don't blame me.' And he was right. He couldn't give the line what it needed. You can't blame Wayne, you can't blame George; you can only blame the assholes

who made the decision to use Wayne —
and all the other actors who were in that
scene just so the names would bring in the
crowds — which they didn't."

Playing John the Baptist was Charlton
Heston, Hollywood's most prolific star of
epics. He said, "There are actors who can
do period parts and there are actors who
can't. God knows Duke Wayne couldn't
play a first-century Roman."

In June 1963, Wayne was due to start
work on *Circus World*, a large-scale and expensive film about the adventures of an
American owner of a European circus.
Samuel Bronston was producing it at his
studio in Madrid, and Frank Capra was set
to direct. David Niven had been announced as Wayne's costar.

Wayne decided to fly to Bermuda where
he would board the *Wild Goose* and sail on
to Portugal to pick up Pilar and their children; Pilar had decided not to brave the
transatlantic crossing. From Portugal they
flew to Madrid, but by the time they arrived at the Bronston Studio, plans for
Circus World had changed. Frank Capra
told me, "I'd been approached by Samuel
Bronston to make a film initially called
Circus which would star John Wayne and

David Niven. Philip Yordan and Nicholas Ray had written the story, but there was no script. The next thing I knew, James Edward Grant had arrived in Madrid to write the script because Wayne had demanded it.

"I'd been hesitant about working with Wayne because we'd had a few cross words back in the late 1940s, but I hoped we could work well together. The biggest problem with *Circus World*, as it came to be called, was that it was the merging of two empires. One belonged to Samuel Bronston who'd been making his epic films in Spain since 1959. He'd been raising money for his past few films by making complicated deals, one with Paramount to distribute the film in certain territories, another with the Rank Organization in Britain, and he had money coming from various quarters. Because he had a deal with Paramount, who had a deal with John Wayne, they wanted Wayne in the film, and with Wayne came his own little empire.

"I quickly began to see I would have trouble, especially when Jimmy Grant told me, 'All you gotta have in a John Wayne picture is a hoity-toity dame with big tits that Duke can throw over his knee and spank, and a collection of jerks he can smack in the face every five minutes. In between all that, you have gags, flags, and cases. That's what his fans want.'

"I said I'd write my own script, and Grant said, 'Duke won't like it,' and he went off to play golf. I had a screenplay that had quality to it, I thought, but when Duke turned up in Madrid, he looked at my script and Grant was right — he hated it. Sam Bronston was faced with the choice of either me or Wayne, and he needed Paramount's money, so he chose Wayne. I told Bronston, who was a very nice man for an independent producer, he ought to get Henry Hathaway to direct the film, and I headed for home.

"In fact, I met Henry Hathaway who said, 'Why are you walking out on Duke Wayne?' I said, 'Henry, I'm not walking. I'm *running*.' And I believe that when I walked, David Niven made his excuses and said he would not be turning up for work."

When I interviewed David Niven at Pinewood Studios on the set of *Candleshoe*, he explained his reasons for quitting *Circus World*. "I loved the idea of making a film for Frank Capra, and had no problem that John Wayne would be the star of the film. The story had been written by Philip Yordan and Nicholas Ray, and I'd worked with them on Bronston's *55 Days at Peking*, which had Charlton Heston as the hero and me as the sensible Englishman, and I knew what they wanted, only instead of Chuck, they had John Wayne.

"But when Capra told me what was happening, I realized this was going to be a typical John Wayne movie which was wonderful for his fans, but I would simply be superfluous. And I was right. Lloyd Nolan got my part, and it wasn't much of a part."

The part in question was that of Wayne's second-in-command, and Niven was right; it was a minor role. Lloyd Nolan had little joy making it. He said, "That was a terrible way to make a movie. And it turned out terrible. It wasn't all bad. We had some fun making it. You can't work with Duke and not have some fun. He wanted the film to be good, Hathaway wanted the film to be good, Sam Bronston wanted the film to be good, but it was just full of problems that nobody could solve."

Hathaway conceded: "Capra was right about the script. Grant was an alcoholic and a great friend of Duke's, and I liked him too. But he was . . . on his way out. He was past his best workwise, and past his best in all respects. So I had Ben Hecht come in and work on the script. But we were stuck with a lot of what was already written because Bronston had gone ahead and had sets built and props acquired. We had a ship that we could overturn. We had a big top. We had circus performers from all over Europe. We had the beautiful Claudia Cardinale. We had a Wild West show. We had wild animals. We had everything but a good ending, and I don't care how great a film might be — and this wasn't great — nobody's gonna go home happy if you don't give 'em a good ending. A showstopper.

"And worst of all, we had Rita Hayworth. Duke became increasingly frustrated with her. She'd turn up not knowing her lines. She'd drink and insult people. And Duke had to play love scenes with her, and he just had no rapport with her. He loved working with Claudia. She was young and full of life, and he treated her like she was one of his daughters."

The director of photography on this one was not Clothier but British cinematographer Jack Hildyard, whom Clothier described as "one of the best in the business." When I had the chance to meet Hildyard, on the set of *The Beast Must Die* in 1973, I asked him about his work on *Circus World*. He told me, "There's a story that goes something like this. For the scene where the big top catches fire, Duke insisted on doing his own stunts. That's true. He worked close to the flames. That's true. The fire got a little out of control. Also true. The blaze became dangerous. Yes, true. Duke carried on working, fighting the fire and turned around to find everyone — the director, the cameraman, the crew — had all gone and left him to nearly die in the flames and smoke. *Not* true. What happened was, when it got bad, Hathaway told everyone to clear out. Nobody left Duke behind. But he was in danger, and he emerged from the smoke coughing badly and his eyes all red. It made for a great scene, but that's not how films should be made. Duke had a bad cough and smoked all the time, and the smoke in the fire scene just made it worse. He was always coughing after that. We'd have to wait before we could shoot sometimes until his coughing had subsided."

Apart from the hazards of filming the fire scene and having a hacking cough, Wayne's biggest problem was Rita Hayworth: "I tried to make Rita feel comfortable, and we took her to dinner: Pilar, Aissa, and myself. She hadn't drunk much and already her speech became slurred.

She was rude to the waiters, which was just goddamn embarrassing, so I gave them all big tips and handed out autographed cards. I said to Aissa, 'Never think anyone is better than you, and never think you're better than anyone else. You have to try to be decent to everybody — unless they give you a reason not to.' "

Nobody knew it then, but Rita Hayworth would suffer from Alzheimer's, and some who had worked with Hayworth and later criticized her for her behavior have suggested that it is possible that she was in the early stages of that disease. Henry Hathaway, however, was convinced the troubles she caused — and suffered — were of her own making. In 1981, he commented, "Rita didn't have Alzheimer's until recently. We're talking about almost twenty years ago when we made that fucking circus picture. It's sad to say, but Rita was a faded film star who drank too much and thought she was above everybody else.

"She got the part because Samuel Bronston's people insisted she was still a major attraction for European audiences. She also looked just old enough and Duke young enough for the two of them to be lovers. It would have looked stupid to have someone like Angie Dickinson, who's the better actress, to have played that part.

"I always said to Duke, 'Wouldn't it be great if we could get rid of this fucking awful so-called climactic scene where Rita and Claudia [Cardinale] twirl about on the ropes?' It was a terrible scene and it needed an aging movie queen who still had the figure. I said to Duke, 'Let's find some unknown aging actress who's going to fat and cast her in the part. Then we can have her save *you* from the fire, and we could have her eaten by the lions, and *that* would be an exciting ending to the film.' Duke wasn't sure if I meant it, or if it would have been a good idea, but he said, 'What the hell, we're stuck with Rita. Let's just finish the goddamn picture.' "

It was a long production, with some final scenes shot at Pinewood in England in the autumn — "Something to do with the deal with Rank," said Hathaway — but the weather was so cold and damp, it made Wayne's cough even worse. Pilar begged him to see a doctor but he refused.

With the last scenes of *Circus World* in the can, Duke and Pilar flew from London to Acapulco to meet the *Wild Goose*. By then, Wayne was coughing up blood.

Henry Hathaway found himself with a

problem when Samuel Bronston told him that he'd made a deal to have *Circus World* presented in Cinerama. Hathaway told me, "I could have strangled Bronston. I said, 'If you'd decided even halfway through the production, I could have put some exciting stuff in.' I knew what people expected from a Cinerama film. I'd shot most of *How the West Was Won*. They have to have exciting high points filmed from the audience's point of view, so they'd feel like they were on a runaway wagon or whatever. We had nothing like that, except where the ship overturns, which was effective in Cinerama. We could have made it the best Cinerama film since *How the West Was Won*. Instead, the public must have felt cheated."

As a Cinerama road-show production, *Circus World* did not do particularly well in America. In Britain, Rank had the good sense to change the title to *The Magnificent Showman*, and it did good business at the London Coliseum. But when it went on general release worldwide in 1964, it found its audience. It was Wayne's only release of 1964, and it was successful enough to keep Wayne in the top ten American box-office stars.

It was a period of his life Duke recalled

with irony. "I did Pappy's last film which went nowhere and I was all wrong for it; I played a Roman soldier, and I was all wrong for it; and I did the worst circus film ever made, and thinking back, I have to concede that my life was like a fucking circus. But I'll tell you something. I wouldn't have had it any other way."

23

Licking the Big C

In 1964, Paramount wanted another picture from Wayne before he made one of his own pictures. They had *In Harm's Way* for him, a large-scale drama set against the bombing of Pearl Harbor. Otto Preminger was directing, and Wayne's costars included Kirk Douglas, Tom Tryon, and Patricia Neal.

Following a compulsory health check (which all film actors have to undergo to qualify for insurance) at Scripps Clinic in La Jolla, he was, surprisingly, pronounced fit and healthy. Paul Fix said to me, "How the hell could they have said he was healthy? Why didn't they find the lung cancer he had?"

Duke arrived in Honolulu with Pilar and the children and checked into the Ilikai Hotel on Waikiki Beach. Apparently, Wayne did not look as healthy as Scripps had declared him. Tom Tryon told me later, "You know, Duke really wasn't well. He *looked* ill. I was told that he'd been making one film after another for the past four years, and there was talk that his wife was getting concerned about him. When I saw him, I could understand her concern. He was coughing badly. I mean, *really* awful. It was painful to see and hear, so God knows what it was like for him. He'd begin coughing and he wouldn't stop, and it sounded just horrendous. He'd begin coughing in the middle of a scene and Preminger would have to stop filming. If it was anyone else, Preminger would have yelled some kind of abuse at him, but he never yelled at Duke."

Preminger had the reputation of being a bully, earning him the nickname "Otto the Ogre." But he was not able to bully every actor.

Over two interviews with Kirk Douglas, the first in 1975 and the second in 1988, he talked about Wayne and the films they made together. "Otto Preminger was in private and on a social level a charming man. But when he was working, he was a bully. I always thought he looked and be-haved like the sadistic Nazi commandant he played in *Stalag 17*. He never treated me badly on the set, and he didn't treat

Wayne badly, but he was cruel to Tom Tryon. Just unendingly cruel. He would come right up to Tom and scream until he was spitting saliva."

In Harm's Way was the first of three films Douglas made with Wayne. Said Kirk, "I like John Wayne. We don't see eye to eye on a lot of things, but I've got tremendous respect for him. To me, Wayne is a real professional. He's a much better actor than he's often given credit for.

"Wayne has very prescribed concepts about what parts he should play, whereas I feel an actor should play anything. He didn't like it when I played van Gogh in *Lust for Life* because he would have preferred me to be more like one of the boys, so to speak. He saw the picture at a special screening, and after it, he said to me, 'Kirk, how in the hell could you play such a weak character like that?'

"I said, 'What do you mean, John?'

"He said, 'Fellers like us are the tough guys of movies. We're in a certain class.'

"I said, 'But John, I'm an actor. I try to play all different kinds of parts.'"

After Wayne's death, Douglas told me, "He was the kind of star that really doesn't exist anymore. He had an image and I think he believed in that image. He developed that character he played on screen and he sincerely believed in it."

Tryon said, "I admired Duke for his determination and I liked him as a human being."

The last time Wayne had worked with Patricia Neal, they had not really warmed to each other. "When we made *In Harm's Way*, it was the first time I'd seen Duke since we made *Operation Pacific* and I was surprised to find him a lot warmer, a lot more relaxed, and a lot more generous," she said. "We had both been through a lot in our respective lives since then and perhaps that's why we got along on our second picture. My husband [Roald Dahl] and I spent a lot of time with Duke and Pilar in Hawaii."

When *In Harm's Way* finished in August 1964, Pilar finally persuaded Duke to have another checkup at Scripps. He drove to the clinic alone, and when he later called to tell Pilar that he would be there for a few days for observation, she became understandably alarmed.

In fact, he was kept there for five days. He returned home and told Pilar, "I've got a little problem. I've got a spot on my lung. I've got lung cancer."

Wayne was due to start filming *The Sons*

of Katie Elder for Henry Hathaway. Michael recalled, "JW came into our office where we were meeting with Henry Hathaway to discuss *The Sons of Katie Elder*, and my father said, 'Sit down. I've got something to tell you all.' I had no idea what it was. Then he said, 'I've got the Big C.' Henry thought the Big C meant the clap and he said, 'Oh, don't worry about it, Duke. They've got penicillin now.' And JW said, 'Not that. I've got lung cancer, Henry, and I've got to have my lung removed.' Henry had also had cancer, so my father was talking to the right guy, and Henry said, 'Well, we'll just postpone the picture for a few weeks, and by then you'll be okay.' And so Henry postponed the picture for about four weeks."

Hathaway told me when I spoke to him in 1975, "I'd had cancer of the colon, and I knew the worst thing was for someone to say, 'Well, that's that then. No point in making plans.' You've *got* to make plans, and I knew I had to make Duke believe that the operation he needed was just a setback. He *needed* his work. I knew that. So I said, 'You go and have your operation and we'll wait around a few weeks and then we'll start shooting.' "

On 16 September 1964, Wayne was admitted to Good Samaritan Hospital, where a tumor the size of a golf ball was found in his left lung. The diseased lung was completely removed in a six-hour operation.

The next day he woke up and began coughing, ripping open stitches and damaging delicate tissue. His face and hands began to swell from a mixture of fluid and air, but the doctors didn't dare operate again so soon. Five days later he was back in surgery where doctors repaired stitches and drained the fluid.

Michael said, "He didn't show that he was afraid, but he's not stupid, so I knew he was worried — more than he'd ever say."

While still in the hospital, Duke received the news that his brother Robert had lung cancer.

On 19 October Wayne left the hospital and, knowing the press were outside waiting for him, he somehow found the strength to get out of his wheelchair and walk out. He chatted to reporters, smiled for the cameras, and walked out to a waiting car with blackened windows. When he got inside, he groaned in agony and used an oxygen tank that had been smuggled into the car without the press noticing.

He had been told by doctors to rest for six months but, after three weeks of inactivity, he got on board the *Wild Goose* and took a cruise down the Mexican coast. He started to drink again and chewed tobacco. An oxygen tank and mask were always close by.

The true nature of his illness had been kept secret from the press and public. They had been told he had been in the hospital to be treated for lung congestion. Against the advice of his agent and his advisers, on 29 December 1964, Wayne held a press conference in his Encino home, and announced he had been treated for lung cancer — or the Big C, as he preferred to call it.

"I licked the Big C," he told the press. "I know the man upstairs will pull the plug when he wants to, but I don't want to end my life being sick. I want to go out on two feet — in action."

When the press conference was over, he collapsed with exhaustion in his bedroom. But he had told the world, and contrary to the fears of his agent and advisers, the legend of John Wayne simply loomed ever larger. If anyone could beat lung cancer, it had to be John Wayne.

Henry Hathaway had some good advice

for Duke: "After the operation, I told Duke, 'Don't baby yourself or you'll become a psychological cripple. The only way to get over this thing is to forget it ever happened and get on with your life. That's what I did, and I'm just fine. And you'll be fine too.' "

Although he'd been ordered to rest for six months, four months after the operation in early January 1965, Wayne began work on *The Sons of Katie Elder*. Hathaway recalled, "Everyone wanted to baby Duke. When we came to film the scene at the bridge over the river, Chuck Roberson said to me, 'I think I ought to double Duke in this scene.' I said, 'What the hell for?' He said, 'That water's freezing. It'll kill Duke.' I said, 'You think I'd let Duke get killed making this picture? He'll do it himself.' Then Duke started up with 'I don't think I can do the scene, Henry,' so I said, 'Duke, you gonna be a baby now? Afraid of a little cold water?' I kind of shamed him into doing the scene, and people think I was cruel.

"I knew it was hell for him to do because that water *was* freezing, but Duke fell into the water like he was supposed to, and he got soaked and frozen through, and when we stopped, he finally climbed out of the water and he had to have oxygen. I knew how hard it was on him. I knew he was suffering. And everyone hated me and thought I was the devil for making him do it. His wife hated me. The other actors hated me. But Duke didn't. He told me, 'I thought I was gonna die in that water, but I didn't. Now I know I can do anything.'

"You watch that picture and what do you see? The same John Wayne he was before the cancer. He knew he had to go on and show the public he hadn't changed. And here we are, ten years later, talking about a man who beat the odds and, as far as the public is concerned, is as tough and strong as he ever was. He's not getting any younger, for God's sake, but he's still working and pleasing his fans, which I think is the second most important thing in his life. The first most important thing is his family. But even they come second to his work sometimes, and that's because he's working *for* his family. He's got Michael working as a producer, and Patrick has done well as an actor, but he really gets most of his work with his father. He's got a son-in-law running his business affairs, and so the boys in his family really kind of need him to keep working. I'm not sure the ladies feel the same . . . but then women don't feel the same as men about these things.

"And apart from his family, he's got a whole load of other people working for him on a regular basis. It was never a problem for me because I made hundreds of films without Duke and I don't need him. But a lot of other people do need him. He doesn't want to let those people down. So Duke'll keep working till he drops, I guarantee it."

In 1965 Wayne had two films in cinemas. The first was *In Harm's Way*, which should have been better than it was, but was nevertheless good enough to do reasonably well at the box office. Audiences were naturally drawn to it by Wayne's presence more than anything else, especially now that everyone knew that Duke had licked the Big C. Then came *The Sons of Katie Elder*, which earned a respectable $12 million worldwide. The two films kept Wayne in the top ten American box-office stars, where he would remain for the next four years.

Early in 1965, Duke surprised his family by announcing he wanted to move out of Encino and live at Newport Beach. And in May 1965, the Waynes left Los Angeles behind and moved into their new home at Newport.

Wayne told me, "I love Newport . . . walking around the bay early in the morning . . . driving to the local store . . . it's a slower kind of life there than in Hollywood."

Claire Trevor thought that it did Duke a lot of good moving to Newport Beach. She said, "He loved the water and he loved his *Wild Goose,* and so it was perfect for him. I live nearby so me and my husband [Milton Bren] saw a lot of Pilar and Duke. I think Pilar was relieved that there wasn't the endless stream of Duke's old drinking friends passing through all the time.

"But even back then I could sense that Pilar and Duke were growing apart. He still wanted to keep working more than he had to. So Pilar had to find other interests. There was her charity work, and she joined a tennis club. When Duke's not working, he often spent time playing chess or cards at the Big Canyon Country Club.

"I tried talking to Duke sometimes. I'd tell him that Pilar wasn't happy just to be Mrs. John Wayne, and he'd say, 'Hell, Claire, I don't know what to say. I'm a movie actor, and it's all I know. When I married Pilar I asked her if she was willing to give up any ideas about a career and be my wife, and she said she was.' I told Duke, 'People can't see into the future. Pilar knew only that she loved you and that you loved her, and she wanted to be with you. She didn't know what life with John Wayne was going to be like. Why do you think it's been so hard on her?' And we talked a lot about the problems they were having, but he couldn't change his ways. I wouldn't criticize him for that. But I hated to see them growing slowly apart."

There was no letup in Wayne's work schedule. He took an interest in an idea for a film Melville Shavelson had called *Cast a Giant Shadow*. Shavelson told me, "I'd been trying to get this picture about the formation of modern-day Israel for a long time, but no studio wanted to back it. I told Duke I was having problems and he wanted to know what the problem was. So I told him the story, and he said, 'An American army officer helps a little country fight for its independence. That's the most American story I ever heard,' and he asked why I couldn't get financing. So I told him that I'd been told by every studio that nobody wanted to see a movie about a Jewish general. I told him, 'I just want to make the picture Gentile by association. If your name is attached to it, they can't say it's a Jewish movie anymore.'

"I wanted Wayne to agree to be in the picture as General Mike Randolph because it was a ploy. If this icon of Gentile culture would agree to be in the movie, I figured the studios would show interest. So he read the first thirty pages of draft script, which I'd written myself because I couldn't afford to pay another writer, and Duke said he would appear in the movie but only if I wrote the entire script. And he said Batjac would coproduce, which gave me the muscle I needed to go to the Mirisch Brothers and get them to finance the picture."

It was actually a little more complicated than that. Kirk Douglas explained how he became involved: "The reason I made *Cast a Giant Shadow* was because Wayne called me and said, 'Listen, I've got this script which I think is perfect for you. If you play it, I'll play the small part of the general.' And he *did*. Wayne is an amazing institution. They don't make that kind anymore."

John Wayne said that he had two reasons for going to Douglas: "I knew that the role of David Marcus was just perfect for Kirk. And I knew that if Kirk would star in the lead role, we'd have a bigger chance of getting the money to make it. But I also knew that Kirk had his own company, Bryna, and that if Bryna came in along with Batjac, we'd be able to convince Walter Mirisch to put up some money, and then we'd be able to get United Artists to back it and distribute it.

"It's a goddamn shame sometimes that making something that is a creative process is also a matter of making deals. I don't want to make deals, I want to make pictures, but you can't do the one without the other.

"Once Kirk said he was in, we were able to get Frank Sinatra and Yul Brynner to be in it.

"I wanted to make it because there were people saying the United States was sending in our troops all over the world just to hurt little countries where we have no right to be. I wanted to remind people at home and abroad who we are and what we've done. I wanted to remind the world how we helped this little country of Israel get its independence . . . and how it was an *American* army officer who gave his life for it."

Shavelson said, "Duke was so high on the Americanness of the picture that Kirk, who is of course a Jew, said to him, 'Don't forget that David Marcus was Jewish.' And Duke said, 'Jesus Christ was Jewish too, but he didn't go to West Point.' "

While filming in Rome, news came through of riots between Negroes and the police in Los Angeles. Shavelson told me, "Duke said, 'Those blacks got what they deserved.' I was shocked. I was furious. It was the only time we had an argument. It wasn't that Duke was prejudiced because he's not. He's just got his own idea of what Americanism is. He said that the rioters had disturbed the peace and there had to be order in his country. What's important to Duke is whether something is good or bad for the country, and to him the riots were bad."

Wayne had a curious point of view on ethnic, or any minority, groups: "The white man made the black man a slave, and that was an evil thing to do. We've all got to live side by side. What's past is past. I'm just saying that people should stop bellyaching about how bad they've got it because there are still white people who don't like black people, but the Negro has got to rise above that and say, 'I'm an American first and foremost and I'm damn lucky to have been born here where I can get an education and enjoy my liberty.' Because there are a lot of black people who aren't so lucky. Look at South Africa. Look at the African nations that have civil wars. I'm tired of hearing the words 'black American.' I don't go round saying 'I'm a white American.' I'm just an American, goddammit.

"So-called minority groups need to stop being in the minority and join the majority. They shouldn't let what other people say keep them in the minority because that's what happens. Someone says, 'You're black so stay in your place.' The black guy should say, 'I'm an American' or 'I'm an Englishman' or whatever free country they are lucky to live in, and they should say, 'I'm going to show you what I can do,' instead of saying, 'Treat us better because we're browbeaten and downtrodden.' I got no time for that."

Apart from Wayne's lack of sympathy for minorities, Shavelson had no complaints with the performance Wayne gave him. He said, "Duke was able to give me the one thing I needed and couldn't film authentically, and that was the horror of the death camps. I didn't want to use the color newsreels that were shot — some of them by George Stevens. I felt to use that kind of footage in a movie would have been plain disrespectful to the victims. And I couldn't re-create it because there is no way the most brilliant makeup artist in the world could make even the thinnest extras look like the survivors of the death camps. The only way to do it was to tell the audience what Wayne's character was seeing when he comes across the death camp by showing it in his eyes. It was a feat of acting I wasn't sure Duke could bring off. He needed to begin with a look of disbelief which gradually grows to outrage. And he did just that. I didn't realize how effective it was until I saw the rushes, and what Duke produced was not only effective but profoundly moving. Don't anyone say that John Wayne can't act."

Considering Wayne's contribution to the film, it comes as a surprise to realize he worked only four days on the film during August 1965, in Rome, and while the rest of the unit continued to film in Italy and then move on to Israel, Wayne returned home.

Work was waiting for him in Old Tuscon, Arizona, in October 1965. It was another Western, *El Dorado*, directed by Howard Hawks, who would never admit that the film was a virtual remake of *Rio Bravo*, with a few twists. Hawks would argue that *El Dorado* didn't tell the same story as *Rio Bravo* or feature the same characters. Both films, however, featured a bunch of lawmen, one of them being a drunk, trying to keep order in a border town and finding themselves holed up in the jail. And instead of having a sober sheriff Wayne with a drunk deputy Dean Martin as in *Rio Bravo*, *El Dorado* featured a drunk sheriff, played by Robert Mitchum, with Wayne playing pretty much the same kind of character he did in *Rio Bravo* but without a badge. In place of old-timer Walter Brennan there was old-timer Arthur Hunnicutt, and instead of Ricky Nelson as a young man deadly with a gun, there was James Caan as a young man who was lousy with a gun. In *Rio Bravo* Wayne was still young enough to have a girlfriend, played by Angie Dickinson in corset and tights. In *El Dorado* Hawks has a joke at the expense of Wayne's age by allowing him to "know a girl," this time played by Charlene Holt in corset and tights.

Later, in 1970, Wayne and Hawks would virtually retell the same story in *Rio Lobo*, and so any suggestion that Hawks remade *Rio Bravo* twice, let alone once, was met with a strong rebuke.

"I *never* remade *Rio Bravo*," he said. "I *stole* from *Rio Bravo*, just like Hemingway always stole from himself. There were a lot of similarities between his stories.

"If a film director has a story that he likes but when he looks at it again he thinks he can do it better, he'll do it again but in a different way. If I think, I could do that better if I did it again, I'd do it again and keep on doing them. When we made *Rio Bravo*, we found places where we could go in one direction or another, and we made our choices but made a note of trying the other direction in another picture. We ended up with enough good choices from *Rio Bravo* to make a whole new picture, so we did *El Dorado*. I said to my writer [Leigh] Brackett who had worked on *Rio Bravo*, 'We had a boy who was a very good gunman in *Rio Bravo*, so let's have a boy who can't shoot at all in *El Dorado*. So that wasn't the same, was it?'

"And in *Rio Bravo* Wayne was the sheriff and his deputy was the drunk. In *El Dorado* Mitchum was the sheriff and *he* was the drunk, and the deputy was stone-cold sober. So we changed a lot. We did everything by opposites. I don't think there's any connection between the two stories.

504

There is a similarity, but that comes in style. I think people who say there is a connection between the two stories of *Rio Bravo* and *El Dorado* haven't actually seen both films."

Robert Mitchum, however, had a different view from Hawks's: "It's a case of making a successful formula and jumping on your own bandwagon. Normally, it's other directors who jump on the bandwagon, but Howard's the only guy I know who jumps on his own."

Hawks had a high opinion of Mitchum: "Robert Mitchum is one of the few actors who can work with Wayne without Wayne blowing him off the screen. But I don't think Mitchum has the power Wayne has. He can't carry a picture as well as Wayne can, and Wayne knows this, which is why I give people like Dean Martin and Robert Mitchum the more interesting characters. Wayne says to me, 'You give everybody else the fireworks, but I have to carry the damn thing.' I said to him, 'That's right, Duke.' "

Wayne had incredible trust in Hawks, even though they only made four films together. "I never read a script for one of Hawks's films," Duke said. "Mostly he'd say, 'Duke, do you wanna make a

Western?' and I'd say, 'Let's do it.' I'd get around to asking what the story was later. He'd start telling me the story and I'd say, 'Don't tell me. I never like your stories but they always turn out to be good.' I didn't need to see his script. We'd get to a scene and I'd say, 'What do I do?' and he'd tell me what he wanted. Then I'd take the script, read the lines and learn 'em, and we'd do the scene. It makes working real easy that way. But you can't work with most directors that way. I don't always trust directors if I haven't worked with them before. But Hawks I trust with my life."

Playing the chief villain was Christopher George. When I interviewed him over the telephone in 1980, he talked of his experience working with Wayne and Hawks. He said, "I liked working with Howard Hawks, and I liked working with Duke Wayne. *El Dorado* was my first with either of them, and I did a few more with them, but not on the same pictures. With Duke, if he likes you, he'll make sure you get to work with him again. When we were making *El Dorado* he said, 'You know, Chris, you're supposed to play this mean son of a bitch I want to kill all through the picture, but you play it with such charm that I told Howard that the character I play has to have a sneaky regard for him.' So they had this scene where I said to Duke, 'You don't give me a chance,' and he said, 'You're too good to give a chance to.' That didn't mean his character liked the guy I played, but he respected him. But Duke kept saying to me, 'Chris, you're just too goddamn nice,' and I said, 'Duke, the best villains are always the ones that have charm. Not those guys who snarl and sneer.' He grinned and said, 'You're right. By God, you're gonna work with me again.' And I did, in *Chisum* and *The Train Robbers*."

El Dorado didn't get released until June 1967, because Paramount didn't want it going up against their other big Western of the time, *Nevada Smith*, starring Steve McQueen and directed by Henry Hathaway. *El Dorado* got good notices and earned around $12 million worldwide, the same amount as *The Sons of Katie Elder*.

Although this demonstrated that there was still a steady audience out there eager for John Wayne in Westerns, Duke now had something else on his mind, and it came to occupy his attention and dedication increasingly. It never became the passion that *The Alamo* had been, but it was a film he *had* to make. It was called *The Green Berets*.

24

The Vietcong Sniper

The world Wayne had grown up in had changed. Even his own country was a place he was beginning to feel a stranger in. There was unrest in America, and there were people protesting against the Vietnam War, which was just beginning to make headlines. But he thought no less of his country: "I thank God every day I wake up as a citizen of the United States. But it seems there are some Americans who don't feel as I do. Things began changing in the mid-sixties and during the Vietnam conflict. I saw it happening for the first time after I'd made *Cast a Giant Shadow*, which I made because I wanted to remind Americans what their country had done for another little country. Well, we were in Vietnam giving lives for another little country.

"I'd gone into Los Angeles to discuss plans for a charity benefit in aid of burn patients at a children's hospital, and there were a lot of meetings. I enjoy being involved but I hate meetings, so I took a break and went over to the old USC campus for a stroll with my secretary [Mary St. John]. I saw a group of students protesting against the Vietnam War. It's only natural that young people should protest against the idea of war. Hell, there were plenty of Americans who opposed our country's entry into the Second World War. But you gotta do what's right. You gotta know what you're protesting about.

"What got my goat was that these students were heckling a young marine, a corporal, who was going by and heading for his car. He walked with his back straight as a rod, and he wore his uniform with pride. Then I noticed that where his right arm should have been there was only an empty sleeve which was neatly folded and pinned down.

"Turned out he was one of the Ninth Marine Brigade which were the first ground troops America sent to Vietnam [in March 1965]. He had a chest full of medals and ribbons. He said his drill instructor had taught him to ignore impolite civilians. He said, 'You don't give them the satisfaction of noticing them.' I waved to him as he drove away. And my blood was boiling."

As Wayne continued his story, he could not hold back the anger he'd felt, and it grew until Duke was yelling the way he must have yelled at those students: "I ran over to the students and I was just so angry, I drummed my fists into their goddamn table and I said, 'You *stupid* bastards! You *stupid* fucking *assholes!* Blame Johnson if you like. Blame Kennedy. Blame Eisenhower or Truman or fucking goddamn Roosevelt. But *don't* you blame that kid. Don't you *dare* blame any of those kids. They *served!* Jesus, the kid lost his *arm*. I mean, what the hell is *happening* to this country?"

It was around that time that Wayne decided he wanted to make a film set against the Vietnam War, and he bought the rights to *The Green Berets*, a novel by Robin Moore.

In December 1965, Wayne wrote to President Lyndon B. Johnson about his plans to film *The Green Berets*. "I told the president that I felt it was important that the people of the United States and also people all over the world should know why it was necessary for Americans to be in Vietnam. And I got the government's support to make the picture."

When I asked Wayne to explain why it was important for America to be there, he looked at me with some amazement as if I should know the answer, but he patiently replied, "When Johnson sent marines to the Dominican Republic in 1965, the liberals said we'd ruin everything and the world would turn against us. But we went in and helped to give them a republic that's as good as any in Latin America. Your own country [Britain] defeated the Communists' attempt to take over Malaya in the fifties. And Indonesia had the good sense *and* the guts to throw the Communists out. Even Kennedy stood up again the Communists when they tried putting their nuclear weapons in Cuba. You just can't let the Communists do what they want, which is to rule the world. Make no mistake. I *know*. Khrushchev told me what he was going to do. And we can't let 'em do it. It's unthinkable. There are people who'll tell you that the Communists are no threat. Believe me, they are. I tell you, I *know*."

That's when I said to Wayne, "Is that because they tried to kill you?"

The long stare was accompanied by a long pause. Finally, he said, "Why'd you say that?" And so I told him what Peter Cushing had told me.

He was clearly bemused as he visibly fussed and fumed in silence except for the muttering that went on under his breath. I couldn't tell if he was going to suddenly lose his temper, or what he was going to do. Finally, he sighed, let his shoulders drop, and just sat there. He raised his eyes and I was relieved to see there was no sign of anger there. He said, "I'll tell you something. I'll tell you why it's got to be like that after I tell you what happened.

"I'd made myself a promise after I realized I'd really licked the Big C that I'd go to Vietnam just to shake hands with those kids we'd sent over. I did it for their fathers in the last world war, and I'd do it for them because whatever war it is, we all owe a debt to the men who fight for our freedom. So I did a three-week tour in Vietnam in June 1966. I spent three days in Saigon where I was put up in a nice hotel where it was safe and comfortable. What really took me by surprise was the number of Vietnamese who recognized me. I'd come out of the Rex Hotel and the Vietnamese people would just stop their cars, and they'd be shouting, 'John Wayne! Number One Cowboy!' I didn't think they'd know who I was.

"You know, there wasn't much I could do to entertain them. I didn't tell jokes the way Bob Hope did, and I certainly wasn't gonna sing to them. I just put on a uniform, took off my rug [toupee], and I went around shaking hands with the troops, joking with them, signing autographs, and answering their questions. I didn't sleep much because I wanted to be at their disposal.

"I wanted to see for myself what was going on out in the boondocks. So they sent me to a little village, and I could hear a lot of gunfire going on not far off. The Third Battalion was based there, and I was signing autographs and the usual stuff when bullets began hitting the ground near us. I didn't notice and just kept signing autographs, but the marines automatically scrambled for cover. So I took cover also, 'cos I'm not stupid enough to stand out there and be a sitting duck.

"I thought, 'Jesus, the goddamn Commies nearly got me again.' Ya see . . . back in the fifties . . ." He was clearly in two minds what to say and how much to say. Finally, he just said, "Look, if you ever see Yakima Canutt, just ask him. He saved my life a couple of times, but he wasn't out there in Vietnam to save me. Fortunately I had the marines, which is the next best thing to Yak."

At the time, I had no idea why Wayne was referring to Yakima Canutt, and I think Duke was unsure how much I knew. So I gave away nothing, hoping Wayne would give me more. And he did.

Wayne continued, "What your friend Mr. Cushing said was true. I don't know for sure how long that goddamn Chairman Mao wanted me out of the way, but it turned out he did. I had an idea there was a Communist conspiracy, but I kept it to myself. Never wanted my family living in fear that anything untoward would ever happen. Thanks to Yak, some of his best cowboys and some men from the government, I was okay on American soil, so I never told my family. And if you ever meet Yak, you can get him to tell you what I mean.

"But out in Vietnam I almost walked into a sniper's bullet that had my name on it. There were a few places I saw in Vietnam, and I can't tell you where I was when me and the marines I was with had bullets whistling past our ears. I tell ya, when you hear the bullets whistle past your ears and you also feel the wind as they fly by, you *know* you've just had a narrow escape. I don't mind admitting, this time I shook. Scared the hell out of me.

"I thought it was just another sniper aiming at Americans, but this was one sniper who didn't get away 'cos the marines caught the son of a bitch. Turned out he was some kind of elite sniper from China working with the Vietcong. I don't know what kind of interrogation they gave him, but they said to me, 'You better come and listen to this.'

"So I went with them into some hut and I have to say he looked kind of all right to me. He didn't have any cuts and bruises, so I guess they didn't have to twist his arm too much. And a South Vietnamese guy told him to tell me what he'd told them. He said something in Vietnamese, and then the translator said, 'I was trying to kill *you*.' I did that thing you see in movies where someone looks behind them to see who he's talking to, and there's no one there. The son of a bitch meant *me*. So I said, 'What the hell have *I* done?'

"He said that I was the big American movie star who his beloved Chairman Mao had said was the chief devil of the great Satan America, or some such Maoist crap. Well, I've been called all kinds of sons of a bitch, but never that. The word had gone out that I was in Vietnam. Seems there was someone who saw me coming out of the hotel in Saigon, who was a spy or something, and the news of me [being there] got back to Mao Tse-tung. He had promised a great reward for the man who killed me. What was so pathetic was this sniper said that Mao had promised that the reward would be great glory, but he also said he had heard there was a financial reward too, and this sniper needed the fortune more than the glory because his family back in China was so poor. So when he saw me, he figured he'd collect on that reward.

"Don't know what happened to the poor bastard. I suspect he didn't live to tell the tale. And if that sounds shocking, you need to know that those Vietcong were doing the most unimaginable things to our men. Things I wasn't allowed to show in *The Green Berets*. But *I* knew what was happening out there."

February 1966 brought good and bad events into Wayne's life. James Edward Grant died, and Marisa was born. Claire Trevor recalled, "Marisa's birth took the sting out of Jimmy Grant's death. I mean, sure, it broke Duke's heart when Grant died, but having a baby when Duke was almost sixty made him feel . . . I wouldn't say young, but he felt that life was there to be enjoyed. He said to me, 'Did you notice how the sunrise gets more and more beautiful as the years go by?' And that's what being a father again at such a late age meant to Duke."

After Wayne's tour of Vietnam, he agreed to help Bob Hope raise funds for the University of Southern California's scholarship endowment. Bob Hope remembered the event just a few years later in late 1969 (when, as a messenger boy, I got to meet the great comic on the opening night of *How to Commit Marriage* at the New Victoria Theatre in London): "Duke Wayne was a former student of USC so it was appropriate that he be among the guests to deliver a short speech before I got up and said my piece. But he was not impressed by some of the students who had staged a number of antiwar protests and boycotts.

"If Mount Rushmore could sprout legs and get up and walk, that's what Duke would be like. You'd want to get out of the way pretty quick. Well, when we were rehearsing, some of the students would look in and shout obscenities and chant their protests, and this was really getting to Duke. He decided he'd make some changes to his speech, and when he showed me, I said, 'My God, Duke, if you say those things, you'll turn those kids into a lynch mob.' And Duke said, 'I don't give a shit!' and I thought, Well, I'm not standing in his way.

"So on the night, there were kids in the audience who gave catcalls as Duke walked on stage. He just stood there and he just kind of subdued them into silence by his very presence. And he told them what he thought, and they gave him a rousing ovation."

When I asked Wayne if he remembered what he'd said at that event, he replied, "I think I can pretty much recall it. I said that a university should be a quiet place where people go to learn, not to destroy property that belongs to someone else. I told them that their teachers and professors are people they should treat with respect. I said that getting an education is a privilege, not a right. I told them, 'We are not going to sit by and let you destroy our schools and our system.' I told them that this was a great university and they owed it their best. Then I said, 'Thank you very much.' Well, there were a lot of people in that audience that obviously didn't feel the same way those who were catcalling did, because I got a standing ovation.

"As I came off I said to Bob [Hope] who was waiting in the wings, 'I hope I haven't stole all your thunder, Bob.' He said, 'The next time I tell you something's a bad idea, just ignore me.' I said, 'I always do, Bob.' Anyway, Bob went out there and entertained the audience, and we raised a lot of money.

"But, you know? I hate to think of our endeavors going to help students who, like me when I was a kid, couldn't afford to attend without a scholarship — but then they turn out to be the ones who go out and burn the American flag."

With John Wayne Westerns continuing to do well, it made sense to do another one, so he made *The War Wagon* in September 1966. Duke's friend and regular costar Bruce Cabot played a crooked mining contractor who owns an armorplated war wagon transporting half a million dollars' worth of gold. Wayne was a man who wants revenge on Cabot for framing him for a crime he didn't commit and for stealing his land. Kirk Douglas played a gunfighter who teams up with Wayne to rob the war wagon of its gold. Also in the cast was Robert Walker as a drunken explosives expert, Keenan Wynn as the wagon driver, and Howard Keel as an unlikely Indian.

Kirk Douglas said of Wayne after his death, "I think he was an artist and a terrific human being. He handled his adversaries with dignity. He was unique.

"We didn't see eye to eye on a lot of things. I was always a Democrat; he was a Republican. He liked to end each day by spending time with the crew and socializing. I only ever had dinner with him a few times. So we weren't really friends. But when he knew you were right for a part, he'd come to you first. He called me to say he was producing *The War Wagon* and wanted me to be in it.

"I had to admire Duke. I didn't realize just how much difficulty he had with just the one lung until we made *The War Wagon*. We were on a plane on our way to Durango, and Duke was having trouble breathing and had to use an oxygen mask.

"He had trouble breathing on location in Durango and often had to use his oxygen mask. But he never let his physical problems get in the way of work. He was extremely professional. He'd be the first on the set. He'd be there looking over special effects and asking what kind of dynamite they were using. He was interested in every aspect of filming.

"He was producing the film, and I'd produced a lot of my films, and he butted into everything, and I've done that too, but he beat me at it by a long shot. I mean, he'd push directors around and he'd say, 'You're putting the camera *there?* Jesus, put it *here.*' Now this was out in the countryside and whichever way you pointed the camera there was beautiful scenery.

"Our director Burt Kennedy was very talented. But he was gentle. Wayne was not very gentle all the time, and he was not a very talented director. And he gave Burt a lot of trouble. I tried to get Burt to stand up to him. I thought of how Otto Preminger had treated Tom Tryon [on *In Harm's Way*] where the director bullied the actor. Here was an actor bullying the director, although Wayne was never as offensive as Preminger."

Burt Kennedy denied that Wayne had bullied him when we spoke in 1979. He said, "Duke was producing the film and he felt responsible for everything that ended up on the screen. I'm sure he would have preferred to have directed it as well because he knew what he wanted. But he'd tried directing and that hadn't turned out well for him. So he chose directors he could trust, which is why he chose Andy McLaglen a lot of times. I only did a few pictures with Duke. *The War Wagon* was the first. I only did one other, *The Train Robbers*. I'm not sure if it was me who didn't want to do too many with him or he didn't want to do too many with me. Maybe he got his own way with Andy [McLaglen] more than he did me. But I wouldn't call him a bully.

"I would say that it seemed to me that Duke and Kirk respected each other but didn't really like each other. They'd argue about politics, and they had such a great rivalry that it produced sparks on the screen which I used to great effect. When they did the scene where they shot two bad guys — where Kirk says, 'Mine hit the ground first,' and Duke says, 'Mine was taller' — that was their real-life rivalry being taken advantage of. And they both thought it was great to play off each other that way. It made the film work as well as it did."

When I asked Wayne about working with Kirk Douglas, he said, "In recent years,

I've worked in partnership with only three actors who I could honestly say I had a chemistry with. One was Dean Martin. One was Mitchum. The third was Kirk. Didn't matter what he thought of me or what I thought of him. He was wonderful to work with, and he is a great actor. I'll tell you something; he would try and hog the scene just as much as I might do sometimes. It didn't happen in the first two films we did, but it did in *The War Wagon*, and Burt Kennedy said, 'That's just the way it should be. You're making the sparks fly. People are gonna love this.'

"That Kirk! I tell ya, I've heard that he says I'm a bit of a bully with directors, but I've heard stories from some directors about *him*. And I heard that his pal Burt Lancaster is the same. I never worked with Lancaster. Would've loved to. Met up with him once or twice, and I said, 'You, me, and Kirk have got to make a picture together.' He said, 'That'd be great. You could push me around and I'll push Kirk around and let's see if he can push you around.' He was kidding, but he had a point. The three of us together in one film would give the director a heart attack."

Kirk recalled one of Wayne's tricks to dominate a scene: "I realized that when there were others in a lineup with him, he'd be in the middle, and he'd have two cowboys to his left and two to his right. He'd turn to the left and say something, and he'd turn to the right and say something, and then they'd all move forward.

"I found myself in that kind of lineup in one scene, standing to his right, and as he turned left to say something, I bent down and poured myself a cup of coffee from the fire. He turned to his right, and I'll never forget the look on his face when I wasn't there, and he looked down and saw me crouching. He said, 'What the hell . . . ?' and I just looked up innocently and said, 'Well, John, we were lined up like the Rockettes. I just thought it would break things up.' He went along with it, but I think he was reluctant.

"He'd get his own back in other ways. It was part of our rivalry, but always with good humor. The character I played never got on a horse the normal way. He always did fancy mounts. There were stuntmen to do all those fancy mounts for me, [but] I decided I should do them and not cheat the audience. So I got a small trampoline which we'd hide behind a rock, and I soon learned how to take a run at it, jump on the trampoline, and land on the horse.

"When John was being interviewed by a reporter who said, 'I hear Kirk Douglas is very good with a horse,' John answered, 'Good with a horse! Hell, he can't even get on a horse unless he uses a trampoline.' You know, *I* thought that was very funny."

The strange thing about hearing Kirk Douglas criticize Wayne for trying to dominate the film is that I've spoken to a lot of directors and actors who have said that Kirk did the same thing. Keenan Wynn was one of them. A regular in Westerns, he played a major supporting role in *The War Wagon*. When I interviewed him over a drink in the bar of a small hotel off Oxford Street, he told me, "I was not one of Wayne's regulars. So I don't speak from any kind of loyalty. I saw that Wayne could impress his opinions on Burt Kennedy, but he never did anything to the detriment of the other actors. Or even to the detriment of Kennedy. Everything was for the benefit of the picture. But Kirk Douglas seemed to feel slighted, I thought. Most of the time he was at ease on the set working with Wayne, but there were times when it was obvious he didn't like something that made Wayne the center of attention, and Douglas would do something to upstage him.

"I sometimes thought, Here we go. It's gonna end in a fight. But Wayne, who towered over Kirk Douglas — and most everyone else — kept his temper in check, and I felt that he had so much respect for Kirk Douglas that he didn't want to get into a fight with him. I don't know if it's coincidence, but they never worked together again after that."

I wondered why Douglas never called Wayne "Duke." He explained, "Everybody else called him 'Duke,' but I called him 'John.' I don't like nicknames unless they mean something special. I didn't know what 'Duke' meant, so John Wayne was always 'John' to me."

When I told Douglas why he was called 'Duke' (although I found it hard to believe he didn't know why), he laughed and said, "So everyone thinks John's a dog!"

The War Wagon was released before *El Dorado* by a matter of weeks. Wayne said, "I hate it when the distributors do that. Universal with *The War Wagon* were in direct competition with Paramount and *El Dorado*." It didn't matter much, because *The War Wagon* made the same at the box office as *El Dorado* and *Katie Elder*.

By then, Wayne was eager to make his Vietnam film: "After I got *The War Wagon* out of the way, I put all my energies into making *The Green Berets*. I went over to Vietnam [in 1965] and when you've been there, when you come back, you can't sit on the fence. Personally, I thought it was right that we should be there as a country fighting for freedom in the world. But that's not why I made *The Green Berets*, even though everyone said I did. I just wanted to make a picture that showed what our guys were doing for others. No one wants war. But there was one, and we had thousands of young men giving their blood and their lives in it. We had thousands of our young men fighting and dying because their country had sent them there. *They* didn't go, 'Hey, we don't want to be here so let's stop fighting and go home.' They were there because their government had told them to be there, and those guys needed our support. We *owed* it to them. It just made me feel sick to my stomach to see our boys getting killed and maimed and then seeing that the people back home weren't behind them. Those protesters weren't just protesting against the war. They were insulting the men who were doing the fighting. I realized that the day I saw those students hurling abuse at that marine with the one arm.

"And to those who say we shouldn't have been there, I say, when it was too late, we realized we should have been in Europe to help the Jews. There was just as much need for us to help the Vietnamese.

"I felt so strongly about it, that I decided I had to direct *The Green Berets* myself. I thought that after *The Alamo*, no studio would back a film I was directing, but Warner Bros. realized that I had the backing of the government and the Defense Department, and they gave the go-ahead.

"We shot the film up in Georgia, at Fort Benning, in 1967. Michael [Wayne] was producing, and we had a good screenplay from James Lee Barrett. I'd lost my dear friend Jimmy Grant the year before, but James Barrett was a really fine writer and I used him on a number of my productions."

When I mentioned that *The Green Berets* didn't benefit from the kind of detailed characterizations that *The Alamo* had, Wayne said, "Let me tell you something. I'd have liked to have given a lot more screen time to developing the characters, but the studio made it clear they wanted a film that had more action than talk, and *The Alamo* was criticized for having more talk than action.

"James Barrett wrote a fine background story to the colonel I played. He had a wife played by Vera Miles, and we shot her scenes, but the studio cut all her scenes out. They just wanted a war picture. And that's what they got.

"I was trying to keep everyone happy and still keep my vision of what *I* wanted. But the studio wanted one thing, and the men from the Defense Department wanted something else. Let me tell ya; it was said I got all the hardware and the real soldiers who were in the picture for free. I paid for everything that belonged to the Defense Department. But I still could only hire the hardware and the soldiers if we changed things in the script. So a lot got changed.

"But I still believe we ended up with a picture that said what had to be said."

Michael Wayne, as the film's producer, told me what it was that the film tried to say: "JW didn't support the war. He supported the fact that we should be there because the war was already going on before the United States government committed so many of our men there, and once that had been determined, then my father felt the soldiers fighting there should get support from the people. He felt that those men were the bravest and best soldiers our country ever put in the field, and he felt the people back home who were protesting were letting those boys down. But JW never supported the conduct of the war.

"So what we did in *The Green Berets* was to show those men as heroes, and obviously that was a terrible thing because the critics tore it apart. But they weren't reviewing the film; they were reviewing my father's politics."

The Green Berets, unfortunately, was not a particularly good film, whatever the reasons. It lacked characterization, and the heroes were of the cardboard type that had once thrilled audiences who flocked to see Second World War movies. The weakness, it would seem, lay in James Lee Barrett's screenplay. Barrett told me, "Duke Wayne took me on with Andy McLaglen's recommendation after I wrote *Shenandoah* for him. I thought Andy would direct *The Green Berets* and maybe Andy thought so too, although he never complained if Wayne did overlook him in the end. I think it was such a personal project of Duke's that he just couldn't let anyone else direct. But we had problems. I had to submit the script to the Pentagon for approval, and they rejected the first draft. I believe Michael [Wayne] kept it a secret from his father because he thought it would be better if I rewrote the script according to their recommendations before the rest of Hollywood got to hear about it. That would have started the rumor that we were already in trouble.

"What the Pentagon objected to was to do with the massive attack by Vietcong on the American base. The officials wanted the South Vietnamese helping to defend the camp, so that was easily rectified.

"They objected strenuously to the second half of the story in which a Special Forces team was to carry out a covert raid in North Vietnam, kidnap a North Vietnamese general, and blow up some of their bridges in the escape back. The Pentagon said that the Green Berets would not invade North Vietnam.

"So I rewrote the script so the second half was about the Green Berets kidnapping a Vietcong general who's inside South Vietnam. But there were hundreds of other changes they kept coming up with. A maverick director would have said, 'To hell with them. I'm making the film my way.' But Duke was no maverick. He believed it was his moral obligation to make a film that represented our government's policies in Vietnam. The problem was, the Pentagon didn't really want the public to know what was really going on, and so the script became just a flag-waving war film. They finally gave their approval to the script. But my typewriter was worn out with the re-writes. I'd say both Duke and I, as his writer, suffered the backlash the film en-countered — Duke more than I. But he stood up to it all. The one thing he would never do is criticize his country, and he wasn't going to blame his country for some of the film's failings.

"And the one thing we were going to get across in the story was that Communism is not an option for Americans — or for anyone. And the critics — especially the ones on the East Coast — saw something distasteful about that. But they thought it was wonderful when they saw American soldiers behaving like Nazis in *Apocalypse Now*. Mind you, wasn't that a great line? 'I love the smell of napalm in the morning.' As a writer I have to admit that's a great line. But as a piece of entertainment for American audiences, I thought it was pretty appalling."

Jim Hutton, who provided the film with most of its more humorous moments as the picture's resident light comedian, and also its darkest moment when he is impaled on a bamboo booby trap, said, "Duke was trying to please too many people who had an interest in what the film finally said. Hollywood is such a fickle place. If *The Alamo* had not created such a storm simply because it had been directed by John Wayne, then Duke would have been able to make *The Green Berets* into *his* film. But what Warner Bros. did was send another director to take over a few months into production, and it caused problems for Duke."

The new director was Mervyn LeRoy who had directed Wayne in *Without Reservations*.

I spoke to LeRoy by phone in 1981 and asked him how he came to codirect *The Green Berets*. He said, "When Duke Wayne was making his Vietnam War film, I found myself fulfilling a family obligation. Before working at Metro, I was at Warner Bros. where I married the daughter of Harry M. Warner. So I became related to all the Warner brothers. Jack Warner agreed to back *The Green Berets* around the time the studio was taken over by Seven Arts, and Warner Bros.–Seven Arts was the company producing *The Green Berets*.

"So Jack Warner called me and said, 'Duke Wayne is making an expensive war picture for us. It's about the Vietnam War.' I said, 'Yeah, I know, and I have to tell you, nobody's ever made a film about the Vietnam War and I think it's risky.' Jack said, 'Yeah, I know. But it could be a good old-fashioned war picture but instead of the Japanese or Germans, John Wayne is fighting the North Vietnamese.' I said, 'Jack, there are people in this country who don't want this war.' He said, 'But there are still enough people in this country who'll see John Wayne in a war picture. And that's what we gotta have.' I said, 'What do you want me to do about it? I'm retired.' He said, 'We've got six million dollars riding on this picture, and I don't think Wayne is coping well.' Actually, Warner Bros. didn't have six million invested. They put up a proportion of the film's six-million-plus budget, and Batjac put up the rest, although what the actual breakdown was, I couldn't say. Anyway, so Warner says to me, 'I think he could do with our help.' I said, 'Has he asked for my help?' He said, 'No. *I'm* asking on his behalf.'

"So I turned up at Fort Benning, and I could see Duke wasn't too happy about it. We'd got on well way back when we made *Without Reservations*, and we'd always

534

stayed friends. So I think he tolerated me, and in the end of what was a very tough production for both of us, he said, 'Thanks, Merve. You got me through this.' I said, 'Good. I'll send you my bill so you can pay for my stay at the home for old movie directors who are getting too old for all this shit.' He laughed and said, 'You're not too old.' I said, 'Duke, we're *both* too old for this. Take my advice. Forget directing and give your fans what they want. John Wayne on the screen beating the shit out of the bad guys.' And I think he took my advice."

Wayne admitted he was initially unhappy about the studio sending a director to take over his production. "Mervyn arrived and said, 'I'm sorry about this, Duke, but Warner insisted I come down here and help you out. I thought I'd directed my last film, so give me the easy scenes, would ya?' And I said to Mervyn, 'You can direct the scenes I'm in and I'll direct the rest of the picture.' He said, 'I've looked at the script and you're in virtually *all* of the scenes.' I said, 'Then you won't sit around getting bored.' "

David Janssen, who played a cynical newspaper reporter who learns what the American soldiers are facing when Wayne's colonel invites him over to Vietnam, told me, "Nobody rides roughshod over John Wayne. Duke tried to forget he had another director there and he'd get on with giving the orders. I'd watch as Mervyn LeRoy would walk over and make some suggestion about something which I couldn't hear, and Duke would nod his head, but I could see he wasn't paying any attention, and then Duke would get the scene the way *he* wanted it. I think Mervyn LeRoy just went through the motions to keep Warner happy. And, anyway, he didn't want his name on the credits."

The film's production values are certainly its strongest points. The special effects and stunt work that went into the battle scenes make for exciting viewing.

There is also a fine score by Miklos Rozsa, best remembered for his music during the 1950s and 1960s for epics such as *Ben-Hur*, *El Cid*, and *Quo Vadis?* I had the rare privilege of meeting and interviewing Rozsa (my favorite of all film composers) when he visited London in 1980. Talking about his unlikely collaboration with John Wayne, he told me, "I think it was Mervyn LeRoy who persuaded Wayne to use me. Not that he did me any favors. I disliked the film, but I've written for many other films I didn't like.

"I watched the film when it was finished. Wayne sat there holding an empty 35mm film can into which he spat tobacco. Not the most pleasant way of watching a film with someone chewing tobacco and spitting it out.

"There was a popular record of the time called 'The Ballad of the Green Berets' and Wayne said he wanted it as his theme. I have always hated songs in films, and I never went for the John Ford school of film music where the cavalry sing as they ride out to fight the Indians. So I said to Wayne, 'You can't have the song being sung by the Special Forces. It would not only be old-fashioned but it would be bad taste.'

"He said, 'People like the song and it'll help sell the picture.'

"I said, 'I tell you what. Let's open and close with the song, but I'll compose a piece that will be the actual theme for the film.'

"He said, 'What kind of piece?'

"I said, 'I presume you want something that says these men are heroes?' He nodded, so I said, 'That's what the music will say.' So I composed the theme which plays throughout the film and gave the picture what I hope was a sense of the heroism Wayne was trying to portray. I also gave a special arrangement for 'The Ballad of the Green Berets' for the opening credit sequence that was different from the record. I have to admit, I liked what I did with it. Then, in the last scene as Wayne walks off into the sunset with the small Vietnamese boy, I used a different arrangement of 'The Ballad of the Green Berets,' which I hope was suitably moving and in keeping with the scene — and the theme of the film. The little boy has lost the soldier he has come to love, and he says to Wayne, 'What will happen to me?' Wayne says, 'You let us worry about that. After all, you're what this war is all about.'

"When I first heard that, I thought, How corny. But I realized that John Wayne was the only actor in the history of cinema who could get away with a line like that. I'd left Hungary and come to America to escape the Communists, so I understood what Wayne was saying. It moved something in me, and I wanted the music to help the audience to be moved. But I had promised to use that damn song, and I used it the best way I could. And in all the reviews, especially the ones which were particularly bad, I don't think anyone mentioned whether the music was good or bad. Some film composers say that an audience shouldn't notice the score, but who didn't notice the music in *Ben-Hur?* I think the critics who hated *The Green Berets* were too shocked and mad at John Wayne to listen to music, so maybe I got off lightly."

There is one particularly curious thing about the film's behind-the-scenes personnel. The credits say that the film was directed by John Wayne and Ray Kellogg. When I asked Jim Hutton who Ray Kellogg was, he replied, "Ah, the director of great classics such as *The Killer Shrews* and *The Giant Gila Monster*. What rare additions to the art of motion-picture making they are."

It turns out those pictures do exist, both of them third-rate, low-budget horror pictures made in 1959, and Ray Kellogg did indeed direct them. But I never could find out what his contribution to *The Green Berets* was. When I asked Miklos Rozsa, he said, "Who's Ray Kellogg?"

All Wayne would say was, "What can I say about Ray Kellogg and *The Green Berets?* Without him, my career would not be what it is today."

Nobody has been able to convince me so far that Ray Kellogg actually had any hand in the making of *The Green Berets*, and because Mervyn LeRoy refused to have his name on the credits, I think Warner Bros. may well have decided that *anyone's* name alongside that of Wayne as codirector would placate the critics. If so, it didn't work. The critics savaged the movie when it was released in June 1968. The *New Yorker* said it was "a film best handled from a distance and with a pair of tongs."

The *Hollywood Reporter* called it "a cliché-ridden throwback to the battlefield potboilers of World War II."

"*The Green Berets* is a film so unspeakable, so stupid, so rotten and false in every detail," wrote Renata Adler in the *New York Times*, "that it passes through being fun, through being camp, through everything and becomes an invitation to grieve, not for our soldiers or for Vietnam, but for what has become of the fantasy-making apparatus in this country. It is vile and insane. On top of that, it is dull."

Despite the critical tirade, the film was a huge success, earning more than $16 million in its first four months and becoming one of the top-grossing films of the year. As James Lee Barrett said, "After all the bad reviews, the public still liked it, and so Duke could thumb his nose at the critics.

It still galled him, though. I said to him, 'Duke, if you upset, say, several dozen critics, but you entertain several million paying customers, you tell me where you're going wrong?' He just nodded and gave me that chin-down-low-and-eyes-looking-up-at-you kind of smile."

25

Oscar

Before *The Green Berets* was released, Wayne was at work on *Hellfighters*, inspired, apparently, by the exploits of oil-fire fighter Red Adair. Andrew McLaglen directed, and the cast included Vera Miles, Katharine Ross, Jim Hutton, and Bruce Cabot.

The plot had little going for it, but the oil-fire scenes were exciting, and there were the usual scenes of Waynesque humor. Jim Hutton recalled, "When we were doing *The Green Berets* Duke said, 'Jim, you're just the kind of guy I need for my next picture which is about fighting oil fires.' I said, 'I don't know anything about fighting oil fires, and I'm sure I don't much like the idea of big fires. I'm just a light-comedy actor at heart.' He said, 'That's why I want you with me. You make me laugh, and the audience loves you.' Well, what could I say? I liked Duke. And if he liked you, you got to do more work with him."

Vera Miles, from *The Searchers* and *The Man Who Shot Liberty Valance*, played Wayne's female foil in what was his last real stab at a romantic role. Duke told me, "When we had to cut her scenes from The *Green Berets*, I told her I'd make up for it by giving her the role of my ex-wife in *Hellfighters*. Since the film was such a bomb, maybe I didn't do her any favors."

For director Andy McLaglen, this was only his second film for Wayne since his first, *McLintock!*, although they would go on to make another three together in the life and career Wayne had left. McLaglen said to me, "You wanna know how tough Wayne is? I had a tubular director's chair with plastic webbing — the kind you can fold up easily. I came over to the camera where we had one of the big fires going which makes you feel like the skin is peeling off your face, it's so hot. And when I went back to the chair, the webbing had totally melted to the chair, even though it was some thirty or forty feet away from the fire.

"And Wayne went into those fires. He said, 'By God, for a million dollars I'll do anything.' But we had to keep water on him the whole time with hoses.

"At one point, I said, 'Stop the water. I can't see Duke with all that water.' But immediately the water on his suit began to bubble and that meant that the heat was so intense he was about to boil. So we hit him right away with more water, and he was fine. But Duke is tough."

Hellfighters didn't set the box office alight. Wayne said, "I had the feeling my career was about to start flagging. I had a hit with *The Green Berets* but I wasn't getting any younger and I knew that *Hellfighters* was not going to be a blockbuster. I was also working with Andy [McLaglen] on *The Undefeated*, which we were planning to shoot in Durango sometime early in 1969, which I hoped would be the kind of Western that people would like.

"But I was getting anxious because there was this young guy called Clint Eastwood making Westerns in Italy and having tremendous success with them. All of a sudden the studios all wanted Eastwood to come and make Westerns for them, but they were not the kind of Westerns I'd been making. They were tough and bleak. One day I said to Bill Clothier, 'I don't get it. What do people see in these films?'

"He said, 'Duke, times change. You gotta change with them. I just don't think *The Undefeated* is a film people will go to see these days.' I didn't like what he was saying and I refused to give in. But he had a point."

It was a point I was able to bring up with Clothier, who told me, "Duke was having trouble adjusting to the changes that came about — especially in the 1960s. He thought things were only just changing, and that he'd been doing things the same as he'd always done them.

"I said, 'Duke, you and the Western have grown up together. The kind of Westerns you used to make in the forties are different from ones you were making ten, fifteen years ago. Look at *The Searchers*. You couldn't have made that in 1939. Look at what *Red River* did for the Western. It made things change.'

"He said, 'Hell, I don't like change.'

"I said, 'But you've been changing along with the genre since you started. That's what I've just been telling you. You can't just get on a horse or knock somebody about and think the public will go for it anymore. You need to change. You've been doing that for years. Don't stop now.' I told him to find something that will show that he could still teach youngsters like Clint Eastwood a thing or two."

Wayne believed he had found exactly what Clothier had been talking about with the publication of a new book called *True Grit* by Charles Portis. He said, "I was able to get hold of a copy of the publisher's galleys and when I read this story of a fat old one-eyed marshal called Rooster Cogburn, I said, 'I was born to play this part.' And it was a character that had never been seen in a picture before. Here was a guy with an eye patch who's survived because he knew you couldn't give an outlaw a chance. You had to use fair means and foul to bring the outlaw to justice. But he always did it for the greater good, if you will.

"And the writing was so good, it read like a movie. So I put in an offer for the rights only to find Hal Wallis had beat me to it. And Henry Hathaway was going to direct it. So I asked Hal Wallis to give me the part. And that was no easy thing for John Wayne to go and ask a producer if he can have a role."

Henry Hathaway recalled: "Hal Wallis already had Wayne in mind for the role of Rooster, and I was in total agreement. The only person who wasn't in agreement was the author, who thought Wayne was all wrong. Apart from that astute observation, Charles Portis was a great writer, and we kept his dialogue in the screenplay because it was perfect."

Wayne admitted that, in retrospect, he didn't realize what an important part the eye patch would play: "I've had a bit of a moustache once or twice in my career, but Hal Wallis told me Rooster not only wore an eye patch but also had a big moustache. I didn't mind the moustache too much, but I said, 'Hal, my fans don't expect to come and see me and find I look like an old pirate.' So Hal said, 'Tell you what. Forget the moustache, but the eye patch stays.' I thought he'd made a bad mistake.

"But then Henry Hathaway told me to eat as much as I wanted and get fat. As someone who'd been trying to fend off a considerable spread since middle age, I was delighted to be able to forget all that and just eat as much as I wanted. I did try to persuade Henry to let me lose the eye patch, but he said, 'You wear that eye patch and give me the performance I want from you and you might even win an Oscar.' I said, 'Henry, you're a great guy — but you're so full of shit.' About the only thing I was right about was that the part *was* one I had to make mine."

A crucial part of the casting was finding a girl to play Mattie Ross, who hires Rooster Cogburn to find the man who killed her father. "Hal Wallis thought Mia Farrow would be perfect," said Hathaway, "but that fucking Robert Mitchum had told her that I was a real son of a bitch to work for, and so she turned us down. Then Wallis saw Kim Darby on some TV show and decided she was perfect for the part. And she was. The only problem was, she was a young unknown actress who started haggling with Wallis who was offering the part of a lifetime in a John Wayne movie that we all had real faith in, and she virtually had Wallis begging her. I'd have told her to forget it and go on being unknown. But Hal got her."

Casting Kim Darby caused upset in the Wayne family. Duke said,

"I was sure Aissa was perfect for the role, and I think she would have been good. I was forgetting this was not a Batjac film and I was working for two tough veterans, Hal Wallis and Henry Hathaway. I made the mistake of telling her the part was hers. Then when I told Hathaway what I'd done, he said, 'You stupid bastard, Duke. This isn't your movie. We got the part cast. So you can go and break your daughter's heart and tell her she can't do it.' And that's what I did. I hated myself for it. Anyway, in the end I told Aissa that acting was no great profession because Patrick had been trying for years to get out from under my shadow, and she saw the sense in that and gave up all ideas of becoming a movie star.

"Kim Darby wasn't too unlike Mattie. She was strong willed, independent, and determined. Problem was, that's great for the character, but not so great for an actor — or actress — to be too much like that. I tried to get some rapport going between the two of us but that didn't work. Henry did his best to get her to work at making our on-screen relationship work, and I think if it wasn't for him, I'd have given up on her. She was a superb actress, no doubt; but was *she* spoiled. Henry said to me, 'I think she's trying to show everyone she's not impressed just because she's working with John Wayne.' Her attitude on me worked the way Mattie's attitude worked on Rooster. It made him go all out, and so *I* went all out. Gave it my best shot. *Better* than my best. But it's not the way I like to work. I like me and my screen partners to get along. Jesus, I got along better with Kirk Douglas!"

The choice of actor for the role of Texas ranger Le Boeuf was a curious one, but one made with commercial rather than artistic reasons in mind. Said Hathaway, "We cast Glen Campbell who wasn't a great actor but he was a popular singer. I figured that he could record the title song from the film, have a hit with it, and it would help the picture. Mind you, if he'd been a really lousy actor, I wouldn't have cast him. And if he had been lousy and Hal Wallis had insisted I use him, I'd have walked off the picture because I don't put commerce before craftsmanship or talent. So that's my way of saying that Glen Campbell gave us the performance we wanted, and no actor can do more."

Despite Hathaway's complimentary remarks about Campbell, the singer, making his film debut, found Hathaway difficult to please, but Wayne, used to Hathaway's tough manner, had nothing but praise for the director. "Henry decided to shoot the picture in Colorado, which kind of upset Charles Portis who said the story took place in Arkansas and complained to Henry. But Henry, in his own sweet way, told Portis that filming was all about illusion, and the audience would believe Colorado was Arkansas. We shot in the autumn so it was extraordinarily beautiful as the leaves changed color and then dropped. The way Lucien Ballard [director of photography] captured the landscape was breathtaking."

Hathaway admitted he could be "a mean bastard": "I haven't got time to make friends. Making pictures is damned hard, especially the older you get. If actors don't like me then that's tough. It's goddamn hard to make a good movie if you're being distracted by actors going, 'Oh, come on Henry, it's a hot day and I'm so tired and . . .' Chickenshit! We got a schedule to meet and a budget to keep. I don't pretend I'm one of those directors who know it all. Jesus, I made enough turkeys to prove that. But when you get a script the quality of *True Grit* and you got John Wayne giving a tour de force performance, you don't get too sympathetic toward actors who can't keep up the pace.

"If there was an actor on that picture giving me any trouble — and I'm not saying there was and I'm not saying there wasn't — I'd be inclined to tell him — or her — to go and watch Duke work at it. He's a man with one lung who had trouble breathing up there in Montrose, Colorado, yet before we shot the famous scene where he single-handedly charges the gang of outlaws, twirling guns in both hands and holding his reins in his teeth, he was up at the crack of dawn before anyone else, practicing how to do that stunt. Duke was sixty-one then, but he never stopped until he could do that ride perfectly, so when we came to shoot it, we didn't have to do take after take.

"When I called it a wrap, I knew I had a picture among all those reels of film."

While Hathaway went to work on the editing and post-production, Wayne took a month off and enjoyed Christmas 1969 at home with his family. Claire Trevor recalled, "When Christmas came around, the biggest kid in the house was Duke. He'd get upset if anyone else tried putting up the trimmings and the tree. He just loved to do all that. And he always made sure he had presents for everyone. In fact, everyone had more presents than they needed. They say Christmas is for children. I always thought Christmas was just for Duke Wayne."

It was a particularly special Christmas that year, according to Duke: "I felt I'd finished a film that was my best in years, and that makes you feel pretty damn good. Just after Christmas I got a call from Hal Wallis to come and look at some of the footage [from *True Grit*] they'd assembled, and, wow! Hal was talking about Academy Awards and telling me this was the *one*. That was enough to send me off to Durango for my next picture [*The Undefeated*], which I'd not really been looking forward to. The only problem I had was that I had to lose all the weight I'd gained to play Rooster, and that's not easy for me over Christmas. But I did it because, I guess, I felt good about myself.

"I think on that one I just enjoyed the whole experience. Andy [McLaglen] was directing and we had a lot of old friends in the cast like John Agar, Ben Johnson, Paul Fix, and Dobe [Harry] Carey. And we had Rock Hudson, one of the most professional guys I ever worked with."

For most members of the public, the revelation that Rock Hudson was gay only broke when he was dying from AIDS in 1985. But it wasn't news to most in the business. Wayne obviously felt a need, in 1974, to quickly establish how much I knew before he spoke out of turn, asking me, "You know about Rock?"

I replied, "He's a homosexual? Yes, I know!"

That opened up a whole side of Wayne I

would never have expected to see. "Who the hell cares if he's a queer? The man plays great chess. We had many a game up there in Durango. And what a good-looking man. I admit, I couldn't understand how a guy with those looks and that build and the . . . *manly* way he had about him could have been a homosexual, but it never bothered me. Life's too short. It wasn't like some of his type who go around saying, 'Poor me, I'm discriminated against.' He just got on with his life in private, and I never cared to know about it. All I cared about was he was on the set on time every day, and at the end of the day he'd say, 'Care for a little chess, Duke?' and I'd say, 'You wanna get beat *again?*' "

When I interviewed Rock Hudson in 1980, he told me, "I was grateful to Duke Wayne because my career was going down the toilet at that time. Then I get a call from Andy McLaglen, saying, 'Me and Duke Wayne want you to make a movie in Durango. Think you're up to making a Western?' I wanted to fall to the ground and give praise, but I didn't want to appear *desperate*. I told them I'd be happy to join them in Durango and said I'd better get some practice getting on and off a horse. I was more used to getting on and off Doris

Day. That sounds terrible, and you know what I meant. I said I did, and we got on well." He went on to tell me, "What crap the film was, but what a great time I had doing it. It came out just after *True Grit*, and that made a lot of people go to see it. John Wayne was then *the* Hollywood legend, and I was on screen with him. The guy is an angel. He saved my life back then when no other filmmaker wanted to know me."

The film was a typical 1960s John Wayne picture, with Duke as a former Union officer rounding up horses to sell to the army but ends up with his herd of horses in Mexico. There he crosses trails with Hudson as a Confederate colonel, who leads a party of around a hundred men, women, and children from the conquered South into Mexico. Making an unusual alliance, Wayne and Hudson find they have a common enemy in the French dictator of Mexico, Maximilian.

I remarked to Wayne that the character he played had a rather unfortunate name — John Henry Thomas. Wayne gave his lopsided grin and said, "What's wrong with being called John Thomas?" I didn't argue.

Durango was a location that Wayne and

Andy McLaglen loved, even though the high altitude meant that Duke had to use his oxygen tank a lot. McLaglen told me, "Both Wayne and I love Durango. People say to us, 'Why are you going to that horrible hole?' But there are some beautiful houses where we always live when we go there.

"In the evenings we eat something of a speciality out there which is a little suckling goat roasted over a spit that they butterfly, and with it you drink a little tequila to keep you relaxed."

About Wayne's legendary "bullying" of directors, McLaglen said,

"I feel that I'm the best director for Duke, and nobody admires Wayne more than I do. Let me say that I feel he really respects me and I certainly respect him. He never tried to take advantage of me. I started directing him when he was fifty-five and I directed him right up until he was sixty-six.

"I always knew how to make him look his best. I never put him in a situation that's gonna make him look bad. When we do a scene I can say, 'Cut!' and he'll say, 'What's wrong?' 'Your stomach is a little bulky.' 'Okay!' Or I can say 'Cut! You slurred over that word,' and he'd say, 'Oh, I did?' and he'd do it again without argument.

"A lot of guys are afraid to say boo to him in case he blasts them out of their director's seat. He's never pushed any of his authority around me.

"It was when we were making *The Undefeated* that Duke fell and fractured a couple of ribs. He couldn't work for almost two weeks. Then he tore a ligament in his shoulder and couldn't use an arm at all. I said, 'Don't worry, Duke. The way we'll shoot this, nobody watching the picture will ever know.' He appreciated that kind of concern. He didn't care that he was in terrible pain. He just didn't want to let his fans down."

Although filming *The Undefeated* started with Wayne in high spirits, he finished it in a somber mood. Rock Hudson told me, "Duke's wife, Pilar, hated Durango, but she was up there with him because he liked to have her with him. And I think she wanted to be with him — but not in Durango. She played chess pretty good, and she, Duke, I, and anybody else we could round up would play chess every night. But I could sense things weren't good between Duke and Pilar. I never interfered. Then, before the picture was over,

Pilar left. Duke told me they'd had an argument. I said, 'If you want to talk about it . . .' He told me a lot about the problems he and Pilar had. It wasn't all her fault, and it wasn't all his fault. But they were going in different directions. She'd become a Christian Scientist, which puzzled Duke. He told me that he could cope with her being a Catholic because he'd had Catholic wives before, and he felt Catholicism was a universal religion. But he didn't get Christian Science. And he didn't *want* to know. I don't have a lot of experience with these cultish religions, but I do know that when you've got one partner involved and the other isn't, there's problems. She didn't smoke or drink, and she didn't really like anyone else doing it. Duke didn't smoke cigarettes, but he certainly liked a drink, and I think Pilar frowned on that but never actually said anything. Those unspoken words can wreck a relationship. I felt sorry for both of them. But I understand they tried to work it out over the next few years, although Duke told me that he and Pilar weren't sleeping together anymore. I told him how sorry I was."

It's no wonder that, in 1974, Wayne told me, "That Rock Hudson. He's a really great guy. The kind you felt you could rely on him if you were in trouble. Damn, how can the guy be queer?"

In June 1969, *True Grit* was released after much anticipation. The critics were virtually unanimous in their praise for the film and for Wayne, although they seemed hardly able to admit to their admiration for Duke. "Can that fat old man be John Wayne?" asked Roger Ebert in his review in the *New York Times*.

William Wolf in *Cue* wrote, "When the John Wayne retrospectives are in full swing, this will loom as one of his finest movie triumphs."

Variety said, "[Wayne] towers over everything in the film — actors, script, even the magnificent Colorado mountains. He rides tall in the saddle as the 'fat old man.' "

Never daring to mention this to Wayne, I thought his performance was over the top and hammy. Wayne gave superb performances in *Red River* and *The Searchers*, and would give at least two more great performances. Acting is a craft that is at its best when it cannot be noticed. But as Rooster Cogburn, John Wayne was seen to be acting his heart out.

Of Cogburn, he said, "That was me letting myself have fun. For the first time, I felt like an actor."

But the problem was that he was trying too hard — and it showed. Screen acting is a craft that requires a realistic approach, unlike stage acting which requires a more grand technique. Suddenly, Wayne was being theatrical, and it seemed false from a man who claimed, "I just try to be sincere. I've been selling sincerity all my life."

To my surprise, Henry Hathaway agreed with me. He said, "I knew Duke was going over the top, but I let him do it because it was a whole different color to any other part he'd played. I thought that he was a pure caricature and not even one of himself, even though some critics said he was a caricature of himself. I thought, Critics are so goddamn arrogant and think they know it all, they're gonna say, 'Good God, Wayne can act.' It was all performance and no realism. But that's okay. That makes the film unique. I wasn't surprised Wayne got nominated for an Oscar for *True Grit*."

I was surprised that Wayne was nominated for an Oscar as Best Actor of 1969 for his role in *True Grit*, especially as he had given superior performances in *Red River* and *The Searchers*, and had not been nominated for either of them. Also in competition for the Best Actor Award of 1969 was Peter O'Toole as Henry II in *The Lion in Winter* (my choice of best performance of 1969), Jon Voight in *Midnight Cowboy*, Dustin Hoffman in *Midnight Cowboy*, and Richard Burton in *Anne of the Thousand Days*.

Wayne was elated to discover he was nominated while making his next Andy McLaglen Western, *Chisum*, back up in Durango in 1969. *True Grit* was, by then, still doing well, earning just over $14 million domestically, making it Wayne's biggest-grossing film at tenth position, where it would stay for many years. An inflation-adjusted account in 1983, which gave a more realistic indication of success, still put *True Grit* high in the list, at number fourteen, not far below *The Alamo* at number ten and *Red River* at number eleven, which were to remain Wayne's most successful films (unless you count *How the West Was Won* which came in at number five).

Chisum was supposedly based on the bloody Lincoln County cattle war *circa* 1878. Wayne was John Chisum, apparently a real character, but the film seemed to have little to do with him and more to do with Billy the Kid, played by Geoffrey Deuel, and Pat Garrett, played by Glenn Corbett. A number of regulars were in the film, including Ben Johnson, John Agar, and, from *El Dorado*, Christopher George.

Ben Johnson and John Agar had been working with Wayne since the John Ford heydays. Johnson was quick to admit, "By the time we were doing those films with Andy [McLaglen], it was all pretty much the same film. The only thing that changed was Duke's weight, which went up and down. I was just happy to be working, but by the time the film was released [in 1970] it was competing with Westerns from Italy and the pictures Clint Eastwood was making in Hollywood. I think if there'd been no *True Grit*, there might not have been such a thing as a John Wayne Western anymore — and they weren't good pictures."

Nevertheless, *True Grit* had given Wayne's career "a much needed kick up the ass," as Johnson put it, but fewer people went to see him in *The Undefeated* when it opened in September 1969, taking $4 million domestically and an estimated $8 to $10 million worldwide, which was still a respectable outcome. In 1969, John Wayne was the top box-office star in America. For a sixty-two-year-old star who'd been going for almost forty years, that was no mean feat.

The films made by Batjac in the late 1960s and early 1970s all cost around $4 million to make under Michael Wayne's close fiscal scrutiny. *Chisum*, when released in August 1970, did better than *The Undefeated*, taking $6 million domestically and at least double that amount worldwide.

Early in 1970 Wayne was in Old Tucson making a non-Batjac Western, *Rio Lobo*, produced and directed by Howard Hawks. Wayne played an ex–Union officer who rids a Texas town of carpetbaggers and settles an old score with a wartime informer in the process. It was very much in the mold of *Rio Bravo* and *El Dorado*, despite Hawks's insistence that it wasn't. Instead of Ricky Nelson or James Caan, it had the lesser-known Jorge Rivero, and instead of Angie Dickinson or Charlene Holt, it had Jennifer O'Neill. The old coot, as previously played by Walter Brennan and then Arthur Hunnicutt, was played by Jack Elam. Curiously, there was no character the equivalent of Dean Martin or Robert Mitchum, although Mitchum's son Chris did play a supporting role. But there was no veteran actor for Wayne to spar with, which surprised even Wayne who asked Hawks, "Do I get to play the drunk this time?"

Rio Lobo was in production when the 1970 Academy Awards ceremony took place in Los Angeles. Wayne flew to Hollywood for the event, meeting Pilar and his children at the Beverly Hills Hotel.

"I really didn't think I had a chance at winning up against all that talent," Wayne told me. "So when Barbra Streisand read out my name, I was as surprised as anyone. I tell ya, when Miss Streisand handed me the little golden man, I was trying hard not to blubber."

Bob Hope was master of ceremonies, as he had been for many years. Over a brief transatlantic phone call in 1979 (which terminated prematurely when the line went dead and I couldn't get him back again), he told me, "I was so glad for Duke — but not as glad as Duke was. *I* didn't cry. I only cry when my fee's too small. But Duke deserved that Oscar."

Wayne told the appreciative audience, "Wow! If I'd known this, I'd have put that eye patch on thirty-five years ago. Ladies and gentlemen, I'm no stranger to this podium. I've come up here and picked up these beautiful golden men before, but always for friends. One night I picked up two, one for Admiral John Ford, one for our beloved Gary Cooper. I was very clever and witty that night; the envy even of Bob Hope. But tonight I don't feel very clever, very witty. I feel very grateful, very humble."

The next morning, Wayne flew back to Old Tucson: "I arrived back on the set of *Rio Lobo* to find everyone wearing eye patches. Even my horse!"

Rio Lobo wasn't one of Hawks's best films, and he knew it. "*Rio Lobo* is a Civil War picture before it's a Western. I didn't think it was a good picture but I made it because I had a good story to start with. But the studio couldn't afford to have another actor alongside of Wayne, so I threw out the original story and quickly wrote a new one."

It seemed to me that Hawks blamed everyone else but himself for the film's weaknesses: "Jennifer O'Neill could have been a lot better, but she was . . . well, a damn fool. She wouldn't let Duke help her, and she was no good. And we had a couple of boys who just couldn't even begin to compete with Duke."

I asked Hawks if he was referring to Christopher Mitchum (son of Robert) and Jorge Rivero. He said, "Chris doesn't even look like his father, and sure as hell doesn't have his father's power. I thought Jorge

Rivero would do all right but he didn't have any authority at all. They just weren't tough enough. So many of these young men of today are too effeminate."

Hawks even blamed Wayne for some of *Rio Lobo*'s faults: "Wayne is getting too old to be worth a million dollars. He had a hard time making *Rio Lobo* just getting on and off his horse because he's . . . well, he can't move like a big cat anymore, and he has to hold his belly in. He's not the same person. He called me and said he wanted to make a movie with me because every picture he'd been doing was lousy. I told him I didn't have a good story. He said he had one. He said, 'I'd play an old gun-fighter, and as he walks down the street, some guy calls him out and he tries to find his glasses because he needs them to see long distances now and he can't see the guy clearly. And then a girl runs up and gives him some glass and he shoots the guy.' I said, 'Duke, you've stood for something all your life, and now you want to throw it away for something like *this?* My God, Duke, it's *pitiful.* You can't play gun-fighters at your age anymore.' He said, 'What about *True Grit?*' I said, 'That was an exaggerated thing, and it got by because the director didn't know whether he was making a comedy or a drama.' Nobody wants to see Wayne as an old gunfighter."

As this conversation took place in 1974, I wasn't able to say to Hawks that Wayne's last two films ever would not only see him revive the role of one-eyed, fat, old Rooster Cogburn to moderately commercial acclaim, and that he would give one of his best performances as the aging gunfighter in *The Shootist*. We did, however, get into a serious disagreement when I said that Wayne had done fine work playing his own age in the two films that followed *Rio Lobo* — *Big Jake* and *The Cowboys*.

Hawks retorted, "*The Cowboys* was awful and *Big Jake* . . . Well, it was okay but I could have done it better."

I had one last question for Hawks: "What did you think of *The Alamo*?" His answer was short: "Bad!"

Rio Lobo only managed just over $4 million domestically.

26

Last Roundup

When *Rio Lobo* was finished, Wayne returned home to shattering news: his eighty-one-year-old mother was very ill, and his brother Bobby was now dying of lung cancer. He lost both his mother and brother within a short span of time. Relations between Duke and Pilar had not improved, belying the appearance of the happy couple they had presented at the Oscar ceremony.

Wayne spent some time away from home, returning to Arizona where he had acquired a twenty-six-bar ranch which was proving to be one of his more successful business ventures. He also owned a farm near Stranfield in Arizona, growing cotton and grain.

The vision of John Wayne as a real-life rancher was appropriate. Although, he said, "I still hate riding horses. I go by truck everywhere if I can. I wish I'd had that ranch earlier in life. I love it out there. It's kind of a regret for me that I didn't start having success in business outside the picture business until recently."

His success in business had only come about since he sacked his son-in-law Don LaCava. He now owned oil wells, hotels, and apartment buildings, and he had investments in numerous other ventures. Yet still he wasn't satisfied with the money he was making. He told me, "I'm damn near seventy and I don't know how long I can keep working as an actor. I don't need much more money for myself, but I have a family of young people and children to think about. When I'm gone, which God willing won't be before I finish this film [*Brannigan*], I want to be sure my family have all they need. Not that I think they won't be able to fend for themselves. But I feel I owe it to them all to give them plenty of money. You see, I've been broke, and I've been rich, and while being rich won't give you everything in life, it sure as hell gives you an advantage. I want my kids to have that advantage."

In October 1970, Wayne was making another $4 million Batjac Western, *Big Jake*, filmed in Durango. He played an aging gunfighter who's been away from home for so long that the film has a good running joke whereby people say to him, "I thought you were dead."

The story centers on the kidnapping of his grandson, played by his own son Ethan. The film was largely a reunion for much of its cast. Richard Boone played the dastardly kidnapper, and Maureen O'Hara appeared all too briefly as Wayne's ex-wife. Wayne leads a rescue party which included Pat Wayne and Chris Mitchum. Old friends like Bruce Cabot and Harry Carey Jr. also appeared. Cliff Lyons directed second unit, and Chuck Roberson was playing a bit part as well as doubling for Wayne, although Duke still insisted on doing as many of his own stunts as possible.

"About the only thing Duke couldn't do was run," said Richard Boone. "He didn't have the stamina anymore, which God knows comes to us all. But his biggest problem was with breathing. He always had an oxygen tank nearby and he used it often. But he never wanted his public to know. It wasn't vanity. He just didn't want to let his fans down, so no one was allowed to take photographs of him using his oxygen."

This was Boone's second film with

Wayne, and one he relished. "When you get to kidnap Duke Wayne's son, you know you've got to be a mean son of a bitch, so I was as mean as I could be. I had a great time, and I had great respect for Duke."

Directing the film was George Sherman, who had produced *The Comancheros* but hadn't directed Wayne since the days of "The Three Mesquiteers." He said, "We'd both come a long way since those early days. I hadn't directed a major film for a long time when Duke asked me if I'd like to do *Big Jake*. I have to admit, I was grateful. But I knew that by 1970 Westerns had changed a lot. I admired Duke for playing a character his own age, yet he was still the same tough character people liked. We only had to establish his age with the fact that he was playing a grandfather, and with a few lines of dialogue. We also established that times had moved on along with Duke by setting the film at the beginning of the twentieth century and having Chris Mitchum ride a motorbike instead of a horse.

"But the biggest change was the violence in films by 1970. Duke disagreed with me on this, but I said we had to make the violence more realistic because audiences had come to expect it. He reluctantly agreed.

But I told him we'd offset the violence with plenty of good humor."

Consequently, *Big Jake* became one of the most blood-splattered films Wayne ever made. And yet it retains a good old-fashioned style by virtue of George Sherman's methods. The result on-screen made for a good John Wayne Western in the grand old manner but without seeming too outdated.

Despite Howard Hawks's criticism of *Big Jake* under Sherman's direction, the film made almost twice as much at the box office as *Rio Lobo*. And Wayne did not have the likes of Robert Mitchum or Dean Martin that Hawks always insisted was needed to play against Duke. Wayne was able to carry the film on his own broad if tired shoulders, and even today the film stands up well. It's not *The Searchers*, but it's superior to films like *Chisum* and *The Undefeated*.

But Duke was beginning to feel that he needed to do something different from the standard John Wayne Westerns. He told me, "I got to a point when I felt that I couldn't go on playing the tough gun-fighter and I was looking for something with a different angle to it. So when Warner Bros. sent me a script called *The*

Cowboys, I saw that it was the kind of thing I was looking for."

The Cowboys cast Wayne as a sixty-year-old rancher whose men quit just when he needs to get his cattle to market. The only men offering their help are a gang of villains led by a particularly nasty character played by the superb Bruce Dern (who'd appeared in *The War Wagon*). Wayne's character knows he's likely to lose his whole herd to Dern and his gang and turns them down. Wayne has no choice but to take on kids for the job.

"I thought it was an interesting idea," Wayne told me. "It also took some of the responsibility off me because it wasn't my own production. Mark Rydell produced and directed it. Did a fine job."

Rydell was an actor who turned to directing for television before directing his third feature film, *The Fox*, in 1967. He followed that with the hugely enjoyable *The Reivers* in 1969. *The Cowboys*, only his third film, began filming in April 1971, on the San Cristobel Ranch, near Santa Fe, New Mexico. It had a budget of $6 million.

Rydell obviously didn't believe Hawks's theory about a major costar because Wayne's major fellow players were the boys. He did, however, have fine support from Roscoe Lee Browne who was excellent as the cook who helps Wayne nursemaid the cowboys on route.

There was also a delightful cameo appearance from noted stage actress Colleen Dewhurst as the madam traveling in a wagon full of prostitutes which some of the boys come across.

Colleen told me, "I wasn't sure what I would make of Duke Wayne, but we got on so well that he said to me when the opportunity arose, he'd like to do another picture with me. I had seen some of Duke's films, and I could see why people liked him. But I felt that in *The Cowboys* he was playing more of a character part, and he seemed to enjoy doing it. I think he had a few disagreements with Mark Rydell, but there was never anything major. Rydell was really trying to get a different kind of performance out of Duke, and I think he succeeded."

The Cowboys was a superior film, with an epic quality that had not been seen in a Hollywood Western since the early 1960s, thanks largely to the stunning Panavision photography of Robert Surtees. But what really sets the film apart is the scene where Bruce Dern shoots Wayne in the back. "Usually when I die in my pictures, I go out in a blaze of glory," said Wayne, "but the character I played in that picture was no gunfighter. Sure, he was a tough old boot, but he was a cattleman, not a gunman. So he turns his back on Bruce Dern — who I have to say was so good he should have been nominated for an Oscar — and gets shot in the back and dies. There's no glory. No heroic death. I liked that. It was a real story.

"The only thing I wasn't sure about was the violent way that the boys avenge my death. I mean, that was almost Sam Peckinpah stuff. But Mark Rydell was a new breed of director, and he had a feel for what the public would go for."

For a man who had spent his early years in films specializing as pathological killers, Bruce Dern was one of the most amiable and good-humored actors I've ever met. When I interviewed him at the Dorchester in London in 1978 (he was over promoting *Coming Home*), he told me, "I had always played small roles as heavies in films before *The Cowboys*. I'd been a villain in *The War Wagon*, I tried to kill Clint Eastwood in *Hang 'Em High*, and I had a go at bumping off Charlton Heston in *Will Penny*, so I figured I might as well be the guy who killed John Wayne by shooting him in the back. But it was a good part. I got to play a really *awful* guy. There's a scene where I grab one of the boys and I drag him into the river and just scare the shit out of him, and he really was scared. And so was his mother, who watched from the sidelines convinced I was going to drown her son. So to do that *and* kill Duke Wayne was something an actor doesn't get to do very often."

The film got better reviews than most of Wayne's recent films. Rex Reed wrote in the *New York Daily News*, "In *The Cowboys* all the forces that have made [John Wayne] a dominant personality as well as a major screen presence seem to combine in an unusual way, providing him with the best role of his career. Old Dusty Britches can act."

When it opened at the Radio City Music Hall in January 1972, it surprised all concerned when it failed to pull in an audience, so it was moved to a smaller theatre. In London, it was premiered at the Casino Cinerama Theatre in a 70mm version, but again it struggled to find an audience despite generally favorable reviews. Only George Melly of the *Observer* seemed to hate it, dubbing the film *Straw Puppies* and calling it "a thoroughly corrupt and nasty film, immoral in the ethical sense, as worthy of an X certificate as *Straw Dogs*." In contrast, Alexander Walker of the *Evening Standard*, who had deplored the violence of *Straw Dogs*, wrote, "The violence is not lingered on or exploited the way the despicable *Straw Dogs* did. It remains an initiation rite, not an evisceration ceremony."

I was working for Cinerama at the time, and the reason for the film's initial failure was obvious to me. Warner Bros. had gone overboard in its publicity campaign by promoting Wayne's death scene, with pictures of him dying all over the newspapers. It removed all the shock and emotional value the film had.

The film also suffered in the West End because it had been given an AA censor's certificate which meant nobody under the age of fourteen could see it. The managing director of Cinerama asked the censor what could be done to make the film available to all ages, and to everyone's surprise, the censor said that if the scene with the wagon full of prostitutes was cut, they would make the film an A certificate, which meant children could see the film if accompanied by an adult. The violence of the final fifteen minutes when the cowboys kill off Bruce Dern's entire gang was left intact. So Warner Bros. agreed to cut the scene, and it went on general release throughout the U.K. in its censored version which meant Colleen Dewhurst's wonderful but brief performance was not seen.

Fortunately, the cut version no longer exists, and the film remains one of Wayne's best, featuring a strong performance superior to his Oscar-winning role in *True Grit*. And it didn't do too badly at the box office after all, taking almost $8 million in America and at least that much in the rest of the world, putting it alongside *Big Jake* as joint number twenty-six in *Variety*'s 1983 list of All-Time Western Champs. But, with age catching up on him, and with little quality material on offer, *The Cowboys* looked like it might be Duke's last roundup.

"You don't often find material of the quality of *The Cowboys* which is also suitable for a man of my years," Wayne said. "It did good enough business for Warner Bros. to commission a TV series. The only problem was, there was nowhere for the story to go with this bunch of boys running a ranch. Someone at Warner Bros. said to me, 'Couldn't we find a way of bringing you back, maybe as your own twin brother.' I said, 'Have you thought about looking for a new line of work because you sure as hell don't know anything about this business.' I was so mad at the really lousy idea I'd just heard, I forgot to say, 'I don't do television.' "

Perhaps Wayne should have considered television. James Stewart found it gave him a new lease on life when he did a series called *Hawkins* in 1973. He said, "It was kind of based on the lawyer I played in *Anatomy of a Murder*. We did a pilot and then when that turned out well, we did a season. But I wasn't happy with the way the network [CBS] treated it by postponing episodes for weeks on end so I decided not to do any more. But I told Duke he ought to consider it. Henry [Fonda] had also done well — better than I did — with a series called *The Deputy*."

Fonda recalled urging Wayne to try TV: "I said, 'Duke, I wish I'd waited until I was a little older before I did *The Deputy*, because my movie career wasn't floundering back then [in 1960], but I think it would be good for you now because you could become the biggest star on television.' And he said, 'I don't want to be the biggest star on television. I'd rather be the biggest star in the movies.' And I said, 'Duke, you *are* the biggest star in movies. But give yourself a break and enjoy the luxury of throwing your weight around on a TV set and make those producers quiver in their shoes. You'll *love* it!' He laughed, but he didn't want any part of it. He thought he could go on making just movies and trying to stay on top. But those of our generation knew we were never going to beat the likes of Burt Reynolds and Clint Eastwood. But if Duke had done a TV series, *everyone* would have watched it."

Wayne was restless. As Ben Johnson noted, "He felt out of place in modern society. He'd not changed his ideas on life, and he didn't like the way films were growing up. Of course, he didn't see them as 'growing up.' He saw modern films as being morally repugnant. But, hell, the American public had watched the Vietnam War on their TVs and there was no going back to the kind of illusions of the old days of cinema. If people couldn't believe a film was being realistic, they didn't go. Even I know that. I did *The Last Picture Show*, and I got myself an Oscar as Best Supporting Actor. I said to Wayne, 'Duke, what do you think of that? I never ever thought I was an actor.' He said, 'I'm delighted for you, Ben. You're a really fine actor and you

580

don't like to admit it. But what kind of movies are these people making?' I said, 'Duke, there's nothing wrong with the movie. You just won't stop living in the past. Life isn't a John Ford picture.' He said, 'You're right, but I can't help feeling lost.' I felt sorry for Duke. Very sad. It seemed to me he had become lonely. Things were bad between him and Pilar, although they were trying to keep their marriage problems out of the public eye. But everyone who knew them also knew it was over between them. Very sad indeed."

If Wayne was sad, he picked himself up, dusted himself off, and climbed back on his horse in early 1972 to star in Batjac's *The Train Robbers*. It was Burt Kennedy's second film with Wayne, and it would also be their last together.

"I wrote the script for *The Train Robbers* and I knew that Wayne would be right for the starring role," said Kennedy. "But maybe I should have taken the script somewhere else because I had to use some actors I didn't want, and I won't offend them by mentioning their names. But they hurt the picture."

The principals in the cast, apart from Wayne, were Ann-Margret, Rod Taylor, Ben Johnson, Bobby Vinton, and Christopher George. Ann-Margret gave a fine performance as the woman who hires Wayne, Taylor, and Johnson to recover gold which she claims her husband stole and which she wants to use to educate her daughter. The trio manage to get the gold and gallantly forgo their fee, only to discover they have been conned by Ann-Margret, who has no husband, has no daughter, but now has all the gold.

Rod Taylor was a friend of Wayne's, but this was their first chance to work together. Christopher George, now a regular in Wayne's films, gave his usual quality performance, as did Ben Johnson. Perhaps Kennedy was referring to Bobby Vinton, who was forgettable, and he may have also disapproved of Rod Taylor, who was also unmemorable. But the whole film is unmemorable. And it was a financial disaster, failing even to make it onto *Variety*'s 1983 list of All-Time Western Champs.

This was followed by Wayne's worst film since *The Conqueror, Cahill, United States Marshal*, filmed in Durango late in 1972. Andrew McLaglen directed from a script that was different from the traditional Wayne Western, but it was not well written. It told the story of a marshal (Wayne, of course) who neglects his sons, played by

Gary Grimes, who'd just had a hit with *Summer of '42*, and Clay O'Brien, who was one of *The Cowboys*. The two youngsters are lured into a life of crime by an outlaw played with scene-chewing relish by George Kennedy. And so Wayne, aided by his Indian friend played by Neville Brand, goes after Kennedy and his boys.

"We rushed that picture, and it shows," Wayne told me. "We should have had a better script. I thought it had a different approach; the story of a man who puts his work before his family. I know what that's like."

George Kennedy, whom I talked to by telephone in 1979, said, "I had a good role and I wouldn't complain about anything except that the film didn't do well. Very often the bad guys are the best parts, and even Duke said to me, 'You got the better role.' He really had nothing much to do in the film. The stars were really the boys, but the writing wasn't good enough to make anyone care too much about them."

When I interviewed Neville Brand in London in 1980, he recalled, "I usually only got to play heavies or the comedy roles. I never got to play heroes, and there I was being John Wayne's sidekick — and an *Indian* sidekick at that. But Duke wanted to show that he wasn't always trying to kill the Indians. He said people were always criticizing him for killing Indians, but he actually rarely ever did. He said, 'I killed far more white men than Indians. I like to have the opportunity to show the nobility of the Red Man.' So I was there representing the nobility of the Red Man, and I said, 'Duke, why didn't you get a *real* Indian to play the role?' and he said, 'I could have done that and I would have done that, but if I did, Warner Bros. would have only said, "We need a known name if you want any money from us." So, no offense, Neville, but I needed your name more than I needed a real Indian.' I said, 'Fine by me. I like working.' "

Wayne had another reason for not enjoying making *Cahill*. "We were shooting *Cahill* when I got word that the Coach was dying . . . of the fucking cancer. I went to see him one last time at his home in Palm Springs. He looked just . . . awful. I had to get back to Durango to finish the film which I really had no stomach for anymore."

Following the disaster and the disappointment of *Cahill*, Wayne realized he had to change with the times, whether he liked it or not. All his career, the Western had been a staple diet of moviegoers. But it was no longer the case. Clint Eastwood had helped to revitalize the Western during the 1960s with his Italian Westerns, but now he was creating a whole new genre, one in which he would play a cop who broke all the rules because he believed more in the victim's rights than the perpetrator's. The first of these films was *Dirty Harry*, and it was a phenomenal success, spawning four sequels.

Thanks to *Dirty Harry*, the fight between good and bad in the modern big city replaced the fight between good and bad in the wilds of the old West.

So Wayne decided to play a cop in *McQ*.

27

Dirty Duke

In *McQ*, Wayne played a watered-down version of Dirty Harry. As he told me, "I thought I could be Dirty Duke. After all, I chose to do it because I turned down *Dirty Harry*. I turned it down for what seemed to me to be three very good reasons. The first is that they offered it to Frank Sinatra first, but he'd hurt his hand and couldn't do it. I don't like being offered Sinatra's rejections. Put that one down to pride. The second reason is that I thought Harry was a rogue cop. Put that down to narrow-mindedness because when I saw the picture I realized that Harry was the kind of part I'd played often enough; a guy who lives within the law but breaks the rules when he really has to in order to save others. The third reason is that I was too busy making other pictures."

Dirty Harry was directed by Don Siegel (who would also direct Wayne's final film,

The Shootist). When I interviewed Siegel in 1979 at Pinewood Studios, where he was preparing to shoot *Rough Cut*, he told me, "Wayne couldn't have played Harry. He was just too old. And he would have objected to many of the things that Clint would do, because Clint was never bothered by image. Wayne was. He was too old to play McQ, which was a poor copy of Dirty Harry."

McQ tells of a tough detective whose friend, also a cop, kills himself. McQ wants to find out why and uncovers corruption within the police force.

John Sturges, famous for films like *The Magnificent Seven* and *The Great Escape*, directed the film in Seattle in the summer of 1973. When I worked for Sturges in 1975, he said to me, "We play a game in the business called Rip-off. You see what makes money and you follow it up with something you hope will repeat its success. In the case of *McQ* we were all just trying to make a Dirty Harry film but with John Wayne instead of Clint Eastwood.

"It didn't bother me that we had a pretty poor script and hardly any excitement. I get paid to do my job, and I do it as best I can. Duke Wayne knew we had problems with it, and we did our best to make it work. I liked Duke, and I think he liked me. He didn't try pushing me around the way I'd heard he pushed other directors around. But then, I've been around a long time. So he respected me, and it was mutual.

"It was one of the few films he made in later life where he didn't have his usual cronies around him, and I think he was kind of lonely and lost. He was living on his yacht while we filmed, and he was pleased when his wife and daughter [Marisa] arrived. But Pilar didn't stay and Duke was furious. That's when he told me his marriage was all but over. I'd heard the rumors.

"There were also rumors that Duke was having an affair with his secretary [Pat Stacy — by then Mary St. John had retired]. I think he found her good company — the *only* company. But I don't know what went on behind locked doors. None of my business. I just wanted to get the film made. I'd say it was just a fling."

The "fling" Sturges thought Wayne was having would turn out to be a lot more than that. Sturges continued, talking about Wayne's age: "He was — what — sixty-seven or something close? He couldn't run. He couldn't fight. He couldn't breathe properly. And he had to wear a dark toupee which never seemed to suit him.

"But what he did bring to the role was his amazing charisma. The fact is, his fans didn't care how old he was or whether his toupee was obvious. I just wished we had a script that gave him more to do, that suited him as he was, rather than try and make it fit his character as it used to be.

"We did have some good moments. The best scenes were between Duke and Colleen Dewhurst, who played an aging prostitute who gives McQ information and gets killed for it. Although we didn't show it, McQ went to bed with her, and the fact that they were both getting on and the incredible rapport the two actors had made it work somehow. Just two scenes, but the best two scenes in the film."

I talked to Colleen Dewhurst by telephone in 1979. She spoke warmly of Wayne, saying, "Duke kept his word about us working together again, and when *McQ* came up, he told John Sturges he wanted me to play the hooker. It was only a couple of scenes, but they were such nice scenes. John Sturges told me that Duke was pretty tense through most of the filming, but when we did our two scenes, he was relaxed and seemed to enjoy the work. I'm so glad I managed to bring something good into Duke's life."

With *McQ* behind him, Wayne returned home to Newport before heading for New York in December 1973 to accept an award from the National Football Hall of Fame. When he returned home, he found Pilar and all her belongings had gone.

"It was just an awful time for Duke," said Claire Trevor. "He never really believed that Pilar would leave him, and he certainly had no intention of leaving her. But suddenly she was gone, and he was mortified. I know she still loved him, and he loved her. When I asked him what he was going to do, he said, 'Well, I sure as hell won't get married again.' I said, 'Duke, she hasn't divorced you yet.' He said, 'I hope she doesn't. Even if we can't live together, I don't want a divorce. But if she wants one, she can have it.' It seemed to me that everything about his life was coming to an end. I felt a foreboding back then [in 1973]. It all seemed to begin with the death of John Ford."

John Ford died in August 1973. I recall sitting in Duke's trailer on the set of *Brannigan* a year later and of him speaking of the death of his friend and mentor. He said, "I felt like I'd lost my father all over again." During the days I spent with him, he never looked so disheartened. Not even when he spoke briefly about his breakup with Pilar.

"Oh Jesus, I know I'm on borrowed time." I could see his eyes welling up, and it was impossible not to feel his tremendous grief — his grief for his lost years, and for the loss of his beloved Coach.

He saw my tears, and it was enough to force him to suddenly perk up and say, "Tell me again why you liked *The Alamo*." So I did, and he seemed happy again. (I know there will be some hard-nosed cynics who will read Wayne's response to my admiration of his film as someone enjoying sycophantic praise, but Wayne never liked or approved of sycophancy. As Linda Cristal told me, "He loved *The Alamo* like a man loves a woman, and so your admiration for *The Alamo* was like a respected admiration for a woman he loved. It pleased him in a sincere way. He didn't wallow in praise. But it delighted him that his work — his labor of love — touched you in the way he wanted it to touch everybody.")

In January 1974, John Wayne rode into Harvard Square in Cambridge, Massachusetts, on a tank. He had received a letter from the president of the *Harvard Lampoon* calling him "the biggest fraud in history" and challenging him to face sixteen hundred students from Harvard University, a campus which was "the most traditionally radical, in short, the most hostile territory on earth."

"It was too irresistible to turn down," Wayne remembered. "I knew they were prepared to give me a hard time, so I rode into town on a tank hoping none of the eggs being thrown by some two thousand people would actually hit me in the kisser. Then I took the stage at the Harvard Square Theatre and they were really ready to let me have it."

It's an event much written about by now, but it's worth highlighting just some of the moments because, as Duke told me, none of his answers were scripted. "There was no way to prepare for it because I had no idea what questions those students would try and knock me down with." Not only were his answers quick-witted, but his ability to laugh at himself won the admiration of sixteen hundred students who had thought John Wayne was just a Hollywood relic with no brains and a political belief that had nothing in common with students of 1974.

"Where did you get that phony hair?" he was asked.

He replied, "It's not phony. It's real hair. Of course, it's not mine, but it's real."

"Is it true that your horse filed for separation papers?"

"He was a little upset when we didn't use him in the last picture."

"What did you use?"

"Three good-looking women."

"Can you do an Ed Sullivan imitation?"

"I'm having a hard enough time imitating people who are imitating me."

"Has President Nixon ever given you any suggestions for your movies?"

"No, they've all been successful."

"What have you done with the Watergate tapes?"

"If anybody is taping this show, I hope it's a Democrat, because the Republicans sure will lose it."

"Do you look at yourself as the fulfillment of the American dream?"

"I don't look at myself more than I have to, friend."

At the end of the debate, sixteen hundred students wildly applauded Wayne, and they awarded him with the Brass Balls Award in recognition of "outstanding machismo and a penchant for punching people in the mouth."

"I got a great kick out of it," Wayne told me. "It was good for all those kids to have the chance to let off steam. When I was a kid we used to tear things apart on Halloween and blow ourselves up on the Fourth of July. I thought those students should have the same kind of opportunity, but maybe they didn't expect me to explode in their faces. They loved it, though. So did I."

Wayne stayed over in Boston for a few days and then flew to London. My hometown. The Duke was coming to town.

When I heard that John Wayne was coming to London, I knew I *had* to meet him. It's not uncommon for anyone to come down with a cold or flu at that time of year. So I caught a cold on Thursday, 17 January 1974, took the day off work from ABC-EMI Cinemas where I was a bored press officer, and headed for Heathrow. I took with me a black-and-white 8 x 10 still of John Wayne, tucked in a manila envelope, which I knew I had no chance of getting signed.

A considerable crowd of fans along with the press had gathered at terminal three to greet John Wayne. I mingled in with various officials at customs, wearing an ABC-

EMI identity pass which a print company I knew had kindly produced for me.

Somebody announced, "His plane's just touched down." The press, the crowd, and I sort of surged forward with nowhere to go, simply because there was a buzz of real excitement all about. Finally, through customs, came the Duke, suitably wearing a white ten-gallon hat.

He called out "Howdy," and handed out cards on which he'd written, "Good Luck — John Wayne." "I wrote them out on the plane coming over," he said. "I figured I ought to have them ready just in case."

As he removed his hat, his toupee looked in need of a quick brush up and his personal hairdresser immediately moved in to smooth it down. Wayne simply kept him at bay and said, "What the hell's the point of that? They've already got their pictures. Jeez, by now I reckon the public can accept any defects I got. I'm not a young man anymore."

That was certainly true. In the flesh, he looked older than his sixty-six years. The face was craggy, the body a little bloated, and the eyes seemed watery. But it did not diminish the man's exceptional charisma.

I pushed my way forward, announced, "Mike Munn, EMI," and shook him by the hand. It was a huge paw of a hand. He smiled, hardly looked at me as others pressed in for a handshake too, and he moved on. I'd met John Wayne. The Duke. And I'd shaken his hand. I was only twenty at the time and, as you can tell, deeply in awe of this living legend.

His PR man, who was called Max, led the way, finding him a chair to sit in — he almost seemed too big for it — and there he held court to answer questions from the British press. When that was over, he rose and walked outside to a waiting Daimler with the press, the fans, me, and the various PR men in hot pursuit. Somehow I managed to get to the car before he got in, and allowing myself the luxury of just being a young fan in the presence of Hollywood greatness, I told him, "*The Alamo* is one of my favorite films, Mr. Wayne."

He grinned, turned back to the reporters, and told them, "It's damn good to see the young people like me."

The reason Wayne was in Britain was to promote *McQ*. He was also in London to record a TV special with Glen Campbell. Warner Bros. were determined to get as much PR mileage out of him as possible and arranged a huge press junket at Grosvenor House in London that same day. I arrived at the Grosvenor to find it packed with reporters and photographers, all seemingly just as excited as I was, awaiting the arrival of John Wayne.

Finally, the moment came when Wayne, accompanied by Max, walked in, and he was immediately ambushed by photographers. "John! Over here!" "Look this way, Duke!" "Smile this way, Mr. Wayne!" "Duke, how about that famous grin?"

He handled it all with aplomb. "Fire that thing!" he said, looking at one camera. He turned to another; "Fire that thing!" He seemed to be enjoying himself immensely.

Max, and several other official bodies, including Eddie Patman, director of publicity for Warner Bros., formed a posse around him as the mass of reporters moved in on him with their questions, most of which he'd answered a hundred times before like, "How did you get the nickname Duke?" and "Who invented the name John Wayne?" Some reporters opted to ask about politics, picking on the fact that he had been an avid supporter of President Nixon and had supported America's involvement in the Vietnam War. He gave solid answers to every question.

Watergate was the topic many reporters asked about, and someone asked him if he blamed the newspapers for Nixon's troubles. Wayne said, "The news media in our country have gotten more power today than the railroad had in 1890. But in 1890 at least they were trying to set up channels of communication. These newspaper fellers today, they keep striking attitudes. Yes, sir, I blame them.

"Of course I blame the papers. The media is too powerful for its own good. Can't blame *all* the papers. Just some. Why don't they put the blame where it belongs. The blame lay on politics. Not on leadership."

Somebody asked if Nixon was innocent or guilty. Wayne replied, "Of what? Tell me. Frame that into a reasonable question and I'll answer it. Look how he brought the boys back from the prison camps. Look how he started a détente with Russia, with China even. He stemmed inflation. He'd done all right. By rights, this should be his hour of crowning glory."

When asked what went wrong, he replied, "Mr. Nixon did his best to keep everyone — liberals, moderates, conservatives — everyone in his government. That's a loony position."

The whole time he was sipping whisky. Max tasted each tumbler first, making sure it was exactly the way Wayne liked it. *That's* what it means to be such a megastar — you get someone to test your whisky. In fact, Wayne was never without a glass in his hand throughout the event. He also, to my surprise, puffed on a cigar.

The questions came thick and fast as he found himself surrounded. Max tried to get between the star and the media, pleading, "Please, ladies and gentlemen, we just got in this morning." Nobody budged, but still Duke grinned and maintained his composure.

Max persevered: "We're understandably a little jet-lagged, so if you can please take it easy and be patient, we'll answer all your questions and sign autographs later."

For a moment, Max's plea kept the press at bay, and Wayne saw his opportunity to move forward. But after just a couple of steps, he was suddenly surrounded again. I saw the strain was beginning to show in his face, and I had the feeling that Wayne was about to explode. Max saw it too. Then through the crowd pushed a Spanish waiter, like a comical Mexican character from an old Wayne Western, saying, "Thees drink ees for Meester Wayne. Give it heem please." Max grabbed the glass, tasted it, pushed it into Wayne's hand while dextrously removing the empty tumbler the Duke had been holding.

This is all part of the publicity machine the public never sees. They get to read the quotes in the newspapers the next morning. But the chaos that ensues at a press reception can get out of control. I've seen it happen many times.

Max was still trying to hold back the ladies and gentlemen of the media but, when Wayne realized his PR man was having no luck, he took matters into his own hands and just began walking forward. Anyone stupid enough to stand in his way would clearly get run down. As it turned out, nobody was that stupid, and Wayne was able to make it to the bar.

As everyone moved in again, he found himself wedged against the bar. I saw how people, women in particular, took delight in touching him, some probably to reassure themselves he was actually real, others just because they wanted to say they had touched John Wayne. It all began to feel a little distasteful.

Finally, Max and Eddie decided enough was enough and announced Mr. Wayne was leaving. He began moving forward once more, and the crowd opened up before him and closed immediately behind him. I'd been carrying my 8 x 10 photo of Wayne around all day, hoping I might get it signed. So I decided it was now or never, and said, "Please, Mr. Wayne, sign this."

"Sure, son," he said.

He wrote, "My best wishes and thanks, John Wayne."

It still hangs, framed, on my wall.

It was a cold, damp London that John Wayne came to in January 1974, and it took its toll on him. He caught a cold which, for a younger man with two decent lungs, would have been a nuisance, but for a man with less than one lung it was serious. The public didn't get to hear about it, but Wayne came down with a viral infection, virtually lost his voice, and began coughing up blood. He taped the TV special with Glen Campbell and appeared on Michael Parkinson's chat show; he was unwell but refused to give in to his weakness. A doctor ordered him to bed for four days.

By the time he returned to California his viral infection had turned into walking pneumonia, and the chronic cough he'd developed — which Wayne shrugged off as mere bronchitis — had affected a mitral valve in his heart. But he didn't know it at the time.

That June, John Wayne returned to

London to film *Brannigan*, by which time I was running the stills department for both Columbia and Warner Bros. in London's Wardour Street. Through a friend of mine at United Artists, I managed to arrange to spend a day on the set for the sole purpose of meeting and talking to John Wayne, and I arrived early at the London location where I met Michael Wayne and unit publicist Mike Russell.

Although Wayne had the reputation of always being up bright and early, this was one morning when he was, for whatever reason, like a bear with a sore head. Michael Wayne came to Mike Russell and said, "JW's late on the set. Someone's got to go and get him. You do it, will ya?"

Mike Russell said, "You're his son. Why don't *you* do it?"

"I may be his son, but I'm still as scared of him as everyone else."

So Mike Russell was sent that morning to the trailer, which was Wayne's home in between takes. He was living at a house in Cheyne Walk in Chelsea. He arrived each morning at the location, usually in London, and went straight to his trailer where his makeup man would go to work on him.

When Wayne appeared, he was smiling

and saying, "Fine morning, Bob," and, "Nice to see ya, Harry," speaking to every member of the crew he passed — and he knew all their names.

I'd somehow been abandoned and left on my own, so I went up to him nervously and said, "I think you were expecting me."

He said, "Oh, yeah. It's Mike, isn't it. I'll call you Michael. It's a damn good name. Well, I got some free time today, so we'll go to my trailer and get some coffee and talk. Sound okay?"

I nodded, quite unable to speak for a moment.

"What's the matter, kid? You look pale."

I owned up and said, "I'm a bit nervous."

"What for?"

"I never met a living legend before."

He roared with laughter, and said, "Kid, you and I are gonna have a fine time."

I followed him back to his trailer which, I seem to recall, was huge; not unlike a home away from home. Stepping inside I couldn't help but notice several toupees hanging on the wall. The press often had much fun at the expense of Wayne's baldness. He was almost completely bald by this time. Unfortunately, his toupees were fashioned for the 1970s and, as everyone who lived through that time will remember, hairstyles in the 1970s were appalling. Consequently, Wayne's hairpieces were also appalling. But he never wore them out of vanity.

He told me, "I never go out in public without a hairpiece because that would disappoint the public." I believe he was right. In the privacy of his own home, he usually left the hairpiece off.

So there I was, sitting with John Wayne and having coffee, and for me it was an unforgettable occasion. There was also a very frightening moment. When he told me about the story of the marine who had been heckled by students from USC, his recounting of the incident had become so animated and loud that he began coughing.

I began to wonder when his coughing was going to stop. It went on much longer than an ordinary cough. I became alarmed at how violent it was as he doubled up, coughing into a huge handkerchief, unable to catch his breath. I became anxious that he was actually going to die there and then, and I was desperate to do something.

"Can I get you something or call someone?"

He waved a hand, making it clear he

didn't want anything. Wanting to do something, I went to the fridge, found bottled water, poured some into a cup, and sat silently by him, waiting until he was ready to take the cup from me. Then I discovered the secret that had been kept from the public. He reached for an oxygen tank and took some deep breaths. Nobody but those who worked with him knew he needed oxygen close by for times like this. It took a while for him to get control again, but he was finally able to take the cup from me and drank it.

"Sorry," he rasped.

"Are you sure you don't want me to call someone?"

"Don't fuss!" he said impatiently. "I'll be okay."

He never allowed anyone to make a fuss of his health problems and always shrugged off any suggestion he was unwell. I realized he was desperate not to give any hint to the public that he was not quite the man he once was. More than that, I think he didn't want to allow himself to believe he was not the strong man he always seemed on the screen.

When, in 1980, I met Don Siegel who directed Wayne in *The Shootist* just several months after *Brannigan*, I told him about the incident in Wayne's trailer.

Siegel told me, "You were with a man who was slowly dying."

I'd had no idea. But in retrospect, I can see that time was, indeed, running out for him.

Thanks to Wayne, I spent several days on the set of *Brannigan* at various locations in London. Mostly I observed director Douglas Hickox, but each day Wayne would come over to me and say, "Tell you what, kid, we'll have a coffee and a talk till they're ready for me."

The premise of *Brannigan* was a good one. A tough American cop comes to London to extradite a villain Scotland Yard have in custody. Unfortunately, Scotland Yard have lost him, so Brannigan sets about finding him with the help of a lovely female detective, played by Judy Geeson.

Geeson seemed to have struck a chord with Wayne. He told me, "Judy's young enough to be my daughter. A lovely girl. I like the irony of the script that she's there trying to look after me."

I didn't get a chance to talk to Judy Geeson on the set, but I did interview her a few years later when I was at *Photoplay*. She told me, "Oh, I *loved* John Wayne. He was just so charming and easy to work with. Although we shot the film in London, it was like making an American movie just because you were working with John Wayne. It was also very funny to see the look on people's faces when we were filming. We'd pull up in a car in a London street, and you'd see these people looking at him and they must have been thinking, 'That man looks just like John Wayne. But, oh, it *can't* be.' I think he got a kick out of that."

Wayne also enjoyed working with Richard Attenborough who played a top Scotland Yard detective. Said the Duke, "I love the way he calls everyone 'darling' and 'sweetie.' Just cracks me up. I like working with English — I should say *British* — actors. Like Laurence Harvey. These guys really know a thing or two about acting. Richard is my kind of movie actor. He doesn't go in for all that violent stuff and nudity. His films are the kind you can go to see without being afraid you'll get embarrassed because you've got your kid with you. And he's a funny guy too. He comes across as all upper-crust, but he's got a wonderful sense of humor."

I had the chance to chat a bit with Richard Attenborough, who said, "I've worked with a few American stars. James

Stewart [in *The Flight of the Phoenix*], for instance, and Steve McQueen [in *The Great Escape* and *The Sand Pebbles*]. I don't suppose all Hollywood stars are like them, but those men are real *pros*. And Duke is just a lovely man. He and I are like chalk and cheese in so many respects, which is why I think we make good casting in our respective roles. He's the big tough cop from America, and I'm the small, gentlemanly detective. It's a caricature, of course, for both of us, but that's what the American financiers want, I suppose. Mind you, I get to do a good fight scene in a pub. It's like one of those saloon brawls in a John Wayne Western. Really good fun."

I was interested to observe Wayne's relationship with Douglas Hickox, a British director with a handful of good films to his credit, plus another handful of not-so-good films. I might have expected Wayne to ride roughshod over his British director, but he didn't. They would talk, just out of my earshot, and their expressions suggested they were generally in agreement. In fact, in retrospect, learning later how tough Wayne could be on directors, my impression was that Wayne liked Hickox and treated him with respect.

Hickox told me on the set, "I thought I

might be in for a tough time because he is
. . . well, he's John Wayne! And I'd been
told all these horror stories about how he's
supposed to be a bully. But there's been
none of that. Fortunately, we've got his son
Michael with us, and he's a good man, and
if there's anything that Duke's upset about,
Michael deals with him. Mind you, Michael's no pushover. He can be tough. He's
got to be. He virtually runs Batjac. I have a
lot of liking and respect for Duke and Michael."

All this backslapping doesn't mean that
Wayne made himself popular with everyone. I met a man who worked on the
film in an administrative position, who
would probably not wish to be identified
(so I'll call him Jim), who didn't like
Wayne. Jim told me that for the first
couple of weeks of filming, Wayne stayed
at the Athenaeum Hotel in Piccadilly before finding the house in Cheyne Walk.
Unhappy with the room he had been
given, Wayne grabbed the surprised and
horrified Jim and literally threw him across
the room.

Jim never knew why — or wouldn't say
why — Wayne had been so angry. But his
secretary Pat Stacy gives a good clue in her
book. It turned out that Pat was to have a

room right next to Wayne's suite. But she had thought it inappropriate to be so close to Duke and moved to a room on the floor above. Wayne liked the original arrangements, and my guess is that he thought the change of room was Jim's fault.

Yet there was a gentle side to Wayne as well, and an exceptionally generous one too. I learned that when Wayne heard that the mother of one of the *Brannigan* crew had been taken seriously ill, Duke immediately had the lady put into private medical care and paid for all the bills himself.

On the day they shot in Piccadilly Circus, Hickox told me I could be an extra in the scene. Many of the people in the scene were not extras but simply people totally unaware they were being filmed and presumably wondering why a Royal Mail pillar-box had suddenly sprung up on a pedestrian crossing. So I mingled with the crowd just so I could say that I had appeared in a John Wayne movie. I never could spot myself on screen, but I have seen a number of other people I know turn up in the film, although they had not realized they had been filmed. I think that *Brannigan* must have been one of the last films shot on location in central London; the local authorities clamped down on filmmakers using the busiest parts of the capital because of the chaos it caused.

My last day on location was in a quiet London street, much of it involving Duke's stand-in doing a lot of running, with the occasional close-up of Duke coming to a halt and catching his breath. Hickox told me, "I don't know if we'll use all those close-ups of Duke. Probably one or two to establish that he's the guy doing the running. I also talked it over with Duke and said, 'Maybe we should show you out of breath,' and he said, 'Sure, let's do it. No point in kidding the audience I'm a young man anymore.'"

At the end of the day and the end of my week with *Brannigan*, I thanked Douglas Hickox, and then I found Duke and thanked him too.

"It's been a real pleasure, Michael," he said. "Hope you had a good time with us."

I told him I had and that I was sorry I had to return to the mundane duties of a publicist in Wardour Street.

"If you come to our good country, you'll come and visit," he said. "Consider that an open invitation."

"I will. Good-bye Duke," I said.

"So long, Michael," he said with gentle sincerity. "I'll always be your friend."

It sounds unsettlingly sentimental, I know. But that was John Wayne.

When he'd arrived earlier in the year, I'd managed to get a signed photo — a priceless tangible memento. But the invitation to visit him and his declaration of friendship are two intangible gifts that I prize more highly than the signed photo.

28

The Last Ride

Sometime in 1977 my path crossed with Douglas Hickox when he was in preproduction on *Zulu Dawn*. He asked me, "Did you know there was something going on between Wayne and his secretary Pat?"

I told him that John Sturges had said Wayne was having a fling with his secretary.

"That was no fling," said Hickox.

I remembered Pat Stacy from the *Brannigan* set, although I never actually conversed with her. She wasn't a great beauty by Hollywood standards, but she had a pleasant face, and seemed a nice lady. She was thirty-two in 1974, less than half Wayne's age. At the time, it seemed to me, being a mere lad of twenty-one, something of a scandal. I was to learn that Pat brought great comfort to Wayne's last years. But when their love affair first began, there was a great deal of heartbreak all round.

Hickox told me, "When we were filming *Brannigan* nobody asked Duke about Pat. But there were rumors. You've got to figure something's happening when two people disappear to Paris on their own. That's what Duke and Pat did in the middle of filming when we didn't need Duke for a couple of days. Then Pilar and the children arrived and I don't know what went on, but it made Duke pretty bad tempered for a while."

I was still unable to believe that John Wayne had fallen for his secretary. As a young fan, I didn't like to think of Wayne as someone with human needs and frailties. I was prepared to accept John Sturges's theory of a simple "fling."

"Anyway," I told Hickox, "Pilar was the one who left Duke. He told me she had."

Hickox said, "Duke told me he still loved Pilar. He never talked to me much about his private life."

Many years later I would experience the trauma of divorce and the devastating effect it has on the children, which I mention only because I think it helps me to understand why Wayne's problems, which were much bigger than mine, would have caused so much grief, and why smoke screens would have been set up.

What I was to discover, through the books by those involved and from speaking to people who knew Wayne well, was that all those people who had an emotional investment in John Wayne all came from different angles.

Pat Stacy wrote *Duke: A Love Story*, an account of her love affair with Wayne which impressed, among others, Wayne's friend James Stewart, who called Stacy's book "a warm, appealing story. It brings out in a very vivid way the warm, dedicated, generous, courageous aspects of Duke's character. It pays honest and loving tribute to John Wayne."

Even Maureen O'Hara said, "Pat has written of those years sensitively, with class and dignity and warmth."

But Aissa, in her memoir *John Wayne, My Father*, thought Stacy had exaggerated her relationship with Wayne and virtually dismissed it. Pilar, in her book *John Wayne: My Life with the Duke*, wrote that when she arrived in London during production on *Brannigan*, Duke made it clear he wanted to start over again with her. When she asked him if he was in love with Stacy, he denied it, and when she offered him a divorce, he said he didn't want one. When she told him she was taking the children back to America, he treated her with "distant politeness." Finally, he told her, "We both have to face it. Our marriage is over."

It isn't difficult to understand why there were conflicting stories. Wayne tried to maintain his dignity and his family connections. And he never criticized or blamed Pilar.

Loretta Young had her own rather blunt opinion but one which has some substance to it. She told me, "You can't be a Christian Scientist and be married to John Wayne."

Duke believed in God. He told me, "I have faith in a supreme being. I don't believe in organized religion because there are too many of them and I just don't think God could be so disorganized as to have that many churches all claiming his authority. My wives have all been Catholic, but while I don't feel any inclination to be a Catholic myself, I can respect those traditions and beliefs.

"I respect the Mormons because they were the great pioneers, and I know John Ford respected them which is why he made *Wagonmaster*. The Mormons are fundamentally American, except they don't drink coffee or alcohol, which is a bad thing in my book, and they don't smoke, which is a good thing.

"It beats me why there are so many movements, especially in America. Our Constitution grants Americans freedom to worship how they like. But like the Communists in the fifties, there have been people who have taken advantage of our Constitution. Something like Christian Science, I just don't understand. They won't even drink wine and I find nothing about them that is fundamentally American. And they don't like to be treated by doctors. I can never understand that. If one of my kids gets ill, I'm sending for the doctor and I don't care what anyone else says."

By "anyone else" he was obviously referring to Pilar, but I have no evidence, anecdotal or otherwise, that Pilar ever refused her children medical treatment. And it can't be ignored that Pilar still looks amazingly beautiful and healthy which is probably because of her way of life, and that Wayne's health problems were largely a consequence of his way of life. Alcohol, especially alcohol, eating well, and smoking, at least up until he had lung cancer, were the true attributes of a man in Duke's eyes.

As Paul Fix told me, "If you didn't drink or smoke or eat heartily, you weren't a real man by Duke's standards. The funny thing is, although he said he didn't trust a man who didn't drink, he really had a sneaking regard for some who were teetotal because secretly he figured that a man who didn't need alcohol — unless he was clearly a weakling — had to be a very strong-willed character. And Duke admired that. He showed it very briefly in *The Alamo*, when he offers Laurence Harvey as Travis a drink, and Travis says, 'I don't drink.' Wayne as Crockett looks surprised and says, 'I've heard of such,' and he goes on to show that while Crockett didn't agree with all of Travis's methods, he had respect for him. Travis was, after all, a very brave man. So Duke was just being bombastic when he'd say, 'I don't trust a man who doesn't drink alcohol because they're not real men.' He was merely boosting his own image because he liked to drink. But he was not an alcoholic. He could go for weeks without drinking. But when he did drink, he *drank*."

Michael Wayne said, "He likes to drink. I've seen him drink a bottle of tequila before dinner, then a bottle of brandy after dinner. But he didn't drink most of the time. If he had a weekend clear, he might drink the whole weekend. But he didn't *have* to drink."

I think the hardest thing for Wayne during his marriage breakup was trying to sustain his relationship with all his children. Claire Trevor, who was able to view the whole situation objectively, told me, "When Duke and Pilar separated, it was only really hard on Aissa, Ethan, and Marisa because Duke and Pilar were their mom and dad. For Michael and Pat and Toni and Melinda it was different. Josephine was their mother, and although they respected Pilar, I don't think they were especially . . . *fond* of her. And that created a great gap between Josephine's children and Pilar's children, which Duke was always trying to bridge. He'd bring them all together for an occasional official photograph which made it look like all his family were as one. But I never thought it was, and I know it pained Duke. He just wanted them to be one family because they all had one thing in common — they were *his* children.

"Then when he got involved with Pat, I think his children by Pilar had trouble accepting it. And it's understandable that they had trouble accepting that their mom and dad were no longer together, without having to come to terms with the fact that their father had a new woman in his life.

"What I can say for certainty about Duke is that he had a great capacity to love. He loved his friends and if you were a friend of his, you could do no wrong and he'd do anything for you. He loved all his children, and to him they were everything. And then there were the women in his life. I don't think he ever stopped loving Josephine, although it had more to do with respect and admiration. In most men — in most *people* — that would have been enough for an ex-spouse. But with Duke it was a kind of love. Pilar he never stopped loving. Of that I'm sure. But they had reached the point where they couldn't get on, and it wasn't for lack of trying. Then along came Pat and she made him feel young and vibrant again. She loved him, not because he was John Wayne, but because he was a man called Duke, and she loved him for all his virtues and in spite of his vices. I believe he loved her because she loved him for himself. But I don't think it would have lasted had he not died as soon as he did. And it wouldn't have been either Pat's fault or Duke's fault. It would have been because she was his secretary, and you cannot have a lasting relationship between a man and his secretary. But for the time he had left, she was great for him.

"For a while Duke was torn between his feelings for Pilar and his feelings for Pat. He later told me he was in turmoil because he was prepared to make the effort to try for a reconciliation with Pilar, but he had also fallen in love with Pat and didn't want to lose her. He told me that when he went back to Newport [after *Brannigan*] he and Pilar discussed reconciliation. But they were just beating their heads against a wall."

According to Pilar's book, this last attempt took place over dinner in a restaurant. When Pilar offered Duke a divorce, he told her, "I don't want a divorce. What the hell gave you an idea like that?"

She asked him bluntly if he was in love with Pat and, according to her account, he answered, "Of course not. She's my secretary — that's all."

"Then why did you take her to Paris?" Pilar challenged him.

He responded with, "Why the hell did you leave London ahead of schedule?"

As Claire Trevor said, they were beating their heads against a brick wall until, finally, as reported by Pilar, Wayne said,

"We have to face it. Our marriage is over."

What had begun as a "fling" during *McQ* had become a real love affair during *Brannigan*.

McQ, released in February 1974, did not do particularly well, taking just $4.1 million domestically. I am sure that had Wayne known that his attempt to emulate Dirty Harry would fail, he wouldn't have done *Brannigan*, because, although it was a better picture than *McQ*, it did even worse at the box office, making less than $4 million. Henry Hathaway recalled, "I thought that was the end of his career. There was no way Wayne was going to become a character actor, but there seemed nothing for him at his age. And he really was gradually becoming unwell.

"Westerns had literally bitten the dust — at least, the kind Duke and me used to make. We'd both struggled in recent years. That's what happens in life and especially in movies. Clint Eastwood had come along and he was the only one making good Westerns, and he could also play a cop like Dirty Harry, but Duke couldn't compete.

"So I thought Duke had had it. Then I got a call from Hal Wallis in 1972, saying he wanted to do a sequel to *True Grit*.

Duke was all for it, and Wallis had got Katharine Hepburn to be in it too. I thought that combination of Wayne and Hepburn would be sensational.

"But then I read the script. Oh boy, was it a dog! It was credited to someone I'd never heard of called Martin Julien. I realized it was actually written by Hal Wallis and his wife Martha Hyer. And it was awful. Just ridiculous. It was *The African Queen* in a Western setting. I turned it down.

"When I took on *North to Alaska* I was not the first choice, which always irked me. They wanted Richard Fleischer to direct it, but he turned it down when he discovered they had no finished script. So this time, I turned the tables and suggested they get Dick Fleischer to direct *Rooster Cogburn*. Wayne had approved Fleischer for *North to Alaska* and I thought there was no reason why he would not approve him for *Rooster Cogburn*. But Wayne rejected him.

"Fleischer assumed Wayne was getting revenge for his having refused to direct *North to Alaska*, but Duke wasn't petty like that. He told me he understood Fleischer's reasons for not doing that picture. By 1975 Fleischer had a good body of work behind him, like *The Boston Strangler*, the Pearl

Harbor picture *Tora! Tora! Tora!* which Duke admired, and *Soylent Green*. Wayne said to me, 'I couldn't let Dick Fleischer take on *Rooster Cogburn* because I thought *you* were the only one who could make that film what it should have been, and, by God, I was right. I thought you'd come to our rescue, but you didn't.'

"So, having lost me and having turned down Dick Fleischer, Hal Wallis chose Stuart Millar, who'd been an assistant to William Wyler for a long time and then began producing films. But he'd only directed one film, *When the Legends Die*, a really fine film with Richard Widmark. I think they all thought that *Rooster Cogburn* would establish Millar as a top director. But he had a lousy script and a star who thought Millar was too inexperienced as a director. And maybe Duke was right.

"He told me that Millar would do so many takes that eventually Duke lost his temper and said, 'Damn it, Stuart, there's only so many times we can speak these lines before they stop making any sense at all.'

"I think Millar was desperately trying to make sense of the script. Wallis had Charles Portis come in and try tidying up the screenplay, but he wasn't able to do much with it, so Wayne and Hepburn made up most of their lines. All Millar had to do was shout, 'Action!' and 'Cut!' It didn't do Stuart's career any good and after that he went into TV."

Richard Jordan played the heavy in the film, and was well aware that his presence would be overshadowed by the combination of Wayne and Hepburn. When I interviewed Jordan on the set of *A Nightingale Sang in Berkeley Square* at Pinewood in 1978, he told me, "It [*Rooster Cogburn*] was a two-person picture, and I didn't mind that. Wayne and Hepburn were the stars, and if anyone was going to come and see the picture, they were coming to see them, not me or anyone else in the cast.

"I never became friendly with Wayne but that's because he was having too good a time spending all his hours with Katharine Hepburn. I thought he was the best screen partner she'd had since Spencer Tracy. She was sometimes giving *him* direction. He was trying to inject whatever he could to recapture the performance he gave in *True Grit*, and Hepburn would quietly tell him, 'You're tipping your mitt,' which meant he was going over the top.

"They had such a respect for each other that the rest of us really were outside of it all. But I never minded because I felt that Wayne should enjoy himself while he was able, and we all thought that maybe Katharine Hepburn might not be around much longer, so she should have a good time too. She only complained because Wayne was bossing everyone — I mean *everyone* — around, just trying to get the film made, which wasn't fair to Stuart Millar, and Hepburn complained that she was the one who usually bossed everyone around!"

Ironically, despite Jordan's seemingly justified theory that neither Wayne nor Hepburn might be around much longer, Hepburn outlived both Wayne and Richard Jordan, who died too early in life in 1993, aged just fifty-six.

Rooster Cogburn (or *Rooster Cogburn and the Lady*, as it was later retitled) was shot in Oregon from September to November 1974. Hal Wallis felt he had a surefire hit on his hands and he decided there would be a second sequel, which Wayne agreed to. When *Rooster Cogburn* was released in 1975, it received bad reviews and did less well than *True Grit*, but it did manage to take a modestly respectable $8 million in domestic sales. "It was one of the highest-grossing Westerns of all time," said Richard Jordan, "but everything about it was compared either to *True Grit* in its quality and its box office, or to *The African Queen*. I heard that the second sequel got canceled because *Rooster Cogburn* didn't do well, but I think there wasn't a third Rooster Cogburn film simply because Wayne's health began to fail quickly and he would have been too ill to do it."

But *Rooster Cogburn* was not enough of a success to compete with other releases of that year, such as *Jaws* and *Airport 1975*. Of the few Westerns released in 1975, *Rooster Cogburn* was the most successful, but, for the first time since 1959, John Wayne was not listed in the top ten box-office stars. He had been in the top ten since 1949, except for 1958, and had been number one in 1950, 1951, 1954, and 1969, and had been number two in 1956, 1957, and 1963. It was a crisis, one which would have caused lesser stars to opt for character parts or retirement. But neither was an option for John Wayne.

There suddenly loomed a solution to Wayne's dilemma. He was offered *The Shootist*, a film which took Wayne out of the old West and placed him in a new time, opening, as it does, in 1901 with Wayne as J. B. Books, an aging gunfighter, riding into town to see a doctor, played by James

Stewart. The doctor diagnoses Books with terminal cancer. The story would follow Books's final days, living in a boarding-house run by Lauren Bacall whose son, played by Ron Howard, idolizes the legendary Books.

The town becomes a magnet for several men who have scores to settle with Books; the film moves toward its inevitable tragic climax when Books takes them all on in one final gunfight in which he prefers to go down fighting rather than wait for the cancer to end his days in misery and pain.

Richard Boone, who played one of Books's old enemies, told me, "Duke never said as much, but I think he knew in his heart of hearts this would be his final film. He always talked of future plans, but he knew. The film is peppered with actors like me from his old films. I don't know if he insisted on us, or if it was a compromise with Don Siegel [who directed] or if Siegel decided we would all get parts, but there was Betty Bacall [*Blood River*], John Carradine [*Stagecoach* and *The Man Who Shot Liberty Valance*], Harry Morgan [*How the West Was Won*], Jimmy Stewart [*The Man Who Shot Liberty Valance*], and me [*The Alamo* and *Big Jake*]. I think Bill McKinney, Hugh O'Brian, and Ronnie

Howard were the only ones who never worked with Duke before."

On the set of *Rough Cut* in 1979, Don Siegel gave me the story of his difficult time making *The Shootist*. He said, "I'd met Wayne back in the late 1940s. For some reason he'd apologized to me, and I didn't know why, and it turned out someone had told him I was a Communist and he'd found out it was a lie, so he'd said, 'Kid, I owe you an apology.'

"When I went to discuss *The Shootist* with him at his house in Newport, he remembered the incident, so I thought that this boded well — I mean, to be remembered by John Wayne after all those years means I'd made some impression.

"I'd gone there with the film's producer Mike Frankovich; we didn't have a finished script then, just a treatment based on the book by Glendon Swarthout. Duke was insisting that all the bad language in the book be kept out of the screenplay, and he asked me what I thought about the changes he wanted. I said that so far the script was lousy. It was being written by Swarthout's son, Miles Hood Swarthout, and it was cold. I said I wanted love between Duke and Betty Bacall. I wanted real tenderness between Duke and Ron

Howard. I wanted to bring tears to the eyes of the audiences.

"What was so funny was that Mike stood up and said, 'Don, you've flipped your wig,' and Duke without a beat said, 'Sit down and shut up.'

"The problem we had was that Mike had allowed this kid to write the script because his dad had written the book, but I told Duke I had a guy called Scott Hale who could make it into a really good script. Mike objected and Duke said, 'You get a writer Don approves of or you can count me out,' and they started having an argument, and I realized they didn't like each other much when Duke called him a liar. He told Mike, 'Be a good fellow and give Don what he wants,' and so I got Scott Hale to fix the script, and he did a great job.

"We had to let Miles finish his script before letting Scott loose on it, and as well as my notes on the script, and Frank's notes, and the censor's notes, we needed Duke's notes. You think a screenplay is a creative process? It's damn hard work getting it so everyone's happy. I brought over the finished script by Miles and about seventy pages of my own notes, and all the other notes.

"Duke had a wonderful house by the bay at Newport, and I suddenly became aware of how beautiful it was. Duke said to me, 'Wanna buy it?' I knew he was joking, but then he surprised me by saying it was all he had left. I don't know how rich or how broke he really was, but he'd lost a lot of money. He said, 'Two lousy crooked business managers done me in.'

"He moaned a lot about how much taxes he'd paid, and I knew he'd made a lot of money and he wasn't living in poverty, but I felt some sympathy for him because he felt he deserved to keep more of the money that he earned than he could. Taxes and bad business deals — but mostly taxes — took a lot of it from him.

"It was easy to like Duke. I felt he was on my side from the beginning. He asked for a day to read the script and the notes, so we arranged to meet the next day. Turned out he had plenty of his own ideas, which I'd expected, and some I liked which gave me inspiration, and some I didn't like. But we didn't fight over any of it. We liked each other and we respected each other.

"What was so funny about Duke was his colorful language. He said to me, 'Why does Clint Eastwood make films that have so much violence and profanity?' I said,

'There's really very little gratuitous violence or bad language in Clint's films. He's got kids of his own.'

"Now, we were having lunch and he had all his grandchildren around him, and he said, 'Bullshit! His films are full of fucking obscenities,' and he let loose a tirade of his own obscenities, and I noticed that not one of his grandchildren paid any attention to what he said. They must have been used to it. And I said, 'Duke, you're wrong about Clint's films, and besides, listen to yourself speak.'

"He laughed and said, 'But you'll never hear me use profanity in a picture.' I never understood his double standards, but I admired him for making some two hundred or whatever films and never using bad language. Anyway, after he'd run down Clint, I said, 'Actually Clint wants to make a picture with you,' and Duke said, 'Well, I never said he was a bad guy.'

"Some days later I took Scott Hale over to Duke's house and we all worked together really well. Duke even showed us his gun room. For some reason, Duke started having problems breathing and couldn't get up out of his seat, and Scott made the mistake of offering his hand to Duke and saying, 'May I help you?' Duke didn't have enough breath to shout, but he said, 'God-damn it, no!' Duke was too proud to accept help, which I admired.

"Anyway, we worked on the script, and it all fell into place. People sometimes think Duke is a big dumb guy with no brains, but he could talk a good script as well as any director. He just needed a good writer to bounce ideas off.

"We filmed in Carson City much of the time, and on a good period street on the back lot at Warner Bros. We started off filming on location, doing the opening scene where Books is held up, and Books shoots him. Until then Duke had been great to work with, but suddenly he lost his temper with the stills guy and almost got his horse to knock him down. It turned out that Duke had his own photographer, which Mike Frankovich should have known, and the photographer wouldn't be there till the next day. But I was shocked by Duke's violent response.

"Then we started filming the scene, and Duke took over completely. All I did was holler 'Action!' and 'Cut!' Actually, he directed the scene very well. But at the end of the day, I simply announced, 'We'll be back here tomorrow. We lost half a day.'

"The next morning before we left for the

location Duke asked me to come and see him, and he threw his arms around me and there were tears in his eyes as he said, 'I don't know what came over me yesterday. I'm sorry, Don, and I swear it will never happen again.'

"I said, 'It's okay Duke. Actually, you had a lot of good ideas. But I have to work loose, or I'm no good.' And he was just so sorry, that when we got to the location, he announced so everyone could hear, 'Mr. Siegel, there's only one director and thank God it's you. What's your pleasure?' And we got on with the scene and whenever Duke had an idea, he'd say, 'Mr. Siegel, is it all right if I look more startled but not afraid of the robber?' Or, 'Sorry to bother you, sir, but can I . . . ?' And it was like that . . . for three days.

"We'd shot some scenes with Duke and Ron [Howard] and now we were shooting the scene where Duke and Betty Bacall ride in the buggy, and we got some fine shots. My cameraman was Bob Surtees who's good and he's fast. We needed a dolly [tracking] shot and so Bruce was seeing to the track being laid which took a little time. And suddenly Duke just exploded. 'What the fucking hell are you doing? You'd do a damn sight better if you stopped fucking around with dollies and concentrated on the lighting.'

"I jumped in and said, 'You should be ashamed of yourself for criticizing Bruce. You haven't come to watch one foot of the rushes, so don't you dare to open your big mouth.' And he tries to say something but I don't give him a chance, and I said, 'I want to see you as soon as you can get to the projection room. Then you can see what Bruce has shot and then I'll hear your criticisms.' Then I said to everyone, 'That's a wrap. Be back here tomorrow morning.'

"Back at the hotel we went to the projection room and we ran the latest dailies which were of Duke and Ron. Bruce was there, looking pale. When the lights went up, I stood up and faced Duke. He had tears streaming down his face, and he took Bruce in his arms and said, 'That's the best damn film of me I've ever seen. I love you and hope you'll forgive me.' Bruce was so overcome he couldn't speak, so I said, 'None of us could be happier with the results, Duke. Let's go to the bar. The drinks are on me.'

"We managed to get all the location work done without any further outbursts from Duke. But I was puzzled by whatever demons were driving him, and in the last week on location it was clear he wasn't feeling well. So I told him if he should be feeling tired anytime to let me know and we'd work around him. He said, 'Thanks for your consideration, but I hate people worrying about me, so cut it out.' We finished on schedule, and Duke's performance was really great.

"So then we moved to the Burbank studio [Warner Bros.]. Our first scene, an interior, was the doctor's office, and there I met James Stewart who was worried about his old friend Duke. Jimmy was very funny. He said, 'Are you shooting the left side of my face?' I said, 'Yes. Is anything wrong with that? Do you have a better side?' Some actors do, you know. But Jimmy just smiled and said, 'Nope. Whichever side the camera points is my best side.'

"Then Duke came on the set and he and Jimmy embraced. The last time they'd worked together was for John Ford. I knew that Ford shouted a lot at his actors, but I said, 'Gentlemen, this scene is very touching. But I hope you agree we should play against that. If you play the scene very matter-of-factly and don't allow the sentimentality to creep in, all the pain, the suffering, and the pathos will be there.' And

Duke said to Jimmy, 'Don't you hate it when the director's right?' And Jimmy said, 'I just hate it.'

"They did their scenes perfectly. The only problem was that Jimmy was rather deaf so I found myself shouting directions at him. And Jimmy said, 'What are you shouting for?' Duke just laughed.

"When we came to film the final shoot-out in the saloon, I went over every shot with Duke so he'd know as much as I did. He didn't have to be there as I set all the blocking with Richard Boone, Hugh O'Brian, William McKinney, and Charles Martin [who played the bartender].

"I finished all those shots by the end of the afternoon, and Duke stopped by so I could show him how I was going to film him entering the saloon. And it was obvious he wasn't happy. He argued with me but he didn't get loud or lose his temper, but I had to explain everything and justify my every decision. It seemed to me he wasn't well. He had been coughing badly. There were times when he had to have an oxygen tank on the set. When he coughed, it wracked his whole body. It was really painful. But you never dared show him sympathy or he'd get mad.

"We shot the scene the way I'd explained

and it was difficult for Duke, who spent a lot of time on the floor. I decided he'd had enough and said we'd do some pickup shots the next day. But the next day he didn't show, and Mike Frankovich turned up and announced Duke was sick. I didn't know — nobody knew — how long we'd be without Duke, so I shot the rest of the sequence without him, working out how I could insert all his shots when he was back.

"I finished the saloon scene, except for Duke's shots, and went to work on scenes that I didn't need Duke for. And then I got the news that the production was shutting down due to Duke's illness. He'd been suffering from an ear infection, but he'd never complained about it. But it had become so bad he was in excruciating pain and he was ordered to stay in bed and pumped full of antibiotics. I was put on immediate suspension and was told the suspension would be lifted if I finished the film without Duke. Basically, I was told that legally I *had* to finish the picture if the studio told me to, whether Duke was there or not.

"We continued filming, using a double for Duke, but we were not going to get the sort of shots I wanted, and we weren't going to get the shots of Books dying. I needed the shot where Books looks up at the boy [Ron Howard] who's just shot the bartender in a futile effort to save Books's life, and I wanted Books to show in his face that he's glad when the boy is not going to become a shootist. And so Books dies. But without Duke, that would all be missing. And yet I had no choice but to do what the studio told me.

"Thank God Duke got better and returned to the studio. He looked pale but he was the same old John Wayne. I had a private talk with him, explaining how I had continued filming using a double. I assumed he knew that the studio had ordered me to work that way. The more I explained about the scene, the angrier I could see him growing. But he hadn't said a word.

"I said, 'I'd like to reshoot the entire sequence now that you're back.'

"He paused a moment, the way he does in his pictures, and said, 'Really?'

"I asked him if he'd like to see everything we'd shot and if there's anything he doesn't like, we'd reshoot it. But he said nothing. I said, 'Look, Duke, surely you knew what we were doing? It wasn't a secret.' He said, 'Nobody told me.' I said, 'I was sure you'd be told. I told Frankovich that I didn't want to shoot anything while you were ill, but my agent and my lawyer looked at the contract and they told me I had to shoot anything they told me to shoot. I just wanted you to come back.'

"But he wasn't happy. He just looked at me long and hard. It was like an older Ethan Edwards glaring at me. I didn't like the situation at all and so I made the grand gesture and said, 'Would you prefer another director?'

"He ignored my question and said, 'Let's get on with it.'

"So we did, and we were doing fine until he learned that Books shoots the McKinney character in the back. I said, 'Duke, he tried to shoot you in the back,' and Duke said, 'I don't care. I never shoot anyone in the back. It's unthinkable for my image.' We argued about it, and in the end I said, 'I've never asked you for a favor but I am now. *You* direct McKinney any way you want.'

"He said, 'No, goddamn it. *You* fix it!'

"I stormed out and went and told McKinney we were going to reshoot his scene. He couldn't believe it. He said, 'If I get shot in the gut and I'm struggling to get out of the saloon, my back's going to be to Wayne. I am not going to turn to face

Wayne just so he can shoot me in the gut, and I'll tell him that.'

"I said, 'Not a good idea, Bill.' And then I told him my idea, which was he'd be shot in the belly and he'd clutch at the wound, staggering to the door. He'd stumble and that would make a natural half-turn and Duke could shoot him then. So Bill liked that idea.

"We still had about two more days to go, when suddenly Duke blew his top at Bruce [Surtees]. He yelled, 'You don't know your ass from a hole in the ground. I've never looked worse.'

"Bruce yelled back at him and I stopped Duke in his tracks by saying, 'Stay right there. We're ready to shoot.' But in fact I went over to Bruce and said I was prepared to walk out and take the whole crew with me and leave Duke behind the bar on his own. Thank God Bruce talked me out of that, and we finished the picture two days later.

"By then all was peaceful again and Duke invited me to his trailer to toast each other with tequila. Somehow we made a good picture and ended up friends. But it was hard work. Duke was ill and he was frustrated by his illness. He took it out on others, but he never meant to."

Richard Boone, an old friend of Wayne's, said, "Duke was angry at everything because he couldn't smoke, he couldn't drink, he couldn't have any fun. And poor Don Siegel took the brunt of it all. But I think there was something about the film, and about his death scene, that put him in a bad frame of mind. He was suddenly faced with a moment in time when he must have been wondering, 'Is this my last scene? Will I ever work again? Is this really my last ride?' It was that damn cough he had. I am positive he thought the cancer had returned, and that colored his whole attitude. He could get mad on any film, but on *The Shootist* he was just a nightmare for Don. Duke never admitted he felt that way, but I sensed it was in his head."

The Shootist wrapped behind schedule, on 5 April 1976, and was rushed through postproduction so it could be released in American cinemas in August. It was almost as though Paramount had no faith in it. Maybe there was even a sense of foreboding about it.

When I reviewed *The Shootist* in *Film Review*, I wrote, "It's as if the Duke is saying good-bye." I had no idea how right I was.

Few other critics noticed that *The Shootist* appeared to be some form of a celluloid eulogy to Wayne — and, indeed, the Western — although Don Siegel insisted that it was never intended to be such. Arthur Knight wrote in the *Hollywood Reporter*, "Just when it seemed the Western was an endangered species, due for extinction because it had repeated itself too many times, Wayne and Siegel have managed to validate it once more. It's a film to remember."

Variety said, "*The Shootist* stands as one of John Wayne's towering achievements. Don Siegel's terrific film is simply beautiful, and beautifully simple. Wayne and Bacall are both outstanding."

Such was the praise heaped upon it that Paramount may have thought they had a blockbuster on their hands. It's a shame that nobody thought to put forward Wayne or Siegel or even the film itself for Oscar nominations as it might have made all the difference to its performance at the box office which was, to say the least, surprisingly disappointing. Its domestic earnings of a mere $5.9 million were, in 1976, so low that it failed to make it into the 1983 inflation-adjusted list of *Variety*'s All-Time Western Champs.

My feeling, as a film journalist at the time (I never considered myself a true critic), was that there was a distinct lack of publicity surrounding the film, due, perhaps, to a perception by Paramount that the Western was an unpopular genre by 1976, or simply due to the failure by the distributors to realize that they had a potential classic on their hands. There was certainly no adverse publicity about Wayne's ill health during filming, which some could have said was the cause of the film's commercial failure. Some have suggested that the film failed because nobody wanted to see John Wayne die on screen, especially from cancer.

Time, fortunately, has rectified some of the damage, and *The Shootist* is now rightly considered a magnificent film, and one of Wayne's finest. Only his performance in *The Searchers* is superior, but, nevertheless, Wayne should have been nominated as Best Actor, and because somebody goofed by not putting his name forward, he was robbed of a second and more deserving Oscar. His last film should have been recognized in 1976 as his crowning achievement. The same is also true for Don Siegel.

It was in 1976 that I met Yakima Canutt and heard how the Hollywood Communists and Russian agents had tried to kill

Wayne in the 1950s. And from Duke himself, I heard how the Chinese and Vietcong had tried to kill him in 1966. I asked Canutt if he felt the danger had now passed for Wayne.

He said, "I certainly don't think the Communists are a threat to John anymore." Then he added ominously, "I do reckon John's got other battles to fight though." Only later did I realize that Canutt was talking about Wayne's health.

I finally asked Canutt why he always referred to Wayne as "John" and not "Duke." He said, "When I'm with him I call him 'Duke,' but when I talk about him, I never use the name 'Duke.' I always say 'John' because people know him as *John* Wayne."

I said, "He told me to call him 'Duke.' "

Canutt replied, "In that case, he considers you his friend. Isn't that something — to be a friend of Duke Wayne?"

I had to admit, it was.

29

The Absolute All-Time Movie Star

John Wayne took a long rest and Claire Trevor said that he seemed better than he had for a long time. She said, "Late in 1976 there was a television show called *An All-Star Tribute to John Wayne* which at first he was reluctant to do. But when he found out that this was the Variety Club's way of raising funds for a new cancer wing on a children's hospital in Miami, he agreed to do it, and he turned up with his children and he enjoyed the whole show. Frank Sinatra, who had not always been his best friend, hosted the event and sang 'You Are the Sunshine of My Life' to him. Maureen O'Hara sang 'I've Grown Accustomed to His Face.' I said my piece about him being my dearest friend. Jimmy Stewart read a poem. Rowan and Martin were there — it was a great show and he had a great time, and he looked better than he had in years."

Ava Gardner told me, "Frank and Duke had only become friends in recent years, and when Frank was asked if he would host the tribute to Duke, he said, 'Just try asking someone else to do it.' That's how much Francis had come to think of Duke."

Claire Trevor said she felt Wayne was looking healthier because "he wasn't rushing headlong into another film. In fact, he couldn't find another film to do. The scripts were not coming in as quickly as they used to, and the ones he read he detested. I told him, 'Duke, put your feet up and take a break.' He said, 'I *am* taking a break. I've got no choice.'"

But Wayne wasn't as well as he looked. He went into the hospital in December 1976 to have corrective surgery on his prostate gland, which, fortunately, was only a minor operation. But what had still gone undetected was a problem with a mitral valve in his heart. And he was still prone to terrible coughing fits.

With no films on offer, he accepted a series of TV commercials extolling the virtues of a substitute aspirin substance called Datril, produced by the Bristol-Myers Company. It was the six-figure sum they offered him that persuaded him to do it, and since he was allowed to make suggestions, he said the first commercial should be shot in Monument Valley.

"He felt he had lost his way," said Claire Trevor. "He had been the biggest film star in the world, and he was humiliated by having to make money doing TV commercials. But he never gave up hope that he'd work again. In fact, he had a script that was being worked on called *Beau John*, and he wanted Ron Howard to be in it with him. But as time went on, his health deteriorated, and *still* he made plans to make his film."

In 1977, Howard Hawks died. At the funeral, it was Duke who delivered the eulogy.

Throughout 1977 his only film work was making TV commercials for the Great Western Savings and Loan Association. As the year went by, his voice grew weak. Thinking he simply had bronchitis, he checked into a local hospital in February 1978. His problem, they discovered, was the faulty mitral valve. In March, he flew to Boston to have the valve replaced with a valve from a pig's heart. The operation lasted twelve hours, during which time his heart was literally removed and his life maintained by a pump.

It was a major operation for anyone, let

alone a man of seventy with one lung. During Wayne's three-week stay in the hospital, Bob Hope delivered a message from the 1978 Academy Awards ceremony, saying, "We want you to know, Duke, we miss you tonight. We expect you to amble out here in person next year, because there is no one who can fill John Wayne's boots."

"That message from Bob," said Claire Trevor, "made Duke determined he *would* be there the following year." Speaking after Duke's death, Claire said, "When he was in hospital to have that pig valve put in his heart, none of us who loved him dared to believe he wouldn't come out of that hospital alive. But I know in my heart of hearts, I feared the worst. So when he did come out it seemed like a miracle. He was definitely looking older and thinner, but we all thought he'd put weight back on and be back to his old self. We all felt better when he joked, 'Now I can oink with the best of them.' But Duke later told me he was scared because he had always feared the cancer would return, and every time he was unwell, and especially when he had to go to the hospital for his prostate and then for his heart, he was truly scared it was cancer.

"He lived with that fear probably every

day for the two years left of his life, but he never let it show except to those closest to him."

Not all of those closest to him seemed to be aware how afraid he was — or they simply didn't want others knowing. Such as Andy McLaglen. Shortly after Duke had returned home from the hospital, I met McLaglen and his daughter Mary at Pinewood Studios. Over lunch, most of the conversation was about Wayne.

"He looks thin, but I'm sure he's in pretty good shape," McLaglen said optimistically. "Duke is Mary's godfather, and even though we might go months without communicating — because he lives in Newport and I'm in Europe a lot — we are very, very close.

"When he was in Boston having his heart operation, I decided to go back and see him. The first day after the operation they had him sitting up in a chair. I came in. He said, 'Hi,' and we talked for about five minutes, and then I had to go out.

"I saw him just before I came over here [to England], and he said, 'You wanna hear something funny? Back in Boston about a week after the operation I said to Michael and Patrick, "I forgot to tell you, but you know what I dreamed the other

650

day? I dreamed that Andrew was here." '

"I'd hate to think that *The Shootist* was his last film. But give him time to get his strength back and put on a little more weight."

I told Andy that I desperately wanted to have the chance of seeing Duke again. "I'd hate it if anything happened to him and I was never able to accept his invitation to come and visit him."

I don't know if Andy was just trying to cheer me up or himself and Mary, but he said, "Don't worry about him. He's really indestructible."

Mary was closer to the mark when she said, "He has a really strong will to live."

He needed that strong will because, while I and Andy would have liked to believe that Wayne really was indestructible, by Christmas 1978, Duke was experiencing excruciating pains in his stomach. He described the pain as feeling like jagged glass had been raked across his stomach. On 10 January 1979, he was admitted to the UCLA Medical Center and two days later underwent exploratory surgery.

He had cancer of the stomach. His entire stomach was removed in a nine-hour operation.

"It was just devastating news," said

Claire Trevor. "It was bad enough for his friends, but what must his children have been going through?"

Although Wayne had survived, he had little to look forward to in however much life he had left. He had always loved to eat, but could now only eat minute amounts of bland food which went straight from the esophagus into the intestine. He loved to drink, but he could never again drink alcohol. His final months of life were spent in torment which was manifest by constant bouts of bad temper. And yet, he wasn't strong enough to really blow his top the way he had characteristically done so many times.

Loretta Young told me, "I thanked God with all my heart when I heard that Duke had survived the surgery. How else can you explain it? Duke told me that he had faith in God, and I believe God rewarded him."

When I questioned why God would have allowed Duke to survive cancer only to live in painful misery until his death, Loretta Young said, "All Duke wanted to do was to be able to be at the Academy Awards show that year."

If Loretta Young was right, then God had blessed John Wayne because on 9 April 1979, Johnny Carson introduced

John Wayne on stage at the Oscars ceremony at the Los Angeles Music Center. I remember watching the show on television and, when I saw Wayne, I was moved, I was shaken, and I was elated. He looked unbelievably thin, and I didn't know it then, but he was in incredible pain. That morning he had undergone his daily dose of radiation treatment, so he began the day feeling sick.

When he turned up at the Music Center for rehearsal, he was told they would do his segment immediately so he wouldn't have to wait around. Being treated like an invalid only made him mad. But, having rehearsed his entrance and the speech he would give, he retired to a nearby hotel where he took a nap but was unable to eat anything.

His makeup man, Dave Grayson, arrived early that evening to put some realistic color into his face. His body was so emaciated, he wore a wet suit under his tuxedo to fill him out — and *still* he looked painfully thin.

Then it was time for him to come on stage to announce the Best Film of 1978. As he walked out, the audience gave him a truly loving standing ovation. He found it difficult to stand for any period of time but, when the applause finally died down, he said, trying to hold back the tears, "That's just about the only medicine a fella'd ever really need. Believe me when I tell you that I'm mighty pleased that I can amble down here tonight. Oscar and I have something in common. Oscar came to the Hollywood scene in 1928 — so did I. We're both a little weather-beaten, but we're still here, and plan to be around a whole lot longer."

He announced that the Best Picture of 1978 was *The Deer Hunter,* a film Wayne was not fond of, and made his way to the pressroom, to be greeted by many old friends, including Yul Brynner and Sammy Davis Jr.

Ava Gardner told me, "Sammy felt really bad because he'd given Duke a really tight hug, not knowing that Duke was in such terrible pain. I said to Sammy, 'I'd bet Duke wouldn't have missed that hug for anything.'"

John Wayne had just two more months to live. The details of his decline given to me by his friends are painful and emotional.

Maureen O'Hara recalled, "I spent three days with him at his house, and the whole time I never let him know how upset I was for him because I know he would have hated that. So I made him laugh as I told him stories, and we remembered some of our hair-raising adventures. But when I left . . . I *knew* I would never see him again."

Claire Trevor said, "Milton and I arrived one Sunday and we were shocked to see how much more he had deteriorated since the Oscars ceremony. He could barely walk. It just killed me to see him like that."

On 2 May 1979, Duke fell to the ground in agony. Ethan drove him straight to the UCLA Medical Center. There doctors discovered new cancer cells had spread, and they immediately operated to remove most of his colon. But it was all in vain, and within ten days his intestines were almost completely blocked. Duke was put on morphine intravenously and spent most of his remaining days unconscious with moments of semiconsciousness.

Barry Goldwater introduced a bill in Congress to authorize the minting of a special medal as a tribute to Duke. Since the Congressional Medal had been introduced in 1776, only eighty-seven people or groups had received it. On 23 May, Maureen O'Hara and Elizabeth Taylor flew to Washington to attend the hearings.

Many tributes were read out by Barry Goldwater; they had come from such luminaries as Frank Sinatra, James Stewart, Kirk Douglas, Gregory Peck, and Katharine Hepburn, who wrote, "I understand that the United States Congress and our president are giving John Wayne a gold medal. Asked for a comment, I can only say with a heart full of love for all concerned, 'About time.'"

The bill was passed unanimously, and it was decided that one side would bear a portrait of Duke as Davy Crockett, and on the other side would be a landscape of Monument Valley. Maureen O'Hara insisted that the inscription should read, "John Wayne, American."

On 9 June, the archbishop of Panama arrived and Wayne was baptized into the Catholic Church. Michael declared that his father did it for his family because all his wives were Catholics, although Pilar had become a Christian Scientist.

The tension that had always existed between the two sets of Wayne children really began to show over the matter of their father's bedside conversion to Catholicism. Aissa maintained her father was so opposed to organized religion that she couldn't believe he would have gone through with the ceremony. She also said her father "was too drugged up to know a conversion was even being attempted."

Claire Trevor said that it was a terrible time for the family. "Not only was their father dying, but rather than bringing his two sets of children together, it only served to widen the gap between them. I don't know what was behind it all, but Michael, as the senior son and a fine man, liaised with the doctors, and he made all the decisions which I think the younger ones — Pilar's children — took some exception to. Decisions were being made they didn't agree with. Guards were put outside his door and nobody but certain people — approved by Michael, I suppose — were allowed to see him. I understand Pilar was not on that list.

"Neither was Henry Fonda, but he turned up and refused to leave until he'd seen Duke, so he was allowed in. But even Mary St. John wasn't permitted to see him. I couldn't see him. Very few people were allowed to visit. I suppose Duke really wasn't up to visitors."

Ava Gardner told me, "Francis was on the so-called approved list, and he went — with Barbara, I think — and he told me that when he saw Duke lying in bed with tubes running through him and looking nothing like the man he'd once squared up to, he just cried. He kept saying, 'I had no idea. I had no idea.' "

On Friday, 11 June 1979, the doctors told Duke's children that the end was very near. Michael couldn't be there, having to deal with lawyers. But all the other children were around his bed. Aissa took hold of her father's emaciated hand. He stopped breathing. Patrick said, "Good-bye, Dad." The time was 5:23 P.M.

Paul Fix told me, "A lot of his friends would have liked to have attended the funeral to say good-bye. But we weren't invited. A lot of us were puzzled because Duke never made a secret of his final wish — that he be cremated and have his ashes scattered over the ocean. He said, 'For God's sake, don't bury me in a box and put me in the ground for the worms. Let me become a part of the ocean.'

"He also wanted something engraved somewhere that said, '*Feo, fuerte, y formel*,' which was Spanish for 'ugly, strong, and with dignity.' He wanted that as his epitaph. But he never got it."

Duke was buried on 15 June 1979, in an unmarked grave on a hilltop in Pacific View Memorial Park, overlooking the

658

ocean. Only his family know where their father's remains lie because, understandably, they didn't want his grave to be desecrated. But the fact that he was buried instead of cremated further increased the tension between the two sets of children.

Michael said that his father had died a Catholic, and had received a Catholic funeral. Aissa said her father's wishes to be cremated were ignored.

I have no doubt that both sets of children had the best interests of their father at heart. I never met Aissa or Pilar, but their respective memoirs seemed to expose the delights and the despair of being daughter and wife of John Wayne. Michael and Patrick I did meet, and despite Duke's lifelong belief that none of his children by Josephine had ever forgiven him for leaving them and their mother, all I saw and heard convinced me that Michael and Patrick loved their father, respected him, and never had a bad word to say about him. In fact, I would say that their father was their role model, and each of them had certain of their father's attributes. Michael is the tough man, making tough decisions. Firm, but gentle. Patrick has the humor of his father. He is the actor rather than the businessman. He developed a certain kind of grace in his movements, a trait he learned from his father. Somehow, combined, Michael and Patrick are the two sides of their father.

But there is no other John Wayne.

Among the many tributes I was able to acquire was one from a star who never worked with Wayne, who barely knew him, and had no anecdotes to offer, only his heartfelt personal tribute. Charlton Heston told me, "He created a permanent niche for himself as *the* American film actor. Beyond any question, beyond any doubt, John Wayne is the *absolute* all-time movie star."

John Wayne was a legend long before he died in 1979 at the age of seventy-two. In a career spanning more than fifty years he made almost two hundred films. Most of those films, even by his own admission, were lousy. His more successful films were often little more than moderately good. The number of outstanding films he made can be counted on two hands. Some might argue they could only be counted on one hand. And yet he became a living legend.

There were many critics who said he couldn't act. Yet he has somehow managed to top poll after poll of the all-time top movie stars. He came to be looked upon by generations of Americans as the ultimate patriot. Yet his ultraconservative politics, such as his support of the Vietnam War, made him unpopular with a whole generation in the 1960s. To many he was the hero who won the war against the Nazis and the Japanese. Yet he never served in the armed forces. And most of all, he was the embodiment of the Westerner: sometimes as a lawman, occasionally as an outlaw, sometimes as the killer of countless Native Americans who were portrayed as marauding "Injuns."

And yet today, in a world of political correctness, his films continue to thrill and entertain. There are still young men who join the American marines because they are inspired by John Wayne's heroics in *Sands of Iwo Jima*. In 1995, a poll among Americans put John Wayne at the top of a list of the most popular film stars — and that was sixteen years after he died and nineteen years since his last film had been released.

His legend lives on in many forms. The airport in Orange County in southern California, a tennis club, a cancer clinic at the University of California in Los Angeles, and a school in Brooklyn, have all been named after him.

On video and DVD his films continue to sell more than any other star's, living or dead. You could put forward the argument that he sells more videos because he made more films than just about anybody else. In fact, there are many of his films which have never been made available on video or DVD. Certainly the few outstanding films he made are available, and many of the modestly good films too. You can even buy many of his pre-*Stagecoach* B Westerns, few of which could even be considered moderately good. But people continue to buy them. They buy them simply because John Wayne is the star.

Perhaps because he made so many bad movies, perhaps because of his right-wing politics which made him unpopular in many quarters, the critics of the past refused to take him seriously because John Wayne usually only ever played John Wayne. Yet today, critics delight in dissecting his varied characterizations because now they have a complete body of work they can look back on and analyze, and they see that there are exceptions to the rule.

When his most personal film, *The Alamo*, was released in 1960 the critics slaughtered it. Yet today, the same film, like many of the epic films of the early 1960s which also came in for heavy critical flack, is recognized as an example of an art form now lost and treasured, and which can only hope to be imitated by the use of computer-generated images and MTV-style editing. *The Alamo* is constantly being reissued on video and DVD, as well as turning up on television, as the critics of today see something in it that those of 1960 failed to notice.

I admit that I have long been a Wayne aficionado. I have scrapbooks on Wayne that I pasted up when I was a boy. I've seen most of his films, although I can't claim to have seen them all because there are still some of his movies that have not been shown in my lifetime. I have interviewed many people who knew and worked with him. And I've had the privilege to spend time with him.

What I learned about him — the secret he kept from many, even from his own family, as far as I could tell — has only served to reinforce my admiration and my fondness for him.

When he died, I grieved. I was a staff writer at the British version of *Photoplay* at the time, and my editor asked me to write a tribute. I had collected many interviews about Wayne from his friends and colleagues over the years. Now I set about making contact with more of them on the other side of the Atlantic, to get, at my own expense from my own home telephone, the memories and emotions of those who knew him best.

In his lifetime his style of patriotism came in and out of fashion with the times. He was a man who was proud to be an American, and a man America was, at times, proud to have represent its purest virtues. He believed that there was no greater country in the world than America, and that it bore the heavy responsibility of maintaining peace in the world.

When he died in 1979, his style of patriotism had become somewhat outmoded, especially his seemingly negative attitude toward civil rights. But then came the war in Iraq in 1991, and Americans began to remember Wayne's ideals about Americanism. Then there was 11 September 2001, and America began to remember John Wayne more than ever. A long-playing record of patriotic poems and monologues he had made in the 1970s was reissued on CD and became a bestseller. The patriotism John Wayne had preached became the doctrine again for most Americans.

I mention all this, not to validate America's position as the world's superpower, nor to praise its morals — indeed, there have been enough events to prove that America is neither incorruptible nor omnipotent — but to merely point out that its ideals, while not necessarily invented by John Wayne, were certainly propagated by him. You don't have to be an American to appreciate John Wayne, but you can understand why Americans appreciate and even revere him.

It is always sad when an actor you admire dies. We somehow feel that we know these people, even though few of us ever do meet them. But I did meet John Wayne and I believe he *was* my friend. When he died, I really could not believe it was possible. I just assumed that he would once again pull through.

I never got to visit him, and I daresay he forgot all about me. But Claire Trevor told me, "If you'd suddenly turned up on his doorstep and said, 'Remember me?' he would have, and he would have told you to stay forever — or however long you wanted to."

I have an abiding memory of Wayne to

close this book with. It's a memory that makes me smile.

You may recall that when on my first day on the set of *Brannigan* I told him I'd never met "a living legend" before. Being called that had made him laugh.

A problem arose concerning the filming of a car chase across Tower Bridge just as it was opening. I have no idea what arrangements had been made, but for some reason the police had stepped in and said that if they filmed on Tower Bridge, Douglas Hickox would be arrested.

Wayne had said to go ahead and shoot the scene, and he would take care of the police. I wasn't able to be there to see this scene, which involved professional stunt drivers, but, according to the film's unit publicist, the scene went ahead, complete with the bridge being opened.

As the police moved in to arrest Douglas Hickox, Wayne ambled over to the British police officers and began signing autographs and chatting to them.

Finally, he said, "You don't want to arrest my director, do you, fellers? Without him, I can't finish the picture." They let Hickox off with a caution — as if he was ever likely to film another car chase across Tower Bridge.

I would have loved to have seen it all happen, but I only caught the moment when Duke was told that the police had forbidden them to shoot on the bridge, and Duke had told them to shoot the scene anyway.

I said to Wayne, "Is that a good idea? Can you do that?"

He looked down at me kind of sideways, grinned and said, "Who the hell's gonna argue with a living legend?"

Postscript

By sheer coincidence but perhaps appropriately, I completed this manuscript on 11 September 2002, in between joining the world in observing the silent tributes to commemorate the first anniversary of 11 September 2001.

So much of what I heard that day, from eyewitness accounts and moving tributes to fallen heroes, to the seemingly endless list of names read out in memoriam, reminded me of the words spoken by John Wayne as Davy Crockett in *The Alamo*: "It's good to feel useful in this old world. To hit a lick against what's wrong or to say a word for what's right, even though you might get walloped for saying that word. I may sound like a Bible-beater yelling up a revival at a river-crossing camp meeting, but that don't change the truth none: there's right and there's wrong. You've gotta do one or the other. You do the one and you're living. You do the other and you may be walking around, but you're dead as a beaver hat."

Filmography

The abbreviations are as follows: *P* producer; *D* director; *S* screenplay; *C* cinematographer (director of photography); *Lp* leading players. Studios, production companies, and/or distributors are named in parentheses.

Early films in which John Wayne was known to feature as an extra are as follows:

The Great K & A Train Robbery (Fox Studios). *D* Lewis Seiler. *Lp* Tom Mix, Dorothy Dwan, 1926.
Mother Machree (Fox). *D* John Ford. *Lp* Belle Bennett, Neil Hamilton, Victor McLaglen, 1928.
Hangman's House (Fox). *D* John Ford. *Lp* Victor McLaglen, June Collyer, Hobart Bosworth, 1928.

Films in which John Wayne, sometimes known as Duke Morrison, had featured, starring, and cameo roles are as follows:

Salute (Fox). *D* John Ford and David Butler. *S* John Stone and James K. McGuiness. *C* Joseph H. August. *Lp* George O'Brien, Helen Chandler, Stepin Fetchit; Wayne, then known as Duke Morrison, was unbilled, 1929.

Words and Music (Fox). *D* James Tinling. *S* Frederick Hazlitt Brennan and Jack McEdward. *Lp* Lois Moran, David Percy, Helen Twelvetrees, William Orlamond, Elizabeth Patterson, Duke Morrison, 1929.

Men Without Women (Fox). *D* John Ford. *S* Dudley Nichols. *C* Joseph H. August. *Lp* Kenneth MacKenna, Frank Albertson, Paul Page, Pat Somerset; Wayne was unbilled, 1930.

Rough Romance (Fox). *D* A. F. Erickson. *S* Elliott Lester and Donald Davis. *C* Daniel B. Clark. *Lp* George O'Brien, Helen Chandler, Antonio Moreno, Noel Francis, Eddie Borden, Roy Stewart, Duke Morrison, 1930.

Cheer Up and Smile (Fox). *D* Sidney Lanfield. *S* Howard J. Green. *C* Joseph Valentine. *Lp* Arthur Lake, Dixie Lee, Olga Baclanova, Whispering Jack Smith, Johnny Arthur; way down in the cast list is Duke Morrison, 1930.

The Big Trail (Fox). *D* Raoul Walsh. *S* Hal G. Evarts, Jack Peabody, Marie Boyle, and Florence Postal. *C* Lucien Andriot and Arthur Edeson. *Lp* John Wayne, Marguerite Churchill, El Brendel, Tully Marshall, Tyrone Power Sr., David Rollins, 1930.

Girls Demand Excitement (Fox). *D* Seymour Felix. *S* Harlan Thompson. *C* Charles Clarke. *Lp* Virginia Cherrill, John Wayne, Marguerite Churchill, Helen Jerome Eddy, 1931.

Three Girls Lost (Fox). *D* Sidney Lanfield. *S* Bradley King. *C* L. William O'Connell. *Lp* Loretta Young, John Wayne, Lew Cody, Joyce Compton, Joan Marsh, Paul Fix, 1931.

Men Are Like That [aka *Arizona*] (Columbia). *D* George B. Seitz. *S* Robert Riskin and Dorothy Howell. *C* Teddy Tetzlaff. *Lp* John Wayne, Laura LaPlante, June Clyde, Forrest Stanley, 1931.

The Range Feud (Columbia). *D* David Ross Lederman. *S* Milton Krims. *C* Ben Kline. *Lp* Buck Jones, John Wayne, Susan Fleming, Edward Le Saint, 1931.

Maker of Men (Columbia). *D* Edward Sedgwick. *S* Howard J. Green and Edward Sedgwick. *C* L. William O'Connell. *Lp* Jack Holt, Richard Cromwell, Joan Marsh, Robert Alden, John Wayne, 1931.

Haunted Gold (Warner Bros.). *D* Mack V. Wright. *P* Leon Schlesinger. *S* Adele Buffington. *C* Nick Musuraca. *Lp* John Wayne,

Sheila Terry, Erville Alderson, Harry Woods, 1932.

Shadow of the Eagle (a Mascot serial in twelve chapters). *D* Ford Beebe. *P* Nat Levine. *S* Ford Beebe, Colbert Clark, and Wyndham Gittens. *C* Ben Kline and Victor Scheurich. *Lp* John Wayne, Dorothy Gulliver, Edward Hearn, Richard Tucker, Yakima Canutt, 1932.

The Hurricane Express (a Mascot serial in twelve chapters). *D* Armand Schaefer and J. P. McGowan. *P* Nat Levine. *S* Wyndham Gittens, Colbert Clark, Barney Sarecky, Harold Tarshin, George Morgan, and J. P. McGowan. *C* Ernest Millar and Carl Wester. *Lp* John Wayne, Shirley Grey, Tully Marshall, Conway Tearle, 1932.

Texas Cyclone (Columbia). *D* David Ross Lederman. *S* William Colt McDonald and Randall Faye. *C* Ben Kline. *Lp* Wallace MacDonald, Tim McCoy, Shirley Grey, John Wayne, Wheeler Oakman, 1932.

Lady and Gent (Paramount). *D* Stephen Roberts. *S* Grover Jones and William Slavens McNutt. *C* Harry Fischbeck. *Lp* George Bancroft, Wynne Gibson, Charles Starrett, James Gleason, John Wayne, 1932.

Two-Fisted Law (Columbia). *D* David Ross Ledermann. *S* William Colt MacDonald and Kurt Kempler. *C* Benjamin

Kline. *Lp* Tim McCoy, Alice Day, Wheeler Oakman, Tully Marshall, Wallace Mac-Donald, John Wayne, 1932.

Ride Him, Cowboy (Warner Bros.). *D* Fred Allen. *S* Kenneth Perkins and Scott Mason. *C* Ted McCord. *Lp* John Wayne, Ruth Hall, Henry B. Walthall, Harry Gribbon, 1932.

The Big Stampede (Warner Bros.). *D* Tenny Wright. *S* Marion Jackson and Kurt Kempler. *C* Ted McCord. *Lp* John Wayne, Noah Beery, Mae Madison, Luis Alberni, Berton Churchill, 1932.

The Telegraph Trail (Warner Bros.). *D* Tenny Wright. *S* Kurt Kempler. *C* Ted McCord. *Lp* John Wayne, Marceline Day, Frank McHugh, Otis Harlan, Yakima Canutt, 1933.

Central Airport (First National). *D* William A. Wellman. *S* Rian James and James Seymour. *C* Sid Hickox. *Lp* Richard Barthelmess, Sally Eilers, Tom Brown, Glenda Farrell, Harold Huber, John Wayne, 1933.

His Private Secretary (Showmen's Pictures). *D* Philip A. Whitman. *S* Lew Collins. *C* Abe Schultz. *Lp* John Wayne, Evalyn Knapp, Alec B. Francis, Natalie Kingston, 1933.

Somewhere in Sonora (Warner Bros.). *D* Mack V. Wright. *S* Will Levington Comfort and Joe Roach. *C* Ted McCord. *Lp* John Wayne, Shirley Palmer, Henry B. Walthall, Paul Fix, 1933.

Life of Jimmy Dolan (Warner Bros.). *D* Archie Mayo. *S* Bertram Milhauser, Beulah Marie Dix, Erwin Gelsey, and David Boehm. *C* Arthur Edeson. *Lp* Douglas Fairbanks Jr., Loretta Young, Aline MacMahon, Guy Kibee; way down in the cast list can be found Mickey Rooney and John Wayne, 1933.

The Three Musketeers (a Mascot serial in twelve chapters). *D* Armand Schaefer and Colbert Clark. *P* Victor Zobel. *S* Norman S. Hall, Colbert Clark, Wyndham Gittens, Barney Sarecky, and Ella Arnold. *C* Ernest Miller and Ed Lyons. *Lp* John Wayne, Ruth Hall, Jack Mulhall, Raymond Hatton, Francis X. Bushman Jr., Noah Beery Jr., 1933.

Baby Face (Warner Bros.). *D* Alfred E. Green. *S* Mark Canfield, Gene Markey, and Kathryn Scola. *C* James Van Trees. *Lp* Barbara Stanwyck, George Brent, Donald Cook, Margaret Lindsay, Henry Kolker, John Wayne, 1933.

The Man from Monterey (Warner Bros.). *D* Mack V. Wright. *S* Lesley Mason. *C* Ted McCord. *Lp* John Wayne, Ruth Hall, Nena Quartaro, Luis Alberni, Francis Ford, 1933.

Riders of Destiny (Mongram). *D* and *S* Robert N. Bradbury. *C* Archie Stout. *Lp* John Wayne, Cecilia Parker, George "Gabby" Hayes, Forrest Taylor, 1933.

Sagebrush Trail (Monogram). *D* Armand Schaefer. *S* Lindsley Parsons. *C* Archie Stout. *Lp* John Wayne, Nancy Shubert, Lane Chandler, Yakima Canutt, 1933.

West of the Divide (Monogram). *D* and *S* Robert N. Bradbury. *C* Archie Stout. *Lp* John Wayne, Virginia Brown Faire, Lloyd Whitlock, Yakima Canutt, George "Gabby" Hayes, 1933.

Lucky Texan (Monogram). *D* and *S* Robert N. Bradbury. *C* Archie Stout. *Lp* John Wayne, Barbara Sheldon, George "Gabby" Hayes, Lloyd Whitlock, Yakima Canutt, 1934.

Blue Steel (Monogram). *D* and *S* Robert N. Bradbury. *C* Archie Stout. *Lp* John Wayne, Eleanor Hunt, George "Gabby" Hayes, Edward Peil, Yakima Canutt, 1934.

The Man from Utah (Monogram). *D* Robert N. Bradbury. *S* Lindsley Parsons. *C* Archie Stout. *Lp* John Wayne, Polly Ann Young, George "Gabby" Hayes, Yakima Canutt, Edward Peil, 1934.

Randy Rides Alone (Monogram). *D* Harry Fraser. *S* Lindsley Parsons. *C* Archie Stout. *Lp* John Wayne, Alberta Vaughn, George

"Gabby" Hayes, Earl Dwire, Yakima Canutt, 1934.

The Star Packer (Monogram). *D* and *S* Robert N. Bradbury. *C* Archie Stout. *Lp* John Wayne, Verna Hillie, George "Gabby" Hayes, Yakima Canutt, Earl Dwire, 1934.

The Trail Beyond (Monogram). *D* Robert N. Bradbury. *S* Lindsley Parsons. *C* Archie Stout. *Lp* John Wayne, Verna Hillie, Noah Beery, Iris Lancaster, Noah Beery Jr., 1934.

'Neath the Arizona Skies (Monogram). *D* Harry Fraser. *P* Paul Malvern. *S* B. R. Tuttle. *C* Archie Stout. *Lp* John Wayne, Sheila Terry, Jay Wilsey, Yakima Canutt, George "Gabby" Hayes, 1934.

The Lawless Frontier (Monogram). *D* and *S* Robert N. Bradbury. *P* Paul Malvern. *C* Archie Stout. *Lp* John Wayne, Sheila Terry, George "Gabby" Hayes, Earl Dwire, Yakima Canutt, 1935.

Texas Terror (Monogram). *D* and *S* Robert N. Bradbury. *P* Paul Malvern. *C* Archie Stout. *Lp* John Wayne, Lucille Browne, LeRoy Mason, George "Gabby" Hayes, Buffalo Bill Jr., 1935.

Rainbow Valley (Monogram). *D* Robert N. Bradbury. *P* Paul Malvern. *S* Lindsley Parsons. *C* William Hyer. *Lp* John Wayne, Lucille Browne, LeRoy Mason, George "Gabby" Hayes, Buffalo Bill Jr., 1935.

Paradise Canyon (Monogram). *D* Carl Pierson. *P* Paul Malvern. *S* Lindsley Parsons. *C* Archie Stout. *Lp* John Wayne, Marion Burns, Yakima Canutt, Reed Howes, 1935.

The Dawn Rider (Monogram). *D* and *S* Robert N. Bradbury. *P* Paul Malvern. *C* Archie Stout. *Lp* John Wayne, Marion Burns, Yakima Canutt, Reed Howes, 1935.

Westward Ho (Republic). *D* Robert N. Bradbury. *P* Paul Malvern. *S* Lindsley Parsons. *C* Archie Stout. *Lp* John Wayne, Sheila Mannors, Frank McGlynn Jr., Jack Curtis, Yakima Canutt, 1935.

The Desert Trail (Monogram). *D* Cullin Lewis. *P* Paul Malvern. *S* Lindsley Parsons. *C* Archie Stout. *Lp* John Wayne, Mary Kornman, Paul Fix, Edward Chandler, 1935.

The New Frontier (Republic). *D* Carl Pierson. *P* Paul Malvern. *S* Robert Emmett. *C* Gus Peterson. *Lp* John Wayne, Muriel Evans, Mary McLaren, Murdock MacQuarrie, Warner Richmond, Sam Flint, 1935.

Lawless Range (Republic). *D* Robert N. Bradbury. *P* Trem Carr. *S* Lindsley Parsons. *C* Archie Stout. *Lp* John Wayne, Sheila Mannors, Earl Dwire, Frank McGlynn Jr., Jack Curtis, Yakima Canutt, 1935.

The Lawless Nineties (Republic). *D* Joseph Kane. *P* Paul Malvern. *S* Joseph Poland. *C* William Nobles. *Lp* John Wayne, Ann Rutherford, Lane Chandler, Harry Woods, George "Gabby" Hayes, Cliff Lyons, 1936.

King of the Pecos (Republic). *D* Joseph Kane. *P* Paul Malvern. *S* Bernard McConville, Dorell McGowan, and Stuart McGowan. *C* Jack Martin. *Lp* John Wayne, Muriel Evans, Cy Kendall, Jack Clifford, Yakima Canutt, 1936.

The Oregon Trail (Republic). *D* Scott Pembroke. *P* Paul Malvern. *S* Lindsley Parsons and Robert Emmett. *C* Gus Peterson. *Lp* John Wayne, Ann Rutherford, Yakima Canutt, E. H. Clavert, 1936.

Winds of the Wasteland (Republic). *D* Mack V. Wright. *P* Nat Levine. *S* Joseph Poland. *C* William Nobles. *Lp* John Wayne, Phyllis Fraser, Yakima Canutt, Lane Chandler, 1936.

The Sea Spoilers (Universal). *D* Frank Strayer. *P* Trem Carr. *S* George Waggner. *C* Archie Stout and John P. Fulton. *Lp* John Wayne, Nan Grey, Fuzzy Knight, William Bakewell, 1936.

The Lonely Trail (Republic). *D* Joseph Kane. *P* Nat Levine. *S* Bernard McConville. *C* William Nobles. *Lp* John Wayne, Ann Rutherford, Cy Kendall, Etta McDaniel,

Yakima Canutt, 1936.

Conflict (Universal). *D* David Howard. *P* Trem Carr. *S* Charles A. Logue and Walter Weems. *C* Archie Stout. *Lp* John Wayne, Jean Rogers, Tommy Bupp, Eddie Borden, Ward Bond, 1936.

California Straight Ahead (Universal). *D* Arthur Lubin. *P* Trem Carr. *S* Herman Boxer. *C* Harry Neumann. *Lp* John Wayne, Louise Latimer, Robert McWade, Tully Marshall, 1937.

I Cover the War (Universal). *D* Arthur Lubin. *P* Trem Carr. *S* George Waggner. *C* Harry Neumann. *Lp* John Wayne, Gwen Gaze, Don Barclay, James Bush, 1937.

Idol of the Crowds (Universal). *D* Arthur Lubin. *P* Paul Malvern. *S* George Waggner and Harold Buckley. *C* Harry Neumann. *Lp* John Wayne, Sheila Bromley, Billy Burrud, Russell Gordon, 1937.

Adventure's End (Universal). *D* Arthur Lubin. *P* Trem Carr. *S* Ben Ames Williams. *C* Gus Peterson and John P. Fulton. *Lp* John Wayne, Diana Gibson, Moroni Olsen, Montague Love, 1937.

Born to the West [aka *Hell Town*] (Paramount). *D* Charles Barton. *S* Zane Grey. *C* J. D. Jennings. *Lp* John Wayne, Marsha Hunt, John Mack Brown, John Patterson, Monte Blue, 1938.

Pals of the Saddle (Republic). *D* George Sherman. *S* Stanley Roberts and Betty Burbridge. *C* Reggie Lanning. *Lp* John Wayne, Ray Corrigan, Max Terhune, Doreen McKay, 1938.

Overland Stage Raiders (Republic). *D* George Sherman. *S* Luci Ward. *C* William Nobles. *Lp* John Wayne, Louise Brooks, Ray Corrigan, Max Terhune, 1938.

Santa Fe Stampede (Republic). *D* George Sherman. *P* William Berke. *S* Luci Ward and Betty Burbridge. *C* Reggie Lanning. *Lp* John Wayne, June Martel, Ray Corrigan, Max Terhune, William Farnum, 1938.

Red River Range (Republic). *D* George Sherman. *P* William Berke. *S* Stanley Roberts, Betty Burbridge, and Luci Ward. *C* Jack Marta. *Lp* John Wayne, Ray Corrigan, Max Terhune, Polly Moran, Kirby Grant, 1938.

Stagecoach (United Artists). *D* John Ford. *P* Walter Wanger. *S* Dudley Nichols. *C* Bert Glennon and Ray Binger. *Lp* Claire Trevor, John Wayne, Thomas Mitchell, John Carradine, Andy Devine, Louise Platt, George Bancroft, Donald Meek, Berton Churchill, Tim Holt, Yakima Canutt, Chief Big Tree, 1939.

The Night Riders (Republic). *D* George Sherman. *P* William Berke. *S* Betty Burbridge and Stanley Roberts. *C* Jack Marta.

Lp John Wayne, Ray Corrigan, Max Terhune, Doreen McKay, 1939.

Three Texas Steers (Republic). *D* George Sherman. *P* William Berke. *S* Betty Burbridge and Stanley Roberts. *C* Ernest Miller. *Lp* John Wayne, Carole Landis, Ray Corrigan, Max Terhune, Ralph Graves, 1939.

Wyoming Outlaw (Republic). *D* George Sherman. *P* William Berke. *S* Jack Natteford. *C* Reggie Lanning. *Lp* John Wayne, Ray Corrigan, Raymond Hatton, Adele Pearce, Donald Barry, 1939.

New Frontier [aka *Frontier Horizon*] (Republic). *D* George Sherman. *P* William Berke. *S* Betty Burbridge and Luci Ward. *C* Reggie Lanning. *Lp* John Wayne, Ray Corrigan, Raymond Hatton, Jennifer Jones (billed as Phyllis Isley), Eddy Walker, 1939.

Allegheny Uprising [aka *First Rebel*] (RKO). *D* William Seiter. *P* and *S* P. J. Wolfson. *C* Nicholas Musuraca. *Lp* John Wayne, Claire Trevor, George Sanders, Brian Donlevy, Wilfrid Lawson, 1939.

Dark Command (Republic). *D* Raoul Walsh. *P* Sol C. Siegel. *S* Grover Jones, Lionel Houser, and F. Hugh Herbert. *C* Jack Marta. *Lp* John Wayne, Claire Trevor, Walter Pidgeon, Roy Rogers, George "Gabby" Hayes, Porter Hall, Marjorie Main, 1940.

Three Faces West [aka *The Refugee*] (Republic). *D* Bernard Vorhaus. *P* Sol C. Siegel. *S* F. Hugh Herbert, Joseph Moncure March, and Samuel Ornitz. *C* John Alton. *Lp* John Wayne, Sigrid Gurie, Charles Coburn, Spencer Charters, Helen MacKellar, 1940.

The Long Voyage Home (United Artists/Argosy). *D* John Ford. *P* Walter Wanger. *S* Dudley Nichols. *C* Gregg Toland. *Lp* Thomas Mitchell, John Wayne, Ian Hunter, Barry Fitzgerald, Wilfrid Lawson, Mildred Natwick, John Qualen, Ward Bond, 1940.

Seven Sinners (Universal). *D* Tay Garnett. *P* Joe Pasternack. *S* John Meehan and Harry Tugend. *C* Rudolph Maté. *Lp* Marlene Dietrich, John Wayne, Broderick Crawford, Mischa Auer, Albert Dekker, Billy Gilbert, Anna Lee, 1940.

A Man Betrayed [aka *Wheel of Fortune*] (Republic). *D* John H. Auer. *P* Armand Schaefer. *S* Isabel Dawn. *C* Jack Marta. *Lp* John Wayne, Frances Dee, Edward Ellis, Wallace Ford, Ward Bond, Harold Huber, 1941.

Lady from Louisiana (Republic). *D* and *P* Bernard Vorhaus. *S* Vera Caspary, Michael Hogan, and Guy Endore. *C* Jack Marta. *Lp* John Wayne, Ona Munson, Ray Middleton, Henry Stephenson, Helen Westley, Jack Pennick, 1941.

The Shepherd of the Hills (Paramount). *D* Henry Hathaway. *P* Jack Moss. *S* Grover Jones and Stuart Anthony. *C* Charles Lang. *Lp* John Wayne, Betty Field, Harry Carey, Beulah Bondi, James Barton, 1941.

Lady for a Night (Republic). *D* Leigh Jason. *P* Albert J. Cohen. *S* Isabel Dawn and Boyce DeGaw. *C* Norbert Brodine. *Lp* John Wayne, Joan Blondell, Ray Middleton, Philip Merivale, Blanche Yurba, 1941.

Reap the Wild Wind (Paramount). *D* and *P* Cecil B. DeMille. *S* Alan LeMay, Charles Bennett, and Jesse Lasky Jr. *C* Victor Milner. *Lp* Ray Milland, John Wayne, Paulette Goddard, Raymond Massey, Robert Preston, Susan Hayward, Lynne Overman, 1942.

The Spoilers (Universal). *D* Ray Enright. *P* Frank Lloyd. *S* Lawrence Hazard and Tom Reed. *C* Milton Krasner. *Lp* Marlene Dietrich, John Wayne, Randolph Scott, Margaret Lindsay, Harry Carey, Richard Barthelmess, William Farnum, 1942.

In Old California (Republic). *D* William McGann. *P* Robert North. *S* Gertrude Purcell and Frances Hyland. *C* Jack Marta. *Lp* John Wayne, Binnie Barnes, Albert Dekker, Helen Parrish, Patsy Kelly, Edgar Kennedy, 1942.

Flying Tigers (Republic). *D* David Miller. *P* Edmund Grainger. *S* Kenneth Gamet and

Barry Trivers. *C* Jack Marta. *Lp* John Wayne, John Carroll, Anna Lee, Paul Kelly, Gordon Jones, Mae Clarke, Addison Richards, 1942.

Reunion in France (MGM). *D* Jules Dassin. *P* Joseph L. Mankiewicz. *S* Jan Lustig. *C* Robert Planck. *Lp* Joan Crawford, John Wayne, Philip Dorn, Reginald Owen, Albert Bassermann, John Carradine, Ava Gardner, 1942.

Pittsburgh (Universal). *D* Lewis Seiler. *P* Charles K. Feldman. *S* Kenneth Gamet and Tom Reed. *C* Robert DeGrasse. *Lp* Marlene Dietrich, John Wayne, Randolph Scott, Frank Craven, Louise Allbritton, Thomas Gomez, 1942.

A Lady Takes a Chance [aka *The Cowboy and the Girl*] (RKO). *D* William A. Seiter. *P* Frank Ross. *S* Robert Ardrey. *C* Frank Redman. *Lp* Jean Arthur, John Wayne, Charles Winninger, Phil Silvers, Mary Field, Don Costello, 1943.

War of the Wildcats [aka *In Old Oklahoma*] (Republic). *D* Albert S. Rogell. *P* Robert North. *S* Ethel Hill and Eleanor Griffith. *C* Jack Marta. *Lp* John Wayne, Martha Scott, Albert Dekker, George "Gabby" Hayes, Marjorie Rambeau, Dale Evans, Grant Withers, Paul Fix, 1943.

The Fighting Seabees (Republic). *D* Howard Lydecker and Edward Ludwig. *P*

Albert J. Cohen. *S* Borden Chase and Aeneas MacKenzie. *C* William Bradford. *Lp* John Wayne, Susan Hayward, Dennis O'Keefe, William Frawley, Addison Richards, Paul Fix, Grant Withers, 1944.

Tall in the Saddle (RKO). *D* Edwin L. Marin. *P* Robert Fellows. *S* Michael Hogan and Paul Fix. *C* Robert de Grasse. *Lp* John Wayne, Ella Raines, Ward Bond, George "Gabby" Hayes, Audrey Long, Paul Fix, 1944.

Flame of the Barbary Coast (Republic). *D* and *P* Joseph Kane. *S* Borden Chase. *C* Robert de Grasse. *Lp* John Wayne, Ann Dvorak, Joseph Schildkraut, William Frawley, Virginia Grey, Russell Hicks, 1945.

Back to Bataan (RKO). *D* Edward Dmytryk. *P* Robert Fellows. *S* Ben Barzman and Richard Landau. *C* Nicholas Musuraca. *Lp* John Wayne, Anthony Quinn, Beulah Bondi, Fely Franquelli, Leonard Strong, Richard Loo, Paul Fix, 1945.

Dakota (Republic). *D* and *P* Joseph Kane. *S* Lawrence Hazard. *C* Jack Marta. *Lp* John Wayne, Vera Hruba Ralston, Walter Brennan, Ward Bond, Ona Munson, Paul Fix, 1945.

They Were Expendable (MGM) *D* and *P* John Ford. *S* Frank Wead. *C* Joseph H. August. *Lp* Robert Montgomery, John Wayne,

Donna Reed, Jack Holt, Ward Bond, Marshall Thompson, Paul Langton, 1945.

Without Reservations (RKO). *D* Mervyn LeRoy. *P* Jesse L. Lasky. *S* Andrew Solt. *C* Milton Krasner. *Lp* Claudette Colbert, John Wayne, Don DeFore, Anne Triola, Phil Brown, 1946.

Angel and the Badman (Republic). *D* and *S* James Edward Grant. *P* John Wayne. *C* Archie Stout. *Lp* John Wayne, Gail Russell, Harry Carey, Bruce Cabot, Irene Rich, Lee Dixon, Tom Powers, 1947.

Tycoon (RKO). *D* Richard Wallace. *P* Stephen Ames. *S* Borden Chase and John Twist. *C* Harry J. Wild and Howard Greene. *Lp* John Wayne, Laraine Day, Anthony Quinn, Sir Cedric Hardwicke, Judith Anderson, James Gleason, Grant Withers, Paul Fix, 1947.

Fort Apache (RKO/Argosy) *D* John Ford. *P* John Ford and Merian C. Cooper. *S* Frank S. Nugent. *C* Archie Stout. *Lp* Henry Fonda, John Wayne, Shirley Temple, Pedro Armendariz, Ward Bond, Irene Rich, John Agar, Anna Lee, Victor McLaglen, Grant Withers, 1948.

Red River (United Artists/Monterey). *D* and *P* Howard Hawks. *S* Borden Chase and Charles Schnee. *C* Russell Harlan. *Lp* John Wayne, Montgomery Clift, Walter Brennan,

Joanne Dru, Harry Carey, John Ireland, Coleen Gray, Harry Carey Jr., Noah Beery Jr., Paul Fix, Shelley Winters, 1948.

Three Godfathers (MGM/Argosy). *D* John Ford. *P* John Ford and Merian C. Cooper. *S* Laurence Stallings and Frank S. Nugent. *C* Winton Hoch and Charles Boyle. *Lp* John Wayne, Pedro Armendariz, Harry Carey Jr., Ward Bond, Mae Marsh, Mildred Natwick, Jane Darwell, Ben Johnson, Hank Warden, 1948.

Wake of the Red Witch (Republic). *D* Edward Ludwig. *P* Edmund Grainger. *S* Harry Brown and Kenneth Gamet. *C* Reggie Lanning. *Lp* John Wayne, Gail Russell, Gig Young, Adela Mara, Luther Adler, Paul Fix, Grant Withers, Eduard Franz, Henry Daniell, 1948.

She Wore a Yellow Ribbon (RKO/Argosy). *D* John Ford. *P* John Ford and Merian C. Cooper. *S* Frank S. Nugent and Laurence Stallings. *C* Winton Hoch. *Lp* John Wayne, Joanne Dru, John Agar, Ben Johnson, Harry Carey Jr., Victor McLaglen, Mildred Natwick, George O'Brien, 1949.

The Fighting Kentuckian (Republic). *D* and *S* George Waggner. *P* John Wayne. *C* Lee Garmes. *Lp* John Wayne, Vera Hruba Ralston, Oliver Hardy, Philip Dorn, Marie Windsor, John Howard, Grant Withers,

Paul Fix, 1949.

Sands of Iwo Jima (Republic). *D* Allan Dwan. *P* Edmund Grainger. *S* Harry Brown and James Edward Grant. *C* Reggie Lanning. *Lp* John Wayne, John Agar, Adele Mara, Forrest Tucker, Wally Cassell, James Brown, Richard Webb, 1949.

Rio Grande (Republic/Argosy). *D* John Ford. *P* John Ford and Merian C. Cooper. *S* James Kevin McGuiness. *C* Bert Glennon. *Lp* John Wayne, Maureen O'Hara, Ben Johnson, J. Carrol Naish, Victor McLaglen, Chill Wills, Harry Carey Jr., Grant Withers, 1950.

Operation Pacific (Warner Bros.). *D* and *S* George Waggner. *P* Louis F. Edelman. *C* Bert Glennon. *Lp* John Wayne, Patricia Neal, Ward Bond, Scott Forbes, Philip Carey, Martin Milner, 1951.

Flying Leathernecks (RKO). *D* Nicholas Ray. *P* Howard Hughes. *S* James Edward Grant. *C* William E. Snyder. *Lp* John Wayne, Robert Ryan, Don Taylor, Janis Carter, Jay C. Flippen, William Harrigan, 1951.

The Quiet Man (Republic/Argosy). *D* John Ford. *P* Merian C. Cooper. *S* Frank S. Nugent. *C* Winton C. Hoch. *Lp* John Wayne, Maureen O'Hara, Victor McLaglen, Barry Fitzgerald, Ward Bond, Mildred Natwick, Francis Ford, 1952.

Big Jim McLain (Warner Bros./Wayne-Fellows). *D* Edward Ludwig. *P* Robert Fellows. *S* James Edward Grant, Richard English, and Eric Taylor. *C* Archie Stout. *Lp* John Wayne, Nancy Olson, James Arness, Alan Napier, Gayne Whitman, Hans Conreid, 1952.

Trouble Along the Way (Warner Bros.). *D* Michael Curtiz. *P* Melville Shavelson. *S* Melville Shavelson and Jack Rose. *C* Archie Stout. *Lp* John Wayne, Donna Reed, Charles Coburn, Tom Tully, Marie Windsor, Sherry Jackson, Tom Helmore, Leif Erickson, Chuck Connors, 1953.

Island in the Sky (Warner Bros./Wayne-Fellows). *D* William A. Wellman. *P* John Wayne and Robert Fellows. *S* Ernest K. Gann. *C* Archie Stout and William H. Clothier. *Lp* John Wayne, Lloyd Nolan, Walter Abel, James Arness, Andy Devine, Allyn Joslyn, Harry Carey Jr., Paul Fix, 1953.

Hondo (Warner Bros./Wayne-Fellows). *D* John Farrow. *P* Robert Fellows. *S* James Edward Grant. *C* Robert Burks and Archie Stout. *Lp* John Wayne, Geraldine Page, Ward Bond, Michael Pate, Lee Aaker, James Arness, Rodolfo Acosta, Paul Fix, 1953.

The High and the Mighty (Warner Bros./Wayne-Fellows). *D* William A. Wellman. *P*

Robert Fellows. *S* Ernest K. Gann. *C* Archie Stout and William H. Clothier. *Lp* John Wayne, Claire Trevor, Laraine Day, Robert Stack, Jan Sterling, Phil Harris, Robert Newton, David Brian, Paul Kelly, 1954.

The Sea Chase (Warner Bros.). *D* and *P* John Farrow. *S* James Warner Bellah and John Twist. *C* William H. Clothier. *Lp* John Wayne, Lana Turner, David Farrar, Lyle Bettger, Tab Hunter, James Arness, Paul Fix, Claude Akins, 1955.

Blood Alley (Warner Bros./Batjac). *D* William A. Wellman. *S* A. S. Fleischman. *C* William H. Clothier. *Lp* John Wayne, Lauren Bacall, Paul Fix, Joy Kim, Berry Kroeger, Mike Mazurki, Anita Ekberg, 1955.

The Conqueror (RKO). *D* and *P* Dick Powell. *S* Oscar Millard. *C* Joseph LaShelle. *Lp* John Wayne, Susan Hayward, Pedro Armendariz, Agnes Moorehead, Thomas Gomez, John Hoyt, Leo Gordon, Ted de Corsia, Lee Van Cleef, 1956.

The Searchers (Warner Bros.). *D* John Ford. *P* Merian C. Cooper. *S* Frank S. Nugent. *C* Winton C. Hoch. *Lp* John Wayne, Jeffrey Hunter, Vera Miles, Natalie Wood, Ward Bond, Ken Curtis, Harry Carey Jr., Hank Warden, Walter Coy, Pat Wayne, Lana Wood, 1956.

The Wings of Eagles (MGM). *D* John

Ford. *P* Charles Schnee. *S* Frank Fenton and William Wister Haines. *C* Paul C. Vogel. *Lp* John Wayne, Maureen O'Hara, Dan Dailey, Ward Bond, Ken Curtis, Edmund Lowe, Kenneth Tobey, James Todd, 1957.

Jet Pilot (RKO). *D* Josef von Sternberg. *P* and *S* Jules Furthman. *C* Winton C. Hoch. *Lp* John Wayne, Janet Leigh, Jay C. Flippen, Paul Fix, Richard Rober, Roland Winters, Hans Conreid, 1957.

Legend of the Lost (United Artists/Batjac/Panama/Dear Films). *D* and *P* Henry Hathaway. *S* Robert Presnell Jr. and Ben Hecht. *C* Jack Cardiff. *Lp* John Wayne, Sophia Loren, Rossano Brazzi, Kurt Kaszner, Sonia Moser, Angela Portaluri, 1957.

I Married a Woman (RKO). *D* Hal Kanter. *P* William Bloom. *S* Goodman Ace. *C* Lucien Ballard. *Lp* George Gobel, Diana Dors, Adolphe Menjou, Jessie Royce-Landis; John Wayne and Angie Dickinson played uncredited cameos, 1958.

The Barbarian and the Geisha (Twentieth Century Fox). D John Huston. *P* Eugene Franke. *S* Charles Grayson. *C* Charles G. Clarke. *Lp* John Wayne, Eiko Ando, Sam Jaffe, So Yamamura, Norman Thomson, James Robbins, Morita, 1958.

Rio Bravo (Warner Bros.). *D* and *P* Howard Hawks. *S* Jules Furthman and

Leigh Brackett. *C* Russell Harlan. *Lp* John Wayne, Dean Martin, Ricky Nelson, Angie Dickinson, Walter Brennan, Ward Bond, John Russell, Claude Akins, Harry Carey Jr., 1959.

The Horse Soldiers (United Artists/ Mahin-Rackin). *D* John Ford. *P* and *S* John Lee Mahin and Martin Rackin. *C* William H. Clothier. *Lp* John Wayne, William Holden, Constance Towers, Althea Gibson, Hoot Gibson, Anna Lee, Russell Simpson, Stan Jones, 1959.

The Alamo (United Artists/Batjac). *D* and *P* John Wayne. *S* James Edward Grant. *C* William H. Clothier. *Lp* John Wayne, Richard Widmark, Laurence Harvey, Richard Boone, Frankie Avalon, Patrick Wayne, Linda Cristal, Joan O'Brien, Chill Wills, Joseph Calleia, Ken Curtis, Denver Pyle, Aissa Wayne, Hank Worden, Chuck Roberson, Olive Carey, 1960.

North to Alaska (Twentieth Century Fox). *D* and *P* Henry Hathaway. *S* John Lee Mahin, Martin Rackin, and Claude Binyon. *C* Leon Shamroy. *Lp* John Wayne, Stewart Granger, Capucine, Ernie Kovacs, Fabian, Mickey Shaughnessy, Karl Swenson, Joseph Sawyer, 1960.

The Comancheros (Twentieth Century Fox). *D* Michael Curtiz (and John Wayne uncredited). *P* George Sherman. *S* James Edward Grant and Clair Huffaker. *C* William H. Clothier. *Lp* John Wayne, Stuart Whitman, Ina Balin, Nehemiah Persoff, Lee Marvin, Michael Ansara, Patrick Wayne, Bruce Cabot, Joan O'Brien, Aissa Wayne, Jack Elam, 1961.

The Man Who Shot Liberty Valance (Paramount). *D* John Ford. *P* Willis Goldbeck. *S* James Warner Bellah and Willis Goldbeck. *C* William H. Clothier. *Lp* John Wayne, James Stewart, Lee Marvin, Vera Miles, Edmond O'Brien, Andy Devine, Woody Strode, Jeanette Nolan, John Qualen, Lee Van Cleef, 1962.

Hatari (Paramount). *D* and *P* Howard Hawks. *S* Leigh Brackett. *C* Russell Harlen. *Lp* John Wayne, Hardy Kruger, Elsa Martinelli, Red Buttons, Gerard Blain, Michele Girardon, Bruce Cabot, 1962.

The Longest Day (Twentieth Century Fox). *D* Andrew Martin, Ken Annakin, and Bernard Wicki. *P* Darryl F. Zanuck. *S* Cornelius Ryan, Romain Gary, James Jones, David Pursall, and Jack Seddon. *C* Jean Bourgin, Henri Persin, and Water Wottiz. All-star cast included Richard Beymer, Richard Burton, Red Buttons, Sean Connery, Henry Fonda, Jeffrey Hunter, Curt Jurgens, Robert Mitchum, Kenneth More,

Robert Ryan, Richard Todd, Robert Wagner, and John Wayne, 1962.

How the West Was Won (MGM/ Cinerama). *D* Henry Hathaway, John Ford, and George Marshall. *P* Bernard Smith. *S* James R. Webb. *C* William H. Daniels, Milton Krasner, Charles Lang, and Joseph LaShelle. All-star cast included Carroll Baker, Lee J. Cobb, Henry Fonda, Karl Malden, Gregory Peck, George Peppard, Debbie Reynolds, James Stewart, Eli Wallach, Richard Widmark, and John Wayne, 1962.

Donovan's Reef (Paramount). *D* and *P* John Ford. *S* Frank S. Nugent and James Edward Grant. *C* William H. Clothier. *Lp* John Wayne, Lee Marvin, Jack Warden, Elizabeth Allen, Cesar Romero, Dorothy Lamour, Patrick Wayne, 1963.

McLintock! (United Artists/Batjac). *D* Andrew V. McLaglen. *P* Michael Wayne. *S* James Edward Grant. *C* William H. Clothier. *Lp* John Wayne, Maureen O'Hara, Patrick Wayne, Stefanie Powers, Yvonne de Carlo, Jack Kruschen, Chill Wills, 1963.

Circus World [aka *The Magnificent Showman*] (Samuel Bronston/Paramount/ Rank). *D* Henry Hathaway. *P* Samuel Bronston. *S* Ben Hecht, Julian Halevy, and James Edward Grant. *C* Jack Hildyard and

Claude Renoir. *Lp* John Wayne, Claudia Cardinale, Rita Hayworth, John Smith, Lloyd Nolan, Richard Conte, 1964.

The Greatest Story Ever Told (United Artists). *D* and *P* George Stevens. *S* James Lee Barrett and George Stevens. *C* William C. Mellor and Loyal Griggs. All-star cast included Max von Sydow, Charlton Heston, David McCallum, Roddy McDowall, Sal Mineo, Ed Wynn, Claude Rains, Telly Savalas, Martin Landau, José Ferrer, Dorothy McGuire, and John Wayne, 1965.

In Harm's Way (Paramount). *D* and *P* Otto Preminger. *S* Wendell Mayes. *C* Loyal Griggs. *Lp* John Wayne, Kirk Douglas, Patricia Neal, Tom Tryon, Paula Prentiss, Brandon de Wilde, Jill Haworth, Dana Andrews, Henry Fonda, 1965.

The Sons of Katie Elder (Paramount). *D* Henry Hathaway. *P* Hal Wallis. *S* William H. Wright, Allan Weiss, and Harry Essex. *C* Lucien Ballard. *Lp* John Wayne, Dean Martin, Martha Hyer, Michael Anderson Jr., Earl Holliman, Jeremy Slate, Paul Fix, George Kennedy, Dennis Hopper, 1965.

Cast a Giant Shadow (United Artists/Mirisch-Llenroc/Batjac/Bryna). *D*, *P*, and *S* Melville Shavelson. *C* Aldo Tonti. *Lp* Kirk Douglas, Senta Berger, James Donald, Gordon Jackson, Yul Brynner, Frank Sinatra, John Wayne, 1966.

The War Wagon (Universal/Batjac). *D* Burt Kennedy. *P* Marvin Schwartz. *S* Clair Huffaker. *C* William H. Clothier. *Lp* John Wayne, Kirk Douglas, Howard Keel, Robert Walker, Keenan Wynn, Bruce Cabot, Valora Nolan, 1967.

El Dorado (Paramount). *D* and *P* Howard Hawks. *S* Leigh Brackett. *C* Harold Rosson. *Lp* John Wayne, Robert Mitchum, James Caan, Charlene Holt, Michele Carey, Arthur Hunnicutt, R. G. Armstrong, Edward Asner, Paul Fix, Christopher George, 1967.

The Green Berets (Warner Bros.–Seven Arts/Batjac). *D* John Wayne and Ray Kellogg (and Mervyn LeRoy uncredited). *P* Michael Wayne. *S* James Lee Barrett. *C* Winton C. Hoch. *Lp* John Wayne, David Janssen, Jim Hutton, Aldo Ray, Raymond St. Jacques, Bruce Cabot, Jack Soo, George Takei, Patrick Wayne, Irene Tsu, Mike Henry, Luke Askew, 1968.

Hellfighters (Universal). *D* Andrew V. McLaglen. *P* Robert Arthur. *S* Clair Huffaker. *C* William H. Clothier. *Lp* John Wayne, Katharine Ross, Vera Miles, Jim Hutton, Jay C. Flippen, Bruce Cabot, 1968.

True Grit (Paramount). *D* Henry Hathaway. *P* Hal B. Wallis. *S* Marguerite Roberts. *C* Lucien Ballard. *Lp* John Wayne, Glen

Campbell, Kim Darby, Jeremy Slate, Robert Duvall, Dennis Hopper, Alfred Ryder, Strother Martin, 1969.

The Undefeated (Universal/Batjac). *D* Andrew V. McLaglen. *P* Robert L. Jacks. *S* James Lee Barrett. *C* William H. Clothier. *Lp* John Wayne, Rock Hudson, Antonio Aguilar, Roman Gabriel, Marian McCargo, Lee Meriwether, Bruce Cabot, Ben Johnson, Harry Carey Jr., Paul Fix, John Agar, 1969.

Chisum (Warner Bros./Batjac). *D* Andrew V. McLaglen. *P* and *S* Andrew J. Fenady. *C* William H. Clothier. *Lp* John Wayne, Forrest Tucker, Christopher George, Ben Johnson, Glenn Corbett, Andrew Prine, Bruce Cabot, Geoffrey Deuel, Pamela McMyler, John Agar, 1970.

Rio Lobo (Cinema Center-National General Pictures). *D* and *P* Howard Hawks. *S* Leigh Brackett and Burton Wohl. *C* William H. Clothier. *Lp* John Wayne, Jorge Rivero, Jennifer O'Neill, Jack Elam, Victor French, Christopher Mitchum, Mike Henry, 1970.

Big Jake (Batjac/Cinema Center-National General Pictures). *D* George Sherman. *P* Michael Wayne. *S* Harry Julian Fink and Rita M. Fink. *C* William H. Clothier. *Lp* John Wayne, Richard Boone, Maureen O'Hara, Patrick Wayne, Chris Mitchum, Bobby Vinton, Bruce Cabot, Glenn Corbett,

Harry Carey Jr., John Agar, 1971.

The Cowboys (Warner Bros.). *D* and *P* Mark Rydell. *S* Irving Ravetch and Harriet Frank Jr. *C* Robert Surtees. *Lp* John Wayne, Roscoe Lee Browne, Bruce Dern, Colleen Dewhurst, Slim Pickens, Sarah Cunningham, 1972.

The Train Robbers (Warner Bros./Batjac). *D* and *S* Burt Kennedy. *P* Michael Wayne. *C* William H. Clothier. *Lp* John Wayne, Ann-Margret, Rod Taylor, Ben Johnson, Bobby Vinton, Christopher George, 1973.

Cahill, United States Marshal (Warner Bros./Batjac). *D* Andrew V. McLaglen. *P* Michael Wayne. *S* Harry Julian Fink and Rita M. Fink. *C* Joseph Biroc. *Lp* John Wayne, George Kennedy, Gary Grimes, Neville Brand, Clay O'Brien, Marie Windsor, Royal Dano, Denver Pyle, Jackie Coogan, 1973.

McQ (Warner Bros./Batjac). *D* John Sturges. *P* Michael Wayne. *S* Lawrence Roman. *C* Harry Stradling Jr. *Lp* John Wayne, Eddie Albert, Diana Muldaur, Colleen Dewhurst, Clu Gulager, David Huddleston, Julie Adams, 1974.

Brannigan (United Artists/Batjac). *D* Douglas Hickox. *P* Michael Wayne. *S* Christopher Trumbo, Michael Butler, William P. McGivern, and William Norton. *C* Gerry

Fisher. *Lp* John Wayne, Richard Atten-
borough, Judy Geeson, Mel Ferrer, John
Vernon, Daniel Pilon, John Stride, James
Booth, Barry Dennen, 1975.

Rooster Cogburn [aka *Rooster Cogburn and
the Lady*] (Universal). *D* Stuart Millar. *P* Hal
B. Wallis. *S* Martin Julien. *C* Harry Stradling
Jr. *Lp* John Wayne, Katharine Hepburn, An-
thony Zerbe, Richard Jordan, John McIntire,
Strother Martin, 1975.

The Shootist (Paramount). *D* Don Siegel.
P Mike J. Frankovich and William Self. *S*
Miles Hood Swarthout and Scott Hale. *C*
Bruce Surtees. *Lp* John Wayne, Lauren
Bacall, James Stewart, Ron Howard, Bill
McKinney, Richard Boone, John Carradine,
Scatman Crothers, Harry Morgan, Hugh
O'Brian, Sheree North, 1976.

Sources

With an occasional exception, I acquired all the quotes in the book firsthand, either in face-to-face interviews, speaking on the telephone, or through informal conversations. I have listed the names of these people alphabetically, and the circumstances of when and where and why, as far as I am able to recall.

Where I refer to conversations by telephone in 1974, these were with the people that John Wayne recommended I talk to. Where I refer to conversations by telephone in 1979, these were for a tribute I wrote for *Photoplay* which was never published.

John Agar: by telephone (1979).
Claude Akins: for general interview in London (1980).
Richard Attenborough: on the set of *Brannigan* (1974).
Lauren Bacall: a casual conversation while I was visiting the set of *Murder on the Orient Express* at Elstree Studios (1973).

Carroll Baker: a general interview (and a game of Battleship!) at her London home during a break in her filming schedule of *The World Is Full of Married Men* (1979).

Ina Balin: by telephone (1979).

James Lee Barrett: by telephone (1979).

Noah Beery Jr.: by telephone (1979).

Budd Boetticher: by telephone, on John Wayne's recommendation (1974) and for planned tribute (1979).

Richard Boone: for general interview while he was filming *The Big Sleep* on location in London (1977).

Neville Brand: for general interview in London (1980).

Rossano Brazzi: for general interview while he was filming *The Final Conflict* on location in London (1980).

Red Buttons: by telephone (1979).

Yakima Canutt: in London for general interview (1976).

Frank Capra: by telephone for general interview (1980).

Capucine: for general interview while she was filming *Arabian Adventure* at Pinewood Studios (1978).

John Carradine: for general interview while he was filming *House of Long Shadows* (1982).

William H. Clothier: on John Wayne's recommendation (1974) and for planned tribute (1979).

Linda Cristal: by telephone (1979).

Ken Curtis: by telephone (1979).

Dan Dailey: general interview by telephone (1977).

Sammy Davis Jr.: social event at a party thrown by Peter Lawford (1974).

Bruce Dern: for general interview at The Dorchester hotel, London, where he was promoting the film *Coming Home* (1978).

Colleen Dewhurst: by telephone (1979).

Angie Dickinson: by telephone (1979).

Edward Dmytryk: for general interview in London (1975).

Kirk Douglas: for interviews at The Dorchester hotel, London, to promote his film *Posse* (1975) and his autobiography *The Ragman's Son* (1988).

Paul Fix: by telephone (1979).

Henry Fonda: general interview while he was in London to perform in the play *Clarence Darrow* (1976).

Carl Foreman: general interview at his London office (1978).

Ava Gardner: a casual conversation at her home in London (1979).

Judy Geeson: for general interview on location at Chiselhurst Caves while she was filming *Inseminoid* (1979).

Christopher George: by telephone, for general interview (1980).

Stewart Granger: for general interview at his London home while he was promoting his autobiography *Sparks Fly Upward* (1981).

Laurence Harvey: informal conversation at a social event in London (1972).

Henry Hathaway: by telephone, on John Wayne's recommendation (1974), for planned tribute (1979), and follow-up phone call (1981).

Howard Hawks: by telephone (1974).

Charlton Heston: general interview at The Dorchester hotel, London, while he was promoting his book *The Actor's Life* (1979).

Douglas Hickox: on location for *Brannigan* (1974) and in London (1977).

Jack Hildyard: an informal meeting while he was filming *The Beast Must Die* (1973).

William Holden: for general interview while filming *Damien: Omen II* on location in London (1977).

Bob Hope: special meeting on opening night of *How to Commit Marriage* at the New Victoria Theatre, London (1969), and by telephone (1979).

Rock Hudson: for general interview while he was filming *The Mirror Crack'd* at Elstree Studios (1980).

John Huston: at Shepperton Studios while he was filming *The Macintosh Man* (1972) and while working for him at Claridge's, London (1974).

Jim Hutton: for general interview by telephone (1976).

Sam Jaffe: for general interview by telephone (1981).

David Janssen: for general interview while he was filming *S.O.S. Titanic* in England (1978).

Ben Johnson: by telephone (1979).

Richard Jordan: for general interview while he was filming *A Nightingale Sang in Berkeley Square* at Pinewood Studios (1978).

Burt Kennedy: by telephone (1979).

George Kennedy: by telephone (1979).

Dorothy Lamour: for general interview in London (1980).

Jesse Lasky Jr.: for general interview at his London home while he was promoting his book *Love Scene* (1978).

Anna Lee: by telephone (1979).

Mervyn LeRoy: for general interview by telephone (1981).

Roddy McDowall: for general interview while he was filming *The Thief of Baghdad* at Shepperton Studios (1977).

Andrew V. McLaglen: general interview over lunch at Pinewood Studios and in production offices while he was in preproduction on *North Sea Hijack* (1978).

John Lee Mahin: for general interview by telephone (1980).

Joseph L. Mankiewicz: while visiting the set of *Sleuth* at Pinewood Studios (1981).

Lee Marvin: general interview while he was filming *The Dirty Dozen: The Next Mission* on location in England (1984).

Ray Milland: visit to the set of *The House in Nightmare Park* (1972).

David Miller: by telephone (1979).

Robert Mitchum: general interview outside a pub in London while he was filming *The Big Sleep* (1977).

Patricia Neal: by telephone (1979).

David Niven: general interview at Pinewood Studios while he was filming *Candleshoe* (1977).

Lloyd Nolan: by telephone (1979).

Maureen O'Hara: by telephone on John Wayne's recommendation (1974) and for planned tribute (1979).

Geraldine Page: general interview by telephone (1975).

George Peppard: for general interview in London (1987).

Anthony Quinn: for general interview while he was filming *The Greek Tycoon* at Elstree Studios (1977).

Ella Raines: by telephone (1979).

Donna Reed: by telephone (1979).

Cesar Romero: general interview by telephone (1988).

Miklos Rozsa: general interview in London (1980).

Telly Savalas: general interview (1984).

Melville Shavelson: by telephone (1979).

George Sherman: by telephone on John Wayne's recommendation (1974) and for planned tribute (1979).

Don Siegel: for general interview while he was in preproduction of *Rough Cut* at Pinewood Studios (1979).

Bernard Smith: by telephone from the offices of Cinerama (1969).

James Stewart: for general interview in London (1980).

Woody Strode: general interview in a London hotel (1976).

John Sturges: while working with him at The Dorchester hotel, London (1975).

Dimitri Tiomkin: informal meeting while in London for premiere of *Tchaikovsky* (1970).

Claire Trevor: by telephone (1979).

Tom Tryon: general interview by telephone (1988).

Lee Van Cleef: for general interview on location while he was filming *The Hard*

Way in Ireland (1978).

Raoul Walsh: by telephone (1974).

Michael Wayne: on the set of *Brannigan* (1974).

Patrick Wayne: for general interview while he was filming *The People That Time Forgot* at Pinewood Studios (1976).

Orson Welles: general interview over dinner at a London restaurant (1983).

William Wellman: by telephone (1974).

Stuart Whitman: for general interview while he was filming *The Monster Club* at Elstree Studios (1980).

Richard Widmark: for brief interview while he was filming *Bear Island* at Pinewood Studios (1979).

Natalie Wood: for general interview at The Dorchester hotel, London (1980).

Keenan Wynn: for general interview in London (1974).

Gig Young: over dinner at The Dorchester hotel, London (1970).

Loretta Young: by telephone (1979) and on the set of *Brannigan* (1974).

Bibliography

The following is not a comprehensive list of books about John Wayne or related subjects, but it names the relatively few books I referred to.

Dietrich, Marlene. *Marlene.* U.S., Grove, 1989.

Fernett, Gene. *Starring John Wayne.* U.S., Fernett, 1970.

Ford, Dan. *The Unquiet Man: The Life of John Ford.* U.K., William Kimber, 1982.

Hardy, Phil. *The Western: The Aurum Film Encyclopedia.* U.K., Aurum Press, 1983.

Higham, Charles. *Cecil B. DeMille.* U.S., Scribner, 1973.

Place, J. A. *The Western Films of John Ford.* U.S., Citadel Press, 1974.

Ricci, Mark, Boris Zmijewsky, and Steve Zmijewsky. *The Films of John Wayne.* U.S., Citadel Press, 1970.

Stacy, Pat, with Beverly Linet. *Duke: A Love Story.* U.S., Atheneum, 1983.

Wayne, Aissa, with Steve Delsohn. *John

Wayne, My Father. U.S., Random House, 1991.

Wayne, Pilar, with Alex Thorleifson. *John Wayne: My Life with the Duke*. U.S., McGraw-Hill, 1987.

Wills, Gary. *John Wayne: The Politics of Celebrity*. U.K., Faber and Faber, 1997.

About the Author

Michael Munn has written eighteen previous books, including biographies of Frank Sinatra, Charlton Heston, Gregory Peck, Gene Hackman, and Sharon Stone.

We hope you have enjoyed this Large Print book. Other Thorndike, Wheeler or Chivers Press Large Print books are available at your library or directly from the publishers.

For more information about current and upcoming titles, please call or write, without obligation, to:

Publisher
Thorndike Press
295 Kennedy Memorial Drive
Waterville, ME   04901
Tel. (800) 223-1244

Or visit our Web site at:
www.gale.com/thorndike
www.gale.com/wheeler

OR

Chivers Large Print
published by BBC Audiobooks Ltd
St James House, The Square
Lower Bristol Road
Bath BA2 3SB
England
Tel. +44(0) 800 136919
email: bbcaudiobooks@bbc.co.uk
www.bbcaudiobooks.co.uk

All our Large Print titles are designed for easy reading, and all our books are made to last.